For Such a Time as This...

*G*od has a wonderful way of answering our prayers; and often His ways are not anything we have prepared for. I was seeking His direction during January of 2007 and questioning whether to keep the doors open in my Bible and gift store, His House. Business was not what I had hoped for in our first year and I was discouraged. On Saturday, January 27th, at 5:00 a.m., I came fully awake and sat up in bed. My eyes watched as a vision played out before them. This is not the first time this has happened to me as you will read in some entries of this book. In the vision I was typing on my laptop and two friends, Gail and Esther, were typing in the background. Surrounding me were journals I had written over the last 12 years. God told me to write a book called *For Such a Time as This...*, and to "make better use of my time at His House." He showed me the name, the front cover photo and the format for the pages of a daily devotional. Why would God put these two women into the vision? He obviously knew they would be willing to participate; and that their skills with typing, punctuation, grammar and spelling would be needed. I emailed them about the vision asking if they would be willing to type and edit for me. Within minutes both had replied offering their services!

I began to write entries that same day without knowing specific format needs or a complete plan for the publishing. When God moves, I listen; and I act! I printed off the pages of a blank calendar and began to write topics, favorite Scripture verses, character profiles, life lesson ideas and the names of people who have had great influence in my spiritual walk. With ease, I filled over seven months of days with teachings! I can tell you there were some entries the enemy did not want written. I struggled with each word in those passages. As I finished each chapter it was sent to Esther who would format, check punctuation and spelling, lightly proofread it, and then send it back. I would forward that copy on to Gail who would do the heavy proofreading for text flow and anything Esther missed, and then send the fully edited copy back to me. Seventy days later the writing was finished.

I recommend you pray each day before you read *For Such a Time as This...* Ask God to give you insight and wisdom. Use the Scripture verse at the top of the page to take you into the Bible. Read around that verse to see what other treasures God has there for you. Apply the second portion—the applications which follow the teachings. Pray the prayers as written—then add your own words to them. God gave this vision so that you could grow in your comfort with the words of the Bible. I will be praying as you read each day's entry.

Author Acknowledgements

*H*ow can I ever thank my husband Dan enough for his constant encouragement and support? He has stepped up and worked for me at the store, cleaned the house and done all the grocery shopping since January! God has truly blessed me with a soul mate to share my life with.

I owe a huge debt of gratitude to Esther Dodson and Gail Schultz who have painstakingly pored over these pages. If you knew how bad my penmanship and typing are, you would realize this is indeed a labor of love. God places friends in our lives *for such a time as this...*

In order for a project like this to come together in such a timely manner, there is much effort required. I thank the His House team of volunteers: Marna, Karla, Bonnie, Elaine, Esther and Marta... for their willingness to serve in the ministry God has put us into... without financial gain, but with great heavenly reward.

To my "Seekers" who have encouraged me and been willing to be used as my 'guinea pigs' for some of these entries... you will never know what your hunger for the Word and your support of His House mean to me. God is raising up a great army of Bible driven disciples... and you are all a part of that army!

To my parents, who always supported and encouraged me (though I know you had doubts about this project), thank you. I know you believe in the cause of Christ and my service in the kingdom. I love you both and am glad God chose you to be my parents.

Finally, to my Heavenly Father, my Savior Jesus, and the indwelling Holy Spirit... thank You. You have breathed life into these dead, dry bones, hope into this broken heart and strengthened me to face each trial. Thank You for twelve of the most amazing years any believer could live. May Your Names be lifted up by all who partake in the words of this devotional.

For Such a Time as This…
by Vicki Renee Bryant

January 1ˢᵗ <u>God's Word</u> *(I Timothy 2:15)*

*Be diligent to present yourself approved to God as
a workman who does not need to be ashamed,
accurately handling the word of truth.*

As we begin this year with a full year of daily devotionals before you, relax and enjoy these teachings. Some are personal experiences, some are life lessons and many are teachings of the Word of God. Let us come into agreement to grow deeper in our faith walk in the year ahead of us. My first recommendation is that you spend daily time in the Word. The following words are taken from a 2006 entry in my journal. "I am pretty consistent in my Bible time. I do not miss mornings with Your Word. Each way I study has taught me different things. At this time, I am writing the New Testament out by hand on legal paper. I am thinking, learning and applying it to my life. This has been great, but not as much fun as when I first marked every word and wrote all over the pages of my Bible." Many of you are asking the obvious question of where to start reading in the Bible. I would recommend the book of Matthew, the first book of the New Testament. This section of the Bible teaches us of Jesus' life, His teachings, and His miracles and of the growth of the early Christian church. The Old Testament is a wonderful written history of God's provision for His people. Throughout this book you will find stories from the first portion of the Bible. Feel free to take the Scripture at the top of the page and begin to read the verses or stories around it. I will share other Bible study tips and techniques in these January lessons.

Time in the Word is a commitment all Christians should make. Unfortunately, that is not the practice of many believers. The Bible is God's instruction manual for us. Have you ever tried to put something together without reading the directions? Have you tried to bake a cake from scratch without a recipe? Instructions guide us through processes in the right order; and then keep us from making mistakes. My greatest wish is that you would use this devotional book hand-in-hand with a daily Bible study.

Lord, my passion for Your Word does not wane. I love its truths. I thank You for the ones who centuries ago were faithful to Your inspiration and command to write down the words which are alive and applicable for us still today. Thank you for teaching me of Your past faithfulness, Your unequaled love, Your hope for tomorrow, Your promises for eternity and Your worry over my lost soul. Amen.

January 2ⁿᵈ   Gospel In A Nutshell   *(John 3:16)*

For God so loved the world that He gave His only begotten Son, that whoever believes in Him shall not perish, but have eternal life.

Sin (our inherent selfishness and outward actions) separates us from the perfect God of all creation. The chasm is deep and God cannot look upon evil for He is holy. In this time of separation, He will send witnesses to sow seeds to us and His Spirit to convict us of the wrong we do. God so wanted us to fellowship with Him and be reconciled to Him, that He came to earth as a man (like us) to experience all of the same things we experience—love, hate, betrayal, loneliness. He came as Jesus. He walked the earth for 33 years and remained unblemished through it all. He was despised and rejected for His claims about who He was. Jesus was crucified, buried and resurrected to new life and now sits at the right hand of God. His shed blood washes us clean (blood sacrifices for sins). He has prepared a place in heaven for all who believe in and accept His pardon. All who refuse to believe will be judged and punished eternally for refusing God's gift of reconciliation. We must all make a choice. Being a good person is not enough. None of us are truly "good" when measured against a holy Jesus.

What we tend to do is to compare ourselves to others in order to prove ourselves good. "I don't kill people like Charles Manson... I don't steal like the looters in the L.A. riots... I don't cheat on my husband like my friend Sue." I hate to break your bubble; but we are not rewarded for that which we don't do. Doing right is expected! Our heavenly reward is for the right we do, not the wrong we don't do. Salvation is a free gift—it should then change our hearts to live a holy and godly life. Let us all look this year at the life Jesus modeled for us... and then begin to emulate Him.

Holy Jesus, I have lived my life comparing myself to others. I need to honestly hold my life up in the reflection of Yours. Only then can I see where work is needed. Your holy life of grace, mercy, kindness, compassion and love is the life I need to model mine after. Amen.

January 3rd <u>His House: The Vision</u> *(Psalms 93: 5)*

Your testimonies are fully confirmed; holiness befits Your house,
O Lord, forevermore.

*T*oday I begin to share with you the amazing story of how I, a former blasphemer of the things of Christ, became the owner of a Christian bookstore. If you don't believe that God still works miracles and is involved in every aspect of our lives... stay tuned. In the fall of 2005, as I was praying before my fireplace during my early morning devotions, a vision began to play before my eyes. In the vision, which was just as real as me sitting here writing this entry, I was walking into the door of a small Christian bookstore called His House. In the vision, I could see specific furnishings (most of which were from my house.) Central in the vision was a table with people sitting around it, talking, praying and praising God. One woman was crying, as another offered prayer over her. I knew I owned the business from conversations with the people at the table. Let me say that I have longed for this type of business since I left the local Christian bookstore six years ago, but knew I did not have the means to make my dream come true. After the vision I felt a peace—a warm calm—wash over me. I stood up and told the Lord that I loved the idea, but He would need to work miracles in order for the vision to happen. I emailed all the "prayer warriors," telling them the vision and asking them to pray about it. Jokingly, I added that my furniture was in the store, so it must be that I was to sell my house and move in with one of them. Not twenty minutes later, one friend offered her basement for Dan and me to live in. The vision was real, the passion was there, the money wasn't... so I moved back into the life I was used to. One thing I did was begin to share my vision with everyone; because you never know how God will work. If the vision was His, then He could be trusted to provide for its fulfillment.

Has God ever worked in this way in your life? I cannot explain why it happens to me. One thing I know is that I am receptive to the working of the Holy Spirit... and absolutely believe He still works in the lives of those who call upon His name. As we begin this journey together for the next twelve months, open your hearts to the truths I will try to represent here. You will need to still your heart, silence your voice and focus on Christ. This is a new year; how about making a new start? Enjoy the His House story as it unfolds and watch the amazing promises of His provision.

You are an amazing God! I know You provide for all of my needs... and may I never take those provisions for granted. Help me this year to begin to hear You more than ever before. I am ready for You to transform my life. Amen.

January 4th   <u>His House: David</u> *(Matthew 6: 33)*

"But seek first His kingdom and His righteousness,
and all these things will be added to you."

In yesterday's entry I spoke about the vision for His House. I also said I began to share my vision with everyone; "because you never know how God will work. If the vision was His… He could be trusted to provide for its fulfillment." His ways are not our ways; and His amazing pathways blow my mind. Around the time of my vision, three new realtors came to work at the realty office where I am office manager. One of them is a single, successful businessman in our city. I had never really witnessed to David; but sometimes we have to trust our actions and words to be our witness. Just a few short months later, David initiated a conversation about the strange weather in the southern part of our nation. He said to me, "It seems like something strange is going on." I asked what he was talking about, as I kept writing and doing work at my desk. His next statement stopped me in my tracks, "Like God is trying to get our attention or something." The next hour was amazing as we talked about faith, the Bible, its importance in our lives…and about my vision for His House. David had every opportunity to stop the conversation, but those who are seeking are "heart hungry" for meaning in life. Just three days later David offered me a little building he owned near his office. He also offered to partner with me to make my "vision happen." From all of the possible scenarios for His House to happen I would never have imagined that God would act so quickly or use this kind man to bring His plans into action. David remodeled the building, adding a kitchenette and provided for all we would need. He has remained a very "silent partner." I thank God for the way He used David. I thank David for the way he allowed himself to be used.

I hope you realize from the circumstances of this entry, that God had a plan for His House long before He gave me the vision. He was raising me up to where I could be used, grooming David to be the man he is and putting the two of us in one another's path... each thing not unique in itself... but undeniably God ordained when put all together. Stop here and look at your life. Has God placed people in your paths... *"for such a time as this?"* Our encounters are rarely by accident. I call them God ordained meetings... watch for them in your life.

Lord, open my eyes to realize that the people in my life are not put there by accident. Each one is placed for Your time and Your service... just as I am placed in theirs. Your plans will always be fulfilled because Your will shall be done on earth as it is in heaven. Amen.

January 5th   His House: God's Provision   *(Psalms 89:1)*

I will sing of the loving kindness of the Lord forever; to all generations I will make known Your faithfulness with my mouth.

The last two entries related that I had my vision, my partner and my building. God was putting all of the pieces together for His House to become a reality. Our next need was fixtures, furnishings and display pieces, and over the next month He began to drop those things in our laps. One of my agents had purchased two display pieces when another company went out of business. When I asked her why she bought them, she said, "Because they were cheap!" We made a trip to my parents' house in northern Michigan— because they shop garage sales for a living. We hauled home a truck-load of antique dressers, cabinets, tables—even a beat-up ladder to hold baby quilts! A friend found a tiered greeting card rack for $10 and donated the gathering tables, which are the most important fixtures at the store. I sent an email asking if anyone had an old desk, office chair or file cabinet. Within a few hours I had them. Someone purchased our coffee maker; another all our coffee and supplies; and yet another some teaching curriculum for the store's lending library.

We were down to needing a checkout counter. The basic ones I found at supply companies were $500-$1200! One day my boss from the real estate company called and asked if I was looking for a checkout counter! He told me there was one in a building he was leasing and it needed to be out right away. I asked how much, and he said, "Free, if you will take it today!" The greatest blessing came when two very special friends, Karla and Marna, offered to work half days, so that I could still work my paying job! That number has now grown to six wonderful His House friends who sacrifice of their time because they understand the vision... just like David did.

Once I said 'yes' to the vision, He provided everything we needed to open the business. Several times people handed us $100 bills. Each time this happened it was when we were barely able to make ends meet. Friends Geri, Laura and Marsha would show up with goodies for all to enjoy. Janet would supply the coffee cupboard. Jim would plow... for free. My logo was designed by a local artist... for free. Hear my story and realize it could be yours. Let Him give you a vision... and then follow that dream.

Lord, You really do care about every little detail of my life. Help me to acknowledge Your provision and Your faithfulness. Jesus, breathe a vision into me, via Your Holy Spirit, and show me how to remain faithful in all I do. I praise Your name. Amen.

January 6th <u>Means of Escape</u> *(I Corinthians 10:13)*

No temptation has overtaken you but such as is common to man; and God is faithful, who will not allow you to be tempted beyond what you are able, but with the temptation will provide the way of escape also, so that you will be able to endure it.

*O*nly by Jesus being between heaven and earth for our sins are we able to live in the "freedom" my Pastor talked about

15

recently. Jesus doesn't keep us from sinning or remove sin from the world. He instead gives us the wisdom to deny our flesh and choose not to sin! That promise is a gift and a great blessing. I <u>don't have to do</u> the things I used to do. It isn't that I can't do them. It is that I choose not to repeat the same mistakes.

I had a student in my "Seekers" Bible study group who was actually angry that God gave us the choice to sin or not. She kept asking why He would do that. Remember, *His ways are not our ways.* I told her He wanted us to come willingly to Him... and that requires choice. We all have the choice to accept or deny the grace of Christ. If not given the choice, we could have been made to be mindless idiots! Does this mean He wants some of us not to choose Him? Of course not! It means He wants a willing believer to come without force... wouldn't you want the same?

We <u>always</u> have a choice to sin or not. We are <u>always</u> given a choice to take the way out which God provides. When we choose not to obey, there are always consequences...some short ranged... and some which follow us for years to come. Can you think of a time when you were given a means of escape and didn't take it? What were the consequences of your decision? Now, think of a time you denied your flesh and took the right road. That decision gave you victory... victory in righteousness.

Thank You, Lord. Your obedience brings me freedom! Your sacrifice is my hope! Your love is more than I can comprehend. Thank You that Your promise is a means of escape from all my temptations. Today, I choose to walk in obedience. Amen.

January 7th   <u>Awesome Creation</u>   *(Psalms 19:1)*

The heavens are telling of the glory of God;
And their expanse is declaring the work of His hands.

I have always been awed and amazed by Your creation around me. I hear Your whisper as the pines by Mom and Dad's house sway in the breeze. I see Your sense of humor in the creation of the camel and in animals at play. I see Your unfathomable imagination in how the regrowth of the plant system works. Lord, I love to see the mighty strength of Your mountains, the fragile delicacy of your daffodils, the vastness of the star strewn heavens and the beauty of a smooth as glass lake with the clear blue sky reflected on its surface. I am taken aback by beautiful color splashed sunrises and sunsets, awesome starry night skies and the fresh smells of spring.

Think about the characteristics of God reflected in His awesome creation. He is a God of humor... think of the giggles of a child at play, the silliness of monkeys or the fun of diving into a cool, clear lake on a hot humid day. He is a God of order... think of the miracle workings of the human eye, the cycle of the sun, moon and stars or the DNA specific to every created thing. He is a God of love... think of the natural instincts for animals to care for their young, the warm sunshine on your face to brighten a dark day and the passion between a man and a woman. He is a God of faithfulness...think of the promises He made and kept to Abraham, Isaac and Jacob, the promise of hope to Noah and the ark and the promise of a Messiah. Our God is the only God who is living, makes and keeps His word and cannot be out-given. His generosity is endless.

Lord, Your character is revealed in creation's wonder. You are love. You created it with love—and You love for us to enjoy it along with You. Every thing our eyes can see is a gift from You. Unfortunately, we take much of it for granted. I want to thank You today for simply being my Lord. Amen.

January 8th   Heaven 'n' Hell   *(I Timothy 2:4)*

*...who desires all men to be saved and to come to
the knowledge of the truth.*

I think most people have a concept of Heaven and plan to be there. Those same people don't believe in Hell. It is funny because if there is one, there must be the other. Just as there is light and dark, hot or cold, sweet and sour, love and hate... there must be a polar opposite of the place of eternal life and blessed peace. The personal belief that Hell does not exist does not make it so. As a Christian we are given the choice to believe or disbelieve the teachings of the Bible. The Bible refers to Hell by several other names: Hades, Gehenna, Sheol and the pit. Fortunately, God provided a way for us to not spend eternity in the lake of fire. That "way" is through the cleansing grace of Jesus Christ. There are many more references in Scripture to Hell than there are to Heaven. Why do you think that is? I believe each is a warning for us to not choose that path.

I absolutely believe in Hell. I absolutely believe that up until my 38th year I was bound for there. My life was all about fun, things, love, Vicki, my needs, my wants, my emotions, my emptiness and my sadness... until the day when Christ so clearly sent me to Home Interiors and to the Christian leaders there. How can I doubt His Word on any topic, when He is always there for me... encouraging and giving me strength? Yes, Hell is real. My mission is that no one I know goes there.

How do you respond to "good" people who sincerely believe they are going to heaven? One common statement people use to refute hell's existence is that God would never send a good person to perish in the eternal lake of fire. That statement is right! God will not **send** anyone to hell; but we must **choose** for ourselves not to go there. It should be our personal responsibility to warn others of the reality of these truths. If they deny Christ, that is their decision. You will not be held responsible.

Father, I earnestly believe that if You provided a heavenly home for those who choose to serve You, then You, as a God of justice, would prepare a place for those who deny You. Lord, we hate to think about realities like this... but that does not make them untrue. Amen.

January 9th <u>Christians and Politics</u> (*Romans 13: 1*)KJV

Let every soul be subject unto the higher powers. For there is no power but of God; the powers that be are ordained of God.

I recall telling my mother a few years ago how horrible it was that our nation was so clearly divided between Democrat and Republican, conservative and liberal and left and right opinions. She said it has to be that way. Then, I began to apply the verse where God says in paraphrase, "Oh, I wish that you would be either hot or cold. But, because you are lukewarm, I will spew (spit) you out." Yes, we will be divided; that is what keeps us hot! If the whole nation was equally on one side, we (as believers) would be compromising our Christian principles in order to keep peace...all moral absolutes would be gone. We as Christians should take an active part in our society, our government and our communities. How else will the voice of God's moral absolutes be heard?

Never believe that we are to take ourselves out of the public forum. Actually, Christians have set back and not fought to keep prayer in our schools, God in our government and faith out of our cities. Shame on us! We are called to stand for truth...not bow to political correctness. We hold a degree of responsibility to show the statutes of God to a Scripturally illiterate society.

Christians are called to action. Scripture tells us to '*go into all nations making disciples...*' We cannot do that in our own nation if we refuse to get involved in our communities and in the political arena. I am not foolish enough to believe we will win every battle. However, we need to at least be heard. Our nation is in horrible moral decay... and we need to stand up and fight. Are you involved in the process in your community? We must stop the compromising, which has removed the hedge of protection our nation used to be blessed with.

Lord, I have failed to be a voice in my community. I have allowed the "politically correct police" to silence my voice. Lord, it is my desire to represent You and Your moral certainties in a dark, dark world. Please show me how and where to get involved. Amen.

January 10th Prayer *(I Thessalonians 5:17)*

Pray without ceasing.

"Lord, my biggest problem is stilling myself to hear your voice in my prayer time. I feel like I always have a huge, long list of very serious requests and by the time I have waded through them—prayer time is over. Maybe I need to simply acknowledge You and then sit before You waiting for Your lead in our very personal time. One thing I don't know the truth or correct action on is whether I should continue to repeat or request the same prayer requests? I have heard 'pray once and believe' and also hear to 'pray without ceasing until I see a result.' Please direct me to become a better prayer warrior this year." Think about the resolutions you make each year...always with the best of intentions. How good are you at keeping those resolutions and promises? I wrote the above passage in a journal entry for January 2, 2006. My goal was to keep my promise to be a better prayer warrior in the year to come. Let me honestly tell you that my prayer life didn't change much during that year. If prayer is so elemental in our walk with Christ, why does it take such a back burner to everything else in our lives?

I believe one of the answers to how to improve our prayer life is to do exactly what the verse at the top of the page says and never cease praying. Our lives themselves should be a form of prayer. Prayer is a form of worship, as is singing. Think of how different your life would be if you were to pray constantly, for your needs, for the needs of others, for strangers you encounter, for leaders, for our military, for a stronger relationship with Christ...your life could be a living prayer. One of the things I addressed in the journal entry is silence before God. Try something this week. Sit in silence, maybe light a candle to keep your focus, and listen for God. Rebuke other thoughts or interruptions. If you feel He is speaking something to you, talk back to Him. This may sound very strange; but it works for me every time. I am not crazy; but God and I have great conversations.

Lord, I want to be a prayer-warrior but don't know how to grow in that area. Please calm my spirit to really hear You speak. This is the desire of my heart and will result in a closer faith walk. Help me to 'be still and know that You are God.' Amen.

January 11th Witnessing *(John 14:6)*

Jesus said to him, "I am the way, and the truth, and the life; no one comes to the Father but through Me."

How do you share the gospel with an unbeliever? What about those who say the Bible is written by a bunch of men and is surely not the 'word of God?' If they are arguing that way, they likely don't accept Scripture as divine or God-breathed. My first response is if the Bible is written by a bunch of men, why is it finished? Where is the book of Billy Graham or the gospel of Charles Stanley? In the application, I will give you an example of a logical challenge to use with Bible detractors. I would tell them that I do believe the Word is God's perfect ordained and sanctioned word and that His Word tells us that He does direct our paths. I never let them think they have changed my mind. It is natural for people to deny the faith you try to share with them. People can argue with your theology, deny the validity of the Word and reject your witness; but **they cannot deny your story**. The three point witness—where I was before Christ, how I found him (or He found me) and how my life has changed since that moment—is powerful and may sow more deep seeds than any sermon we can give. Simply tell of the differences Christ has made since you trusted Him with your heart. This is especially powerful for those who have had a drastic life change. Those who knew them in their former life will surely be intrigued by the changes.

Here is the word picture I paint to try to explain why the Bible is God ordained word written at the hand of men. "Let's say I get the diagnosis of liver cancer next week; and I want to leave a legacy, a life plan and a last will and testament for my grandchildren and my son. I am too weak to write, so I gather four of my closest friends together and tell them stories, share my dreams and tell of my testimony. Each is assigned the task of going home and writing my testament for my family. Each of the four copies will be different. The stories will be similar; but will be written from the viewpoint and perspective of each author. Because they are not identical, does that mean they are not my words? Are the stories untrue? Do the slight variations disprove all of the text?" As you can see by this illustration; God could clearly direct the writers of the Bible to place the information which is important to Him in its pages for us.

Your word is truth. Your provision of it is undeniable. The one who denies its validity cannot sway me; because I am committed to You and Your place in my life. Lord, embolden me to be Your mighty witness. Amen.

January 12th Adoption *(Romans 8:15)*

For you have not received a spirit of slavery leading to fear again,
but you have received a spirit of adoption as sons
by which we cry out, "Abba! Father!"

*A*re you an adopted child? Were you raised by the people who gave birth to you? I was adopted when I was in kindergarten by the man who raised me. I am adopted in my real life; but am also spiritually adopted into the kingdom of God. If I am an adopted child of God, I hold the same rank as does my "Brother" Jesus Christ. My heavenly Father wants to do all the same things in my life as my earthly father does. He wants to clothe me, feed me, and help me to trust Him. He wants to protect me, correct me and teach me. I have the same access to Him through prayer and worship. He longs to hear my heart speak to Him. Even though He knows what I am going to say. He loves me speaking it to Him in faith. That communion and those conversations grow us closer to one another, expand my level of trust, faith and belief that He cares about everything in my life. When I praise, he is glorified. When I worship, He is edified and when I request; He knows I believe He is able to fill each need. Mostly, I learn that, like in any relationship, sometimes I need to be silent and give Him the chance to speak back His responses. I need to *"be still and know"* that He is God.

What benefits do you have as an adopted child of God? He wants to clothe you…and His word tells us He will clothe you *like the lilies of the field.* He wants to feed you… Scripture tells us *"man can not live on bread alone; but on the very word of God."* He wants to teach us trust… *"trust in the Lord with all your heart and soul."* He wants to protect you… He is your *"refuge and your shield."* He wants to correct you and advises… *"spare the rod and spoil the child."* He also wants to teach you… *"Study to show yourself approved… a workman rightly dividing the word of truth."* These are your provisions as an adopted child of God… reach out and receive them.

Here I am Father God; adopt me willingly into Your family. Help me to act like my brother Jesus acted and to walk like He walked. Adoption into this family holds no fear for me… I am glad to finally be home. Amen.

January 13th <u>Leroy's Saturday Visit</u> *(Isaiah 5: 20-21)*

Woe to those who call evil good, and good evil; who substitute
darkness for light and light for darkness; who substitute bitter
for sweet and sweet for bitter! Woe to those who are wise
in their own eyes and clever in their own sight.

*E*arly in 2007 I answered the bookstore phone before we had opened for the day, to hear a desperate sounding young man who had the wrong number; and because he was on a cell phone, I looked the correct number for him. Our conversation included the fact that I was in Owosso at a Christian bookstore. Leroy asked for directions and said he was coming to see the store. Judy and Debbie, two of our Saturday regulars, were there when he arrived. He carried a Bible in his hand and joined us at the table. He was questioning a Scripture he had heard the night before and wanted help finding it. He continually talked about how "wise and clever" he was; and told us how he figured out how to get around the laws. He also told us that he used to "be a Christian" but had walked away from his faith. Leroy told us that he owned a taxi service and had bought a bus in order to get around municipal laws, which forbade full nudity strip clubs with alcohol within the city limits. Our visitor "wisely" discovered that the statutes did not cover a touring strip club. However, his next statement wiped the shock off our faces. He said he found the above verse while searching for another; and in his words, "it sobered me up." I told him of another verse I recently read, which paraphrased says *"Hell and destruction are never full, so the eyes of a man are never satisfied."* Leroy left after prayer around the table... hopefully a changed man.

Judy, Debbie and I were stunned when Leroy told us about his strip club plans; but we didn't condemn or cast him out. You see, the enemy was working his hardest to get our friend to fall face first into the pit of hell! What Satan didn't plan on was a Scripture verse coming to mind and haunting a lost soul until God could put a bookstore owner in Owosso in a position to help him. These are God

24

ordained moments and encounters. May we all be ready to speak truth and Scripture... *for such a time as this!*

Jesus, You never fail to amaze me as you place people in my paths who minister to me... or who I am able to minister to. I will never forget how You orchestrate special encounters, feed my spirit the right words and lead me to pray against the forces of evil. Leroy learned a lesson about thinking he was smarter than You. May that bus, which was purchased for evil, be used for good in Your kingdom. Amen.

January 14th <u>Persecutor Now Persecuted</u> *(John 15:18-20)*

"If the world hates you, you know that it has hated Me before it hated you. If you were of the world, the world would love its own; but because you are not of the world, but I chose you out of the world, because of this the world hates you. Remember the word that I said to you, 'a slave is not greater than his master' 'If they persecuted Me, they will also persecute you; if they kept My word, they will keep yours also'."

*P*ersecution is a byproduct of sharing Christ. Reread the verse above. Jesus doesn't sugar coat what will happen to us when we witness His name before men. Also notice that He tells us they will hate us because they hated Him first. Does that mean that people who reject our witness actually "hate" Jesus? That question, only they can answer. We must remember that *'the enemy comes to kill, steal and destroy.'* The enemy is Satan; and it is HE who hates Jesus. The unbelieving world around us is serving Satan... period.

I clearly remember the things I thought and said about people with a deeply committed faith before I believed. I told my son, Brent, we didn't go to the old church because "we didn't need to be churchy." I laughed behind my Mary Kay Consultant's back after she invited me to Christian Women's functions. I rebuked (very rudely) my Home Interior Displayer when she— with Bible in hand—tried to share the Gospel with me. I said that if a friend had a better marriage

25

she wouldn't need to be so involved in her church. We all laughed at her faith and church work. How these things haunt me, make my witness more effective and make me realize just how hurtful rejection for faith feels. I hate persecution… how much more Jesus must have hated to have His teachings rejected.

We really don't know what persecution is here in America. Some of us have relatives or friends who aren't as close since we became followers of Christ. We might be treated poorly in the public forum. We might be made fun of for standing for what we believe. These are minor things compared to what Jesus suffered. If Christ is truly first in our lives, we can expect ostracism, persecution and even hate. This is actually somewhat reassuring to me. It tells me that I am on to something right!

Lord Jesus, You were persecuted, belittled, spit upon and blasphemed. What I need to acknowledge is that You did that for me! I was valuable enough for that suffering. How amazing is that truth? Give me the fortitude to suffer persecution for Your name. Amen.

January 15th Children of Light *(Ephesians 5:8)*

…for you were formerly darkness,
but now you are Light in the Lord; walk as children of Light.

One thing I believe is that we are to walk as "Jesus with skin on" everywhere we go. He had kind eyes, gentle words, healing hands, obedient feet and a heart filled with love. Jesus wasn't critical, nasty, cussing or unkind. He shone a spiritual *"light"* by His goodness and mercy, which poured from around Him. Light reveals evil, enhances good and removes darkness. If we walk as light, then the evil of this world will be exposed in comparison to our "lightness." When we walk as light, we enhance what is good in ourselves and in others. We compliment and encourage more light bearing activities, and others see Jesus in us! Light also dispels fear of the dark unknown. Light, which comes from Jesus, is not afraid of darkness. Why? We have overcome darkness, death and fear.

One of my favorite verses of Scripture tells us *'what is done in darkness will be revealed in light.'* I love that truth. Darkness provides great cover for 'dark works' to be done, especially those we try to hide from others. But, God sees all! Nothing is hidden from His eyes...and in His time, He will reveal all darkness. Yes, in His time-not ours. Many of us spend too much time worrying about what others appear to be getting away with. It becomes our obsession and keeps us from being "Jesus with skin on" to our world. How is your focus? Are you more ready to do that which you are called to do...and thus be light? How can you *"light"* your little sphere of influence today?

Father, I love the warmth of sunshine on my face on a summer day and the amazing works of light and color in sunsets. Light makes our lives so much easier. I would love to have walked with Your Son as He walked the earth bringing light in the darkness of illness, handicap and death. Make me a light in this dark world. Amen.

January 16th   <u>End of Self</u> *(Isaiah 43:25)*

*"I, even I, am the one who wipes out your transgressions
for My own sake, And I will not remember your sins."*

I relate to this Scripture because I spent thirty-eight years running the other way and trying to live my life the way I wanted to. I ran from God's love to men, to things and to gaining people's approval. I ran towards money, popularity, and doing anything to fit in and be accepted. I thought 'skinny' would help, new furniture or purses would help or all A's would get people to love me. Unconditional love was my goal. Loss of self-esteem was what I received. I certainly didn't need a God telling me not to have "fun" anymore and laying a bunch of restrictions on me. That is why I rejected those who tried to tell me that the answer to my need was Jesus. Then, I came to the end of myself. I realized how futile and unproductive my life was and how much I needed hope in my days. When I stopped running, JESUS reached out—touched me—and allowed me to rest in someone else for the first time in my life. He never stopped seeking me; but He is also a gentleman and would not force Himself on me.

These are painful passages to write. They sort of bare me before you and still cause me a great degree of shame. Have you come to the end of self? Have you realized that money, career, kids and a big home will never satisfy the deep hunger of your soul? I could have saved myself a lot of humiliation, financial hardship and wasted years if I had made wiser choices. I never considered the Christian walk as a viable choice. It was too restrictive; and I was having too much fun... wasn't I? If you are under fifty, don't waste as long as I did to come to end of self. If you are older than I am, what are you waiting for? Self will never satisfy.

Thank you, Lord, for the grace and the new start in my life. I am far from perfect... actually just a work in progress. I do know that You long for me to walk with You. Today, I choose to do that which is important to You. I want desperately to come to the end of self. Amen.

January 17th He Is My Refuge *(Philippians 4:6-7)*

Be anxious for nothing, but in everything by prayer and supplication with thanksgiving let your requests be made known to God. And the peace of God, which surpasses all comprehension, will guard your hearts and your minds in Christ Jesus.

hen I take my burdens to Jesus, He shoulders them. When I carry them myself, they steal my peace and rob me of my joy. God's peace guards my heart and mind. Why would anyone choose to carry burdens, which can be lightened? I belong to the Lord. Only He can lift my stress, calm my stomach, remove a headache, direct my paths and give me peace. How do you react to this statement? "Fear, worry and anxiety are all sins against God." Ouch, that one has to touch home with most everyone who reads this book. The above Scripture gives us a command... to not be anxious. It also gives us a promise... for peace beyond comprehension.

Have you ever been around a believer going through a horrible time of testing? I remember a great number of people coming to me after a wonderful Christian woman in our congregation died. Those people, to a number, told me 'the way Pat died, touched my heart and made me want to join her in heaven." What a statement... what a legacy. As this believer was suffering in final stages of cancer, she was witnessing the truth of Jesus to doctors, nurses, janitors and friends. She knew this life was short; but her eternal refuge waited just around the corner.

———————————

Does fear or anxiety plague you? Both are great tools of the enemy. He loves to keep you in bondage... and does a great job. Another verse tells us worrying about that which may happen will never add one minute to your life; but it will certainly ruin the minutes of today. I fully understand worry and fear. Been there, done that and bought the t-shirt! Worry has never once helped me through any situation. How can you better learn to trust God? My advice is time in His Word. Take the verse above, read it and a few verses around it. Read them slow, preferably out loud. Ask yourself what they mean. Then ask yourself what they mean to you. Dwell on them all day today. Begin today to really feed upon God's love letter to you.

———————————

Father, I have allowed worry and fear to keep me from walking in full faith. When I allow them into my life, they cause me to try to lean on myself to get away from them. I need to lean on You, You and only You, Lord. Help me to find promise verses to memorize. I can call them to mind when fear, doubt and anxiety try to move into my life. Amen.

January 18th <u>Peter's Denial</u> *(John 18: 25)*

Now Simon Peter was standing and warming himself.
So they said to him, "You are not also one of His disciples,
are you?" He denied it, and said, "I am not."

*P*eter had been in the place most Christians would say they would love to be. He had physically walked beside Jesus, held the honor of being one of his three closest friends, watched Him feed the multitudes and seen Him heal the blind, deaf and lame. Peter watched as Jesus was transfigured on the mountain — a glimpse of the glory of Christ as King of Kings. Peter was the only disciple who clearly stated that Jesus was *"the Christ, the Son of the living God."* Peter had seen it all... so what could make him deny Jesus as we see in the Scripture above? FEAR! Peter was afraid that what he was seeing done to Jesus would be done to him if the Jews knew that he was one of Jesus' closest allies. To make matters worse, Jesus had predicted this denial just hours before. Peter, immediately after his third denial, hears the crowing of a rooster, which fulfills Christ's prediction. Luke 22: 61 begins with these words, *"The Lord turned and looked at Peter."* Peter, devastated by his cowardice and ashamed of his betrayal goes outside the building and weeps bitterly. How could it be so easy to say he would never deny Jesus, even offering that he would be willing to die for Him, and turn around and commit this horrible act?

It is easy for us to condemn Peter and judge his betrayal of Jesus. We might even believe we would never do the same thing. Let me ask you this: How many times have you been threatened with death because you are a Christian? Most of us, fortunately, will never face this moment of decision. Most of us will not be persecuted, hunted or murdered for our faith. Unfortunately, that lack of threat often results in a lack of commitment. Christians in other parts of the world face these threats every day... yet they proclaim Christ at the risk of life and limb. Before we judge Peter, we need to reflect on how many times we have failed to speak out for our faith, our fellow Christians and Christ Himself. Are there times when you knew you should take a Christian stand; but fear of embarrassment held you in check? Thankfully, we know by this passage that we are not the only ones to ever deny Him.

———————

Jesus, I am quick to judge Peter. I have been quick to judge others for not taking a bold stand for You, but I too have failed You when I haven't stood up for my faith. I have allowed political correctness, peer pressure and embarrassment to stop me from speaking truth. I confess my shortcomings, receive Your mercy and move forward striving to please You. Amen.

January 19ᵗʰ   Peter's Restoration   *(John 21:16)*

He said to him again a second time, "Simon, son of John, do you love Me." He said to Him, "Yes, Lord; You know that I love You." He said to him, "Shepherd My sheep."

Yesterday's entry explained Peter's denial of Jesus and his shame at his lack of courage and loyalty. Today's Scripture picks up days later as Jesus and Peter speak for the first time face to face after the betrayal. During the period in between, Jesus has been tried, crucified and buried for three days. On the third day Jesus' tomb was found empty; and Mary Magdalene was sent to tell *"His disciples and **Peter**"* to meet Him in Galilee. Jesus singling Peter out must have been balm to Peter's wounded heart. How long those days in between must have been as Peter relived his failure and wished he could turn back the hands of time. A short time later Jesus did meet with the disciples as a group; but now we come to Jesus and Peter face to face. Remember, Peter denied Jesus three times. The above Scripture details the second of three questions Jesus asked Peter. Each question reaffirms to Peter that Jesus' grace is full and all encompassing. Three denials-three commands for Peter to lead the early Christian church! Jesus reinstates Peter to his former "best friend" status. Jesus prophecies that one day Peter will die for the cause of Christ… and indeed, the denier becomes a martyr for his Lord.

Before this conversation between Peter and Jesus, Scripture tells us that Peter had gone back to his old life and profession as a fisherman. He and several other apostles are fishing on the Sea of Galilee when they see a man on the shore preparing food over a fire. They have caught no fish; but the man tells them to cast the net on the other side of the boat. John realizes it is the Master on the shore. Peter, when he hears it, dives overboard! When I first read the entry, I thought he was committing suicide! I really needed to learn about grace! Peter was so excited to see Jesus again, he swam to shore faster than the others could row the boats… he needed to make things right with his Lord. Once Jesus restored him, Peter was determined to never let Him down again. You see, God will use even the weakest vessel once the vessel realizes it is useless on its own.

Holy Spirit, please help me remember where I was before Jesus reconciled me to Him. May I walk every day in remembrance of the fact that without Him I am of no use in this world. Any good thing I do without your grace and counsel is only good for my pride. Peter learned the hard way. Help me to not have to fall so far before I am humbled. Amen.

January 20th   God's Promises   *(Hebrews 7:2)*

Therefore He is able also to save forever those who draw near to God through Him, since He always lives to make intercession for them.

*W*hat does God promise me? He offered me sanctification—set apart holiness to serve Him. That makes me realize that I am able not to sin. He intercedes for me. When I mess up, He cleans me up to stand before the Holy Father. My faith makes me believe that He is able to take the little I offer Him and keep it safe and protected for when I will see Him face to face. He promises me that no one and no thing can separate us from the love He gives to us. The greatest promise is that when I leave this earth, either through death or from the gathering of the church, I will instantly be with Jesus and will always be with Him. These words bring one comfort in my hardest days. Most of us would love to have a written set of promises between us and God. Like a contract between two people. Actually, we do have that! It is called the Bible. God's many promises for His children are captured within its pages. This contract has one special clause: we need to read it frequently in order to be reminded of the promises within.

———————

How do we go about mining these gems and promises? One of my favorite ways to claim scripture is to have a set of colored Bible markers, which I use to highlight key verses in my Bible. For instance, I use yellow markers to highlight promise Scriptures. I use green to mark the things I need to remember to walk fully before God. I might use blue to highlight consequences for sin and pink for verses I want to be able to go back and find again. If you take the time to do this, it will make you truly slow down and think about what you are reading. The Bible is a treasure trove of God's words. It is not a dime-store novel meant to be read as such. Don't try to go too fast. I do not recommend reading the Bible through in a year. You need to feed upon its words—and they are not fast food!

———————

Father, I want to mine all of the promises Your word holds for me. I fully realize this will take dedication and discipline. I am committed to giving both to You and to getting to know You more. Please open my eyes to Your truths. Amen.

January 21st **Christian Contentment** *(Philippians 4:11)*

Not that I speak from want, for I have learned to be content in whatever circumstances I am.

The above words are absolutely opposite of the world's philosophies. They are also absolutely opposite of how I often act and feel. I need to talk about what is good, not what is bad in my life. Why would anyone want to have what a glum-faced Christian has? The world is full of unhappiness and dissatisfaction; and the last thing they would need is to find that in church! Why do we find it so difficult to find positive things to talk about? I am just as guilty as the next person. Recently, I was in a heated (and quite negative) debate about local political issues with a fellow believer. I have to confess that I am a born arguer and take great pleasure in stirring it up a little. Later that same day, the other person called me to apologize for getting so passionate! I was so convicted; because I never thought to call him and make sure we were okay in our relationship after the discussion. He acted in a much more Christ-like way; and I was left with egg on my face! I need to be praising His name to high heaven—not lamenting low sales. I need to be telling of His mercy, love, provision and goodness—not carrying on about things which aren't perfect. The Lord has always provided enough for us.

———————

How content are you? Do you allow the things of the world to steal your contentment? Here is a great example. Dan and I went to get our income taxes done recently. We had a specific amount of credit card debt for the bookstore, left over from Christmas, 2006. I kept "reminding" God of how much we owed; and that I would love to get enough back to pay the cards off. Remember, we had nothing toward paying the bills when we walked into the tax office. The total refund was approximately $1100 less than the total debt. And, I was having a world famous "Vicki Pity Party." Dan let me stew for a bit and then told me that the reality was we had "nearly enough to eliminate the debt, what was I complaining about?" OUCH! I hate it when he is right. I wasn't content when God gave "nearly enough." I wanted it

34

all! I am not the only one like this... Let's learn to be content with what we have instead of always longing for that which we want.

___

Father, Thank You for this reminder. I have been ungrateful and demanding—childlike in my attitudes. I needed this attitude check. Lord, give me an "attitude of gratitude" and wisdom to discern between my wants and needs. Amen.

January 22nd <u>Power of the Word</u> *(Deuteronomy 6:6-9)*

"These words, which I am commanding you today, shall be on your heart. You shall teach them diligently to your sons and shall talk of them when you sit in your house and when you walk by the way and when you lie down and when you rise up. You shall bind them as a sign on your hand and they shall be as frontals on your forehead. You shall write them on the doorposts of your house and on your gates."

One of my favorite reasons for knowing the word of God is to bring stories or Scriptures to mind when I need them. As we were preparing to open the store, Bonnie (my boss at the realty office) worked on the jewelry display. As she placed each piece, she read the Scriptures aloud. They made me think of the stories or verses around them. I know that my power to overcome the onslaught of the enemy lies in verses like: *"No weapon formed against me shall prosper. I am more than a conqueror in Jesus Christ. He who is in me is greater than he who is in the world. I can do all things through Christ who strengthens me. There is no condemnation in those who love Christ Jesus."* These Scriptures reveal some of the promises I referred to in the entry for January 20th. Yes, this Word is our strength and our hope.

___

Are you taking the time to really read the verses for each lesson? The Scriptures are chosen specifically to lead into the teachings

35

and the applications. One idea to help you to better assimilate Scripture into your vocabulary may be to reread the verse after you have completed each entry. Another thought might be to reread the verses at the end of the day. See if they are still fresh in your mind. The promise verses in the above teaching can be looked up using a concordance. Most Bibles have a basic one in them. You choose a key word from the verse and try to find it that way. If you don't know how to use a concordance, find assistance from someone in your church or at a local Christian Bookstore. Like everything else in life, this will require some effort. I promise you... it is worth every ounce you put into it. There is nothing sweeter than being able to recall and recite a verse, which you have hidden in your heart...*for such a time as this.*

Lord, I need to know these promises from Your word. How else can I call upon them in a time of testing? Lord, one verse says, "No weapon formed against me shall prosper." That is an amazing statement. I claim it for myself and choose it as my own. Open my eyes, ears and mouth to see, hear and taste the wonder of Your precious Word. Amen.

January 23rd Walking with God *(Proverbs 3:5-6)*

Trust in the LORD with all your heart and do not lean on your own understanding. In all your ways acknowledge Him, and He will make your paths straight.

In case you think I never have dry times in my faith walk, note this entry from my April, 2006 journal: "I need to laugh and be joyful again. I have allowed complications over work, stress and life in general to destroy my life and my peace. I rarely laugh like I used to. Lord, I am still breathing; things are still funny; and I still have teeth in my mouth; help me to laugh. My fellowship with God is in direct parallel to my mindset. Lord, I need to have a word picture burned in my mind of the "Footsteps" poem, knowing that when I walk, You walk beside me; when I dance, You take the lead and when I am hurting, You carry me. I praise You so very much for all the good in my life. Lord, help me to improve our walk together through life."

That entry was written less than a month after the official opening of His House, my Christian bookstore. This was the dream of my heart. Why did life seem so heavy at that time in my life? PRESSURE! I was working 60-hour weeks, dividing my focus between two jobs, keeping the accounting for our home and two businesses and worrying about how to pay the bills for the store. Business hadn't taken off as I had hoped. This was a hard time in my life... because I had lost focus and perspective. God gave me the vision for His House. He supplied the partner, the building, the fixtures and wonderful volunteers. This was clearly God's vision and God's business. I was trying to make it all mine! As bad as all that seemed, I was walking in one of those "Footsteps" periods where He was carrying me!

Is pressure getting to you today? Some pressures like illness, financial loss and family struggles cannot be avoided. However, we bring many unnecessary ones upon ourselves and cling to them like they are our lifeline. Some of us thrive on having "issues" in our lives. It gives us a purpose... or so we think. God didn't design us for this stress. My life has calmed down; because I gave control of my hours to God. Give Him your schedule; let Him carry you and show you where you need to be. He is faithful.

Holy Spirit, my life is confusing and hard. I confess that some of it is because of my own doing. Lord, help me to allow You to pick me up and carry me through the hard times. May there only be one set of footprints... Yours... as we walk into the tomorrows of my life. Amen.

January 24th <u>Names of God</u> *(Proverbs 18:10)*

The name of the LORD is a strong tower;
the righteous run into it and are safe.

*T*he **<u>Lord our Righteousness</u>** tells me that even though I am flesh, I can be righteous when I realize that my righteousness comes from the Holy Lord. He is my ideal to aim toward.

<u>Wonderful Counselor</u> tells me that He hears my cries, knows my heart and advises me when I seek His way.

<u>Everlasting Father</u> encourages me my resurrected life will be eternal, as He promised—and unlike life here which is painful and temporary.

<u>Able</u> tells me that all I entrust to Him (money, time, family, my job, my gifts and abilities) He will protect.

<u>Peace</u> is one of the things I so drastically seek from Him. My life is crazy, and only true heart deep peace will keep me on an even keel.

<u>Strong tower</u> reminds me that when I start to lose my peace, need refuge, am attacked by the enemy or am weak and afraid, He is where I run. No man, drink, drug or material possession can provide the refuge I need.

Look again at the above descriptions of our Father God. Which means the most to you? Think about why that is. Has He provided counsel, refuge or peace in your life? Do you most look forward to eternal life with Him? Is His righteousness what you base your life upon? Let's work together from this day forward, to dwell upon these descriptions and begin to apply their truths in our lives. Here is another thought for applying and understanding the Word of God: Write each of these titles upon a separate recipe card. Use them in prayer to acknowledge Him for what He is in your life. I will make the prayer below an example of how to do this. You are learning more every day about how to walk with the Lord.

Sweet Jesus, You are more than able to bless and care for every-thing I entrust into Your capable hands. I lift my money, my time, my family, my talents and my praises into Your hands. Use them, use me, and cause Your light to shine through me. Amen.

January 25th Ransomed *(Psalms 49:6-7)*

*...No man can by any means redeem his brother
or give to God a ransom for him...*

*M*y first thought about ransom in the above verse was for hostages held in bondage against their will, with a price on their heads—which, when paid, will buy their release. I think of the people captured and held in Iraq and the fact that as a nation we cannot negotiate with terrorists. Once we give in to the demands of one group, the capturing will never stop. How much is one person worth? It is interesting what kidnappers would guess a life to be worth... $100,000... 50,000... 1,000,000. I think the victim's life is worth whatever the kidnapper's needs are. How much was my life worth in Satan's hands—working against Jesus, against the church and toward a horrible world? I guess it was worth whatever it cost Jesus to buy me back on Calvary. Satan wanted to keep me tied up in sin; Jesus wanted to buy my freedom... and the price was high, but Christ's love was higher.

Do you fully understand how Jesus redeemed you? Let me take you back into history as a way of explanation. Most of us know the story of Adam and Eve in the Garden of Eden. The serpent (Satan) tempted Eve to eat fruit from the one tree in a huge and fertile garden, which God told them not to eat from. Eve fell for the charm of the enemy, ate the apple, and then generously offered a bite to Adam. As soon as they did this, they felt the separation from God caused by sin. Prior to this they walked with God in the Garden. When God came for their time together they hid; because they realized they were naked. Their sin had exposed them and made that which was natural into something vulgar. God detailed the consequences for their sin. Today we can blame having to work for a living, the pains of childbirth and fear of SNAKES on Adam and Eve. They were cast out of the Garden, never to return. Before God sent them away, He slaughtered animals and made them clothes from the hides. The innocent animals shed their blood to hide the shame of those who had sinned. From that time on, animal sacrifices were used to reconcile God to His sinful creation. Jesus put an end to animal sacrifices when He offered "innocent" blood on a sinner's cross to cover our sins with His righteousness. He actually assumed the sin of every man in the world. He washes us clean; but <u>we must receive His pardon</u> by coming to Him in faith. If you have already accepted Christ, stop and praise His name—giving Him thanks. If not, please turn to **August 6-9** and read the **plan of Salvation in Christ**. He is waiting for you.

Thank You, Jesus that I have such value and worth in your eyes. Amen.

January 26th <u>Darkness or Light</u> *(I John 1:7)*

...but if we walk in the Light as He Himself is in the Light,
we have fellowship with one another, and the blood of
Jesus His Son cleanses us from all sin.

I find darkness and light in myself. I know they cannot inhabit the same heart. We are called to be *'salt and light'* in a bland and very dark world. <u>My darkness</u> traits are criticism, dissention, fear and unbelief, judging others, pride, self-promotion, gossip, exaggeration and competitive ways. <u>My light</u> characteristics are my willingness to smile, listen, encourage, and pray with others. I also have faith enough to see where Your clear direction is coming from and follow the paths You open up for me. Jesus is called the Light of the World. Think about the light characteristics I listed above. Jesus lived all of them, didn't He? When He wanted time alone to pray, He stopped to bring healing to others. When He wanted to spend time with His closest friends, He was called to feed the multitudes. He was "Light shining" everywhere around Him. Reread the Scripture verse. *"but if we walk in the Light as He is in the Light, we have fellowship with one another..."* We are commanded to walk in light; because only when we do will we have full fellowship with one another! No wonder there is such division, hatred and animosity in our world. There is a shortage of light!

I hate to break the news to you, but you cannot save or change the whole world. Let's try something new today and for the next week. Let's be lights in the dark world we walk in. Smile at grouchy people! Say kind words to those who are not kind to you. Stop gossip before it starts! Do something nice for someone who would not expect it. Send a card of encouragement. Offer prayer to someone with a need. Tell someone in the service sector, "Thank you for the job you do." You cannot change the whole world, but you can surely light up a part of it. Let's walk this week as Jesus with Skin on! Stretch yourself... you may be more blessed than those you are shining upon!

Jesus, Your word tells us that in Your eternal reign there will be no need for sun, moon or stars because You will be the light! No darkness! No sorrow! No tears! Just light—light—light! Thank You for showing me ways to be more Christ like. Please open doors for me to shine this week. Amen.

January 27th Word is Light *(Psalms 119:105)*

Your word is a lamp to my feet and a light to my path.

*T*he passage above and *"Trust in the Lord with all your heart, and lean not on your own understanding; in all your ways acknowledge Him, and He shall direct your paths"* are two of my favorite verses in Scripture. I use them to teach others the absolute value of knowing Your unfailing Word and listening for Your *still, small voice* to speak direction to them in a time of need. Jesus, just last week as a friend and I talked and I told him that yes, we are given gifts and abilities to go out and use in this life; but we are to ask God's direction and guidance by *'leaning on His wisdom,'* not ours, and allowing Him to *'direct our paths.'* Think about a pitch dark room. Most of us are uncomfortable in that kind of darkness unless we are trying to sleep. Have you ever lit a single candle in a dark room? How amazing it is that as our eyes begin to adjust, we can see quite clearly, at least in the area near the flicker of the candle's flame. That is how the word of God is in the heart of those who believe its promises. Scriptures can be like small flickers of light in the darkness of our world. God's promise to never leave or forsake us is a light. His covenant to save us if we believe upon His Son is a light. All of these little lights come from His word. Surely, after two lessons in a row on light we must realize that He is sending us a message.

Think of the darkness as someone who is totally blind. They have no need to turn on lights to move about in their familiar surroundings. We could walk into the same place and stumble over all the things hidden in darkness. Why can the blind soul find its way around? He has become familiar with where things are. I am that blind person... and so are you. We walk around with stumbling blocks before us every day. When we know where the word of God is hidden and pull it out when needed, we can maneuver safely through this life. God's promises are light for our feet... a flashlight in a pitch black forest. We need to dwell more upon the Light of His precious Word.

Light of the World, I stumble and fall as soon as I get out of the safety of Your hedge of protection. I have failed to seek Your truth and Your promises. Open my eyes to see the very real need I have for Your Word, written upon the chambers of my heart. Amen.

January 28th   <u>Lost Sheep</u>   *(I Peter 2:25)*

For you were continually straying like sheep, but now
you have returned to the Shepherd and Guardian of your souls.

I have always heard about the fact that sheep are very stupid animals who if they fall over don't get up or who would drown before they would move away from deepening water. The following comes from my April 23, 2006 journal entry. "I have to ask myself if I am any smarter. I fall into gossip, spending sprees, criticism, judgment and selfishness and am not wise enough to get up and move over. I would drown in my debt if You didn't provide ways for me to get out of it. I allow doubts to pile up to the point where I cannot function and I nearly drown in them. Thank You for the Shepherd. When I am stupid, He convicts me and reminds me of wiser choices. When I am afraid, He calms me and makes me remember past faithfulness. When I am lost, He comes after me— restores me and loves me. I am that foolish sheep. You are my loving Shepherd. Because of that, I am never lost. Amen."

Have you ever felt like I did when I wrote that entry? Do you continue to make the same mistakes over and over again? Do your words, spending habits and selfish ways convict you? Has God bailed you out of a mess, only to have you get back in it? Why don't we learn? The answer is really quite easy. We are creatures of habit…and it usually takes a 2x4 up side the head to break the habit. That doesn't mean it is impossible to change. Remember, *"With God all things are possible; for nothing is impossible with God."* Are you ready to begin to let Him make the changes, which will seem quite painful at first; but will ultimately make you a better person and a more effectual witness for Christ? The process is called pruning. He will need to lop off the useless things in your life in order for the good things to produce in abundance. He will never begin the process until you acknowledge your need. Call upon Christ and let the changes begin.

Father, I am afraid of the pruning process, though I do trust You with all I hold dear. I ask You today to begin a good work in me, removing the wrong things which sap my strength and energy. May I always know that "all things work together for the good of those who love the Lord and are called according to His purpose." Amen.

January 29th Sacrifice *(Philippians 2:6-7)*

... who, although He existed in the form of God, did not
regard equality with God a thing to be grasped,
but emptied Himself, taking the form of a bondservant,
and being made in the likeness of men.

Jesus was the ultimate volunteer, physician, psychologist, nurse, teacher, pastor and friend. He came to serve and save... never to laud His authority over men. He washed feet, cleansed hearts, removed blinders from eyes, cleaned houses and slept where He found room to sleep. The hardest part for most of us to understand is why He left the glory of heaven to do these things. He left the peace, ease and comfort of heaven plus the constant presence of His Father to come to a place where He would be despised, forfeited, blasphemed, rejected, manhandled, beaten and crucified.

Why would anyone do that? It is love... love much greater than our tiny human brains can comprehend... more love than I have ever felt... love like I want to show to others. Can you understand that kind of love? Maybe if we think of a parable, a word picture, we can better understand. Let's picture ourselves walking down the street with a tiny child we love holding tightly onto our hand. That child, in a moment of impulse, releases our hand and runs straight toward the road and into oncoming traffic. In lightning like speed, you reach for the child, toss him back to safety and fall into the path of the car. You lose your life; but you save the life of the child who you love so dearly.

What do we learn from the parable? We are the precocious child, running headlong into sin and oncoming danger. We do this, letting go of the hand of the One who created us and loves us more than life itself. That One is Jesus, the lover of our souls. He ran into the traffic, which would condemn us to certain death... and took the hit for us. That is love. That is sacrifice, and the two cannot be separated. Sacrifice for wrong motives—popularity, financial gain or notoriety is not real sacrifice. Sacrifice in the name of love is pure and holy.

Lord, I now have a clearer understanding of why You would sacrifice Your life for me. You love me. You love me. You love me... even when I am that undeserving, naughty child. How can I ever thank You for stopping my certain death and giving me eternal life? Amen.

January 30ᵗʰ <u>Peace</u> *(I Chronicles 22:9)*

Behold, a son will be born to you, who shall be a man of rest;
and I will give him rest from all his enemies on every side;
for his name shall be Solomon, and I will give
peace and quiet to Israel in his days.

As He did in the days of Solomon, God wants to give us peace. He gives it and we allow the world to take it away from us. Jesus was peace. He loved everyone, forgave those who hurt him, was merciful, kind, patient, self-sacrificing and peaceful. He sought quiet time to fellowship with the Father in prayer and communion. We must seek to *"dwell in peace"* and to return to that haven when the horrors of the world seek to rob us of our peace. The world loves division, dissention, animosity and hatred. That's why Jesus is such a foreign idea to them. The concept is beyond their greatest imagination; those who have never known peace cannot begin to understand it or its changing effect on our lives. Look at the evening news. Do you think the people in the Middle East wouldn't like peace? Of course there are always those who thrive on trouble and insurrection. Peace is not always possible. If we must compromise our beliefs in order to have peace...it is peace purchased at the wrong price. It is better for a Christian to be in separation from those who disbelieve, than to compromise principle for the sake of peace. Even in the midst of those storms we can have inner peace because we know we are right with the Lord of our souls.

Who and what steals your peace? There are times when friends, coworkers and busyness are our peace stealers. We need to look deep, seek God's direction and see if the job might not need to be changed, the friendship might not need to be sacrificed or the busyness might not need to be eliminated from our schedule. Only then can we calm our spirits and seek the face of God. Are your spouse, children and siblings your 'peace stealers?' Obviously, you can't quit them, though sometimes we quite honestly would love to! Seek counsel from godly advisors. Seek God's answers in His Word. Seek and find quiet time to calm your spirit. Find a prayer warrior to come into agreement with you. Do whatever you need in order to find peace. Turn off the phone, the television and the internet. Sit before Him in prayer and allow Him to cover you with His blanket of calm.

Lord, I need Your peace and the calm only You can bring into my life. I will surely need Your help. Sometimes I feel like I cannot keep my head above water. I simply need more of You, less of the world and a deeper faith walk. May I find the "peace, which passes all understanding." Amen.

January 31st <u>What is "The Church?"</u> *(Ephesians 5:25-27)*

Husbands, love your wives, just as Christ also loved the church and gave Himself up for her, so that He might sanctify her, having cleansed her by the washing of water with the word, that He might present to Himself the church in all her glory, having no spot or wrinkle or any such thing; but that she would be holy and blameless.

I was reading the book, "The Body" by Chuck Colson; and in it he states that "The Church" has never been a building. When we say "let's go to church" we are talking about a place, but we should be talking about going to gather with a group of people, like-minded in obedience and service to the Lord. The Church is described often in Scripture as "The Bride of Christ" arrayed and awaiting his return to take her to eternal reward. That is not talking about a big and beautiful building. It is the true and righteous body of believers who serve His purposes, who will meet him in the air. I think of this like a home. A house becomes a home not by how it is decorated or how big it is, but rather by the love, fellowship, support and encouragement of those who live within its walls. Fancy light fixtures and brass door knobs are not the things which make our houses into homes. If they are, we are headed for disaster. Likewise, church programs, a great narthex or awesome stained glass windows, do not make a church building the church. We need to think hard about what church really is.

Many church bodies have divided over the issue this passage brings to mind. Building expansion programs can lead to huge division within a congregation. I have heard it said that after the loss of a child and money problems, building a home is the third most cited cause of divorce. If it is that stressful on a marriage, of course it will be stressful on a church body. We need to worry less about space and numbers, more about serving one another, and mostly about taking our church body outside the four walls of any building and into the *'highways and byways'* in our cities. If you are part of a body of believers, start using your influence for change in ministry outreach. If you are not part of a local congregation... become a part. You need them; and most assuredly they need you.

Father, when Jesus died and the temple curtain was torn in half, You came to live in our hearts... not in a building. WE should be like-minded with other believers. Your church began in small groups, in homes and on the streets corners. WE need to get back to that kind of unity. Amen.

February 1ˢᵗ <u>His Glorious Appearing</u> *(Colossians 3:4)*

When Christ, who is our life, is revealed,
then you also will be revealed with Him in glory.

*C*hrist's coming means the end of trials and labors on this earth. It means peace, complete peace, which is something I have never known. It means the end of darkness, where evil hides and practices its deeds to hurt the innocent. It means that those alive in Christ will be lifted to Him; and those who died the first death while walking with Him, will rise up from their graves to meet Him in the air. His coming proves to the denier and blasphemer that the Word was true, the sacrifices for faith were worthy, the obedience to a doctrine was not foolish and the hope of the faithful is to be rewarded. Blasphemers will see Him just as believers will... except blasphemers will find no joy in what they see. He is coming; and we must be ready!

Can you imagine the emotion in your heart when you first see Jesus? If you have accepted Him and are one of His children, you will be abundantly blessed and excited to see your Savior face-to-face. You will know that your faith was not unfounded and that every minute you served Him was well spent. Think though, about others who have denied Christ, blasphemed believers and lived their lives in sin and separation from the things of God. They will fall to their knees before a Holy Lord; and regret will wash over them like tidal waves. Suddenly, every verse of Scripture they have denied will play before their eyes. They will wish they could turn the hands of time backward and relive the choices they made.

Jesus, on the day of Your glorious appearing we shall all see the face of the One who died for each of us. Those who never asked You to live within their hearts will wish they could have one last chance. Lord Jesus, I would like to know that no one I care about will see the terror of that day. Use me to ensure that this may be the case. Amen.

February 2ⁿᵈ <u>Junk Food</u> *(John 4:34)*

*Jesus said to them, "My **food is** to do the **will** of **Him**
who sent Me and to accomplish His work.*

*T*he first verse *"My food is to do the will of Him who sent Me"* sounds alien to our ears. What does "food and work" mean? Jesus was sent for a purpose; and He was to feed upon fulfilling that purpose. Jesus fed upon serving His Father, healing the sick, delivering the captives, casting out the demons, showing mercy to those who least deserved it and dying on the cross for our sins. That is not a very pleasant way to live or die! Or is it? He was feeding His soul with each soul He helped. What do I feed upon? I feed upon junk food, candy, fast food and everything that harms my body. I am without discipline for most of my days. Then I look in the mirror in horror and decide it's time for a diet. I stick to that for about a month; and if I haven't lost 40 pounds, I quit. What if I was to 'feed upon' the same things Jesus did? What if I fed the poor, instead of the mouth? What if I talked the truths of the gospel, instead of talking about whether I want Doritos or Fritos? Jesus fed on that good service; it fueled His passion. I'll bet if you asked a professional athlete, they would tell you they 'feed' upon the physical aspect of the game... and it is their passion.

Let's talk seriously. I know I am not the only one who feeds on junk food! Honestly, this lesson isn't about food but about feeding on the works of our hands, the Word of God and the refueling of the Holy Spirit. How are you feeding? Do you spend daily time serving in God's business? Are you reaching out to others? Do you ever reach beyond that which is comfortable for you? Think of the things we could accomplish if our *"food was to do the will of Him who sent us to accomplish His work!"* Let's make an effort to grow in our acts of service.

Help me to feed upon serving You, Lord. I want to be of good service to Your kingdom. I confess that laziness, fear and selfishness have held me back. Help me to feed upon that which is good, perfect and righteous. May that—instead of gossip or complaining—be my purpose. I failed yesterday—renew me today! Amen.

February 3rd A Bad Taste in God's Mouth *(Revelation 3:15-16)*

"I know your deeds, that you are neither cold nor hot; I wish that you were cold or hot. So because you are lukewarm, and neither hot nor cold, I will spit you out of My mouth."

When I first became a Christian, I can remember a coworker telling me that she would never read the book or Revelation because it scared her to death. My response was that God chose to have it written by the Apostle John, so why would it be any scarier than the rest of Scripture? I came to realize that we are afraid of that which we do not understand. I never professed to be a Bible scholar; but I love a challenge. So I tackled the last book of the Bible. The imagery was confusing, but some of the teachings were absolutely clear... even to a woman in the first few months of personal Bible study. The verse at the top of this page was one which hit me right where I was. Think about it. Do you like warm soda pop or lemonade when you are thirsting for a drink on a hot day? Do you want to eat lukewarm, congealing gravy on your mashed potatoes? We have definite expectations and lukewarm isn't acceptable. Would your marriage or friendships be rewarding if they were lukewarm? God feels the same way! I would have to believe (because it is written in Scripture) that God despises lukewarm "pew potatoes." Why? They don't know they are lukewarm and are thus rendered useless in growing the kingdom of God.

———

God wants us to be passionate about Him. He wants us to be excited, so that we will tell others what He has done for us and can also do for them. He would rather have someone ice-cold and totally walking contrary to Him than a lukewarm, part-time Christian. These are hard words; truth can be that way. When I became a believer in 1996 you couldn't shut me up! I was hungry to learn everything I could and told everyone what I was learning. I have the same fire today. Why? I spend daily time in the Word of God, feeding upon His truths and listening to what He wants for my life. I would never want to stand before the throne of judgment and be deemed "tepid" in my faith walk.

Sweet Jesus, I want others to see the fire I have for You. Lukewarm people aren't contagious—and I want this "faith disease" to be highly contagious, infecting everyone I come in contact with! Lord, help me to be as excited to run to You as a child running to a favorite friend. If I ever begin to cool off, please place this Scripture verse before my eyes as a not-so-gentle reminder. Amen.

February 4th <u>Bless Me, Indeed!</u> *(1 Chronicles 4: 9-10)*

*Jabez was more honorable than his brothers, and his mother named him Jabez saying, "Because I bore him with pain." Now Jabez called on the God of Israel saying, "**Oh that You would bless me indeed** and enlarge my border, and that Your hand might be with me, and that You would keep me from harm that it may not pain me!" And God granted him what he requested.*

The Old Testament books of Kings and Chronicles are not for the faint of heart! They are a telling and a retelling of the history of the tribes, leaders and kings of Israel. Why are they there? They are the historical record, proving the heritage of those born into the nation of Israel. In the midst of these seemingly endless lists of unpronounceable names fall the verses at the top of this page. How horrible to be named Jabez, meaning born in pain! What a legacy he had to live up to! (Personally, I believe that all children are born in pain; just ask the one giving birth!) Scripture tells us that Jabez was honorable—maybe to make up for all that pain! It also tells us that he was a man who sought God. Today we look at the first of his requests,

"Oh that You would bless me indeed." Does that seem like a selfish request? Would it seem more humble to say, "If it is Your will, please send me good things today?" We ask God these kinds of things in our prayers all the time. "I really need that new job, God. Could you help me out?" or "Lord, if it is Your will, please help us buy this new house." Hmmm, those requests don't seem quite so bold, do they?

Maybe Jabez was a tither. You know, taking his first fruits to the Lord as commanded in the early books of the Old Testament. If he was, this verse might explain his request. *"Bring the whole tithe into the storehouse, so that there may be food in My house, and test Me in this," says the Lord of hosts, **"if I will not open for you the windows of heaven and pour out for you a blessing until it overflows."*** What is Jabez really doing here? He is acknowledging the very real truth that all good things come from the Lord above. He is admitting that he needs God's provision. How often do you do the same? Are you God sufficient or self-sufficient?

Father God, You are the source of every blessing in my life—my relationships, my finances, my health, my faith walk...my very life. I believe You have abundant blessings with my name on them just waiting for me to ask for them, thus professing my confidence in who You are. May I take nothing for granted, and may I never think that things come because of my power. You are my Provider... and You have done a great job so far! Amen.

February 5th Expand My Outreach (1 Chronicles 4: 9-10)

*Jabez was more honorable than his brothers, and his mother named him Jabez saying, "Because I bore him with pain." Now Jabez called on the God of Israel saying, "Oh that You would bless me indeed and **enlarge my border**, and that Your hand might be with me, and that You would keep me from harm that it may not pain me!" And God granted him what he requested.*

*A*s we continue in our study of Jabez, let us look closely at his second request to God. **"Enlarge my border."** This is my favorite of Jabez's supplications. Other versions translate the word border into territory. "The Bible according to Vicki" says, "Make my sphere of influence and my ministry bigger than I could ever imagine!" Likely, you prefer the border expansion to mine! Jabez was asking for expanded land which equates to more work, so we really aren't so far apart from one another. Maybe I have "CRAZY" carved in my forehead, but I say the same to the Lord every day, "Put someone new in my path so I might minister to their needs today." "Provide me with a building, a partner and a bunch of money so I can minister through a Christian business." Or, "Make me sit still long enough to write 366 devotionals...so that one person (maybe you) will grow in their faith throughout the next year." If God is going to bless me (from yesterday's devotional), then I want to use the gifts and abilities He has given me. The more I use, the more He will bless. Luke 19:26 begins, *"I tell you that to everyone who has, more shall be given..."* I have been given gifts... and I surely want to use them to His glory.

Are you afraid to ask God to expand your ministry? Are you afraid that He may take you to places you are not equipped to go? Are you comfortable right where you are? I can honestly share here that I did pray about each of the ministry opportunities written above. God faithfully provided that partner, building, business, 366 devotional entries and hundreds of opportunities to minister to those in need. I am still waiting for the "bunch of money;" but I never close a door God wants to open!

Heavenly Father, I admit that I am apprehensive about where you might send me—because in myself I am not equipped to minister to the needs of those around me. Please, help me to overcome my fears, step out in faith and allow You to "direct my paths." I know in my heart of hearts that You would never send me anywhere that I cannot be Your hands and feet. Amen.

February 6th <u>Your Hand Upon Me</u> *(1 Chronicles 4:9-10)*

*Jabez was more honorable than his brothers, and his mother named him Jabez saying, "Because I bore him with pain." Now Jabez called on the God of Israel saying, "Oh that You would bless me indeed and enlarge my border, and **that Your hand might be with me**, and **that You would keep me from harm** that it may not pain me!" God granted him what he requested.*

*J*abez realizes that abundant blessings and expanded borders could easily be the very things which could cause him to move down wrong paths. He asked God to keep His hand upon him, directing his paths so that he wouldn't walk away from that which God had planned for him. I fully understand this request. As a business owner, a Bible teacher and a mentor to young believers, I could easily make a misstep which would impact the lives of others. Jabez called from his righteous heart for God to keep him from any pain he could inflict on himself or innocent bystanders. In the 23rd Psalm (one of the rare Bible verses most people could recite) we are told that God *"makes us lie down in green pastures, leads us beside still waters, and guides us in the paths of righteousness."* That is the difference between the God we serve, the Living God of Israel, and the stone idols of other nations. Our God cares... and because He cares, He loves us enough to keep us on right paths. Jabez was taking out a spiritual insurance policy, guaranteed to keep his blessings and outreach focused on his Master.

What do we learn from Jabez' request? How does his hunger for God's touch speak to our hearts? Many of us like to compartmentalize God, keeping Him in a nice little Sunday morning box. We don't make Him part of our marriages, our parenting, our careers or our entertainment. Actually, He might be pretty ashamed to be called our God if He were with us in our day-to-day lives. Jabez wanted to avoid that possibility. He wanted to march 100% to the beat of God's drum. He knew that failure or sin in his life would reflect poorly on the God he served... and would hinder the blessings He wanted to send.

Lord, I need to acknowledge You in the same way Jabez did. I want to be Your child, Your adopted daughter. I have tried to direct my own paths before... like a foolish sheep without a shepherd. Each path led me to failure and disappointment. Your paths aren't always straight, but we surely have fun going around the curves and over the hills. I wouldn't want any other tour guide. Amen.

February 7ᵗʰ Letter of Apology *(Psalms 103:13-14)*

Just as a father has compassion on his children, So the LORD has compassion on those who fear Him. For He Himself knows our frame; He is mindful that we are but dust.

One of my favorite stories of how God's sense of humor has been revealed in my life began at a wedding Dan and I attended three years ago. At the reception we shared a table with my uncle and his wife. Before I became a Christian, I lived a very ungodly life. A good part of that life took place in a local bar. My uncle had been involved in some of those times and we began to laugh about old times and the funny memories we shared. Several times during the night I felt the nudging of the Holy Spirit to tell this couple that while it was okay to relive these memories, it was not good to glorify them. He also urged me to tell how my life had changed once I began to walk with Christ. I was sick with conviction all the way home, walked in the door and sat down to write a letter apologizing to my aunt and uncle. I confessed that I had been outwardly disobedient in my omission of my faith and told them exactly how Jesus had changed my life. I had Dan take the letter to the mailbox... so I wouldn't change my mind and not send it at all. On Wednesday, I told my Bible study class about it... and on Friday **it came back in the mail** marked as incorrect address! Believe me; the spiritual struggle to re-mail the letter was harder than the first decision. I finally placed it in a new envelope and sent it off again. What a chuckle God must have had!

You may wonder why I felt so convicted by my actions that I would write a letter sure to cause a stir in others' lives. I have spent time in the Word of God every day for 11 years (to date). Many times in Scripture a character feels the separation from God caused by sin in their life. My glorification of sin and failure to tell who brought me the freedom to deny those actions is sin in itself. One of my theories has always been that the commandment *"do not take the Lord's name in vain"* doesn't only mean using Jesus or God in inappropriate ways, but that as Christians we are given the command and authority to use Jesus' name to change our world. When I failed to tell of his awesome work in me, I took His precious Name in vain.

Jesus, Your convicting Spirit is not a burden in my life. You prove to me time and again the truth that it is easier to walk with You first, than it is to walk in my own volition and go back to make things right later. I long to walk fully in Your light every day of my life. I still fall down, but You always pick me up, dust me off and restore me to Your grace. Amen.

February 8th <u>Righteous Anger</u> *(Matthew 21:12)*

And Jesus entered the temple and drove out all those who were buying and selling in the temple, and overturned the tables of the money changers and the seats of those who were selling doves.

*R*ighteous anger does have a part in our lives. I love the story about Jesus overturning the tables of the moneychangers who were using the faithfulness of temple worshippers to make a fortune. These people were abusing the needs of the Jewish populace as they came to offer sacrifices at the temple. The moneychangers would insist that the worshippers' coins were not the correct ones and would cheat the people with an exorbitant exchange rate. Another practice they used was to find a "blemish" on the animal brought to sacrifice (whether it was there or not). They would sell them a more 'perfect' animal to sacrifice, then turn around and sell that 'blemished' animal to the next person. Jesus saw all these things they were doing in the light of day with no shame or apology! Jesus' anger was a righteous anger. He was furious that what was to be a house of prayer had become a "place of commerce." I do wonder if Jesus would think the same thing about today's churches. Are we there to worship our Savior, or to pay a duty with our limited time for God? Are we there because the church is our family; or because the words tickle our ears and give us a good start for the week? Time for soul searching!

_____

If you are a regular church attendee, why do you go? Is it to worship? Maybe it's to fellowship with other believers. Is it because the music is good? I ask these things for your own benefit. We are to go to the "temple of God to meet with Him and offer Him our sacrifices." Those sacrifices can be a lot of different things—worship, prayer, tithes or service. We need to stop treating our churches like Christian Community Gathering Places. The church is God's house! Doesn't that require a degree of reverence? I love fun and fellowship. I love laughter and (obviously) potlucks! Mostly, I love to hear the Word of God taught and defined. I remember a pastor long ago telling us that if we came to be entertained, we came for the wrong reason. He was right!

_____

Heavenly Father, help me to control my fleshly anger. It has controlled me in the past. Help me also to see where righteous anger is needed. The removal of Your name from the public forum is a great example of a place to tunnel my energy. Keep me focused on You, and You will direct my paths. Amen.

February 9ᵗʰ <u>Weight of the World</u> *(Matthew 21:12)*

Surely our grief He Himself bore, and our sorrows He carried; Yet we ourselves esteemed Him stricken, smitten of God, and afflicted.

*J*esus suffered in ways I can't even imagine because His suffering included carrying the weight of all my sins (and the sins of the entire world) on His shoulders. He was delivered to enemies, betrayed by His closest friends, beaten, spit upon, blasphemed, persecuted, made fun of, shuffled from one court to another, separated from His mother, abandoned by those He trusted most, crowned with thorns, struck in the face, flogged to near death, burdened by the weight of the cross, led up Golgotha hill, crucified, made fun of there, died, was pierced and was laid in a borrowed tomb. If it had been any other way, no one would remember the story today. Yet we take it so lightly. How often do Christians really think about Jesus' suffering, other than during the Easter season? I doubt there are many readers of this book who would willingly sacrifice one of their children for anything they had done wrong; let alone for the sins of someone else's children. We need to realize what this cost God. How would you handle watching your child spit upon, blasphemed and falsely accused? We owe Him every-thing... and so often give Him nothing but a passing glance, an hour of our week and a few dollars in the offering plate. Had God cared for us as we care for Jesus, every one of us would be headed for eternity in hell.

Do the words in the teaching section seem too harsh or convicting to you? I believe with all my heart that a great number of the people within the Christian community take Jesus' sacrifice too lightly. If that were not the case, we would be doing all the things we are commanded to do... feed the poor, care for the widows, adopt the orphans and pray for one another. Instead, we walk in the doors on Sunday, distracted by Saturday and worrying about Monday. We go through the motions, and we fool some people. We cannot, however, fool God. He knows where our hearts and thoughts are. I am not condemning you... I am just as guilty as the next person. He carried the weight of our sins on His shoulders...

Jesus, from Your humble birthplace to Your borrowed tomb You stayed focused on that which was important. How can I be so distracted by the inconsequential things of this life? Holy Spirit, move into my spirit and help me to keep my focus on what is truly important in my life. Amen.

February 10ᵗʰ <u>Bright Eyes</u> *(Mark 10: 14-15)*

"Permit the children to come to Me; do not hinder them;
for the kingdom of God belongs to such as these.
Truly I say to you, whoever does not receive the
kingdom of God like a child will not enter it at all."

September 11, 2001 was a day that changed the world as we knew it. It was also the day our first grandchild was due to be born. I remember telling God I didn't want Tyler to be born on a day of such destruction and evil. He made it clear to me that the decision wasn't mine! Tyler was born six days later on September 17, 2001. Our lives have never been the same! Tyler was a beautiful baby who captured our hearts from the first moment we touched him. Tyler began having sleepovers at our house the week he was born. I remember so clearly holding him and singing this little song, his very own Grandma written lullaby: "Bright eyes, bright eyes, such a beautiful boy; bright eyes, bright eyes, you bring us such joy. Little Tyler bundled in blue; Grandma's so happy, just to be with you." He would smile... my heart would melt... and I would think maybe all the frustrations his dad gave us were worth it!! We learn as much from Tyler as he does from us. We learn that "old people" can climb on monkey bars, that hot chocolate in front of the fireplace is delicious, and sticks of Big Red gum are the perfect size to split with Poppa. Tyler loves church and prays the same prayer before meals and at bedtime: "Hey, Jesus thank you for this food and all my people... even my grandma and grandpa."

Children, no matter the situation of their birth, are gifts from God. Ever since Tyler's birth he has lain on the other end of the sofa and watched me do my Bible study in the early mornings. Recently, he asked what I was studying. I taught him about confession and repentance. Is that too heavy for a five year old? Maybe not! Two weeks later he was told not to go near my new laptop. When I walked back in the room he was in the chair holding it. I scolded him and asked why he does the things he is told not to. A little while later he called me to where he was and very seriously asked me, "Grandma, would this be a good time for repentance?" What a memory he has! Thank God for the privilege of being Tyler's grandmother.

Lord Jesus, thank you for children. How I wish I could be as honest, open, passionate and fearless as they are. I would love to have that energy, imagination and unrestricted love. Help me to never push them away, consider them an inconvenience or ignore their questions. I too am but a child in the arms of my Loving Father. Amen.

February 11th Blue Eyes *(Psalms 127: 3-4)*

Behold, children are a gift of the Lord, the fruit of the womb is a reward; Like arrows in the hand of a warrior, so are the children of one's youth.

*Y*esterday you learned about the doting grandma side of me. Today you will learn about the other little "heart stealer" in my life. Hailey Nichole arrived on June 1, 2005, as her mother, under the influence of lots of drugs, grinned her way toward childbirth. Hailey was tiny, petite and beautiful... and I helped with her delivery! She is the polar opposite of her big brother. She is fair haired with blue eyes; he has brown hair and big brown eyes. She is dainty and feminine; he is the proverbial bull in a china shop. She squeals; he yells. She is a daddy's girl; he is a mommy's boy. They prove to me the wonder of how God created each child to be unique and special. No cookie cutter kids here. Hailey is more pensive, more of a thinker... and she lights up the room with her grin. We want the best for this adorable child. We pray daily for her and look forward to the day she gives her heart to Christ. Hailey is a blessed little girl with a beautiful Mommy and a dedicated Daddy. If you have no grandchildren, you may not understand my gushing on these two entries. If you do, you understand completely.

———————————

God's Word tells us children are His gift. How often we forget that truth. I believe He watches us spoil them with too many toys, clothes and luxuries. Surely He would rather see us give them godly homes, proper discipline and love revealed by our commitment to care for their needs. I am led to think of Hannah and Elizabeth—Bible characters who were both childless. They asked God to remove their shame, give them a child and then promised to dedicate their sons into God's service. Both women conceived, held the child they longed for more than life itself, and kept their word. Hannah's son, Samuel, became a prophet of God who was used to appoint and anoint King David. Elizabeth's son was John the Baptist who paved the way for the gospel of grace preached by our Jesus. We sell our children short when we don't expect big things from God for them.

———————————

Father God, before time began You had a plan for each child to ever be conceived in this world. You hold their lives in Your hands. We have fallen so far short in "training them up in the way they should go." Lord, help me to make the difference in the life of one child today. Help me to touch them, hug them and listen to them. I receive them as a gift from above. Amen.

February 12th <u>Holiness</u> *(Psalms 51:60)*
Behold, You desire truth in the innermost being,
and in the hidden part You will make me know wisdom.

*H*ave you ever had a 'beat me up' kind of day? I must have had one on May 3rd, 2006, from the sound of this entry! "Filthiness of flesh and spirit are not present in holiness; and I am far from holy. Truth (with no compromise) is holiness. I fail here also. Wisdom is part of a holy walk. I rely more on human wisdom and book smarts. Holy people are able to deny worldly lusts; a look at my body shows that I haven't conquered that either. Purity of body, mind, words and the flesh reflects holiness. I am very impure." One thing is true: God isn't finished with me yet! When I fail to be the woman God calls me to be in all aspects of my life, I am hurting myself as much as Him. Some would say that holiness is an unachievable goal. They may be right in the sense that Jesus alone has been holy and perfect. That should never stop us from striving to be holy and Christ-like in all our ways. Why strive for holiness? Your walk is watched by others every day. They are waiting for you, a Christian, to fall on your face or fall away. Your walk must reflect Christ's goodness, or else it will reflect the agenda of the enemy. Let's strive together to do better every day.

How would you describe your holiness level? Others would discount the things I wrote in the first paragraph of this entry. Unfortunately, I know myself and God knows me even more. I am pretty honest about my shortcomings. Why wouldn't I be? I can't fool the only One who really matters in the long run! Contrived holiness is distasteful to God. Jesus talked often about putting on a false front by acting religious. God would rather have a struggling seeker than a religious pretender working in His name. The seeker is at least trying to grow and is not satisfied with the status quo. Let's commit our hearts to strive for holiness, Christ-likeness and humility.

Lord, I ask You to complete in me the good work You began. Strengthen me to overcome fleshly lusts, to seek always to be more *like You in my spirit and in my Christian walk. I need a new infilling of Your Spirit to make me exactly who You want me to be. **Amen**... and thank You for loving me in spite of me.*

February 13th <u>Clear Conscience</u> *(Isaiah 43:25)*

I, even I, am the one who wipes out your transgressions for My own sake, and I will not remember your sins.

here are still days when I am afraid to face the throne of judgment. In those moments I realize that unconfessed sin holds me in bondage. I confess the sin and bring back to my mind Your Scriptures like 1-John 1:9, *"If we confess our sins He is faithful and just to forgive our sins and cleanse us from all unrighteousness."* I must confess my sins, and then He <u>will</u> cleanse me from <u>all</u> unrighteousness. Note that the Scripture assures that Jesus WILL, not might, cleanse me. Notice also that the cleansing is for ALL, not some, of my sins. Christ's blood doesn't only cover some of our sins. When this fellowship is restored and I am back in the circle of His love, then I get very excited to see the face of my Holy Father, my Precious Savior and the Holy Spirit. I believe that one of the hardest things for Christians to understand is grace. Grace is 'unearned, unmerited favor." What does that mean? We can't earn it by being good or doing good things. We can't buy God's love. We also don't deserve His mercy. That sounds harsh, but we must remember that our sin may seem little compared to that of others. However, we are not judged against one another. Your sins are measured against Christ's life. I remember years ago teaching about grace being the same for my gossip as for a convicted felon's murder. We see the sins in degrees of our own making. God sees sin as sin; and all of it separates us from His good graces.

We need to stop measuring ourselves against our neighbors. We all do it, don't we? "I may not go to church every week, but at least I don't swear like Sue."—"Bob was busted for drunk driving, so my own adultery doesn't seem so bad."—"Mom, yes, I got a D in science, but at least I'm not out doing drugs like my friends are." Each of these illustrates my point. We cannot weigh our sins against someone else's. A clear conscience before God exists when we can lay our head down at night knowing we walked our entire day for Christ. Even so, we need to confess any sin we may have inadvertently committed. Let us all seek to start and finish today with a clear conscience.

Jesus, I cannot wait to look in Your eyes and have You look at me for the personal touch and emotional healing I so crave. I long for a clear conscience, a full restoration, and a life dedicated to service until You come for me—Come, Lord Jesus! Amen.

February 14ᵗʰ <u>My Salvation</u> *(Romans 10:9-10)*

...that if you confess with your mouth Jesus as Lord, and believe in your heart that God raised Him from the dead, you will be saved; for with the heart a person believes, resulting in righteousness, and with the mouth he confesses, resulting in salvation.

On February 14, 1996, I sat in a five-dollar garage sale chair in an upper level bedroom of our home and gave my life to Jesus. That is the day when I finally responded to His calls on my heart. Ten years later, I wrote the following journal entry as I remembered the significance of my Salvation anniversary. "I am excited to write on this special day in my life. I think of a lot of things I treasure about my relationship with Jesus. I treasure the presence of the one who <u>never leaves me</u>. I can call on Him at any time in my life and He is there. I also treasure grace, mercy and forgiveness for the things I do (still today), the things I have done in the past and the things that I will do in the future. I surely need grace. I treasure the truths of Your Word—a love letter written to me so that I might dig in, feast upon and be directed by Your teachings. I love how alive it is, how applicable it is and how much easier life is when we simply obey Your teachings and mirror Your ways." I truly believe it was no mistake that I came to Christ on Valentine's Day. While everyone else was obsessing about how to show someone they loved them, I was offering my heart to the One who loves like no other has loved. I love Jesus; He is my Valentine. Dan bought me a card on February 14, 2007. I was irritated because we had agreed not to waste money on Valentine's gifts or cards. I opened the card... and it was for my Salvation anniversary! How special is my husband? How special is my Lord!

Do you have a salvation anniversary? I have been given the privilege to lead several people to Christ; and I keep track of their Salvation anniversaries, so I can send a note or make a call. Do you understand the significance of knowing the day you were born again? That is the 'birthday' we should celebrate...the day of our **"new birth."** Here is an idea. If you don't know the exact date of your new birth experience, make today your recommitment day and make it your anniversary. Spend time with the Lord, get in touch with His truths, find a Scripture verse to call your own and begin a whole new walk.

Jesus, I treasure the knowledge that when this life is over, I will see Your face, be held in your arms and enter my eternal reward! Thank You for saving me. Amen.

February 15th Yesterday & Forever *(Hebrews 13:8)*

Jesus Christ is the same yesterday and today and forever.

Do you ever think about what the home Jesus has prepared for you in Heaven will be like? I don't mean how big or fancy it will be. I am talking about what will not be in that home, as compared to our earthly homes. I look forward to the heavenly home because I believe that the plumbing won't leak, the furnace will always work and the walls will not need repainting! I look forward to no dissention, no anger and no sibling rivalry! My heavenly home will be the place the Lord has prepared for me, so it will be perfect. I am not worried about size, shape or feature because a straw hut with Jesus is better than a mansion with discord. The Scripture verse above tells us that Jesus is always the same. He loves us today as He loved us at creation. His mercy endures forever. He will rule and reign for all of eternity. I am so grateful that Jesus never changes—because He is the one constant in my life. He is my all in all. He is my hope in things to come. He is the **Son**shine of my life. He is peace in a peace-less world.

Think about the fact that Jesus never changes. Now think about how people change. We see the passion of a young married couple turn to cold indifference. We see that adorable toddler become an obnoxious teenager and think they must have mixed up the babies at the hospital! We see excited new believers become indifferent to the things of Christ. We allow the things of this world to change and influence us. Sexual temptation, money problems and kids affect the marriage. Peer pressure causes our children to separate from us. Faith, not fed by the Word of God, becomes lukewarm. Jesus never changes. He is the baseline we can measure everything else against.

Lord, prepare a place for me and come soon and take me there. Humble and modest or huge and fancy, You choose and I will worry more about seeing Your face than what place You are preparing. How grateful I am for the unchanging love You give to me. Help me to measure all other things against You and Your character. Amen.

February 16th   After God's Own Heart   *(1 Samuel 16:7)*

The LORD said to Samuel, "Do not look at his appearance or at the height of his stature, because I have rejected him; for God sees not as man sees; for man looks at the outward appearance; but the LORD looks at the heart."

When Samuel the prophet was sent to anoint the future King of Israel, he went to the house of Jesse the Bethlehemite, as instructed by God. There he proceeded to be introduced to each of Jesse's sons. The eldest, Eliab, was handsome, as was Abinadab, the second oldest. After Samuel had heard the Lord reject each of Jesse's seven strong sons, he was confused. The Lord had given clear instructions for this journey, and Samuel was doing exactly as commanded. In frustration, Samuel asks Jesse if he has other sons. Jesse's response is basically that the seven important ones were here and only David, his youngest son who was at work with the flocks, was left. Samuel had them bring David in from the field. Immediately the Lord revealed to him that David was the one to be anointed. Samuel did as God instructed, but wondered why this young, relatively weak boy was God's choice. *But the LORD said to Samuel, "Do not look at his appearance or at the height of his stature, because I have rejected him; for God sees not as man sees; for* **man looks at the outward appearance***; but* **the LORD looks at the heart.***"*

How reassuring this should be to us! God doesn't care about your chic hair style, your designer clothes, or your nicely manicured nails. He cares about the condition of your heart. That extra 10 pounds you gained in the last year doesn't turn Him off. Man will surely judge you by appearance... but God judges the goodness, kindness, dedication and faithfulness of your heart. Even though outward appearance (and physical health) should hold some degree of importance in our lives, they certainly do not determine our identity. What does your heart look like? Would the condition of it cause God to call you "a person after His own heart?"

Father God, how grateful I am that I don't have to be perfect to be loved. How wonderful to know that You didn't cast off David, that lowly shepherd boy... nor will You cast me away. Help me to remember that You look at the heart, and that I need to do the same in my dealings with others today. Grow my heart to be more like Yours. Amen.

February 17ᵗʰ <u>A Heart of Grace</u> *(2 Samuel 9:1)*

Then David said, "Is there yet anyone left of the house of Saul, that I may show him kindness for Jonathan's sake?"

*W*e see the heart of David, which made him God's choice as the future king of Israel, in this verse. History teaches us that in Old Testament times when a new king was placed upon the throne of Israel, all members of the former king's family were slain. This sounds harsh to us, but this prevented the heirs of the first king from mounting an insurrection and trying to take the throne back. David, seeking to fulfill a promise he made to his best friend Jonathon, seeks to find if there is anyone of the house of Saul left alive. The King is told that there is one son of Jonathon who survives. He seeks further information and finds that Mephibosheth survived, but is crippled in both feet. His nursemaid had dropped him while trying to flee when word came that Saul and Jonathon had died in battle. He is now a grown man, living in exile for fear of the King's wrath. David sends for Mephibosheth, who comes to him fully expecting to be killed. He falls at the feet of the king, who tells him, *"Do not fear, for I will surely show kindness to you for the sake of your father Jonathan, and will restore to you all the land of your grandfather Saul; and you shall eat at my table regularly."*

Wow! Not only is David showing mercy to the grandson of his enemy, but he is accepting him into his household as a member of his family! Mephibosheth, the crippled man who was living in fear of King David every day of his life, is going to sit at the King's banquet table! He will eat among the "beautiful people." Imagine the apprehension as he makes his way to that table for the first time... as he seats himself among the princes and daughters of David... as they look at him in pity or judgment. None of that matters—because he is dining with the King!

Father God, I am not so unlike Mephibosheth. I am crippled in my own ways—most of them don't show on the outside. Who am I that I am allowed to feast upon the blessings of Your kingdom? Lord, I am ever mindful of my shortcomings. May I look with eyes of mercy upon all who would come before me, no matter their appearance, attitude or status. Amen.

February 18ᵗʰ In the Wrong Direction *(2 Samuel 11: 2-3)*

*One evening David got up from his bed and walked around
on the roof of the palace. From the roof he saw a woman
bathing. The woman was very beautiful,
and David sent someone to find out about her.*

David should have known that something was amiss as soon as he decided not to leave home and go out to battle with his troops. What would cause a great military hero to stop doing what he loves and what has brought him great acclaim? Scripture tells us that *"Hell and destruction are never full, so the eyes of man are never satisfied"* (Proverbs 27:20 KJV). Even when cautioned that the woman, Bathsheba, was married to one of his soldiers, he still followed the lust of his flesh. David and Bathsheba conceive a child from their union, and suddenly David is faced with the realization that his sin is about to be exposed. He schemes to have Bathsheba's husband, Uriah, brought in from the battlefield— thinking that he could be deceived into believing the child is his own. Unfortunately for David, Uriah is very honorable and refuses to go home while his soldiers sleep in tents. David, in order to save his own reputation, commands that Uriah be put on the front line of battle and abandoned, in order that the enemy will slay him. Other innocent men die due to this poor military move, but David doesn't care. He thinks he has gotten away with his sin. In the next entry we will discover that sin carries consequences... sometimes long-range consequences.

David, a man after God's own heart, has everything going for him. It is easy for us to judge him because of his adultery with Bathsheba and for his scheming against Uriah. Yes, that is surely contemptible. It is sin. Sin by any other name is sin... and all sin is ultimately against God. Psalm 51 is a great picture of the depth of David's shame. He cries out for restoration, cleansing, and a return to the day when he did have a heart like God's. Before we judge him too harshly, we need to remember that all sin separates us from God. Our sins have different labels. They are still sins.

My Heavenly Father, I confess that I have been like David, caught in the web of my own sin and powerless to go back and undo what I have done. Knowing that You forgave him helps me to know that I can bring my sins before the God of mercy, confess them, run the other way from them and receive the restoration I so long for. Amen.

February 19th   Heritage Shattered   *(2 Samuel 12: 10-12)*

"Now, therefore, the sword will never depart from your house, because you despised me and took the wife of Uriah the Hittite to be your own. This is what the LORD says: 'Out of your own household I am going to bring calamity upon you. Before your very eyes I will take your wives and give them to one who is close to you, and he will lie with your wives in broad daylight. You did it in secret, but I will do this thing in broad daylight before all Israel'."

$\mathcal{K}$ing David had fallen far from the place God had elevated him to as a "man after His own heart." Now, Nathan the prophet has been sent to give him the dire prophecy of what the consequences of his sin will amount to. David has been ignoring the needs of his older children. The sword mentioned above is the attacking of everything he holds dear. His son, Amnon, rapes his half sister, Tamar, and then casts her out like a harlot. When her brother Absalom realizes that their father is not going to punish the sin, he takes matters into his own hands and kills Amnon. Absalom ends up living apart from his father for five years as his anger toward his father burns. Absalom devises a plan to overthrow his weak father and become the king of Israel. It isn't hard to do, because a distracted leader isn't working on serving and knowing his subjects. Absalom gains the loyalty of many in Israel, chases his father out of Jerusalem and fulfills the prophecy above by lying with his father's concubines in the sight of the entire city. David is reduced to a fleeing vagrant living in caves to try to stay alive. Eventually, Absalom is slain by David's military leader, but the dream is shattered. David has lost both of his sons and the respect of the people God sent him to lead.

———

Once sin has separated us from God, it is easy to get caught up in the things of the world and to lose our focus of what is really important. David was disrespected by Absalom because of his weak response to Amnon's sin against Tamar. Absalom was wrong, but we can clearly see why he would think that a king should be stronger and more ready to discipline. Do you think God's consequences were too harsh? Remember, the Word tells us that what is done in darkness will be revealed in light. Sin is like cancer and must be destroyed before it continues to spread.

———

Dear Lord, I confess to being easily distracted by the "stuff" in my life. I need your Spirit to guide and direct me, keeping me focused on what is really important. Help me to keep my eyes on the things I am responsible for. Consequences can be so hard to face... help me to avoid them in the first place. Amen.

February 20th Death of a Dream *(2 Samuel 23: 3-5a)*

*"The God of Israel said, The Rock of Israel spoke to me,
'He who rules over men righteously, who rules in the fear of God,
is as the light of the morning when the sun rises... when the
tender grass springs out of the earth, through sunshine after rain.'*

Truly is not my house so with God? For He has made an everlasting covenant with me…"

avid is nearing the end of his life. He has been richly blessed with military victories over mightier armies, wise counsel through some of God's most anointed teachers and prophets, and wealth beyond his wildest imagination. He has many children and has chosen Solomon, his son born with Bathsheba, to sit upon his throne. All that God promised him has happened… yet, the picture of perfection is marred by the consequences of a decision made years before. God kept His part of the everlasting covenant mentioned above, but by David's own actions he failed to "rule over men righteously." He has lost three sons, been made a laughing stock by one of them, been betrayed by his close friend and military commander Joab, and now, another son, Adonijah, wants to fight Solomon for the throne their father is soon to vacate. Surely by this time David wants it all to end. Hasn't he paid a high enough price? David wants to build a temple for God. Israel has never had a brick and mortar building to worship in… a place for God to reside among Israel, His chosen nation. When David shares his vision with the prophet, he is told that God doesn't want him to build the temple. His only consolation is that Solomon is chosen to fulfill the dream and build the temple in the future.

All of David's successes cannot bring him peace at the end of his life. The dreams he had for his kingdom and his legacy are compromised. He will abdicate the throne with a black mark on his name. Does David give up and forsake his walk with God? Absolutely not! He has had many victories and God still calls him *"a man after My heart."* 2 Samuel 22 is an entire chapter dedicated to thanking God for His protection, provision and forgiveness. David learned many lessons, some the hard way, but will never forget the amazing way he was taken from the sheepfold and made a King!

Father God, may my mistakes never keep me from walking close to You. Make me willing to accept my consequences and move on in fullness of faith. Others may criticize or condemn me, but You love me back into right standing and tell me to simply go and sin no more. Amen.

February 21ˢᵗ Still Small Voice *(Psalms 85:8)*

I will hear what God the LORD will say; for He will speak peace to His people, to His godly ones; but let them not turn back to folly.

"*I will hear the Lord when He speaks, for He speaks peace to His people.*" We have to hear His spoken peace in order to receive it. How can we hear amid the noise and clamoring of this life? We must still ourselves and wait for the still small voice. Think about Matthew 7:7, a verse which says, "*Ask and it will be given to you, seek and you will find, knock and the door will be opened.*" He is standing and knocking at our heart's door, but are we too busy to open the door? We are so caught up in doing busy-work, getting involved in programs and focusing on our earthly wants that we don't hear His knocking. We are too busy seeking new ways to get closer to God when we should simply quiet our lives, open His Word and listen. We must remember that prayer is dialogue and is a two way action. He wants to speak, but often cannot get a word in edge-wise because we are bringing a laundry list of requests. Like any other relationship, our dialogue with God requires give and take. How can we ever find out what He has to say if we are doing all the talking? God speaks when we listen.

Do you know how to hear the "*still small voice* of God?" Do you truly want to hear it? This will never happen until you make (take) time for the conversation to happen. Here are a few tips to help you: Find a place... if not a whole room, then a corner of a room, which is your Bible study and prayer area. Set a time when you can focus without distraction. I prefer early in the morning, but some choose nighttime. Light a candle if possible; it will help you to focus. I pray before I begin to read the Word, asking the Holy Spirit to reveal truth to me. I begin to read <u>slowly</u> as I think about what I am reading. I turn off the reading light, focus on the candle and begin by praising God for who He is. Move from there into confession of sin, then thanksgiving for our blessings and finally into our supplications or prayer requests. Gradually allow yourself to leave prayer time by listening for God's voice—maybe in a Scripture verse or in a line from a song, or sometimes in a clear-cut statement to your conscience. Learn to do this and your prayer life will grow.

Father, teach me to hear Your voice, to calm my spirit and to really communicate with You. This is one area I will really need help with. I must learn to turn off the pressing things of the day in order to be fully focused on You and the words You have for me. Amen.

February 22nd <u>Building a Dream: Vision</u> *(Genesis 37:19)*

They said to one another, "Here comes this dreamer!"

*I*t's really funny how we admire some dreamers like Henry Ford, Thomas Edison, Benjamin Franklin and the Wright Brothers, and we make fun of someone we know who has an inborn vision. We think they can never do what they see in their minds. There were likely doubters in the life of each of the men I mentioned above, but they didn't allow doubt to stop them from achieving the things God put in their souls. Dreams can burn in the heart for years with no life breathed into them. The Scripture above comes from the story of Joseph, a favored son of Jacob, who fathered the twelve tribes of Israel. Joseph had a dream...a vision birthed into his spirit by God. Unwisely, he shared the dream with his brothers who hated him for it and for his favored status with their father. The words above are spoken in derision and hatred. Shortly thereafter, Joseph would be sold into bondage by his siblings. That surely wasn't how his dream had looked! Does that mean the dream was not really from God? No, just a mere detour! My Dad is a dreamer. Ever since I was a young child he has talked of building a log home. He drew pictures, talked of how he would do it, and put it on hold because he had a family to support. The thing he wanted most and which burned in his heart required planning, money, time, and a series of events, which would put him in the place for the dream to happen. God knew the dream. He gave it to him...and in His timing the dream would come true.

What is the dream born in your heart? Do you have the great American novel hidden there? What about an invention you need to develop or a business you wish to open? What is your dream? Why haven't you chased after it? Let me ask you this: Is the dream contrary to God's will or His Word? That is not a dream from God! Did you know that we are usually given a dream which works well with the gifts He has given us? Dad was a lumberjack as a young man. He knows trees. That is his gift. Surely, it is not mine! He couldn't sit and write this book, but that is my gift! What is your dream?

Father, You placed passions and dreams in my heart at the time You knit me together. I confess that I haven't acted on some of them because I allow fear, doubt or insecurity to quench my desires. Please show me what my dreams mean, where they can be used in Your kingdom, and how they can come to fruition. Help me to close my ears to those who doubt. Your will be done. Amen.

February 23rd   Building a Dream: Preparation   *(Genesis 3:19)*

"By the sweat of your face you will eat bread,
'til you return to the ground, because from it you
were taken; for you are dust, and to dust you shall return."

*Y*esterday we talked about two dreams. Let's look first at what happened to make Joseph's dream come true. After being sold into bondage by his hate filled brothers, Joseph ended up in Egypt being trained in service to Pharaoh. He was a diligent student, but he never wavered in his faith of the God of his people. Joseph learned to do all for the glory of God. Was the work hard? Yes! Would he rather have been with his family in Canaan? Yes! He chose to make the best of it. Each thing he learned would later be used in situations God would place him in. My father's dream didn't just fall into place by itself. Dreams require effort. About 10 years ago, he began to put his ideas into action by designing a saw mill to build the log home. That wouldn't be a stretch for a design engineer... he is not that. He then began to machine the parts for the mill in his brother's manufacturing shop. That wouldn't be a stretch for a machinist... he is not that. He figured out how to use hydraulics to run his machine. Again, not hard for someone who worked in that field... but he did not. Remember though, our dreams usually have something to do with our strengths...and my dad knows trees! He cut, hauled, debarked, oiled and shaped every log used in the house! Not a big deal for a 20 year old, but amazing for someone in his sixties! None of that mattered. His dream was going to happen... as long as the saw mill worked!

This seems daunting to most of us who never stretch ourselves out of our comfort zones. Why would a man Dad's age undertake this seemingly impossible task? Are you good at preparing for the needs in your life? A couple months before I had the vision for this book, someone purchased a laptop computer for me. Later, I felt it was a waste of money because it wasn't being used as it should. Little did I know the plans God had for my computer! Like Joseph and my Dad, God prepared me for years to be able to come up with enough journal entries and teaching to write this book. He birthed the dream into them... and into me.

Lord, how amazing that You would care enough to give me a dream, prepare me for its eventual fulfillment and equip me with what I need in order for my dream to come true. May I never doubt that "all things work together for the good of those who love the Lord and are called according to Your purpose." My dream is part of Your plan... prepare me to follow Your calling on my life. Amen.

February 24ᵗʰ <u>Building a Dream: Foundation</u> *(Proverbs 10: 25)*

*When the whirlwind passes, the wicked are no more,
but the righteous have an everlasting foundation.*

A builder will tell you that the foundation is the most important part of any building. Yes, a roof keeps out the rain and
the walls keep out the wind. Yes, the furnace warms us and the electric service brings us light. But, the whole thing will tumble down
without a proper foundation. Joseph's foundation was built upon
the promise God made to his great grandfather, Abraham. God had
promised Abraham that his seed (heirs) would inherit the promised
land and that no enemy could completely destroy them, as long as
they kept an eye on the laws of God, walking in His ways. Joseph's
faith supported him in all his times of testing. It was the foundation
for his life. He held to the promise, knowing God would not lie. The
foundation for my father's log home had to be strong, sturdy and well
anchored. The weight of the massive logs (some 18" through) would
easily topple a weak base. After the hole was prepared he began to
lay each block, checking for square and level, placing just the right
amount of concrete between the blocks and the tiers. This is heavy,
dirty and backbreaking work, but how would the house stand if the
foundation crumbled? Broken blocks couldn't be used. Improperly
mixed concrete is not strong. Uneven spacing was not acceptable.
This was the foundation a dream was about to rest upon.

As I wrote this lesson I was led to think about believers who are
walking in faith without a foundation. Faith must be supported. The
support is the Word of God. Without that support we will crumble
or fall away when times get tough. God's Word holds promises to
see us through testing. It shares words of encouragement and hope

and His vision for each of us. Why is the church not focusing on teaching the Bible <u>as written</u> to its new believers? Is it because they might leave if something was required of them? Shame on us! This is the foundation our lives are to be built upon; how tragic to not have it in our hearts. My advice to you today is to get yourself into the living Word of God... allowing it to teach, convict, direct and discipline you.

Jesus, Your prayer is that every believer would hunger, thirst and crave quiet time with You... that they would desire to turn off the T.V., give up some recreation and bury themselves in Your Word. Scripture tells us that Your Word is a lamp unto our feet and a light unto our path. May it become the hardened and strong foundation of every one who is called by the name Christian. Amen.

February 25th   Building a Dream: Taking Shape
(Ephesians 2: 20-21)

"...having been built on the foundation of the apostles and prophets, Christ Jesus Himself being the corner stone, in whom the whole building, being fitted together, is growing into a holy temple in the Lord."

How exciting it is when a dream finally begins to take shape! We can see where God's hand is directing us, His provision blessing us and His vision growing us! That happened with Joseph. His loyalty, hard work and faithful service to the King of Egypt had earned him a position of great authority. He was second only to Pharaoh himself in overseeing Egypt. He had amassed wealth, power, and most importantly, respect for his unfailing faithfulness to God's laws. God used Joseph to interpret Pharaoh's dream, a foretelling of years of great harvest followed by many years of severe famine. Joseph began to put his training to the test...and the results kept Egypt from destruction by famine. As for the building of the log home, the sawmill worked! The logs were shaped, the reinforcements were put in place and the walls went up. Long, hard days of back-breaking labor went into each log. Dad built every truss, joist, door frame, window, door and stairway. Those who said the mill would never work were silenced. Those who said he was too old to finish it stood by and watched. The roof went on and the basement became separate living quarters with bath, bedroom, kitchen and living area. The dream of a lifetime was not to be put off any longer!

Though this story sounds quite magical, I'm sure there were many days Dad felt like giving up, as there were numerous setbacks during the building process. Mom had two major open heart surgeries and came to the brink of death. My nephew died at age 21; and my younger brother two years later. Good labor was hard to come by, money ran short, frustrations were overwhelming and Dad's inability to sleep at night didn't help. But, the dream was taking shape. There was no going back. In all of this process God was working in my Dad's heart. He was learning more than how to put in windows; he was learning the importance of family to share his dream with. He was learning that gifts and abilities come from God. He was learning that his legacy had to be more than a log home.

Holy Spirit, how amazing are the methods You use to teach us the real meaning of life. How wonderful to know that as the elements of our dreams take shape, You are always there to guide us. Help me to learn from this log home building process. Dream, Preparation, Foundation and Taking Shape are all vital steps. May I skip none of them as Your dream lives in me. Amen.

February 26th <u>Building a Dream: "Well Done!"</u> *(Matthew 25: 23)*

His master said to him, "Well done, good and faithful slave. You were faithful with a few things, I will put you in charge of many things; enter into the joy of your master."

*I*n this last installment of the Building a Dream series, we need to see what happened with the dreams God gave to Joseph and my father. Joseph carried Egypt through the great famine. The storehouses he filled provided not only for his people but also for those in neighboring countries who came to buy wheat from Pharaoh. Little did Joseph know that God would use this to bring him face to face with his brothers. Yes, the same brothers who sold him into bondage came to buy wheat to save their families and their aging father. Joseph recognized them and through a turn of events revealed himself as their brother. He sent them home to return with Jacob, after telling them that what they meant for evil God used for good. He could save his father from starvation! My parents are nearly ready to move into Dad's dream house. We have celebrated the last two Christmases in that amazing home full of ceramic tile and hardwood floors, intricate wood details, custom-made cabinets in the kitchen and baths, inviting porches and a warm brick fire-place. Strangers may be amazed, but we watched the work from start to finish. We listened as he explained how the mill would work. We watched him labor long nights to build it. We watched as it sat in the yard for three years before the work actually began. We watched the excitement as the first few logs went in place. We worked with him whenever possible...but, it wasn't our dream. He is an amazing man who has been gifted by an amazing God.

I hope you have enjoyed these two interlaced stories. Isn't it amazing how God can use history to teach us lessons which are just as applicable today? Joseph had a gift. My father has a gift. I have a gift... and so do you! What a waste to never seek to follow your dreams, to never stretch your limits. You will never learn what He can accomplish if you never try. Joseph became a powerful man; but he never took his eyes off God. He never considered his kingdom work sacrifice. He proved to Pharaoh what a man of God looks like. Does the way you live reflect God to the unchurched world? Seek to fulfill your dream.

Father, Your giftings and graces are immeasurable and perfect. Your blessings are abundant. Your provisions are always necessary. May I learn from these men. Determination, foresight, planning, hard work and stumbling are all part of getting the job done. Walk with me as I begin today to find my God breathed dream... and to live it to the fullest. Amen.

February 27th   Blood of Jesus   *(Revelation 7:13-14)*

Then one of the elders answered, saying to me, "These who are clothed in the white robes, who are they, and where have they come from?" I said to him, "My lord, you know." And he said to me, "These are the ones who come out of the great tribulation, and they have washed their robes and made them white in the blood of the Lamb."

Many churches refuse to talk about the blood of Jesus because it sounds somehow violent and distasteful. Guess what? We are violent and distasteful...that is why we need to talk about the blood which cleanses us from all sin. The blood of Jesus has the power to justify and to prove us true and faithful. It is also our atonement, which is a process of making things right. On the Day of Atonement the Hebrews were to go to anyone they had a difference with and restore the peace and the relationship. Jesus' blood washes our separation from God away and puts us back in right relationship with Him. The blood marks us as belonging to God and keeps us from being claimed by the hand of the enemy. We cannot imagine taking filthy soiled clothes and dipping them in a vat of red blood only to have them come out whiter than we ever saw them! That is what happens when we claim Jesus as Savior. He *washes our sins white as snow, removing them as far as the east is from the west* from us. Jesus' blood makes all things new. The power of Jesus' blood is to reconcile us to Him for a forever relationship and dominion.

Can you imagine the blood of Jesus washing down over your soiled flesh and making it white as snow? This truth is beyond our comprehension. There was a day when preachers explained how deep our need for grace is. Those were the days of hundreds of sinners being saved at tent revivals. The listener wasn't being beat up. He was being confronted with truth. Once that happened, the sinner couldn't wait to receive the cleansing blood of Christ. We need more of these sermons; instead of the politically correct drivel the mega-churches are using to gain great numbers of members. How sad will be the day when the masses that have never had sin defined, stand before Jesus. Instead, they have heard glossed over sermons for the sake of mere numbers.

Father, we have wandered far from truth. Help me to fully understand the power and impact of Your blood upon my sin. Open my eyes to all truth and clarity of Your message. Amen.

February 28th   <u>Word for Life</u>   *(Psalms 119:140)*

Your word is very pure; Therefore Your servant loves it.

These words are from my May 6, 2006, journal entry: "I know from personal experience that You care about everything I care about! Lord, how You have proven this over and over in my relationships, in shelter (homes), in jobs, in family, in directing my path for ministry and in keeping me hungering for Your Word. I spoke yesterday that I truly believe that a week without journaling and studying the Word would absolutely change my faith walk. *"Your Word is a lamp unto my feet and a light unto my path."* It is my conviction, hope, strength, witness, testimony and proving ground. Jesus, I need it as much as I need to breathe. You fulfill the Word. You <u>are</u> the Word. And, I praise Your holy precious name. Thank You for allowing me to teach the Word." When I was a child, I wanted to be a teacher. Teaching truly is a dream birthed into my spirit by God at the time of my creation. Little did I know it would be the Bible I would spend my time teaching! I started seeking God in the fall of 2005 and was hooked on the Word from the minute I first opened it. Shortly thereafter, I began to teach a group of eight women each week. I was teaching it as fast as I was learning it! Why not? It was my passion and the gift He breathed into me.

Why do I get so excited about the Bible? I am amazed that all Christians aren't excited! Why would you want to give your life to someone you know nothing about? Why wouldn't you want to know the history behind the greatest movement in history? Why wouldn't you want to know the stories of God's past faithfulness to His chosen people? Why wouldn't you want to claim the promises reserved for those who obey Christ? All of those things are held within the precious pages of the Bible… and so much more. If I had one wish for every Christian I know, it would be for them to hunger for the Word of the Living God, to feast upon its sweetness and to drink of its living water.

Father, I have lost—or maybe never really found—the passion Your Word deserves from me. I have let busyness keep me from poring over the Scriptures. The Word of God is as vital as the air I breathe; help me to understand it each day of my faith walk. Amen.

February 29th   <u>He Knows the Heart</u>   *(Psalms 26:1-2)*

Vindicate me, O LORD, for I have walked in my integrity,
and I have trusted in the LORD without wavering. Examine me,
O LORD, and try me; Test my mind and my heart.

I don't know for a fact, but believe that many people think His House came into being because I wished to put another local Christian bookstore out of business. I am unable to explain that we are two very different kinds of businesses, and our city needs more, not fewer Christian retailers! "Lord, I don't need the approval of men, but I confess that I allow their disapproval to bother me." That is my prayer and confession in one statement. The portion of the verse for today's entry which reads, *"Examine me, O LORD, and try me; Test my mind and my heart,"* can be a scary request. Do we truly want God to test and examine the deepest recesses of our minds? He knows our thoughts already; do we want Him to dig deeper? What are we afraid of? King David sinned with Bathsheba, as detailed in several February entries. He was so convicted when confronted with his sin that he wrote Psalm 51. In that Psalm he makes it abundantly clear, that all sin is against God. Yes, he sinned against his family, Bathsheba and his own flesh. But, ultimately the sin was against God, who called him *"a man after My heart."*

Our ministry is very focused; and we would never try to blatantly hurt another Christian retailer. I picked and chose specific product lines which were different, in order that our product lines would not be identical. I intentionally do not carry all of the newest books and music. I have sent numerous customers there, even called for some to see if they had a specific item in stock. It was never my intention to run them out of business. My intention was a place of ministry and teaching. You see, that was God's plan when He gave me the vision. What about you? Have you ever been falsely accused of something? Was your first instinct to lash out and defend yourself? Mine was too. Instead, I sat back (for once) and allowed my actions to speak louder than my words!

Lord, I surely need Your encouragement and peace as I work and minister in Your name. Please help me to keep my eyes on You and my feet planted so firmly in the Word that nothing—nothing—can shake where I stand. You are all I need—and I do need You. Use me this day as Your light in darkness! It does not matter what anyone else thinks, as long as I am right before You. Amen.

March 1st <u>This New Month</u> *(2 Timothy 1:7)*

For God has not given us a spirit of timidity,
but of power and love and discipline.

*M*y journal entry from January 1, 2004, reads as follows. "Lord, this New Year holds so very many things—and today I know none of them. I could fear tomorrow, dread health needs, job losses, death of loved ones, persecution, hunger, abandonment, but I trust You and your promise to never leave me or forsake me. I only need look back on this past year to see the hands of the Lord as we faced potential job loss, Mom's illness, family deaths of Benjamin and Uncle Bob and temptations that needed to be faced. Jesus, You were with me, were my hope and my strength, and will be my Counselor and ever-present Lord as I begin this next adventure!" Today is the first day of a brand new month. Do you look forward to what lies ahead? Are you excited about the plans God has for your life in the next 31 days? Do you trust Him to be with you when you face things like I faced in 2003? I promise you, He never lets us down. God is the same yesterday... today... and forever! He will always carry us through the storms. Did I want to face the near death and open heart surgeries my mother had to face? Absolutely not! Did I want to bury my sweet nephew and my uncle in the same August week? Absolutely not! Did God give me the "spirit of power" mentioned above? Absolutely!

We never know what tomorrow, this month, this year, or the next decade holds. It is funny how the things we think we could never survive are survived when we are faced with hard times. As a young child, I felt that if my Grandma and Grandpa died I would not want to live without them. Guess what? They are both gone and their deaths hurt terribly, but I have continued to live without them. The Scripture above says God didn't give us a *"spirit of timidity."* No, we would be Christians of no value to the lost if we walked around in terror of the unknown. This is really what faith is all about. God's Word tells us that faith believes in what we cannot see. What we see requires no faith! I have faith that whatever comes my way, tomorrow is in His hands. Thus, I have no reason to fear.

Lord, why do we walk in fear of what tomorrow holds, instead of trusting You to carry us through difficult times? Please show me how to grow my faith. I confess my worrying, my fears, and my lack of trusting You. How can I ever be a powerful witness for You if my faith is weak, little, or shallow? You breathed life into me. Please breathe faith in abundance into my spirit. Amen.

March 2nd   Stone Idols   *(Exodus 20: 4)*

"You shall not make for yourself an idol."

Think about the stone idols many nations worshipped in the past and, in some cases, still worship today in much of the world. These are dead gods. Notice I used a small "g" in describing these gods. Only one God, the God of all creation, is the real God. Do not mistake stone gods or idols for our God. This may cause some of you to disagree with me, but I feel called to address this issue. Having worked in retail for many years—including now at His House—I have watched many people worship stone idols. The idols they worship are angels. I am in no way belittling angels, for they are God's messengers, workers and warriors... but THEY ARE NOT GOD. I have seen too many people collect these lovely idols, caring for them, dusting them and spending a lot of money for them. Many of these same people will never open a Bible, pay a tithe into the kingdom of God, or seek a deep and abiding faith. Listen carefully to these words: "Worshipping anything other than God is making that thing your god." This is a vital truth... angels did not create you. Angels cannot save you. Angels in themselves make no one a Christian. I have listened for years to people who talk about their "spirit beings having contact with angels." The only spirit being you need to be in contact with is the Holy Spirit of God.

I have collectable angels in my house. They are lovely; but they do not get my worship.

Please do not be offended by these words. They are affirmed over and over in Scripture. I am not telling you to be afraid of angel figurines or to get rid of the ones you have. Just keep your perspective on figurines and statues. One of the main commandments of God is to not worship any graven images. I think of the stone idols of Bible times and their arms are usually clasped in front of them, or are stiffly down at their sides. I see Jesus exactly the opposite of that. I see His arms wide open, waiting, welcoming, yearning for us to run and seek that embrace.

Father God, You are "approachable" if we only seek You first. Lord, I want to always serve a living God... not a wooden idol or a stone statue. Thank You for being alive, living in my heart through Your Holy Spirit. I am blessed to call You my Father, my Refuge, my Haven, my God... above all *other gods! Amen.*

March 3rd <u>He Cares</u> *(Genesis 16:13)*

Then she called the name of the LORD who spoke to her, "You are a God who sees," for she said, "Have I even remained alive here after seeing Him?"

*D*o you believe God is interested in the little details of your life? Do you see His hand directing your paths and feel Him walking with you through the tough times? I absolutely believe the Scripture above when it says, *"You are a God who sees."* Here is an excerpt from another 2004 journal entry: "Jesus, I have written many, many times about You directing my footsteps. I clearly have a testimony about this subject. You have used that directing to lead me to jobs, friends, deals and church. So many times I find myself somewhere—almost wondering how I arrived—only to look back and see your SPIRIT leading me to that place. Jesus, why do others not see this? Why do they feel weak if they trust You to direct their paths? Why do You even care about the minutia of my life… because You are my Father, taking Your child on a journey over hills, through valleys, around immovable mountains… destination: Paradise!" I sense that He is patiently waiting until we come to the end of ourselves and are ready to include Him in all parts of our lives. Imagine being so ready to advise, direct and carry…and not being asked! Just as we see things our children do and wish they would ask for our help, so must Father God see our futile struggles and wish we would ask for His help. How much easier our lives would be if we believed He SEES EVERYTHING, and then acted according to that knowledge.

How do you live your life? If you are like most, you think God will wink and turn His eyes away from your little indiscretions. He is a holy God. He hates sin and cannot be a part of it. His ignoring the wrongs we do would be participating in them. God cares about the things you care about. He would love to be included in all parts of your life. That may seem far-fetched. Scripture tells us He knows the number of the hairs of our heads! He cares about every sparrow that falls; surely He cares more about you. You are created in His image! My challenge to you is to begin today to share all parts of your life with Him. Ask Him to work with you to remove the bad and carry you through the difficult.

All seeing, all-knowing God... help me to walk through this day knowing that I cannot hide my actions from You. Help me to realize that You care about even the smallest things…my words, my thoughts, my actions. Father, make me like a trusting child who depends on his parents to meet every need. I have tried to do it my way… let me begin today to do it in a way pleasing to You. Amen.

March 4ᵗʰ   Where's the Hunger?   *(John 6: 35)*

*Jesus said to them, "I am the bread of life; he who comes to Me
will not hunger, and he who believes in Me will never thirst.*

As soon as I die and come face to face with my Savior, I am going to ask Him: "Why did Your people not hunger for this BREAD, for PRAYERFUL WORSHIP, and for TIME IN YOUR PRESENCE." They tolerate their faith instead of living it in abundance and feeding on it in every way possible! I don't understand complacency and being satisfied with knowing of Jesus instead of really knowing Him. I don't always believe that real worship happens in a crowded church during timed moments of music and prayer. I worship best at home—in my morning Bible and prayer time. I love to see His face in all things! I will ask Jesus if He had lots of promises for His children who never opened the Word to read them. To me it is like getting birthday or Valentine cards and leaving them unopened in sealed envelopes. I promise you that I cannot remember the words printed in any birthday card I've ever received, but I remember these words from Psalm 139, *"For You formed my inward parts; You wove me in my mother's womb. I will give thanks to You, for I am fearfully and wonderfully made; Wonderful are Your works, and my soul knows it very well."* I can only imagine the sadness I will see on Jesus' face when He tells me that "they were too busy living life to care about the Giver of life."

What is your hunger level? Do you "force yourself" to give God one hour on Sunday…if nothing else is going on? Do you offer your time or service for anything which will grow His kingdom? Do you open His "love letter" and feast upon its promises? Do you hunger and thirst to learn how to be more like Him? Jesus came to die for our sins, but He also came to show us how to live the holy, God centered life, which will set us apart in this filthy world. If I could teach, preach, shout or holler one truth to those who call themselves believers, it would be to **feed upon the Word**. Find someone who can teach you to apply and understand it. Dig for the golden nuggets of wisdom within its pages. If you don't ever hunger for Him… you will never want to leave this world.

Father, I hold within my reach the greatest love letter ever penned. Why do I find it so hard to find time to open its pages and read the messages You sent for me? Lord, I want a burning, passionate hunger for You, Your Spirit and Your holy Word. May this not be a burden or a job… but a blessed time of communion with the One who knit me together. Speak to me; speak to my very soul. Amen.

March 5th   Religion Versus Relationship   *(I John 3:24)*

*One who keeps His commandments abides in Him,
and He in him. We know by this that He abides in us,
by the Spirit whom He has given us.*

In the fall of 1995, I began to seek God (or, He finally caught me after years of running). I began to journal. Many of the March entries are excerpts taken from those journal entries. One thing I quickly learned is the difference between religion and relationship. All religions are definitely not the same! I lived many years separated from anything at all to do with faith or with God. I always believed in God, but I had <u>no</u> desire to know Him or to give Him time, money, and power to direct my steps. I wrote in one journal entry, "Lord, the methodical way in which You removed my walls, softened my heart and "burned that bridge" is amazing to look back on! How grateful I am to be able to see in clear hindsight Your hand in my marriage, my home, my family, my jobs and my changed heart. Only through this "backward looking" can I now look ahead to see a brighter future and an eternal blessing beyond these shores. Thank You." Religion or religious rituals can never fill the very deep hole in our hungering hearts. Ritual never requires communication or interaction; relationship requires both. Religion is about a doctrine or certain actions. Relationship is close, personal and contagious. I know many 'religious' Christians who have never found the secret of relationship... and their lives reflect that. I guarantee you, a pure relationship with Jesus Christ will change you from the inside out.

———————

Believing in God is simply not enough! Saying you have faith, without putting effort into building a relationship with God, will never change your heart. Think about this in the context of marriage. If someone asked you if you are in a loving relationship, and you respond, "Well, I am married," you are not answering their question. Yes, you may be married... but where is the relationship? Marriage is a ceremony, a rite, a ritual ordained by God. That does not mean it will survive without hard work and the growth of a relationship between the partners. Our faith walks are the same. We must communicate, serve, love unconditionally, and include our Lord in all parts of our lives in order for our relationship to grow.

———————

Jesus, I want a personal, intimate, fulfilling relationship with You. Religion alone leaves me empty. Rituals mean little, but conversation between us through Your Word and my time of prayer means everything to me. I do not want to be a casual Christian. I want fire, passion, dedication and interaction... and I will settle for nothing less. Amen.

March 6th <u>Joseph: Sold into Bondage</u> *(Genesis 37:27)*

*"Come let us sell him to the Ishmaelites and not lay
our hands on him, for he is our brother, our own flesh."
And his brothers listened to him.*

In this entry we meet the 12 sons of Jacob who will later be known as the heads of the 12 tribes of Israel. Jacob, who was the spoiled son of his mother, has continued the legacy of picking favorites and has caused great division among his children. Joseph, the son of Jacob and Rachel, has been singled out and shown favor since birth. His brothers have watched jealously and have grown to despise him. Our story opens as Joseph is sent to bring provision to his brothers in Shechem where they are pasturing their father's flock. Joseph is a dreamer and a braggart who previously dreamed of his brothers bowing down before him. Foolishly, he told them the dream and they have been looking for a way to "take him down a peg." Some of them want to kill him; some just want to do him great bodily harm. Judah the second oldest, devises a plan to sell him to a caravan of traders from another country. Joseph is sold to the Ishmaelites, then sold again into bondage in Egypt. The brothers take his multicolored tunic (a special gift from their father), cover it in animal blood, and then go tell Jacob his favored son has been killed by a wild beast. Jacob is devastated! Why did it have to be Joseph? He refused comfort from his other children saying, *"Surely I will go down to Sheol in mourning for my son."* Joseph's older brothers are left to think about the consequences of their impulsive and angry actions.

This is sibling rivalry out of control! Jacob is devastated. The 11 other brothers are hiding a dark secret they hope will never be revealed. Joseph is separated from his entire family, taken to a pagan nation and put into forced labor for Pharaoh, the king of Egypt! Are you more like Joseph (the bragging dreamer), or Jacob (the parent who favors one child over the other), or the jealous and impulsive brothers? Most have done or said things in moments of anger that haunt them, and if brought to light would cause them shame. Thank God that our Jesus brings us pardon instead of what we deserve! Scripture tells us our sins are as far as the east is from the west away from us when we place our lives into the capable hands of our Savior.

Father God, I have been a dreaming braggart like Joseph; I have been the jealous child like his brothers; I have been wrong in not treating everyone fairly and with equity. How grateful I am that You love me in spite of my actions. Help me be the person You want me to be… and to know that no matter how dark the circumstances, You are still in control. Amen.

March 7th   Joseph: Supernaturally Blessed   *(Genesis 39:23)*

"The chief jailer did not supervise anything under Joseph's charge… the Lord was with him; and whatever he did, the Lord made to prosper."

Joseph is serving in the house of Potiphar, the captain of Pharaoh's bodyguard, and everything he does is amazingly blessed. Unfortunately, Potiphar has a wife with a wandering eye… and she likes what she sees in Joseph! Joseph is no fool! He knows that God is blessing all the works of his hands. He flees from her advances; only to have her shout that she has been attacked by him. Potiphar (the doddering fool) has Joseph thrown into prison after Mrs. Potiphar tells her elaborate account of the assault. Is Joseph down and out? No, because God is on his side! In prison, Joseph is used to interpret the dreams of Pharaoh. (God doesn't mess around, does He?) After questioning his own "prophets and wise men" and getting no satisfaction; Pharaoh summons Joseph who clearly tells him, *"It is not in me; God will give you the favorable answer."* Pharaoh believes the interpretation that Egypt would be blessed with seven years of abundance, followed by seven years of devastating famine. Joseph also tells him how to prepare for these times by building storehouses during harvests to carry through the lean years to follow. Pharaoh is amazed and makes Joseph second in command only to himself over all of Egypt! What a great sense of humor God has! The slave sold into bondage becomes the second most powerful man in the nation of Egypt!

If we were faced with the setbacks and circumstances of Joseph's life, would we handle them in the same dignified ways? I know I wouldn't! I would be hosting my now famous pity parties and inviting everyone I know who would tell me how unfair God was being to me. Joseph should be a shining example to us of how to persevere, press on and overcome life's challenges. Joseph didn't waste his time with foolish questions like "Why me?" He just rolled with the punches, ducked the jabs, and became a knockout fighter for God's glory!

Lord, I am so grateful that You have a plan for each of us and that sometimes the road doesn't go in a straight line. I doubt that Joseph would have been used as he was if he had taken his eyes off You and followed his own paths. Joseph was obedient in the little things... and thus was blessed with the big ones. He took the knocks without falling. May I learn how to handle challenges from this man's example! Amen.

March 8th Joseph: A Family Reunion *(Genesis 45:4)*

Joseph said to his brothers, "Please come closer to me."
They came closer. And he said, "I am your
brother Joseph, whom you sold into Egypt."

The storehouses of wheat in Egypt carried that land through years of famine. Joseph had rationed and planned so well that other lands were also able to buy wheat from Egypt. Pharaoh's riches multiplied greatly at the hand of good leadership. Jacob, Joseph's father, and his family were starving in their land. Jacob sent his sons, all but Benjamin (his new favorite), to purchase wheat from Pharaoh. Joseph sees them and immediately recognizes them. They do not recognize him. Why would they ever expect to see their younger brother in charge of the storehouses of Egypt? Joseph has them brought into his house and questions them through an interpreter about their father and other brother. He then devises a scheme to get his younger brother Benjamin brought to him. Joseph finally reveals himself to his brothers. Can you imagine their horror! How will they explain this to their father?

What will he do to them? What if Joseph keeps Benjamin and breaks their father's heart again? Instead of any of these reactions, Joseph begins to weep so loudly that the people outside the palace can hear him! He wants to see his father... he wants to reconcile with his brothers... he wants to bring all of Jacob's family to live in Egypt so he can provide for them!

One of the key verses where Joseph spoke to his brothers says, *"Now do not be grieved or angry with yourselves because you sold me here, for God sent me before you to preserve life."* Joseph could forgive all the suffering he had lived for many years because he trusted that it all was part of God's plan. Pharaoh, because of Joseph's years of faithful service, provides everything needed to move his family to Egypt. Joseph's brothers must go home and try to explain the turn of circumstances to their father and then try to convince him to come away to a new land. Would you be as forgiving, as willing to reconcile without punishment with those who hurt you? Joseph's mercy is a picture of Jesus' love... and we can all learn from it.

God my Father, thank You for the picture of grace I find in the story of Joseph's betrayal, successful time in Egypt, and reconciliation with his family. This shows me that "all things do work together for the good of those who love the Lord and are called according to His purpose." Lord, may I trust You with every event in my life. You are faithful beyond measure. Amen.

March 9th Hearing His Voice *(John 10:4)*

When He puts forth all His own, He goes ahead of them, and the sheep follow Him because they know His voice.

How do we hear the voice of God? He will not shout above the noise in our lives in order to get our attention. He is a gentleman and will not force Himself upon us. I wrote in 2004:

"Jesus, I hear You speak to me, especially in our morning times when the noise is shut off from around me. Sometimes though, You speak in the words of a song, the sermon of a pastor, the words in a book, or in the wise and godly counsel of a friend. Whatever the medium, it is the message which is most important. Your words have the power to allay my fears, calm my nerves, remove my doubts, open my eyes to peace and convict me of my wrongdoing. Jesus, in the days ahead please continue to speak to me, to direct my path and to evermore mold me into the Christian You want me to be. I will listen for Your voice and I will seek Your direction." There are wonderful examples throughout the Old Testament of God's people hearing His voice. Moses heard it on the mountain when God told him to remove his sandals, for he was standing on holy ground. Samuel heard it as he ministered at the temple with Eli the priest. Noah heard it when he was told to build the ark. Gideon heard it when he was "just minding his own business."

Do we really think God has stopped speaking to His children? God speaks all the time. The problem is that we ignore His voice. He longs to speak to you. Each of the characters in the above passage had work to do, lots of distractions, and a certain degree of unwillingness to follow God's command. Actually, there are times when He speaks to me and I wish He would talk to someone else!! How do I know it is God speaking? He always speaks contrary to my selfish human nature. He always takes me to places I would never think to go. He usually takes me out of my comfort zone. He never speaks contrary to His Word. Every time this has happened I have grown and been blessed. Are you ready to stop and listen for His voice?

Holy Father, I confess that I would sometimes rather have noise than the things You would speak into my heart. I confess that I am afraid of the places You may send me, the things You may ask me to do or the conviction our conversation might bring. I know that You know everything about me... including the things I don't know or understand. Keep talking to me... and I will make a better effort to listen. Amen.

March 10th Shepherd's Sacrifice *(John 10:14-15)*

"I am the Good Shepherd, and I know My own and My own know Me, even as the Father knows Me and I know the Father; and I lay down My life for the sheep."

The image of the shepherd and his stubborn flock has always been one of my favorite ways to picture Jesus. I see Him in a shepherd's humble clothing... when He clearly should be clothed in majestic robes. I see the shepherd's hook firmly in His hand to draw wandering charges back to safety. I would love to say to Jesus, "Why do You hold that instead of a royal scepter? I see You with little company other than poor, lowly shepherds—instead of in attendance at royal feasts with the rich and the powerful. I see You summoned by the Father to offer your perfect, sinless life for a mindless, dirty and disorderly flock—and I cannot understand <u>why</u>!" Actually, the sheep—not known for being one of God's smartest creatures—are smarter than most of us are! If the shepherd has food, the sheep come to eat. If he knows where the still waters lie, the sheep come for a refreshing drink. If he has shelter, they come in from the storms. If he has a greener pasture to move them to, they go willingly and in trust. We 'intelligent' human beings, on the other hand, fail to eat from Our Shepherd's hand, choose to stay outside of His shelter and refuge, and balk whenever He tries to move us to more fertile and productive places. He knows what is best for us, what is in His plans, and what tomorrow holds.

Do you balk at the paths the Lord tries to walk you down? Have you missed out on greener pastures and still waters because you chose to ignore His prompting? Sheep are foolish creatures...and so are independent, "self-made" men and women who think they need no shepherd. How simple life would be if we allowed God to direct all of our paths! You know... the old "let go and let God" attitude... accepting His closed doors, climbing through His opened windows, and traveling on His chosen fork in the road. How fun! What a stress reliever! Why don't we do this? Are we afraid of where His leading might take us? Are we so sure of where we are going that we cannot relinquish control?

I thank You, Sweet Jesus, for shepherding this undeserving member of Your flock. Why do I fail to trust the One who knows me better than I know myself? Please take the blinders from my eyes that I might follow You and Your plan for me. Faith is about me trusting that You have no desire to see me fail, see me fall, or see me wander away and be lost. You laid down Your life for this lost sheep. Amen.

March 11th   Our Words Reflect Our Hearts   *(Psalms 85:8)*

I will hear what God the Lord will say; For He will speak peace to His people, to His godly ones; But let them not turn back to folly.

Sometimes I am amazed when I read my previous journals and see where I was years ago. It frustrates me to know I am still worrying about the same problems, battling the same conflicts, and letting the world steal my peace. In January of 2004 I wrote: "I wonder sometimes if my faith is as strong as Dan's. I say all of the right words to others about God's perfect timing. I tell them, "God answers all prayers, and in hindsight you will understand why this is happening." I wonder though if I say them because I am programmed to, or if I really mean those words. How can I truly believe these things and have a bad attitude (which I had because the coffee maker, printer, dryer and truck all died last week)? I spewed to others and had a great pity party! My "misplaced control" needs to be relinquished, or I will never know peace at the hands of a loving God." Guess what? I have the same doubts today, struggle with how deep my faith really is, and wonder how to comfort people in their times of testing. I doubt there is one pastor who has NEVER had doubts or weak moments. Here is a revolutionary thought: Christians are people too! We are not unemotional, mindless robots. We hurt, sympathize and bleed. We have compassion, doubts and fears. We try to flee from danger and the unknown. We have faith, but we are not isolated from the things of this world.

———————————

Can you relate to my statements about wondering how deep your faith really is? How can any of us know how we will react when the medical diagnosis is ours, the death is that of our loved ones, or the job loss hits our home? I know this truth. When the sickness was my mother's, God held me up. When the deaths were my twelve-year-old niece, my twenty-one-year-old nephew and my forty-two-year-old brother; God helped me mourn. When the job loss was Dan's with 26 years of seniority…God drew us to Him. I am still the best host that a "pity-party" ever had. I still fail and fall. But... I am never forsaken or abandoned.

———————————

Lord, when I begin to speak negativity or doubt, please shut my mouth with Your gentle hand. When the enemy tries to steal my peace and bring me grief, help me to be strong in You. When I am faced with a time of hardship in my life, help me to remember that You have never failed me yet! You are always faithful… even when I am weak. Help Thou my unbelief. Amen.

March 12th Gate of Freedom (*John 10:9*)

I am the door; if anyone enters through Me, he will be saved, and will go in and out and find pasture.

Freedom is a word we toss around lightly in our society. We say things like "I have the freedom to speak whatever I want," or "I don't want to become a Christian and lose my freedoms," or "I want a divorce so I am free to do as I please." I used to think some of these same thoughts. I truly believed Christians had no fun... too many rules to follow, and (God forbid) they have to spend all their money on dress clothes instead of blue jeans! I used my "freedom" to pepper the world with profanity, to reject and ridicule those who attended church and to use my money for totally selfish purchases. On February 14, 1996, however, I relinquished my personal freedom and gave my heart totally to Jesus. Amazingly, I found freedom like I'd never known in my life! I am **free** to not have to try to impress people anymore with words or actions which I am convicted for. I am **free** to "not say" the things I used to say. I am **free** from the hunger to "fit in," which led to that. I also am **free** to just live by faith — no matter how foolish the world believes me to be. In chapter 10 of the book of Daniel, Gabriel and Michael (two of God's most powerful angels) reveal to us that they are in a constant battle with enemy forces and evil angels who seek to control the hearts and minds of leaders and those whom they lead. How grateful am I that I have Your Word in my hand and in my heart. The only true key to freedom is to walk with You, for You, and always toward Your destination for me.

I spent 38 years regretting my words, hating my thoughts and apologizing for my actions. What kind of freedom is that? Sin holds us in bondage... period. Think about a day with no regrets... a month... a year. Now, that is real freedom! The gate to that kind of freedom is narrow, and only a few will choose that path. You can have that freedom, but are you willing to give up your flesh to receive it? Freedom requires our willingness to give up the things which control us. What handcuffs are keeping you from being free?

Jesus, my Liberator, thank You for setting this "captive" free! How grateful I am for all the things I no longer have to do to fit in or find love. I can walk through Your narrow gate, choosing the path of righteousness instead of the path of sin. I am free from the bonds which held me. I can hold my head high, not in pride, but in the knowledge that the enemy of my soul no longer controls my destiny! Help me tell others what true freedom is; and how they can find it only in You. Amen.

March 13th <u>Flush of the Spirit</u> *(John 14: 26)*

*But when the Father sends the Advocate as my representative—that
is, the Holy Spirit—He will teach you everything and will
remind you of everything I have told you.*

A 2004 journal entry reads: "Jesus, I have written many times in the last eight years about the warm flush which washes over me when Your Spirit and I really connect. I love the feeling—and I feel it now as **we** write these words. Your Spirit is part of the "we" because He fills me with thoughts, dreams, ideas and convictions. Jesus, I do "wish for Your physical presence" and long to see Your face. I think Your eyes and hands are what I hunger for most. I know that Your eyes see me as I really am; and that can be a very fearful thought. I long to see the hands which held the children, touched the diseased and turned the water into wine." Sometimes when I read my journal entries, I try to remember what led me to write the things I have written. Journaling provides me with the ability to write thoughts, prayer needs, successes, failures and blessings. Before I journal on any given day, I read the journal entry for the same day the year before. This provides a great insight into how God has worked in my life in one year's time. I have found numerous mentions of this 'flush' of the Holy Spirit. I know it is real; I know it is a way God uses to show me He is with me. I never want to rely on emotions or feelings to guide me in my faith walk. That is what leads too many people to get excited about Jesus and then fall away as soon as the "high" wears off. Only a steady diet of time in the Word and focused prayer will keep the believer as passionate as when he first came to know Christ.

The Holy Spirit of God is the portion of Him who inhabits the spirit of the believer. He is our Convictor, our Counselor, our Wise Discerner and our Teacher. He leads us, when we seek His direction. He cautions us when we are about to go astray. He will reveal the truth of God's Word. He will calm the storms in our hearts. All believers need the Spirit. If you don't understand how He works in our lives, use your Bible's concordance to find references on the Holy Spirit.

Holy Spirit, I don't know enough about You and Your work in the life of a believer. Please reveal Yourself to me. I need your direction, Your conviction and Your help to really understand the things of the Lord. You are called the "gift" sent when Jesus left this earth. I want to receive this great "gift." Amen.

March 14ᵗʰ <u>Faith in Nature</u> *(Psalms 8:1)*

O LORD, our Lord, How majestic is Your name in all the earth,
who have displayed Your splendor above the heavens!

The glisten of dew on a thin blade of grass,
The warmth of the sun on a clear summer day;
The call of a bird in the nest in the tree,
Your splendor revealed in nature's sweet way.

The splash of color on the leaves of the oak,
The unfolding petals in the garden by day;
The playing squirrels as they dig for a treat,
Your splendor revealed in nature's sweet way.

The kiss of a puppy on the cheek of a child,
The roar of the ocean as sand seems to sway;
The breeze in the trees as the wind blows on by,
Your splendor revealed in nature's sweet way.

The strength of high mountains with white on their peaks,
A blanket of snow where the kids long to play;
Tornadoes and tempests that blow through the plain,
Your splendor revealed in nature's sweet way.

---

*D*o you take time to stop and see the wonder of nature around you? Dan and I lived for 19 years in a house in the city. I always enjoyed nature, but never realized why people in the country enjoyed being far from town. Two years ago we moved outside the city... and now I understand. The sunrises and sunsets are wonderful. The big sky full of stars is a canopy and the deer along the woods line bring nature to our eyes. Take time to really look around you. I often run for the camera to capture a perfect sunrise, a magical sunset, or the clean, crisp look of newly fallen snow. I love to see the first birds of spring, the full bloom of summer, and the beautiful tapestry of His fall paint brush. I love the crisp, cold mornings of winter, the jacketless days of summer and the sweater days of autumn. I love scurrying baby squirrels, peeping baby birds in the trees near my house and the smell after a soft rain.

Father God, Your majesty is so awesome. I seek to find You in the clouds, You in the mountains and You in the rainbow. These are Your signs of hope and promise. I love the creation; I love more, the Creator. Amen.

March 15ᵗʰ   Faithful Provider   (Psalms 145:13)

Your kingdom is an everlasting kingdom,
and Your dominion endures throughout all generations.

*M*any people feel that God is like a genie... kept in a bottle until the time we choose to release Him, just in time for Him to give us the things we desire. Yes, He is waiting to bless us, but the truth of the matter is that He will never give us anything which is contrary to His Word or defies His holy nature. God seems to be the "fall guy" when we don't get the things we want. I can just hear myself in this passage. When Dan lost his job with twenty six years of seniority, I told a friend that I didn't believe in God because I prayed and prayed for the factory not to close! She very boldly asked me if I ever conversed with God other than when I wanted something! I hated the question because I hated the conviction. I felt we often confuse the promises God makes to provide for us and focus only on the things we wish for and seek from Him. God has always provided income and shelter, as well as food and love in my life. How often have I thanked Him for these blessings? I would love riches without work, a huge, spacious house and a fancy new car. He instead provides for my needs. I am grateful that I don't have every single thing I want. I know myself well enough to realize that I would take credit for all I have and fail to thank Him for my possessions and accomplishments.

What about you? Do you ever have a conversation with God, which doesn't amount to a "wish list" of your needs and those of others? Do you acknowledge that every good and perfect thing comes from God? I believe that most of us never see His hand of direction and His amazing orchestration of events in our lives. Why? We think that all we possess and all we accomplish are because of our own abilities and efforts. I would love to be a great singer... you know, like Shania Twain! (That is a joke for all of you who know what a stretch that really is!) If I had focused and obsessed on that, I would have missed owning a store, teaching the Word and writing this devotional. We need to ask for His will... not our wants. We need to step out in faith and allow Him to direct our paths. Scary thought? Yes! But, oh so worth the sacrifice. His dominion does endure.

Sweet, Sweet Jesus, I am blessed by Your faithful provisions, Your constant support, Your Word to teach me, and the circle of friends You continue to bring into my life. Jesus, You always provide "just enough" to keep me humble— yet sheltered from the wrong things I could seek. Your provision is perfect. You are perfect. I trust You to provide for my needs. Amen.

March 16ᵗʰ Keep it Simple *(Psalms 19:7)*

The law of the LORD is perfect, restoring the soul;
The testimony of the LORD is sure, making wise the simple.

This Scripture verse about "making the simple man wise" is one I love to meditate on. I love to think about the fact that the so-called 'intellectuals' will never understand the pure joy of the Gospel of Christ. They are always looking for a deeper meaning in layers of hidden truths. Where did we lose the **KISS** method of reasoning: **K**eep **I**t **S**imple, **S**illy? I have talked to so many people who think the Gospel is too simple. It is beyond their scope of thinking to believe that simple spoken faith in Christ can save us from our sins. Yes, the words of faith are simple, but their impact in our lives should never be taken lightly. I think of a song on a country singer's first Gospel album about us needing a little old fashioned rock and roll. An older man is telling the younger man that his life is heading nowhere and that he needs to hear what changed the older man's life. He says that what he needs is "a little good old rock & roll." The chorus tells that he put his feet on the Rock and his name on the Roll, and when it's called up yonder he won't have to worry about his soul. I love the simple Gospel truth. You are the Rock— and when we confess Your name in faith our name is in Your Roll Book of Life! Why do we make the simple truth of the Gospel so complicated?

———————

Have you encountered those who believe that Christians are blind fools or mindless idiots for walking in faith? Jesus knew that this would happen. In Matthew 11:25 we find these words, *"At that time, Jesus said, "I praise You, Father, Lord of heaven and earth, that You have hidden these things from the wise and intelligent and have revealed them to infants."* Does this mean we are babies or fools? No, it means that we who seek and find the truth of His Gospel, are recipients of His divine revelation. That kind of revelation doesn't come from books, college degrees or intellectual exercises. It comes from an honest, open, childlike desire to know absolute truth. Does faith come hard for you? Ask the Holy Spirit to grow your faith, reveal His truths, and use your story to lead others to the mercy seat of Christ.

Jesus, I praise You for the day when the truth of the free gift of salvation was revealed to me. If I must be unencumbered like an infant in order to grasp Your truths... make me like a newborn baby. Help me to keep my witness simple, clear and You focused. Help me to be merciful to those who are too burdened by book smarts to understand perfect truths. I thank You, my Rock, because my name is on Your Roll. Amen.

March 17th   Surrounding the Righteous   *(Psalms 5:12)*

"For it is You who blesses the righteous man, O LORD; You surround him with favor as with a shield."

*D*o you believe God surrounds the righteous with a shield of favor? That is the promise given to us in Psalms 5:12... and God is not a man that He should lie. If He cannot lie, then we should claim this promise along with all the others in the Bible. What exactly does a hedge of favor look like? In my life, favor opens doors for jobs, blesses me to understand the Word and produces gifts like the ability to write and teach. I see wonderful Christian people who open their mouths and have awesome vocals pour forth in song. I would love to have that kind of favor! Some people are favored with finances, great wisdom and blessed patience. My personal belief is that God selects the favors we can best use to bless His kingdom. My jobs have done that, as have my teaching abilities. Favor is also a form of protection. I remember after 9/11/2001 when a female Bible teacher responded to the question of a television interviewer who asked her why God would allow these attacks on American soil. She politely replied, "God is a gentleman who will not force Himself on anyone. We have removed Him from our schools, homes, churches and cities. When we remove God, we remove the hedge of protection He provides for His chosen ones. How could we think this wouldn't happen? America is not shielded from her enemies! We live in a blessed nation; yet we forget that every good and perfect gift comes from the Lord."

———————————

Can you think of a time when you knew without a doubt that God's hedge of protection kept you from injury or loss? Did His hedge of favor ever open a door for you? In the mid-June entries of this book you will read an account of how God opened job doors for me over a period of years. How do I know they are doors He opened? Each one involved someone from my past who came forward and offered or found me a job; each job led me down the path toward a faith walk with Christ. If you were to look back over your life in perfect hindsight, would you be able to see Him doing the same in your life?

———————————

Holy Spirit, You are always with me, directing and leading me to places You have prepared for me to go. Why do I often take credit— or give credit to others—for the provisions in my life? Help me to claim this hedge of protection, this shield from the onslaught of the enemy and this favor You wish to pour upon me. I am at Your mercy; ready and waiting for You to bless my walk today. Amen.

March 18th He's My Blesser *(Psalms 29:11)*

The LORD will give strength to His people;
The LORD will bless His people with peace.

*J*n a journal entry on January 23, 2004, I wrote the following words: "I love the line, 'You chase us with your blessings'! How awesome it is to think of You watching from above saying, 'I think Vicki needs a little pick-me-up today—here, I'll send her one.' You are a great God; You love us more than we can imagine. I know that You know my every need. I know that You are my every need. I simply must not ever forget that truth. Thank You for the awesome lessons in the book of Daniel and for the things which I learned about him that I can apply to my own walk with You." Think about God chasing us, waiting to shower blessings upon us! How much greater is He than some stone idol? Daniel, whom I mentioned in the journal excerpt, was blessed by God's supernatural protection because he refused to stop praying to the God of Israel, in spite of great warnings by Nebuchadnezzar, King of Babylon. Daniel was obedient and God chose to bless him by closing the mouths of ferocious lions. Maybe my blessings haven't been quite that amazing, but I have surely felt the power of God as He blessed my life. I have never had a time in 11 years when I couldn't pay my bills. I have good health—in spite of all I do to sabotage it! I have a rock solid marriage, two healthy grandchildren, a loving son, and parents who are still living. I have a roof over my head every night, shelter from the storms, and great friends. I have clothes to wear, food to eat, a bookstore I couldn't afford to open and the God-given ability to write this entry for your eyes. Do I thank Him for the ability to do so? Yes! Do I thank God for direction, guidance, counsel, and His holy Word? Yes!

How has God showered blessing into your life? We fail to ever be completely grateful for the things we would never be able to accomplish ourselves. Pride is a huge part of this problem. Do you want to learn how to thank God? Begin from the first waking moment tomorrow. Thank Him for ears to hear the alarm, legs to walk to the bathroom, water to cleanse you, towels to dry you, lungs that breathe, eyes that see, hands that touch.

Father God, Your blessings are abundant. Your provisions are true. Your love for undeserving people like me is unquestionable. Thank You for this passage and for the reminder of exactly how much I take for granted. Help me not to ignore the blessings I have. Amen.

March 19ᵗʰ <u>**Will I Be Able To Speak At All?**</u> *(Psalms 145:3)*

> *Great is the LORD, and highly to be praised,*
> *and His greatness is unsearchable.*

*T*he contemporary Christian song, "I Can Only Imagine," has been played on secular radio constantly since it was released. I never fail to stop and think of what I will do when I first see His face. The words are to the effect*: I can only imagine what my eyes will see when Your presence is before me. Will I sing, 'Hallelujah?' Will I be able to speak at all?* The singer says he may fall to his knees; he may dance for Your glory; or... he may be unable to speak a word. Maybe if we spent more time thinking about our heavenly home we would have less time to dwell on ourselves here in this temporary home. Look at this powerful Scripture from Revelation, Chapter 5: *"Then I looked, and I heard the voice of many angels around the throne and the living creatures and the elders; and the number of them was myriads of myriads and thousands of thousands, saying with a loud voice, 'Worthy is the Lamb that was slain to receive power and riches and wisdom and might and honor and glory and blessing.' And every created thing which is in heaven and on the earth and under the earth and on the sea, and all the things in them, I heard saying, 'To Him who sits on the throne, and to the Lamb, be blessing and honor and glory and dominion forever and ever'."* Every creature with breath, living or dead, will rise and sing the praises of Jesus. Imagine the sound of that choir! Imagine the volume! Imagine seeing the face of Jesus, the Lamb of God... on the throne He earned by sacrificing Himself for us!

Take time to give this passage some thought. Are you so tied to the things of this world that you never consider where you will spend eternity? Scripture tells us Jesus' words, *"I am the way, the truth and the life; no one comes to the Father, but through Me."* Your money won't pay for your admittance. Your good works can't earn Heaven for you. Your religious practices aren't enough. Only faith in Jesus Christ will earn you admittance to hear this heavenly choir, to see the face of your Savior, and to live forever in the place He has prepared for you.

Oh Lord, I cannot wait to see what Your face looks like and how Your children will react when they first see You! I long for that day, and it keeps me from getting too attached here. I want to be a part of that heavenly choir, singing Your praises and watching You bask in the adoration You so richly deserve. Yes, every knee shall bow, every tongue confess that You are indeed Lord. Amen.

March 20th   Paul: Saul the Persecutor   *(Acts 7:58)*

... they began stoning him; and the witnesses laid aside their robes at the feet of a young man named Saul.

The man we know as the Apostle Paul lived his early adult life in a very different manner than he did in the written chronicles of the New Testament. Paul was born in Tarsus, a busy shipping community known for its commerce. His given name was Saul; he was born into a family of Pharisees. The Pharisees were a division of the Jewish people who were strictly dedicated to the Law of Moses and were absolutely loyal to the nation of Israel. They held fully to the promises of God spoken over His chosen people. Saul trained under Gamaliel, one of the great teachers of the law, and was being groomed as a Rabbi. The role of a Rabbi was to preach, teach the Scriptures, and judge those who had broken God's Law. He also learned the unique style of question and answer used for debate in the synagogue. Saul was passionate about the destruction of the early Christian church. The destruction of these rebels became his sole purpose. As Saul spent time learning and growing in the synagogue, he heard the impassioned speech by one of the followers of the recently crucified Jesus Christ. Peter, just released from prison for preaching the gospel, said that he had to obey God... no matter the cost at the hands of man. Words like that would cause most people to rethink their hatred for these Christians, but not Saul. He was fully dedicated to his purpose.

———————————

Christians in America have no idea what it is like to be a believer in many other parts of the world where followers of Christ are tortured and murdered for their faith. We hate the above story of Saul who stood by and watched Stephen as he was stoned to death for refusing to deny his faith. Paul watched and was unmoved. He and his fellow Jews were threatened by the changes that Jesus' teaching brought among the population. Jesus taught grace, love, mercy, forgiveness and servitude. Paul was protecting everything he held dear. How many of us are as passionate to defend what we believe, like these early Christians? I dare say, very few!

———————————

Jesus, we read this account of Paul and find that we don't like him much. Actually, we would like to have seen him treated in the same way he treated the church. You, on the other hand, died for him! Unfortunately, most of us would be afraid to stand up like Paul did for his beliefs. May I learn, if nothing else, to be bold for You in the face of persecution. Amen.

March 21ˢᵗ <u>Paul: Blinded by the Light</u> *(Acts 9:3)*

As he was traveling, it happened that he was approaching Damascus, and suddenly a light from heaven flashed around him.

Saul was on the hunt. He was traveling to Damascus, Syria, and other nations to find any small groups from the Christian church. This movement of believers was called "The Way." Saul's passion burned; he was a man on a mission and nothing could stop him. Nothing, that is, except a blinding light sent straight from Heaven which shone directly on him and caused his vision to fail. Couple that with a voice booming from Heaven asking why Saul was persecuting Him (Jesus). Saul was on his way to a life changing journey. He was taken to a nearby town where a believer in Christ named Ananias was sent by God to lay hands upon Saul, so that Saul could regain his sight. Imagine Ananias' terror! This was Saul—who ordered the murder of Christians! I am sure Ananias never said, "Here I am, send me!" He however did as commanded, when told by God that *"he is a chosen instrument of Mine, to bear My name before the Gentiles."* Saul received his sight, accepted his Savior and was baptized! After being struck blind and hearing the voice from Heaven... I would believe too! What an amazing conversion! And you thought <u>you</u> had a great story! <u>Paul</u> (God changed his name) immediately joined the church in Damascus, learned how to share his faith, then began to preach in the Jewish synagogues. Paul was **born again** and wanted everyone he knew to receive the same gift.

Can you recall the events which led to your Christian conversion? Many say they just "grew into their faith." My story is very different, and I had more of a Saul type conversion. The passion and fire Saul felt from the moment of his encounter with God was never quenched. He (Paul) was instrumental in getting the gospel of Christ to the Gentiles (non-Jewish). How tragic it is that so few believers ever share their faith. That job is not reserved for pastors, ministers, or prominent Christian leaders. We are equally as equipped to teach others about Jesus' grace as Paul was. Do you share your faith with others? What keeps you from being a witness for Christ?

Jesus, I have failed in Your commission to go into all the world, preaching the gospel, welcoming new believers and baptizing them in Your name. I have let the fear of persecution keep me from speaking to others about the difference You made in my life. I am willing, but my flesh is weak. Make me strong in You. Amen.

March 22ⁿᵈ Paul: Minister of the Gospel *(Acts 9:26)*

*When he came to Jerusalem, he was trying to associate
with the disciples; but they were all afraid of him,
not believing that he was a disciple.*

The above verse is likely a mild description of what
happened when the newly converted former Pharisee went
to Peter, James, John, and the other Apostles and wanted to join
them in their ministry work. Can you blame them? The man who
had watched Stephen stoned for his faith was now claiming to
be a Christian! Would you believe him? Would you trust that he
wasn't a spy? That is bad enough, but now the Jews were trying to
kill the betrayer too. In time, and with the help of Barnabas, Paul
was welcomed into the close knit group and began to witness in
the area of Jerusalem. Predictably, differences started between the
impulsive and rash Peter and the passionate Paul. Today, as we
read the Gospel accounts, we realize that God sent the division.
Paul was called to minister to the Gentiles. Peter held firm to his
belief that Gentiles needed to become Jews first and then be led
to Christ. He also thought converts should all be circumcised (a
Jewish requirement.) Paul fully disagreed, left the area and traveled throughout the middle-east, preaching the Word of God. He
wrote nearly two thirds of the books in the New Testament. Paul's
letters of encouragement, chastisement and caution to the early
churches in Ephesus, Philippi and Colosse, contain some of the
Bible's greatest teaching.

We aren't so different from Peter. We are cynical when we
hear that a celebrity or someone we have known for some time
has become a Christian. I know that my family completely doubted
a real heart change in me. They thought I was "going through a
phase." Eleven years later, they are still waiting for me to grow out
of it! Those who meet me today have no idea of the person I used to
be. Jesus Christ will change lives; but we have to tell people about
Him in order for that to happen! Can others see the difference Jesus

has made in your life? If not, you may need to recommit your life to Him and begin to allow Him to work in you.

Heavenly Father, You have changed my life, but do others see the change? I, like Paul, have differences with other believers. Help me to realize that we all have the same passion, the same faith and the same goal. Peter and Paul had very different stories, but You used each one's gifts to change the world. Make me willing to be used. Amen.

March 23ʳᵈ Paul: Ignorance and Unbelief *(1 Timothy 1:12-14)*

I thank Christ Jesus our Lord, who has strengthened me, because He considered me faithful, putting me into service, even though I was formerly a blasphemer and a persecutor and a violent aggressor. Yet I was shown mercy because I acted ignorantly in unbelief; and the grace of our Lord was more than abundant, with the faith and love which are found in Jesus Christ.

*I*f you read the Scripture above without really understanding it, please read it again. That is Paul's testimony in a nutshell. He admits that only by the strength of Jesus was he able to face his conversion, face his opposition and face eternity with hope. Paul explains that even in his life of hatred, Jesus found him faithful! What a picture that is! Jesus looked at the heart of someone who was a blasphemer, persecutor and violent aggressor against His church, and saw potential there. He knew the fierce determination Paul used against Christians could be instrumental in spreading the gospel throughout the middle-east and into the whole world. Jesus also knew Paul acted in ignorance and unbelief; he didn't know any better! I didn't either! I thought I was okay. I would have told anyone who asked that I was a Christian. I am so glad Jesus looks deeper than we do. If not, I would still be living for myself, worshipping at the altar of pride and having only bad influence within my sphere of friends. I was Paul. I made fun of Christians—some of whom were later instrumental in my conversion. I, too, was shown mercy, faith and love when I deserved none. I had no redeeming qualities, yet He redeemed me. Thank You, Jesus!

Paul is a perfect picture of the life-changing presence of Christ in a heart. He taught on marriage, parenting, friendship, witnessing, and how to maintain unity in the church. He went to the least likely places... wherever God sent him. Think about this: God chose me to teach the Word, minister through a Christian bookstore, lead young seekers to Christ, and to write this book. Fifteen years ago, no one (me included) would have dreamed these things. I am still shocked at how He works in my life. Are you letting God lead you? He has a great plan, but He needs you to give Him complete authority. Give it a try; He is an awesome God.

Lord, I am as undeserving of Your grace as Paul was. I am almost afraid to ask You to examine my heart, but please show me anything at all that keeps me from being effective in Your ministry. I once walked in ignorance and unbelief, but these passages are teaching me how to walk in wisdom and faith. May I make You proud to say, "Well done, My good and faithful servant." Amen.

March 24th Knit Together *(Psalms 139:13)*

For You formed my inward parts;
You wove me in my mother's womb.

What powerful words these are! God knit each of us together with unique characteristics, personality traits and abilities. Unfortunately, most people usually look at the wrapping paper on our outsides and never get beyond that to see the heart of gold inside. In a world focused on looks, accessories and pampering, we have become shallow and vain, which often leads to us comparing everyone else to us. I have often thought that my flaws (outward flaws like my weight, shape and age) kept me from being "hirable" in the job market. I felt like my employer would hire a young, beautiful girl over a heavy, middle-aged woman. God has showed me that I do not want to work for employers who feel that way. He has directed me toward employers who see my abilities more than my body. Because of His direction, I am able to prove my worth in the job market and "reflect Christ's beauty through the light of love showing upon my broken pieces." I often wonder what would happen to someone whose entire self worth was wrapped up in their looks…and then tragedy struck and that look was marred. How would they feel as people looked at them in horror, derision or pity? Would they be willing to walk outside their home? Would they become a scarred hermit with dreams of yesterday? Aren't you glad that your worth is not in your looks, your bank account, or your wardrobe? You have been bought and paid for by the blood of Christ... and that is a dear, dear price. You are the apple of His eye. He knows the real you and still loved you enough to die for you.

Where does your self worth lie? I certainly hope this entry has helped you to understand more fully the place you hold in His heart. Scripture tells us that God knows every sparrow which falls to the earth… and you are worth more than many sparrows. God loved you enough to send His only Son to become your sin, so that He could look at You. God cannot look upon sin. No amount of love from another person can ever give us absolute worth.

Only the One who loved us first can love us best. Thank You, Father God, Jesus my Savior, and Holy Spirit. I am blessed to know that Your face shines upon my life; may others see You reflected in me. Amen.

March 25th <u>Hope in Christ</u> *(I Timothy 4:10)*

For it is for this we labor and strive,
because we have fixed our hope on the living God,
who is the Savior of all men, especially of believers.

"*J*esus, I spent so many years believing in and being afraid of You. I didn't know Jesus; I didn't house Your Spirit; and I usually took Your creation for granted. How grateful I am for the sown seeds, the fertilized seeds and watered plants—which are now the mustard tree of my life! I do see You in the sunsets, the sunrises, the first birds of spring, the butterflies of summer, the face of a newborn baby, the love of a long married Christian couple, and in the people whom You send into my life and put in my path. You were, You are, and yes, You will always be. I am so grateful for the hope I have found in You—and <u>nowhere</u> <u>else</u> in my life!" I love to read my old journal entries like this one above from 2004. Sometimes when I begin to read them, my mind is amazed that I wrote the words. Were it not for my terrible penmanship, I would think someone else wrote some of them. Think about the verse above. Have you "fixed your hope on the living God?" What exactly does that mean? Hope to me is expectation. It is the expectation that I will walk in the light of Christ today. It is the expectation that God's hedge of protection surrounds me. It is the expectation that God's word is true and that I have new life in Christ. Hope dilutes depression. Hope keeps us moving forward. Romans 15: 13 says: *"Now may the God of hope fill you with all joy and peace in believing, so that you will abound in hope by the power of the Holy Spirit."*

Do you have hope? Let me ask you that again. Do you have hope? Life without hope is not life at all. Hope says that your child can get out of the wrong group of friends. Hope says your marriage can be saved. Hope says that God can provide a job. Hope may seem foolish to those who have no hope in their lives. Hope is in Christ. Hope is for a healthy heavenly home.

Father God, my hope is in You and in the power of Your Holy Spirit. This world causes me to feel quite hopeless. Thank You that Your word tells me to fix my hope on You. Thank You for the reminder that hope is my trusting in Your provision. Amen.

March 26th **Creation Declares His Majesty** *(Isaiah 40:28)*

Do you not know? Have you not heard? The Everlasting God,
the Lord, the Creator of the ends of the earth does not
become weary or tired. His understanding is inscrutable.

*Y*ears ago, I traveled to a weekly sales meeting with some coworkers. Michigan in the fall is a wonderful canvas of varied colored leaves, changing trees and splashes of red and orange in surprising places. My friends were so busy talking that they never looked out the car windows to see the "free entertainment" outside. I would challenge them; they would glance, nod and say "nice," then continue on with their conversation. I wrote the following journal entry on January 4, 2004: "Jesus, I love to watch the special programming about insects and animals, and the special and unique characteristics You give to each one. When I see the underwater footage of life in the ocean depths, I am blown away! People come in all sizes, shapes, colors and personalities. Only a God of infinite insight, unlimited imagination, and a great sense of humor could do the job that You did when creating this world." Many times in Scripture when God was challenged for His decisions and choices, He would challenge back with, *"Did you hang the sun? Do you know the paths of the moon? Do you know how deep the oceans are?"* Only the God of creation could know these things. He is a truly awesome God!

I actually think it is harder to believe that the world around us just happened, than it is to believe in a Creator. Anyone who can look at the color and vibrancy of Hawaii, the peaks of the Swiss Alps, the rushing waters of a flowing river and the amazing sprouting of a planted seed... and see only an accidental big bang creating those things... is beyond my scope of understanding. God placed each creature in the proper environment, provided all they would need to function, then gave them unique abilities and characteristics. Why aren't we able to replicate every creature? Why do animals mate within their species only? Yes, my faith is in the Creator of the universe, in spite of "intelligent and educated" disbelievers.

Lord, everywhere I look I am amazed at what You have made. From the tiny ladybug to the largest elephant, Your amazing intelligence is revealed. From the process of conception to the beauty of birth, Your amazing wisdom is laid before us. You are a God of order and purpose, giving meaning to every piece of Your creation. Thank You for eyes to see, ears to hear, and hands to touch the beauty around me. Amen.

March 27ᵗʰ <u>Even Me!</u> *(Ephesians 2:4-5)*

But God, being rich in mercy, because of His great love with which He loved us, even when we were dead in our transgressions, made us alive together with Christ (by grace you have been saved.)

Here is an excerpt from a journal entry in January of 2004, which I find clearly expresses my passion and gratitude for my salvation: "Jesus, I have a hard time comprehending the kind of love that made You willing to die on the Cross for my sins... especially when You've "seen me at my worst!" I have to wonder if at any time You saw us in the cesspool of our lives and reconsidered. I look at it through selfish, judgmental eyes and think that I would have a hard time laying down my life for a brother who is vile, sin filled and ungrateful. Jesus, thank You for overwhelming mercy and goodness, for free and unfettered love which we don't have to earn, and don't even deserve, and for a complete pardon of my pride, selfishness and judgmental ways. You are awesome, Jesus!" If you are a **born-again** Christian, you should be able to say the same things... unless you are a lot more perfect than I am! He does see us at our worst and He still loves us. He does watch the messes we make of our lives, and will still forgive us. He does hear us take His name in vain... and will still give us pardon. I cannot help but think of the things in my past with shame and embarrassment. He looks at them, touches them with a drop of righteous blood and washes them white as snow. It is unexplainable and unfathomable... it is Jesus.

Judging others in the light of our own sins is nothing less than hypocritical. I have a friend who will watch a television special or movie and criticize everything the characters do. Maybe we all do this, but the truth is that most of us do the same things to different degrees or with different rationales. She doesn't see her own actions, only the "wrong actions" of others. How awesome it would be if we looked through love eyes like Jesus does. Instead of criticizing or condemning, we would love unconditionally.

Lord, I am so very grateful that You looked at me through love eyes instead of faultfinding eyes. My salvation is the greatest gift I've ever received... and amazingly, it cost me nothing. May I never forget exactly what it cost You. Help me to reflect Your love to everyone I encounter. Amen.

March 28th Watch Maker *(Psalms 89: 6-7)*

For who in the skies is comparable to the LORD? Who among the sons of the mighty is like the LORD, a God greatly feared in the council of the holy ones, and awesome above all those who are around Him?

Recently, I listened to an interview between James Dobson and Joe Gibbs (football coach & NASCAR owner). Joe said when people ask him if he "really" believes in God that he uses a watch as his witness. He asks the person who is questioning him: "Do you see this? What is it?" The person replies, "Well, it's a watch." Joe Gibbs then says, "How do you know it's a watch? Did you see someone make it?" Of course, the person didn't see it being made. Gibbs then says, "Just because you can't see the watch maker, does that mean he didn't make it? It is the same with God. He is Creator of all. We may not see Him, but what we do see proves that He is!" I loved this wonderful word picture. Are we sure enough of what we believe to even be able to share it with others? Joe Gibbs is a dynamic and influential leader in the sports field. Why does he step forward and talk openly about his faith? It is who he is... **all the time**. Whether at home, at the football field, at the race track or at any public venue, Joe Gibbs is a Christian. We could certainly take our lead from Joe. Think of the impact the Christian community could have on society if we would all take a cue from Joe's "playbook."

How could you use the 'watchmaker' analogy in a conversation? Practice it until you are comfortable. This may be the very tool God will use for your witness in the near future. Have you ever thought of how well prepared atheists, abortion rights activists or conservationists are to defend their positions on their issue? Why are blood bought Christians not as passionate about our cause? Don't we owe Christ our best commitment? After all, He is the Watchmaker who has given us a face, a pair of hands, and working inward parts! What a fine craftsman He is!

Father God, You deserve for me to give You my best in all parts of my life, including and especially in my witness. Bless Joe Gibbs for being dedicated to Your cause and for sharing his faith through thought, word and deed. Help me to be equally as committed. Amen.

March 29th   Desperate For His Touch   *(Psalms 103: 2-3)*

Bless the LORD, O my soul, and forget none of His benefits;
Who pardons all your iniquities, Who heals all your diseases.

*O*ne of my favorite New Testament stories is told in Chapter 9 of the Gospel of Matthew. Here Jesus has been called to restore health to a synagogue official's young daughter. The man exhibited great faith by coming to Jesus, which reflected his belief that He has the power to heal her. As Jesus turns to follow the man, a woman fights the crowd to get near Him...just near enough to touch the hem of His garment. There is more here than a simple cry for healing. This woman has been hemorrhaging blood for 12 years. In Jewish laws, women were considered unclean during menstruation and were strictly forbidden to be near men. This woman is likely very weak, probably anemic, and is risking everything for a chance to touch Jesus. Think about the implications. She could be stoned if someone reveals the truth about her. She is fighting her way into a crowd of people... a place most women know better than to go. Jesus takes a few steps and then stops and asks, *"Who touched Me? I felt the power go out from My cloak."* His disciples respond that in this crowd He is bound to be jostled. *"Who touched Me,"* He asks again. The woman bravely tells Him she did, and why. Jesus is amazed at her faith. He turns to her and says, *"Daughter, take courage; your faith has made you well."* Immediately the blood issue stops; and Jesus then continues on to the home of the synagogue official.

This woman was desperate. Everyone else had forsaken her, but she was not forsaken by the One who could heal her. Everyone else had given up, but He gave her health and restored her ability to feel like a woman again. What is your form of bleeding? Is it childhood hurts, physical needs, emotional burdens, marital struggles or spiritual doubts? The bleeding certainly hurts... and only One can help. How desperate are you for His touch? Will you step out of the crowd and dare to be different, so that you can feel His touch? Be as brave as this woman was; reach out in faith and allow Jesus to stop your bleeding.

Jesus, some of us bleed on the inside and some of us on the outside, but it is still blood. I come before You for Your healing touch and Your caring heart. Others may think I am beyond help, but You know better. You knit me together; You can knit me back together. Amen.

March 30th <u>Walking The Gospel</u> *(John 20:21)*

So Jesus said to them again, "Peace be with you;
as the Father has sent Me, I also send you."

I am passionate about witnessing and doing the things the Lord has called us to do. Here are some thoughts on what I think Jesus would want from us:

(1. His children are called to be "Jesus with skin on." (2. We are not to decide independently how to minister to strangers, or to our brothers in Christ. (3. We are to pore over the Gospel and learn from it how Christ walked. (4. We are to emulate the things He did, and the way He loved. If we were to walk today like Jesus did over 2,000 years ago... our world would be more filled with love. There would be less hate, war and strife; and there would be no hunger, poverty or prejudice. We would not judge, criticize, or forsake one another. We would be healed and be healers. We would give God all the glory.

———————————

Why do you think so many unchurched people believe Christians to be absolute hypocrites? The early Christian church was a ministering body to the widows, the orphans, and the poor. They cared for one another's needs, reached out to the strangers in their midst and emulated Jesus' love. They were inclusive, not exclusive, to anyone who wanted to be part of them. Back to the hypocrite question: Who does your church minister to? Programs and services are wonderful, but the church will never grow unless we reach outside the safe four walls of our building. We must take the Gospel to the streets. Remember, the church is the body of people, not the building. This is where we have messed up. Buildings, programs, music department performances... all are great. However, these things keep us busy doing church work and not ministry work. What would Jesus think of the Christian church of today?

———————————

Lord, we have allowed programs to overshadow ministry. Help me and my local church body to reach outside of our building to be "Jesus with skin on" to a lost world. Show us, teach us, and use us. Amen.

March 31ˢᵗ   <u>He Knows My Heart</u>   *(Psalms 55:2)*

Give heed to me and answer me;
I am restless in my complaint and am surely distracted...

In 2004, family situations had led to a division in my family. Without great detail, I will say that I refused to deny the truth of the Gospel in order to bow to political correctness. I questioned why this could be happening to me. After all, I had not backed off from my time in the Word or my service in the Kingdom. Through it all, I knew one truth. God knew my heart, my intentions and my integrity. Have you ever been in a similar situation? Families are touchy in the best of situations, but they can be really bad when hard times hit. This story makes me think of Moses, one of the great Bible leaders of all time. He was doing everything the Lord was telling him, and in the way He was telling him. Here comes that family thing... Moses' brother Aaron and sister Miriam decided that they should have the same authority as Moses. They didn't want to wait for big brother to make decisions, so they turned the people against him. When God addressed their sins, Miriam ended up with leprosy. Aaron pled with God for restoration from her sins, calling them foolishness. God heard the cry and restored her flesh after seven days. Moses was thrust into family differences... not by his choice, but by the choice of others. Moses' character was above reproach and his abilities were God given. He could have fallen into sin at any time, but he was determined to follow the ways of the Lord.

How are your family relationships? I always think of the Scripture which says that "a friend loves at all times, but a brother is born for adversity." Does that mean we are destined to fight with our siblings? No. I hope it means that there comes a day when family garbage stops, and that when times get hard the brother becomes your lifeline. As Christians, we are called to be examples to those who are in our sphere of influence. Our families are included in that sphere.

Jesus, help me to use Your Spirit, my gifts and these hands to serve others and to be beneficial in Your Kingdom. Thank You for loving all of me—even when I feel very unlovable! You see my heart... and that's all I need to know. Help me to bring healing within my family whenever possible. Amen.

April 1ˢᵗ Comfy, Casual Days *(Matthew 11: 28)*

*Come to Me all who are weary and heavy laden,
and I will give you rest.*

I love casual! In a life where I have to dress up for office work and for church on Sunday, I love my "blue jean" days, or occasionally a day in my favorite gray "holey" sweats. They are full of holes, are loose fitting (not a great diet idea) and have different shades of paint splattered all over them. Why do I love those sweats? I can be myself in them. I can crawl under the bed to grab a dropped earring. I can go for a walk or take a nap without worrying about wrinkles. They are who I am—comfy, battered and bruised, and perfect for a casual day at home. Dan wants me to throw them away—NEVER! Even if only the cuffs remain, the sweats will still be my favorites. They, very simply, are me! Jesus and His disciples had to be casual people. How pretentious can you be when you are homeless, eating wherever you can find a meal, and teaching in the open-air areas around Jerusalem? Jesus wasn't impressed by the rich robes of the Jewish leaders or the military uniforms of the Roman guards. He sought out the poor, the blind, the sick and the cast offs. I have to think He would like me much better in my sweats than in my work clothes. He would want me to come to Him in my most comfortable state. How else could I sit at His feet to learn?

I know that everyone is different. I have friends who insist on getting dressed every day!! Go figure! Why get dressed to hang around the house? Clothes are really a reflection of our personality. Are you always perfectly groomed and neatly dressed? Are you a casual slob like me? We place a lot of weight on how we dress; but we were all born naked! I am kidding here, but Jesus isn't into high fashion. He will take you just as you are, at any time of the day or night. Come to Him now in prayer no matter how you are clothed. Clothe yourself in humility, not finery.

Jesus, if I try to look good before I come to You, I will never look good enough. Help me to be properly, but not obsessively, groomed and clad. You love the homeless soul in cast off rags as much as the Hollywood star in high fashion. Help me to keep my eyes on what is truly important. Amen.

April 2ⁿᵈ <u>An Everlasting Love</u> *(Jeremiah 31: 3)*

"...I have loved you with an everlasting love;
therefore I have drawn you with loving-kindness."

*A*s I prepared for Valentine's Day, 2007, I wrote the following journal entry: "Am I looking for hearts and flowers, or a love that lasts on this Valentines Day? Actually, hearts and flowers don't thrill me much anymore, but I found the love that lasts on February 14, 1996. After months of reading Scripture, poring over books, hearing sermons and talking to other Christians, I met the Love of my Life—My Sweet Jesus! I call Him the lover of my soul... though not like most of us think of a lover. No, He loved me enough to write a long love letter outlining all the best ways to walk and serve Him. He had it printed, and I hold it every day as I read the New Testament. He loved me enough to climb a long, lonely hill, hang on a cross, suffer ridicule and die for me. That is truly a lover!" I remember days early in my adult life when Valentines Day without someone to buy me a card or send flowers was the end of my world. Today, I see it as a holiday inspired by greeting card and candy makers. I have written before about my salvation, but this bears repeating. Jesus became my first love. No man could offer me what He did—eternal life! No man ever loved me enough to sacrifice himself for me. I never want to hear Jesus say to me, "*…I have this against you, that you have left your first love.*" He was addressing the church of Ephesus, who had forgotten who they were supposed to be serving. No, I do not want to hear those words when I stand before Him face-to-face.

Are you someone who feels a deep-seated need to be loved? Do you sell yourself short because of that? Do you settle for less than God says you deserve? Look again at the verse at the top of this page. Is the love you know everlasting? I see way too many marriages falling apart to believe that all man/woman love is ever-lasting. That sort of love is hard to come by—humanly speaking that is. That is the exact type of love Jesus offers to all who call upon His name in faith. Have you called on Him yet?

Jesus, I haven't known that kind of love… and I want it in my life. Lord, I accept Your sacrifice on my behalf and Your unconditional love for me. How do I grow in Your grace and love? Lord, I long to be loved as You offer love. Amen.

April 3ʳᵈ His Essence *(Psalms 45:8)*

All Your garments are fragrant with myrrh and aloes and cassia.

" Jesus, these descriptions are true... and yet the world denied You because You came in poverty and humility instead of royal robes in a regal palace. The garment I picture is a simple tunic... a pauper's clothes... stained with Your shed blood. I see a garment to which I am drawn, not because of its elegance or its richness, but because of its simple goodness... its sturdy practicality and its good fortune to have been worn by God Himself. Jesus, when I reach for You it is for cleansing mercy, forgiveness and pardon. How blessed I am to know the simple part of You before I see You in all Your splendor when You return." Those words were from my journal entry in February of 2004. Do they cause you to picture the humble robes of the Lord? I love to think about how He was so simple in His clothes and life. At His House (my Bible and gift store) I carry a candle line called "His Essence." Each jar has the Scripture for Psalm 45:8 on it. I love to share this product with my customers because they love the fresh, unique fragrance. This candle has equal parts of the three ingredients in the verse: myrrh, aloe and cassia. I often tell my customers, "No wonder we will love to live with Jesus for eternity, if He smells like this!"

Think about how certain scents touch our lives. Have you ever walked into a home or a bakery where fresh bread was baking? How about the smell of homemade soup or chili on a cold winter day? Think about the cold, fresh smell of a child who has been playing in the snow. We love smells. Think about the scent of Jesus… a scent we will recognize as soon as He comes close. His is the scent of comfort and familiarity. Myrrh is generally used in perfume making in Arabia. The aloes here are spices from sandalwood — much like cedar, which we use in closets or chests. The cassia is taken from flowers of the cinnamon tree. The scent is not exclusively male or female like so many are… it is simply His Essence.

Lord, I long to smell the fragrance of Your robes… to see the hands which held the children… to hear the voice which calmed the storms. Come, Lord Jesus, I am ready to see Your face. Amen.

April 4th Faith, Not Works *(Ephesians 2: 8-9)*

For by grace you have been saved through faith;
and that not of yourselves, it is the gift of God;

not as a result of works, so that no one may boast.

*W*hat does the Bible verse for today mean? Let's break it down and see. The first portion says *"For by grace you have been saved through faith."* This tells us that salvation (the profession of faith in Jesus Christ as our Savior, leading to eternal life) is by God's grace (unearned, unmerited favor) when we have faith to claim that gift. The next portion says, *"…and that not of yourselves, it is the gift of God,"* meaning we can't do this ourselves. We do not have the power to save ourselves or anyone else. Only by the greatest Gift ever given—a perfect holy baby born in a manger—can we be saved. God loved us enough, in spite of our sin, to send Jesus to us. Lastly, *"…not as a result of works, so that no one may boast."* This verse tells us that our works or good deeds do not save us. Many religions base their blessings and eternal life on works performed by those who wish to gain grace. This is reassuring to me, because it means that those who do good things in order to receive eternal life will not be saved, only those who come in faith. What is faith? Faith believes that which we cannot see with our eyes. Anyone can believe in something they see; it takes much greater faith to believe in that which we cannot see. I would not recommend that anyone profess faith without seeing the truth of the Gospel. We do this by studying God breathed Scripture. Read it, research it, and understand it. All of us should challenge the things of the faith. If we don't, we are "mindless robots following a dead man," as one well-known media mogul refers to Christians. The steps to salvation in Christ begin on the 6th of August.

Do you understand the teaching above? If not, please reread the passage slowly, maybe several times today. We must understand the concept of grace, salvation, works, faith and boasting. It is a heart change, not a rational brain change! Blind faith is foolish; we are called to dig deeper and find a real and deep belief in who God, Jesus, and the Holy Spirit are. Are you learning from this teaching? Are you hungry for even more? Seek truth from God and He will help you to better understand. I am praying for you to find a hunger you've never had before.

Father, I am grateful that I cannot save myself and that my good deeds don't save me. I could never do enough good to merit Your unbelievable salvation. Help me not to boast of my good doings, but to do these things as a natural fruit of knowing You. Amen.

April 5th Noah: Called of God *(Genesis 6:7)*

The Lord said, "I will blot out man whom I have created from the face of the land, from man to animals to creeping things and to birds of the sky; for I am sorry that I have made them."

*P*oor Noah! He was minding his business, being a godly man and raising his family as he watched the evil grow around him. At the same time we see the very words of God in the verse above stating He regrets ever creating man in the first place! This is only the sixth chapter of the Bible, and it gives us a real picture of how quickly evil can permeate our world. God decides to send a flood to kill all living creatures because they have corrupted that which He called good. *"But, Noah found favor in the eyes of the Lord."* God tells him of the plan and makes provision for Noah, his wife, his three sons and their wives to be spared. Noah is told to build an ark, a huge enclosed boat, of gopher wood. Very specific instructions are to be followed as the ark is built hundreds of miles inland... in a nation which rarely sees rain. The people around Noah must have thought he had lost his mind. But wait, it gets better! Noah finishes tarring the boat and begins to load all species of animals onto it in pairs, so that they can continue to reproduce after the waters recede. Noah must have heard all the jeers and jokes made at him and his family, but only the opinion of God mattered to him.

How willing are you to be different? What would you do if the command God gave you seemed absolutely foolish and you knew you would face great ridicule if you obey? Most of us are more concerned with what people will think of us than of what God desires from us. Few of us truly dare to be different... even though we are called to be different. Actually, God calls us to be a *"peculiar"* people who are in the world, but not of the world. In order for us to be effective in our witness, we must be willing to shed the bonds of political correctness, to speak truth and to stand for what we believe. If we don't do this, the church is of no effect in the world.

Father God, I confess being different scares me. I am much more comfortable with fitting in than I am with standing out. I know You have commanded me to be holy and be bold. Please strengthen me to be able to do that. I long to be in Your perfect will. Make me bold like Noah and willing to withstand the ridicule of those who would persecute me. Amen.

April 6ᵗʰ Noah: At the Helm *(Proverbs 27:15)*

*"A constant dripping on a day of steady rain
and a contentious woman are alike."*

I couldn't resist this entry. Just thinking about Noah locked within the ark with four women, three men and a plethora of animals is more than I can hold in. Think about it. Mrs. Noah is tired, hasn't bathed in 150 days and has to sleep near the elephants. Her daughters-in-law are getting on her nerves; the wombats are on the prowl; and Noah keeps telling her to *"trust in the Lord."* She cannot hold in her anger any longer... drip... drip... drip. The water drips in, the rain hits the roof, and the birds have not stopped dropping while on the fly! Noah is on the receiving end of her words... and they are as grating as the drip... drip... drip of the water. "Who brought the flies on the boat? Don't swat at those mosquitoes! They are the only ones we have, Noah! The pig is in labor and the dog is in heat!" Yes, close quarters with that many people for 150 days is only for the strong of heart. That is why Noah was chosen. God knew He could trust this man to do exactly as commanded. Noah and his family must have felt totally isolated from the world around them before the flood. Finally, finally... the rain stops... the dove has stayed gone and it is time to disembark. Imagine the smell, the noise, and the hunger for sunshine of all on the ark. Noah was surely a man after God's own heart.

Picture here a metal bucket sitting under a drip in the roof. Perfectly timed drops continue to fall into the bucket... there is nothing soothing about the sound. Noah may have listened to that in the ark. Our Scripture tells us how hard it is to live with a contentious woman. The teaching above is mostly fiction, but it could describe the condition of some marriages. Are you contentious? Are you a nagging wife or a harping husband? No relationship can grow in a situation like that. Noah's faith and righteousness saved him. His patience and tolerance made him obedient. How do you measure up?

Jesus, I don't want to be known as a contentious person. My nagging and anger bring no good to my friendships, marriage or relationships. Help me to curb my tongue, speak only kind words and be an encourager. No matter what the situation, You didn't whine or spew venom. Help me to be more like You as I walk through the situations of my life today. Amen.

April 7th <u>Who Moved?</u> *(Joshua 1:5)*

No man will be able to stand before you all the days of your life;
just as I have been with Moses, I will be with you;
I will not fail you or forsake you.

I remember hearing very early in my faith walk: "If you aren't feeling as close to God as you once were... who moved?" That statement piqued my thoughts and made me realize that even in my earthly relationships—I move! I am so grateful that God is steady, constant, faithful, honest, sincere, and of integrity. How could I represent a God who was any less? I know God's word says He will never leave me or forsake me. I am holding on tightly to that truth; and digging into His word helps me to not lose my grip on His hand! Several Bible stories come to mind as I write this lesson. I think of King David who moved away from God and moved into deadly sin. I think of King Solomon who was God's wisest man, yet moved away and allowed the gods of his foreign wives to take precedence in his worship. I think of Noah, the builder of the ark, who got drunk and naked when he moved away from God. What about Judas Iscariot, who walked every day beside Jesus, and then turned on Him? There are many stories about those who moved away from God; and every one brought shame, despair and even death.

Are you as close to God as you once were? Are you as close as you want to be? He hasn't moved. *He is the same yesterday, today and forever.* He is the one constant in our lives. He should be the baseline we adhere to which keeps us from falling into sin. Are you keeping His commands? I am not talking about doing good works here. I am asking if you are lying, cheating, stealing, coveting or "murdering" someone with hatred. Notice the promise in the verse... *"No man will be able to stand before you all the days of your life; just as I have been with Moses, I will be with you."* When we are walking His way we are immune to the enemy's attacks. We must be ever mindful of the slow drift, which leads us away from the things of God. How are you doing in your faith walk?

Jesus, I am so blessed to know Your Presence and Your love. I feel the warm flushes of Your Presence as I write these words. I know that if one of us has moved, it isn't You. Help me to move back, to remove the space between us and to be restored into Your graces. Amen.

April 8th <u>Garden of Blessings</u> *(Genesis 3:8a)*

They heard the sound of the Lord God walking
in the garden in the cool of the day...

We tend to think of gardens full of brilliant, beautiful flowers, relaxing benches and butterflies flitting every-where. Sometimes we think of vegetable gardens, hoed to remove the weeds and producing healthy, fresh produce to feed our families. Gardens have always been such a part of Scripture and have become vital settings used to tell the Biblical story. I think particularly of The Garden of Eden where Adam and Eve walked in pure fellow-ship with God. All of their wants and needs were satisfied. There was no shame, no suffering, only beauty. How tragic that the enemy of our soul was allowed to sneak in and destroy man's fellowship with God. I think of Gethsemane—the garden of prayer, the garden of reluctance, the garden of despair, the garden of sweat drops of blood, the garden of Christ's arrest. These gardens are two lovely places... fertile and lush, but they are also places where evil entered... a serpent to tempt and test man, an enemy to try to fill Jesus with fear. Man won in one, but lost in the other. It isn't always what grows in the garden that makes it beautiful. In Eden's garden, God walked with His creation. He listened to them and they listened to Him. Time was not a factor... life had no end. Then, sin entered the garden and life was given an end point... death. Man was separated from his Creator; and life became hopeless.

Gethsemane's garden carries a very different story ending. Yes, it was a place of betrayal, despair and fear. It was also a place where the reconciliation between God and man was carried out. Jesus prayed for the *'cup to be taken from Him.'* He asked God if there was any other way... maybe another spotless lamb to be offered up. It was also a place of obedience and forgiveness. Jesus knew who His betrayer was. If Judas Iscariot was the only sinner on earth, Jesus would still have gone to the cross. Gethsemane is the garden of grace. Think about these two gardens during your day today. Picture them in your mind. Eden—beautiful and lush—providing every-thing needed for life. Gethsemane—beautiful and lush—providing everything needed to restore life.

———————

Father God, thank You for both gardens. I would likely have made the same sinful choice as Adam and Eve, and spoiled Your created perfection. I would have tried to stop Your suffering in Gethsemane... and would have been stopping the plan You made from the beginning of time. Amen.

April 9th Rosie's Glow *(Ruth 3:11)*

"Now, my daughter, do not fear. I will do for you whatever you ask, for all my people in the city know that you are a woman of excellence."

Have you ever met someone who glows? Seriously, someone who seems to be backlit so their eyes shine and their presence is almost magnetic? Many years ago I met a woman like that. I was waiting tables in a local restaurant when a couple came in and sat at one of my tables. I was immediately struck by how lovely she was—clear skin, bright eyes and a dynamite smile. When she spoke, my opinion did not change. I have met beautiful women before who know how beautiful they are and are not very nice. Rosie wasn't like that. She was kind, gracious and generous with her praises. At the time I was not a believer and never realized her beauty was the Spirit of Christ shining through her. Rosie and I became casual friends from that day forward. I would occasionally run into her at my different jobs. No matter how long between these meetings, she always asked after my family and took time to listen to my answers. Listening is a fine art; Rosie mastered the art. Rosie, now a widow with failing health, never ceases to amaze me. She is as full of fire for Jesus as I was as a baby Christian 11 years ago. She loves the Lord, loves people, and has surely made an impact on the lives of many people besides me. The verse above talks of a *"woman of excellence."* I see

Rosie's picture in the dictionary beside that definition. I thank God for the blessing this sweet, sweet soul has been in my life.

I want to be a woman of influence and excellence like Rosie. She may have been born nice... I wasn't, and have to work to grow that grace. Make no mistake though; these virtues can be developed. Philippians 4:8 tells us to dwell upon *"whatever is true, whatever is honorable, whatever is right, whatever is pure, whatever is lovely, whatever is of good repute and whatever is worthy of praise."* We need to shut out the noise, fill our minds with good thoughts, avoid negativity and gossip, and walk the walk of the virtuous. That will grow our influence in a dark world, in our homes, in our workplaces and in our churches.

Lord, I am not much like Rosie. I confess to You that I have allowed myself to be drawn into negativity and division. I have dwelt upon that which is far from pleasing to You. Please shut my lips from speaking unkind words. Make me an encourager. Use me to influence the nonbelievers in my sphere of influence... like the Rosie's of the world influenced me. Amen.

April 10th   Karen: A Friend for all Seasons   *(James 1:12)*

Blessed is a man who perseveres under trial; for once he has been approved, he will receive the crown of life which the Lord has promised to those who love Him.

Karen has been my best friend for 40 years. We grew up together on the "wrong side of the tracks" and have remained friends through all our life changes. We double-dated, shared secrets, laughed and cried, and we had our share of disagreements. I know her family like my own. High school friends still ask me how she is—almost like one of us wasn't known without the other. We had one identity, like a married couple. There is a comfort in knowing someone so long and so intimately. I have had many 'friends' in my life, spent a lot of time with them, then had them fade away as situations and times changed. Not so with Karen. What is the difference in her friendship and the others who move in and out of my life? Commitment! Even though we don't talk often, each of us knows the other is just a phone call away. I find it frustrating as we face the empty nest phase that life keeps us both too busy to just relax and enjoy one another. <u>Busyness</u> keeps us from the <u>business</u> of being with those we most want time with! What a great tool of the enemy! Keep them busy and keep them from putting forth a united front. About eight years ago a nightmare began to unfold in Karen's life… one that could have destroyed her… and could have really shaken her faith. She went through hell on earth; and we both found out what friendship really means. Tomorrow's entry will tell this story.

———————

Are you a good friend? For some people it comes easier than for others. I confess I get busy and distracted, and time just seems to fly away. Soon I realize I haven't talked to friends in days, even weeks. What does it take to be a good friend? Scripture tells us a friend sticks closer than a brother. That is powerful because we have always heard that blood is thicker than water. Think about it though. Our brothers and sisters bring that whole "sibling rivalry" thing into the picture. Usually it's not the same with a friend. We can confide in them and not expect to have our dirty laundry aired at the next family get-together. We need to work on being better friends.

———————

Lord, My friendship skills need to be developed and improved. I allow things of this world to keep me from being the friend You would have me be. Thank You for loyal friends. Each one is a gift from Your hand. Each is different… kind of like a bouquet of beautiful flowers. During the darkest times of my life they have lifted me up, encouraged me and 'stuck closer than a brother.' None can compare with You, my best friend, Jesus. Amen.

April 11ᵗʰ   Karen: Set the Captives Free   *(Luke 4:18)*

The Spirit of the Lord is upon Me, because He anointed Me to
preach the Gospel to the poor. He has sent Me to proclaim
release to the captives, and recovery of sight to the blind,
to set free those who are oppressed.

*K*aren is a nurse. Ever since she was a child, nursing was her goal. I, who faint at the sight of blood, could never imagine anyone wanting to do what she does. Karen worked for the home care division of a local hospital and was promoted into management. Her nightmare began several years later when charges of Medicare fraud against Karen and two other supervisors were filed. They were led to believe early on that this was nothing serious and that any charges would be against the hospital. Unfortunately, several years into the investigation, this proved to be untrue. Karen, the most honest person I know, was arrested for Medicare fraud. The hospital retained top criminal attorneys, and Karen learned a vocabulary she wished she never heard. Words like affidavit, character witness, deposition and evidence became part of her everyday language. Delay after delay kept them from going to trial, until January of 2004. If my best friend had not been one of the accused, I would have found the legal proceedings to be very interesting. Karen knew she could lose her nursing license and everything she had worked her whole life for. From the start, the government prosecutor made a complete fool of himself. His witnesses were caught in lies. His evidence was ridiculous. His arguments and repetition put the jury to sleep and the judge to the end of his patience. Finally, two weeks later in an all-or-nothing move by the defense attorneys, the charges were all thrown out. If I never did another thing right in our friendship, I was there every day of Karen's trial. Most importantly, I was there to bathe that courtroom with prayers on behalf of my best friend.

Sometimes, as Karen went through her struggle, I literally didn't know what to say to her. Instead, I prayed for my friend. When her nightmare first began, God spoke to her and told her everything would be all right. Karen doubted those words as charges were filed, arrests were made, and meetings with the attorneys made the bad dream a reality. God kept His promise... not in Karen's desired time frame, but in His—maybe to make her learn to trust in Him, not in man.

Lord, when everything is dark in my life, may I remember Your promise to never leave or forsake me. May I look through the storms to see the light of Your peace on every horizon. May I never doubt that You understand my suffering; because You suffered first. Amen.

April 12th   Doubt No More   *(Psalms 121:3-4)*

He will not allow your foot to slip; He who keeps you will not slumber. Behold, He who keeps Israel will neither slumber nor sleep.

*W*e often slumber in a fog of doubt. We doubt for God's provision for our needs. We doubt that He feels our hurts. We doubt that He cares about the things that are important to us. We doubt that He could love us enough to sacrifice His Son for our needs. The above verse is one example of the many promises God gives to us through His book of promises... the Bible. Read the verse, using the punctuation marks to stop or pause. *He will not allow your foot to slip* promises that His hedge of protection is there to keep us from slipping... into sin, off the edge of the narrow wall dividing right and wrong. *He who keeps you will not slumber* tells us He is our keeper, our provider, the one who meets our needs. This verse also tells us He never sleeps. He is always watching, alert, and ready to answer our prayers or act on our behalf. *He who keeps Israel will neither slumber nor sleep* tells us that the promises He made (and kept) to Israel are the same ones He will make and keep for us.

Do these things reassure you? Are you full of doubts? What is your greatest source of doubt? Stop and really think about this answer; these are important questions. If you never look deep enough to really visit the things which cause you to not walk fully with God, you will never grow beyond where you are now. For some of you, that may be fine. You are happy where you are. I know there are others who want more. Let me ask again, "What is your greatest source of doubt?" Do you doubt the paths He might walk you down? Are you doubtful that He will pick you up and carry you through the hard times? Read the breakdown of the verse again... His Word is as Good as Gold!

Lord, I confess my doubts and fears. They have crippled me and plagued my faith walk. You alone love me enough to die for me... even in my filth. I need to claim Your promises as mine. Please send Your Spirit to open my eyes to all truth and hope. Amen.

April 13ᵗʰ Martha of Bethany (*Luke 10:40a*)

"But Martha was distracted with all her preparations..."

The first sermon I ever heard was on the story of Mary and Martha. Just minutes into the message I realized very clearly that I was a "Martha" through and through. Some of us are born organizers and planners. Some of us are dreamers. Some of us don't care what the house looks like as long as we can spend time with a friend. I am surely not that person. I move my living room furniture every other week! I did the same in my bedroom as a teenager—hard to believe isn't it! I am a Martha! Each time I have heard this lesson taught, Mary—her pensive, deep thinking sister—comes out the heroine. I have one question...who cooks the meal for the party while Mary ponders and sits at the feet of the guest? In this story Jesus has come to visit the sisters and their brother Lazarus at their home in Bethany. Martha is planning the meal, which includes feeding those who travel with Jesus too. Mary is sitting at Jesus' feet, listening to the teaching—while Martha slams the pots and pans in the kitchen. (Don't laugh; you know the same thing has happened in your family!) Finally, in total frustration, Martha confronts Jesus. *"Lord, do You not care that my sister has left me to do all the serving alone? Then tell her to help me."* Martha doesn't beat around the bush! She is telling God in the flesh what to do! Jesus tells her, *"Martha, Martha, you are worried and bothered about so many things..."* Well of course she is; there is company for dinner... a great teacher... the One who says He is the Son of God! You can't feed Him a T.V. dinner!

Are you a Martha? Does the preparation and cleanup keep you from enjoying the party? This is so me! I am bossy. I am organized. I am thorough... and people who are not drive me crazy! I think I am fine. But, am I? Does my obsession with perfection keep me from really sitting at the feet of Jesus and hearing what He wants to speak into my spirit? There has to be a compromise where we can get the things done which need done, and also time to calm our spirits for quiet time with Jesus. In the clamor and busyness of life, we can clearly lose focus on what is truly important.

Lord, help me to calm down, take time at Your feet, feast upon Your Word and realize the dirty dishes will still be there tomorrow! Maybe You could send another Martha in to do them, while I spend time with You! Life is short; and obsessing over unimportant details wastes those few precious years. Thank You for the lesson on Martha and Mary. As always, I needed to hear it. Amen.

April 14th   <u>Mary of Bethany</u>   *(Luke 10: 42)*

"...but only one thing is necessary, for Mary has chosen the good part, which shall not be taken away from her."

*T*oday, we look at the Mary side of the Mary/Martha confrontation. A Sunday school class discussion a few years ago led one of my dearest friends and me to tell our views of the Mary/

Martha debate. Rachel said Martha's make her very uncomfortable. She told the class she would rather sit at the table and visit with her guests, even if dinner wasn't ready on time, than to obsess about the work needing to be done. I can honestly say I never saw it from that perspective before. Rachel also stated that Martha's make her feel like she doesn't measure up. Let me tell you here... Rachel is one of the godliest and kindest people I have ever met. If I had a choice to be like one other person, I would choose her! Why would I (a confirmed Martha) want to be a Mary? Stress, blood pressure and frustration, to name a few things! Mary was doing that which Jesus said was right, *"...but only one thing is necessary, for Mary has chosen the good part, which shall not be taken away from her."* She quieted her spirit, probably knowing that whatever she did to help Martha wouldn't be good enough anyway. She chose to risk Martha's wrath because she only had a few precious minutes to share with Jesus. She had different priorities than her sister. Neither sister's priorities were bad, but Mary's were more Christ focused.

Okay, you Martha's, are you still judging the Mary's in your life? What do people remember about your last gathering: perfect food, the immaculate house and the impeccable decorations? Do they remember the fun you shared, the laughter, the times of fellowship and prayer? I can recall parties where I did dishes while my family laughed and played in other room. If you are the Martha personality type you can learn to compromise, relax and enjoy guests. In most cases, they don't care what condition your house is in, unless the cat hair and dust balls in the spaghetti are too much for them! Mary types can stretch themselves to be more organized and more prepared for entertaining. No matter what, take time to sit at the feet of Jesus and just breathe...

Jesus, the Mary part of me doesn't really care about what needs done around the house, but I also know that You would rather my family lived healthy! Help me to learn the necessary organizational skills You deem vital in my life. I may never be a Martha (Stewart), but I can be just who You made me to be. Thank You for these lessons on personality styles. I am glad You didn't make us all alike! Amen.

April 15th <u>**Stepping out in Faith**</u> *(Psalms 109:21)*

But You, O God, the Lord, deal kindly with me for Your name's sake; because Your loving-kindness is good, deliver me.

*O*n April 12th we talked about our doubts keeping us from ever truly trusting God to lead us and direct our paths. The following passage from a 2004 journal entry speaks to the teaching from that past lesson. "Only in perfect hindsight are we able to see where You steered us through the storms, protected us in the battles, and directed us to greener pastures. I believe that the majority of Your intercessions we never even know about. How many times have You kept us from a car accident, directed us from something or someone who would serve to hurt us; or given us a pleasant surprise that we failed to acknowledge as from Your hands? I'm glad I don't have 20/20 foresight; I'm sure it would scare me to death. I love the 20/20 hindsight, for only in this am I able to see Your gifts, blessings, direction and protection." We have all heard awesome stories of God's provision and direction in the life of His children. I shared the His House story... a great example of what is written above. Had I had to stop and think (really think) about opening a business in a sluggish economy, with no extra money to fall back on, with another job I couldn't leave, and with another large Christian store in town, I would never have stepped out in faith. That is exactly why God worked each detail out in His quick and perfect timing. He had to take it out of my hands in order for His purpose to happen.

Have you ever stepped out in faith? Were you afraid before you took the step? How did it work out in the end? Think about the 20/20 hindsight statement. There are so many times when I am going through a difficult time and praying for relief... and it feels like a weight on my shoulders that will never be lifted. Sometimes I wonder when the relief actually came. In that perfect hindsight I see the outcome. If I look closely, I can usually see the very moment the Lord began to turn the tide. There was a very short period of time like that before His House opened. I had major panic attacks and was convinced I would be a failure as a daughter, mother, grandmother and friend... because I would have no time to put into those things. God sent a wise friend who spoke faith into me, calmed my spirit and helped me through it. I see this clearly in perfect hindsight.

Lord, stepping out in faith is not easy for me. My insecurities hold me back and will eventually keep me from ever doing all You want me to do in my life and for Your kingdom. Help me today to take baby steps in faith... to walk into the unknown, trusting You to direct my paths. Amen.

April 16th <u>Draw Near to God</u> *(James 4: 8)*

Draw near to God and He will draw near to you. Cleanse your hands, you sinners, and purify your hearts, you double minded.

I have always loved this Scripture verse, but I couldn't think of a clear picture for the message... until now. One name keeps coming to mind—Zacchaeus. (Hebrew names are difficult, so let's just call him Zach.) He is described in Luke 19 as a *"man small in stature."* This isn't his only shortfall (no pun intended). Zach is considered a traitor by the Jews. At the time of this story, Israel is under Roman authority and is being taxed exorbitant rates to line the pockets of high ranking Roman officials. Zach is a turn-coat tax collector who is not only collecting what he is told, but is filling his own pockets at the expense of his fellow countrymen. He is despised, but reconciliation is just around the corner. Jesus is coming to town! The crowds are filling the street, and Zach, because of his short height, cannot see. He climbs a sycamore tree and onto a branch which extends over the road Jesus will soon walk upon. Jesus looks directly up at him and calls him by name!

"Zacchaeus, hurry and come down, for today, I must stay at your house." What **shock** the people who heard this exchange must have felt! If Jesus was who He claimed to be, surely He would know what sort of fellow Zach was! Jesus didn't care, because He saw potential in even a vile Jewish traitor. The life-changing experience led Zacchaeus to give half of his possessions to the poor, to repay all he had defrauded by four times the amount stolen, and to become a born-again Christian! Hurray! Jesus is coming down the road of your lost loved ones' lives too!

We must judge through the same eyes Jesus judges through. Do you believe convicted felons can become born-again Christians and be powerful instruments in the hand of the God? A Nazarene Pastor, Robert Pickle, was a drug user, a drug dealer, and a convicted felon. Today, he speaks to young people about alcohol, drugs, purity and peer pressure. He became a believer while in Federal Prison! He lived everything we hate as believers, but he now lives each day witnessing, encouraging and evangelizing for Christ.

Lord, I am quick to let appearances or past history discount people who could be power tools in spreading the Gospel of Christ. Help me to remember that I too was a sinner with different sins than Robert Pickle or Zacchaeus. I didn't deserve and cannot earn grace. It is the free gift given to all who call upon Your holy name and receive the cleansing power of Your shed blood. Thank You, from this sinner. Amen.

April 17th Feeding the Multitudes *(Mark 6:41-42)*

He took the five loaves and the two fish, and looking up toward heaven, He blessed the food and broke the loaves, and He kept giving them to the disciples to set before them; and He divided up the two fish among them all. They all ate and were satisfied.

*J*esus and His disciples have been healing, casting out demons and preaching the Gospel in areas surrounding Judea. They are leaving for some much needed rest to a secluded place. The people see them, and because they can't get enough of Jesus and His teaching, they follow them. Jesus, knowing that He has limited time left on earth, and having a heart of compassion for these *"sheep without a shepherd,"* begins to teach them. At day's end the disciples advise Jesus to send them away to their homes or to buy themselves something to eat. Jesus, in absolute seriousness, tells them *"You give them something to eat."* The apostles are stunned. All they find in this crowd are five small bread loaves and two fish. How can this possibly feed a crowd of thousands? Wait... Jesus is going to teach a powerful lesson. Little... with God in it... is always enough! He takes the loaves, lifts them to Heaven, asks for God's blessing, and then hands them to the disciples to distribute. He does the same with the two tiny fish. Read Mark 6: 41-42 again. *"They all ate and were satisfied."* When did the miracle happen? When someone offered the fish and bread? When He called down His Father's blessing on the offering? Or, was it when the disciples touched it and watched it multiply in their own hands? We know that the story ends with 12 full baskets of broken bread pieces and fish left over. Maybe the miracle is in the breaking of bread together.

Think about church potlucks! I take a casserole of baked beans and you bring a chocolate cake. Everyone has brought a dish to pass. People begin to fill their plates. If you are at the end of the line, you see the heaped plates and think there will never be enough by the time you get there. Amazingly, there always is. How can we believe God will not honor our gathering together, multiply the bounty and feed everyone? We are a family! He is our Father, and He always provides for our needs. If you haven't been participating in these kinds of events, you need to start. How else will you ever see the miracle of multiplication at the hand of a powerful God?

Father, You know exactly what I need. Sometimes I have "wants" and "needs." You know the difference. Help me to never forget that little is much when You are in it. I have seen Your awesome provision so many times in my life. Help me to never forget that every good and perfect gift comes from the Lord above. Amen.

April 18ᵗʰ The Tongue *(Matthew 15:11)*

*"It is not what enters into the mouth that defiles the man,
but what proceeds out of the mouth, this defiles the man."*

I absolutely know that I need to curb my tongue. I use it to speak words which divide. I use it to destroy instead of to edify. I use it to boast instead of be humble. I use it to criticize and use it to cuss or speak inappropriate words. I surely need for God to *"set a guard over my lips."* How do I learn to bless and not curse, edify and not destroy, or speak love and not hate? Jesus alone! I need for Him to make me aware of what I am going to say before I speak. Then I can evaluate the words before they ever leave my mouth. I need Him to fill me with love, patience, kindness, goodness; and let it pour forth from my lips. The verse above was spoken by Jesus when the Jewish leaders were accusing Him and His disciples for what they ate and their lack of hand washing before the meals. Jesus is speaking to make a very important point. He might have said to His accusers: "We can worry about how clean our hands are, how presentable we are before our meals, and even about the food we are actually eating; but what goes into My mouth isn't the problem. What comes out in My speech is the problem. What comes out of the mouth actually defiles Me and makes Me filthy." What an amazing thing to say in the presence of Jewish leaders who closely adhered to the Mosaic 'clean and unclean' practices! They were worried about cleanliness. He was worried about godliness. There is nothing wrong with clean, but vile and hateful words destroy.

What do the words of your tongue speak? Are they words of uplifting and encouragement? Or, are they words which destroy and cause pain to others? Spoken words cannot be taken back. The ears which hear them, never forget the pain inflicted. Marriages fall apart, families are shattered, children are scarred and congregations divided... all because of the power of unkind words. Think about your words in the last week. Do you need to go to the Lord in confession? I do as I write this passage. Let us agree to work on our words.

You are awesome; and You always speak in love and truth. Lord, I have let You down in this area. I have the power to curb my tongue and fail to. I am sorry. Please latch my lips to not let bitter words flow. Amen.

April 19th Simon of Cyrene *(Mark 15:21)*

They pressed into service a passer-by coming from the country, Simon of Cyrene (the father of Alexander and Rufus), to bear His cross.

Have you ever felt like you carry the weight of the world on your shoulders? I know I feel that way when pressures bear down, or when I see the way our world is today. These weights cause me sleeplessness, neck pain and stomach problems. I can honestly say though, I have never carried a weight like Simon of Cyrene did. Cyrene is a country in North Africa, which is called Libya today. Simon is a member of the "Synagogue of the Freedmen," slaves who worked off their indenture, became free and chose to live in Judea. He is bringing his young sons to Jerusalem to honor the Passover and is caught up in the masses lining the road as Jesus passes by carrying His cross. We take the carrying of the cross for granted, but depending upon the size of the cross beam, Jesus' cross could have weighed between 200 and 300 pounds! Our Lord is exhausted, beaten almost beyond recognition, and forced to maneuver among the throngs of people. Simon, likely standing at one the city gates, is enlisted to help Jesus. That is the last thing he wants. As a father he doesn't want his sons to see what is about to happen. The choice is out of his hands. Simon shoulders part of the weight. He probably has no compassion for this criminal, but I have to believe that changed when Jesus looked at him with grateful eyes. Simon of Cyrene truly felt the weight of the world as he shouldered the instrument upon which our Savior would die to bear the sins of the world that day.

Jesus' teaching includes several references to us taking up His cross and bearing it each day. We all have different crosses to bear... physical handicaps, poverty, illness, widowhood, family problems, but carrying His cross into the unsaved world is the most important job we will ever do. We can never confront the real meaning of the cross and remain unchanged. This we know about Simon: The Man whose cross he carried became his cross to bear. The blood of the cross was now upon his shoulders. Simon was likely the last kind hand to touch Jesus before the crucifixion. He had to have been changed forever. You see, his sons, Alexander and Rufus became leaders in the early church.

Father God, I hate interruptions in the plans I have for my days. I cannot imagine how "inconvenient" it was for Simon to stop and carry the cross of Your Son. How glad I am today that he was enlisted to help ease the burden of my Jesus. This was clearly a "divine appointment" where You placed Simon at that gate "for such a time as this." May I never fail to realize my plans are never as important as Yours. Amen.

April 20th "If you will, I will..." *(I Kings 6: 12-13)*

"Concerning this house which you are building, if you will walk in My statutes and execute My ordinances and keep all My commandments by walking in them, then I will carry out My word

with you which I spoke to David your Father. I will dwell among the sons of Israel, and will not forsake My people Israel."

The above verse is taken from a portion of Scripture where the temple of God in Jerusalem is being built and dedicated. This is no small matter. God's Presence has been with His people for over five hundred years inhabiting a tent, which was moved from place to place until the nation of Israel finally settled in their promised land. King David's great desire was to build a real temple for his God. Unfortunately, because of past sin, David was embroiled in war during his entire kingship. His son, Solomon, is building that temple; every detail has been seen to. God addresses the nation before He moves into this permanent dwelling place. He lays down the terms of His provision for Israel. Loosely paraphrased, the Scripture above says: "Obey My rules, honor My laws and walk as I have commanded, and I will dwell here with you as I promised my friend David. Do this and I will never forsake or abandon you." The people immediately agree to these terms. The temple is dedicated, the sacrifices are offered, the incense is burned and the Spirit of the Lord fills the temple walls. Finally, Israel has a permanent place to worship; and God has a permanent place to minister to His children. How unfortunate it is that Solomon's foolishness soon casts his nation into sin... a sin still prevalent today. The temple no longer stands in Jerusalem. One day in the "new Jerusalem" God will dwell among His people.

It is very easy for us to fault find the nation of Israel for their disobedience to the laws of God. Do we do any better? Look at the world around us! How many people do you know who accepted Jesus as Lord and Savior, only to fall away when times of testing or temptation came? We think of Israel as a nation of religious people. We picture it like it is in historical Bible films. Israel is no different than America. It is a pagan nation with out-of-wedlock pregnancies, drug abuse, high divorce rates and rampant immorality. Have no fear, God is still in control.

Father God, I fail You and let You down repeatedly. I forsake Your statutes, laws and commandments. I try to live life my own way... and feel like I am doing pretty well until I fall flat on my face. May today be a new start? I will promise to seek Your face, hold Your hand and listen for Your voice. Your permanent dwelling place is now my heart. Amen.

April 21ˢᵗ   Good Biblical Epitaphs   *(Genesis 6:9)*

These are the records of the generations of Noah. Noah was a righteous man, blameless in his time; Noah walked with God.

*W*hat would you like people to say about you after you have died? Most of us fail to realize that we are writing our own epitaphs and legacies by how we live our lives each day. This thought led me to review how some Bible characters were described in Scripture. Take Noah for instance. He was obedient and willing to be called a fool as he followed God's command to build a boat hundreds of miles from the nearest body of water! No wonder we are told *"Noah was a righteous man."* How about Jabez? Scripture tells us he was born in pain and was *"more honorable than his brothers."* That is quite a character reference. Here is another example: King David was called *"a man after God's own heart."* David sinned. How could he be called a man of God? David was convicted of his sin, confessed it before God and repented to keep himself from doing the same thing again. Ruth, who left home and family to care for her mother-in-law, receives this compliment from her future husband, *"...I will do for you whatever you ask; for all my people in the city know that you are a woman of excellence."* Finally, Joash, the king of Judah, was up against mighty enemies when he assumed the throne at only seven years old. He reigned forty years. Scripture says, *"Joash did what was right in the sight of the Lord."* There are many more positive epitaphs throughout the Bible. How wonderful for their legacy to be written in such a positive way.

A good epitaph should be the legacy of every Christian man and woman. The life we live before others determines what they will remember about us. Will they call you a dedicated Christian in a difficult world? Will they say you had the heart of a true servant of God? Will they say you loved everyone and never met a stranger? Will they say you prayed for them, taught them Scripture, or listened when they needed a willing ear? What will your epitaph be? About Noah I once read "if Noah had been truly wise, he would have left off those two flies!"

Jesus, I want my epitaph to be that I walked in full service to You and reflected You in a positive light before all I came in contact with. The words and actions of my today's will determine the memories in others' tomorrows. May I be righteous, excellent, blameless and a believer after God's own heart. Amen.

April 22nd   Bad Biblical Epitaphs   *(Genesis 19: 26)*

*But his wife, from behind him, looked back,
and she became a pillar of salt.*

Just as there are many examples of historical Bible characters who received good epitaphs, there are many who were not so pleasingly lauded. Look at the Scripture from Genesis 19, which refers to the wife of Lot. He and his family are fleeing God's destruction of Sodom and Gomorrah when she turns to look behind her (something she was warned against) and *"becomes a pillar of salt."* Yep, that is the kind of thing I want to be remembered for! NOT! How about Samson? He was handsome, strong, a good leader and a fool controlled by his flesh! His Biblical epitaph reads, *"So the dead whom he killed at his death were more than those whom he killed in his life."* Here is another. Absalom, the son who tried to steal the throne from King David is fleeing on a donkey when his mane of luxurious hair gets caught in a low hanging tree branch. He is slain while hanging over the road. A messenger says, *"Let the enemies of my lord the king, and all who rise up against you for evil, be as that young man!"* Lastly, I bring the epitaph of Judas Iscariot. This man, who walked with Jesus, ate at His table and participated in His earthly ministry—turned around and betrayed Him for thirty pieces of silver. His last moments are described this way: *"He threw the pieces of silver into the temple sanctuary and departed; and he went away and hanged himself."* Our legacy may be the only thing we leave behind. In my case it certainly will not be money!

One of the things I am most grateful for is that my legacy, if I were to die tomorrow, would be totally different than the one I would have left even fifteen years ago. My former legacy would be more like the ones in today's entry. I hope I would be remembered for teaching the Word, being a prayer warrior and being an encourager to friends, family and customers. Are there negatives in your life which would cause you to have a less than glowing epitaph? It is never too late to begin to rewrite it.

Father, Please reveal to me by the work of the Holy Spirit, any thoughts, actions or deeds, which would keep me from being identified as one who walked with God. Your recommendation is most important to me. Will You stand to welcome me home and say, "Well done, My good and faithful servant?" That is the desire of my heart. Amen.

April 23rd   Godly Husbands   *(Ephesians 5:25)*

Husbands, love your wives, just as Christ also loved the church and gave Himself up so that He might sanctify her, having cleansed her by the washing of water with the Word.

*D*ivorces and bad marriages are the norm in today's society? You need only to read the above Scripture to see how husbands you know measure up. (This is not meant to be a "man-bashing" lesson.) At some point in time, maybe even in the Garden of Eden, the understanding of God's plan for marriage was superceded by a "me first" attitude. The above verse and the next seven verses clearly describe what God ordained a husband's role to be. How many husbands do you know who love their wives as Christ loved the church? Exactly how did Christ love the Church? He died for her! He nurtured His followers (us, His church) and healed their hurts. He turned away from His own needs for the needs of others because their needs were more important to Him. He prayed for them. He fed them. He took their shortcomings upon His shoulders. Where is the "me first" attitude of Christ? It is nonexistent. Husbands need to embody these same values. They must be willing to be healers, reconcilers, prayer warriors, feeders and nurturers. Doesn't that make men look like wimps? I am married to that kind of husband. Dan always puts my needs first. He says, "I'm sorry," even when I started the battle. He carries my burdens, prays for me and encourages me in every venture God leads me on. Jesus loved; Dan loves, and all husbands must ask themselves this question: How is your love walk? Do you put your wife's needs first?

You may think it's easy for me to write this entry because I am married to a godly man. Let me tell you, Dan is a dry alcoholic of 22 years. There was a day I would have said he was beyond hope... his first two wives said that! Jesus made the difference in Dan's life. He can make the difference in the life of your husband, too. Start praying now for every part of his life... faith, finances, friendships, parenting and worldly influences. If you are a man reading this passage, please take it to heart. Marriages can never succeed if both partners are not willing to give everything to the union.

Father God, You defined marriage when You created Eve from Adam's rib. The wife is to be a part of her husband; he is to treat her accordingly. Father, we have drifted so far from those truths. Our lives revolve around a serious "I-disease," whose symptoms are 'I want... I need... I like... I don't like." May we learn to put You first, our spouse and family next, and our own needs last. This is a lot to ask. It was a lot to ask of Jesus; yet He did exactly that. Amen.

April 24th <u>Godly Wives</u> *(Ephesians 5: 24)*

But as the church is subject to Christ, so also the wives ought to be to their husbands in everything.

𝓘 can see you ladies' hackles rising as you read the above verse! How we hate the whole submission idea. We picture a dictatorial man commanding his wife to wait on him hand and foot as she cowers and hides from his authority. That is not at all what Godly submission is about. The word submission, when broken down, means to (sub)—come under someone else's (mission)—work. If the husband is trying to lead in a godly way, the job of the wife is to come under him and support him. The word submission can also be defined as "an offering." Why do we find the idea of offering of ourselves to be so unpleasant? Would you like a husband who had a servant's heart toward you? The Scripture also talks about the church being subject to Christ. How are we (the church) supposed to be subject to Him? We are to do nothing which blasphemes His name. We are to follow the common sense teachings of the New Testament. We are to love His followers. We are to share His Gospel. Would it hurt women to love their husbands, give them a good name (by the words we speak of them), teach our children to respect them, and offer our services to make their lives better? This isn't much to give in return for a solid home life, a respectful spouse and common parenting beliefs. Just as Jesus prayed for His church, we need to pray for our husbands... and they need to pray for their wives. Actually, it is very hard to stay angry at someone you are sincerely praying for...and Scripture tells us to not "let the sun go down on our anger."

Unfortunately, many of you are offended by this message. You have been told by the media and the liberated women that you are nobody's doormat, you have to stand up for your rights, and you are to do all things in response to your feelings or emotions. That is precisely why so many marriages fail. There is no pulling together in the same direction, a definite lack of respect between the spouses and a world full of bad examples of marital relationships. We laugh at television sitcoms and series which make men look like blundering idiots; we then treat our husbands the same way; and then we find them unresponsive and uncaring. This is totally contrary to Jesus' teaching... and it needs to stop.

Jesus, I have not been the woman You ordained me to be. I have thought only of myself, my needs and my emotions. None of those things exhibit the selflessness You call us to. I do not have a servant heart. I am not setting a good example for the young people in my life. Help me to be the example they need to see... for there are so few good examples. Amen.

April 25th Godly Marriages *(Ephesians 5:21)*

For this reason a man shall leave his father and mother and shall be joined to his wife, and the two shall become one flesh.

*W*e've heard the cliché many times: "Marriage was made in Heaven... and so was thunder and lightning." Why is this union ordained by God the butt of jokes in television series, movies, and others who seek to destroy it in our nation? We have allowed it. We have cheapened the meaning of commitment. We have forgotten that fidelity should be the norm in marriage. We have found how "quick and easy" divorce is, as opposed to how "long and hard" marriage can be. Why not just give up? Why get married in the first place? Why not just live together outside the bond of marriage and save the hassle of separation or divorce? Why not, indeed! The answer is easy. God ordained marriage between a man and a woman as the ideal fostering environment for the family. There was a day when "for better or for worse" meant never giving up. There was a day when husbands and wives would never have thought to badmouth their spouses in public. There was a day when respect for one another was the norm! Can marriages survive in our world today? ABSOLUTELY! Will it be easy? ABSOLUTELY NOT! So many cases of divorce — especially within the church — are a result of the unequal yoking the Bible teaches. When a believer marries an unbeliever, the yoke which binds one to the other is pulled in two different directions. This causes arguments, parenting problems, values compromise, and often leads the believer away from their faith. As we see from divorce statistics, unequal yoking should be avoided. Marriage choices should be made based on things beside flesh.

———

Are you in a difficult marriage? If you are unmarried, what marriage examples do you see around you? I recently asked a friend how many solid marriages she could name. She named Dan and me only. She told me most of the other marriages struggled, ended in divorce, or resulted in people just existing under the same roof. Marriage must be a life-long commitment. We need to take the word DIVORCE out of our vocabulary and learn to compromise, communicate, pull together, and respect one another! Mostly, we need to make wiser marriage choices before we plan the wedding!

———

Father, the state of marriage in America must break Your heart. This union, ordained in the Garden of Eden, designed for the bonding of two souls as they are joined as one and sanctioned "until death do we part," has been destroyed by selfishness, temptation and compromise. Only with Your help can we begin again to marry for "the marriage, and not the wedding." Amen.

April 26th   How Far We Have Fallen   *(Joshua 23:3)*

"And you have seen all that the Lord your God has done to all these nations because of you, for the Lord your God is He who has been fighting for you."

*T*hose who attend my Bible Study class (Seekers) have heard me say many times that in 50 years America has gone from "Leave it to Beaver" to "Desperate Housewives," and today's T.V. programming clearly parallels our moral fiber. We have removed God from the public forum, and we are paying a serious price. The following is an excerpt from my journal entry of February 3, 2007: "What if we all stop speaking the Word of God, stop buying or carrying Bibles, stop attending church, close Christian schools and totally remove Christ/God from our nation? If we look around us at the garbage taught in public schools and the filth on T.V. and the Internet, just imagine how this evil cancer would grow within a few weeks. Then, imagine a nation like that for years, decades or centuries! The only reason America is not further immersed in this horrendous sin is because there is still a faint moral, godly fiber running through our land. Make no mistake, the secular progressives in our nation want the world I've described, and are more than willing to lay everything on the line to get their way. How hard are we going to fight to stop this?" They spout their "intellectual" garbage and we remain silent. They tell us there is no true moral compass and we think maybe the Bible is outdated.

As Christians, we are to weigh all things against God's Word to determine its validity. We see in today's Scripture that God has fought for us through battles, both within and without our borders. We are a blessed, wealthy and free people. But remember... God will <u>not</u> be mocked. We allowed prayer to be removed from schools and allowed the same-sex marriage curriculum in! Educators tell our children they need birth control pills, instead of teaching them to respect their bodies because God created them before time began. We fail to protest, write congressmen, or even challenge things contrary to the Word that are being forced down our throats. How God must cringe as He looks at what America, the shining beacon of freedom, has become.

Jesus, I am angry at the things I see happening, but feel powerless to do anything about it. These are painful realities for me to face, but unless something is done—unless we stand and fight for what is right, America will become a completely secular society. Lord, I need Your holy boldness to stand up and speak out against all I see. We have lost our hedge of protection. Amen.

April 27th   A House United   *(Joshua 24:13)*

"I gave you a land on which you had not labored, and cities which you had not built, and you have lived in them; you are eating of vineyards and olive groves which you did not plant."

*L*ook closely at the progression of sin over the last 50 years in America. The 1950's... a decade of hot rods, rock 'n' roll music and great family ties. Our nation was strong as we celebrated the victory of World War II and reveled in national pride and in simply being free Americans. The Scripture above applies. Our forefathers worked hard that we might have all the good things of God. In the 50's, T.V. had just come into most homes; families shared meals together; mothers took care of their homes and children; and disrespect was corrected with a swat at the "seat of learning." Lucy and Desi entered our homes, made us laugh and maintained moral integrity on the screen. Ed Sullivan brought Elvis (gasp) into the mainstream, and teens danced the jitterbug—fully clothed! Families worshipped together and God was in the classroom. Never would our parents have imagined that terrorists would attack us, abortion would be rampant, and families would be destroyed.

Today, we look at the 50's as if they were the dark ages. Women didn't have real jobs... What? They stayed home and cleaned, cared for their husbands and children, joined the PTA, and even cooked real meals... What? Blue jeans were not school attire; they wore no low-rider pants or low-cut knit tops; and no 6-year-olds were dressed to look like 25! Actually, God created man and woman to be two different <u>types</u> of people. Man was commanded to care for the woman God created from his rib. Woman's nature was to nurture. (Some of you really hate this entry, don't you?) What a shame that the innocence of the 50's is gone. What a shame that the rat race of life has destroyed the simple pleasures of a cherry Coke and a real hamburger. What a shame we can't turn back the hands of time.

Lord, we have fallen so far from Your perfect plan that we pity women who stay home to parent their families—when we should admire them. We have bought into the belief that it takes two incomes to make ends meet, when the reality is that two incomes are required because we spend too much. Your plan was for women to nurture, men to support, and children to respect their parents. Instead, both parents work, the children are without proper supervision and our nation's moral fiber is destroyed. Amen.

April 28th   Forsaking all Truth   *(Joshua 24:15)*

"If it is disagreeable in your sight to serve the Lord, ***choose for yourselves today whom you will serve****; whether the gods which your fathers served which were beyond the River, or the gods of the Amorites in whose land you are living; but* ***as for me and my house, we will serve the Lord****."*

*O*ur entry today will talk about the legacy of the 1960's and 1970's. The entire makeup of our nation changed during the revolutionary years of the 1960's; where it became "cool or hip" to buck the establishment. Moral restraint was cast off and "free love" became the mantra of our country's youth. As you can likely tell, I am not a fan of this decade. America's loss of moral authority in the world began to take real shape when the family became obsolete. Government welfare programs caused much of this problem when women were offered financial benefits if they would move their husbands out of the homes. Children were now without the supervision of a father. Too much freedom in the hands of young people became a recipe for disaster. Teen pregnancies, due to increased sexual experimentation, were increased. Drug use escalated, morals evaporated and America became embroiled in a war in Southeast Asia. Anti-war protests led to a complete disrespect for our military power and the young men drafted into service. The "shackles" of traditional Christianity were cast off as New Age religious movements began to gain popularity. We forgot the God of our Fathers...

What do we learn as we look back at these difficult decades? What did abortion on demand, drug abuse and the breakdown of families do to our nation? We became cynical, untrusting and hard. We became angry, disrespectful and lost. We replaced that which was good for that which was fully contrary to the Word of God. Unfortunately, we have gained little ground back since then. Good clean fun is gone. Our little ones are forced to grow up long before they should. We have little to be proud of from a spiritual standpoint. America, the shining light on a hill, became a cesspool of sin. How it must break God's heart!

Father, I cannot imagine how it hurt You to watch America forsake Your teaching and turn so blatantly to sin. Disrespect hurts in all ways, but disrespect for our Christian heritage has destroyed our national pride. Lord, we need to fall on our knees in repentance, cast off the shackles of sin and return to You. Help me to be instrumental in that happening today. Amen.

April 29th Worldliness vs. Godliness *(Joshua 24: 16)*

"The people answered and said, "Far be it from us that we should forsake the Lord to serve other gods."

*A*fter the 60's and early 70's, the next two decades seemed much less harsh...much more "user friendly" for all Americans. The problem with that belief is that America was still moving steadily away from God. Fewer families were attending church, fewer children were hearing the truths of the Christian faith, and fewer people were aware it was happening. Drift is dangerous. When we drift away from God we often do not realize it is happening. We skip church a few times so we can enjoy all of the recreation we have at our hands. We let a few cuss words slip into our vocabulary; and we begin to feed the lusts of our flesh. The 1980's and 90's were like this. The spoiled children of the Baby Boomer (1950's) generation came of age with a burning "I want it, and I want it now" attitude. Cable T.V. and the Internet brought everything to our doors. We filled our eyes, ears and spirits with garbage, then acted out the things our eyes saw. Little thought was given to the falling thermostat of our moral register. "Everyone else does it" became our pat answer. Nations around the world began to despise the "weak, spoiled Americans." Alcohol abuse exploded; families continued to be destroyed, and God was literally yanked from the public forum. Our President was immoral in the White House... and we excused it because he was a great communicator. How God must have hated what He was seeing.

Like Israel, God richly blessed this nation. We were thriving with industry, commerce and influence in the rest of the world. During this time we truly became a self-serving, self-centered people. Young people from broken homes sought 'love' wherever they could find it. Where was the influence of the church? By the 1990's, we had dumbed down the sermons, changed churches into "Christian entertainment centers," and allowed the secular humanists in our education system to tell us that God was a figment of our imagination. Where was the church?

Spirit of God, we are a shameful people. Where are our morals, our values, and our sense of self-respect? Why do we allow educators to tell our children they are derived from apes; instead of telling them they are fearfully and wonderfully created? We have dumbed down Your Word, forsaken the gathering together to worship, and allowed the media to make us look like fools. We set no example as Your people to the rest of the world. Spirit, give me Your wisdom and direction to make a difference. Amen.

April 30th <u>A House Divided</u> *(Joshua 24: 20)*

"If you forsake the Lord and serve foreign gods,
then He will turn and do you harm and consume you
after He has done good to you."

*T*his is the final entry in the series on America's fall from God's grace. I understand that you are likely ready to give up on this book because of the hard truths I have spoken. Stick with me. I believe that the church has been weakened, not because God is weak, but because we are unwilling to stand up and fight for what we believe in. The truth of the matter is that most atheists could better defend their reasons for denying God than Christians could defend their faith. We are not in the Word (though I am working hard to get you interested). We entered the new millennium with acts of terrorism in our cities, with illegal immigration out of control, and with abortions allowed to be performed up to the moment of delivery. We have rampant suicide rates among our young people, pornography being thrust down the throats of our children on T.V., and extended families with the wounds of abandonment, betrayal, and all forms of abuse. Our children are raising themselves on a steady diet of violent and sexual video games. Our nation is completely divided on moral and political issues and military engagements. We are a House Divided. Scripture tells us: *"a house divided cannot stand."* Read the Scripture verse at the top again. *"He will consume you after He has done good to you."*

Are we beyond hope? Absolutely not! God is still on the throne; the Holy Spirit is still working in the hearts of His people; the blood of Jesus will still wash us clean...if we but ask. The change has to start within the body of Christ. We will face tough challenges because sin is so pervasive in our society. We must dress our children like children (not porn stars). We must communicate with our youth. We must not give in to the peer pressure our teens are susceptible to. We must work on our marriages. We must tell our children that they are not animals and can control the lusts of their flesh. We must put God back into our homes, our churches and our nation!

Father God, You ordained the family's existence in the Garden of Eden. You teach us how to parent, love and communicate in Your Word. You bless this nation with abundance, and we abuse that blessing. Lord, bring us to our knees, remove our idols, restore our families and help us to walk fully with You. Thank You that You have not given up on the United States of America. Amen.

May 1st Revealed in Light *(Jeremiah 23:23-24)*

"Am I a God who is near," declares the LORD,
"and not a God far off?" "Can a man hide himself in
hiding places so I do not see him?" declares the LORD,
"Do I not fill the heavens and the earth?"

J take comfort in the knowledge that I am never truly alone— no matter where I am, who I am with, what the circumstances are, or how hard life is at any given moment. This is a source of assurance and encouragement in my daily walk. On the other hand, Jesus sees and hears my every word, thought, deed, action and temptation. He sees when I am tempted and allow the temptation to overcome me. He sees all of my flaws—the ones I so adeptly hide from everyone else. I remember speaking to a group of fellow believers one night and saying that one of the men could sit among us, sound very godly and pious and fool us all. He could later go in a dark computer room, spend hours looking at pornography and feed filth into his mind. We may be fooled; God is not! He knows our every thought, word and deed. He gave us rules for living, provided a Savior to redeem us and always provides an escape from the sin which tempts us. The prophet Jonah tried to run and hide from God. Why? He didn't want to do what God commanded him to do. (Does that sound familiar?) Jonah thought hiding on a ship at sea was a good idea, until God sent a storm, which led to Jonah's secret being revealed. In the end, Jonah did what God told him to do in the first place. What a lot of suffering for no reason!

What is done in darkness will be revealed in light. That should encourage those who live by laws. The man who would hide in the computer room and look at pornography will pay a price. If he is married, the bond of trust will be broken. If he isn't, what else will it take to please his lust? God knows the consequence of all our actions. Because of His great love, we are always given the ability to escape the sin. What do you try to hide in darkness? What would you do differently if Jesus was standing next to you? What means of escape has He provided before? Learn to pray against the temptations of the enemy. Satan makes every bad thing look great. Not because he cares about you; but because he doesn't want you to serve Christ.

Guess what, Lord? That is the why I stay focused and intent on Your Word, Your truths, Your spirit, Your direction, and Your love on the Cross. Please keep watch over me. Reveal to me the darkness within. Amen.

May 2nd Forsaken *(Matthew 27:45-46)*

Now from the sixth hour darkness fell upon all the land until the ninth hour. About the ninth hour Jesus cried out with a loud voice, saying, "ELI, ELI, LAMA SABACHTHANI?" that is, "MY GOD, MY GOD, WHY HAVE YOU FORSAKEN ME?"

$\mathcal{T}$he *"why have You forsaken me"* line has always bothered me. I think I can better understand it if I remember that Jesus is God. God forsook Himself—His pride, His power, His control and His authority for our sakes. He could have stopped it at any time; but He chose to be humbled for us. I believe that more people have a hard time understanding the above truths than anything else in Christianity. How can God be man? How could God die on a Cross? Remember how the story of creation in Genesis tells of God's need for companionship? That is why He created man. He wanted one creature from His creation to be able to communicate and fellowship with Him. He created Adam, took his rib and made Eve, and gave them total control over all He created. After the temptation of the enemy, they were separated from Him. From that moment on, creation has been separated from Creator. God had to do something to bring reconciliation. He became man in the form of Jesus, born of the Holy Spirit, lived a pure life and died a sacrificial death. That death allowed God to assume all of our sin, freeing us for reconciliation with Him. Our sin was buried with Him; then He arose sinless and perfect to return to Heaven. Lastly, He sent the Holy Spirit to live in our hearts and guide, direct and convict our spirits.

If I as a mom stop being self focused and "me centered" and spent all of my energy being the best mom, I would still be Vicki. I would just be a more compassionate form of Vicki. God is still God; Jesus was a part of God. God didn't forsake Jesus; He had to forsake Himself. That was God on the Cross—bared before a hateful world—opened to ridicule—suffering in love—God! Can you image this kind of love? Are you self-absorbed like I am? Do you understand that Jesus is God, and that God died on that Cross? If you are having a hard time with this truth, get help. Reread the teaching; seek the help of a Pastor or Bible teacher. This is one of the basic foundations of our faith... and you need to understand it fully.

Father God, Jesus my Savior, and Holy Spirit—I need full understanding of the depths and truths of the Holy Trinity. This is one of the hard things for me to understand. How can I ever thank You enough for assuming my sin and cleansing me with the Creator's blood? Amen.

May 3rd Meet Crystal *(Psalms 121:1-2)*

*I will lift up my eyes to the mountains; From where shall
my help come? My help comes from the LORD,
Who made heaven and earth.*

Let me share a story of an absolutely supernatural mission I was sent on in 2005. One of my agents came to me saying he had talked with a former client who was ill and needed someone to talk to. I went to Crystal's house, having no idea of what I would find when I got there. Crystal had recently been diagnosed with a brain tumor. She opened the door, visibly distraught, and we sat down and began to talk. For the next full hour I held Crystal, recited Scripture over her and prayed for her needs. She confided that she had been a Christian, but had walked away from her faith and allowed the love of things to take place of the love of Jesus. Bible verses kept flowing out of my mouth. After I got back to my office, I wrote to the Prayer Warriors, asking them to pray for this terrified woman. I assured them that Crystal was back with the Lord and would appreciate notes or cards. I asked my Bible Study class to do the same. Within days, Crystal was being showered with love from dedicated Christian believers. Crystal went through the testing, ready for whatever she faced. Her only regret was that she might have to leave her beautiful daughter and her husband. No word could express the euphoria we all felt when word came to us that there was no cancer in the tumor! We were all stunned!

I wrote these words on January 28th, 2006: "Why should we be stunned? You are God—You are the Great Physician and You are the Healer of our body, mind and soul! I am so excited for her! What a testimony for prayer and a walk in faith! Jesus, let them never, EVER forget what happened to her when her doctor declared her to be cancer free!" Where was our faith? Some people I talked to fully believe that Crystal indeed had cancer, and that God healed her because of the flood of prayers and faith. Some said it was because the "lost sheep" returned to the sheepfold. Mostly, I believe God used all of us as her intercessors. We can never use the Word for healing... if we don't have it in our hearts.

Jesus, thank You for using me to make a difference in other people's lives. Use me again to be "Jesus with skin on" in my sphere of influence. Thank You also for the hearts of compassion who reached out to a hurting, frightened stranger and carried her on the wings of their prayers. Amen.

May 4ᵗʰ Burdens *(Matthew 11:28-30)*

"Come to Me, all who are weary and heavy laden, and I will give you rest. Take My yoke upon you and learn from Me, for I am gentle and humble in heart, and YOU WILL FIND REST FOR YOUR SOULS. For My yoke is easy and My burden is light."

I think the thing which makes my life bearable, even in its most testing times, is the knowledge that when I lie down and sleep for the last time on this earth, the new world I awaken to will be burden free and blessing filled. I can hardly imagine a world with no illness, aches, weakness, war, hatred, terrorism, money needs, kid problems, persecution, cancer, diabetes, drug abuse, child abuse, divorce, death of loved ones, shame, unforgiveness, disappointment, poverty, leukemia, colds, hunger or loneliness. Actually, many of these things, if not all of them, could be averted today, if we would call on Jesus and release them into His precious hands. What do you think the portion of the above verse reading *"My yoke is easy and My burden is light"* means? Many people will never become Christians because they think the rules are too burdensome. I have found His yoke to be very light. Actually, His **yoke is lighter than the sin yoke I used to carry around all day**. Acting right in the first place is not burdensome... it is liberating. Freedom is mine... and can be yours, too!

Remember the story of Crystal yesterday? One of the burdens we are called to carry for Christ is to bring love and healing words to those in need. I could have been too busy to go to Crystal that day. God would have still worked in her life, but I would have missed the blessing in my life! When we give in the name of Christ we always receive more in return. Crystal came, unknown to the class, to our Christmas potluck. She hadn't had surgery or test results, but she stood before them, sobbing and telling them what they all meant in her life. She had fed on their Scriptures, read and reread their cards and prayed for each of them, even though at times she was clearly losing her memory. Don't hold back from being used in God's work...you don't know what you're missing.

When I give, You always give in return. When I offer, You always take the little offering and multiply it. When I feel dry, You always water me by using me to feed others. You are the God of miracles... using this broken piece of clay is a real miracle. Amen.

May 5th Take Up His Cross *(Matthew 16:24)*

Then Jesus said to His disciples, "If anyone wishes to come after Me, he must deny himself, and take up his cross and follow Me."

These words were from January of 2006: "Last night, a pastor from a local Baptist Church talked about us needing to speak out our faith without second thought to how others will react to it. We need to carry the Cross in every place our feet fall... school, work, home, the public square, in conversations, in greetings and in our families. How do we do that? We let His ways influence ours. We let His Words be our words. We let His actions be our actions. We let His love be our model for love. We let His willingness to sacrifice be our willingness to help others. We let His obedience before His Father be our model for obedience to the Father. We spend necessary time learning His Word—the Sword of our faith—so we will have it in our hearts and ready to use at all times. Lord, I want to continue to carry that Cross daily." Peter, James and John, Jesus' three closest apostle friends, left everything they had to follow Christ. They were away from home, jobs and family. They surely fulfilled the "deny himself" portion of the verse. Did they carry His Cross? Yes, they surely did! James and Peter died for the cause of spreading the Gospel of Salvation. John was exiled to the island of Patmos, isolated because he refused to stop talking about Jesus Christ. Following Christ cost them everything.

I was at a wedding reception years ago and visiting with the people at our table. One of the women was someone I had gone to high school with, whom I knew as an acquaintance. I had just begun to work at the Christian bookstore in our town and she asked me about my job. Instead of telling her how amazing my job and ministry opportunities were, I was ashamed to let the others at the table know I worked in a Bible store. I made short answers to her questions; but she wouldn't change the conversation. I was immediately convicted. Dan, as usual, sat next to me...and his silence spoke volumes. When these things happen I realize that God is watching and allowing me to be tested. How could I be ashamed of Him, of my job and of my faith? Later, I found that the woman asking the questions was genuinely interested because SHE WAS A CHRISTIAN! Has this ever happened to you? If so, you know how I felt afterwards.

Jesus, how could I be embarrassed or ashamed of the One who gives me life? How could I deny You? I am willing to learn to carry Your Cross, but I will need the help of the Holy Spirit. Help me to be Your burden bearer. Amen.

May 6ᵗʰ Righteousness *(Isaiah 61:10)*

I will rejoice greatly in the LORD, My soul will exult in my
God. For He has clothed me with garments of salvation,
He has wrapped me with a robe of righteousness.

*N*one of us in ourselves are clean or righteous. Jesus alone was righteous. He clothes me in His righteousness, so I can proudly wear it. My bridegroom (Christ) makes me beautiful, not to men who only see the outside, but to God who only sees my heart. We need to walk in our righteousness and be prepared every day for the return of Christ. We would not want to be caught in deep sin on the moment of Jesus' return. I cannot be righteous without my Christian faith. The good things of my past are filth and fodder compared to how Jesus taught us to walk. The leaders of the Jewish faith wore beautiful robes, elaborate headpieces, and carried themselves in traditional religious stoicism. They looked very holy and made sure everyone knew their leadership positions and their righteous heritage. Along comes Jesus, a barn born, homeless vagrant with a band of ragtag followers. He surrounded himself with fisherman, tax collectors, and women of ill repute like Mary Magdalene. He taught things totally contrary to the ways of the critical religious leaders of His day. He talked to everyone, took time to look into the eyes of the blind beggar and spoke of love and mercy. Everything about Him wasn't righteous in the eyes of the "religious elite." Everything about Him <u>was</u> righteous... **in the eyes of a holy God.**

Our clothes and actions don't make us righteous. I heard recently that going to church doesn't make you a Christian, any more than sitting in the garage makes you a car! Actions and church attendance will never prove your faith out. There are lots of people who study the Scriptures diligently... to find things about them to refute. Our righteousness can only come from a "right" walk with Christ. This will always look like a "wrong" walk to the world. If you want to be fully right with the Lord, you must be willing to be fully separated

171

from worldly things which hold you hostage. Pray for guidance in this area of your faith walk.

———————

Lord, fill me with Your righteous heart—so far removed from how mine is. I need You more than words can say, because You are my all in all! Amen.

May 7th <u>False Doctrine</u> *(2 Peter 2:1)*

But false prophets also arose among the people, just as there will also be false teachers among you, who will secretly introduce destructive heresies, even denying the Master who bought them, bringing swift destruction upon themselves.

We are watching the prophetic word be fulfilled in world politics, loss of moral fiber, and the persecution of Christians for their faith. We must dig ever deeper into the Word in order to be able to stand against these things. Some who have proclaimed Christ will reject Him and turn to other faiths, New Age movements and false doctrines. I believe with all my heart that the majority of them will be people ungrounded in the Word. Why are people led so easily astray? Why are they so quick to leave that which they have grown up with to follow a lark? We are always looking for something new and different. There is always something which looks better... a different husband, a new credit card, a less cumbersome faith! John 10:10 tells us that "*the enemy comes to kill, steal and destroy*." New Age religions and Scientology allow us to set our own moral absolutes and to worship ourselves. Who wouldn't love that!?! Doesn't it sound better to be able to decide whether abortion, divorce, theft, or assisted suicides are right for us? "Who needs a bunch of archaic rules in a book written by a bunch of men?" That is what the world is saying. Let me tell you the truth. We need rules and guidelines. Look around you and see the condition of the world. Who is to blame? We are, because we have failed to follow God's commands for safe, healthy and happy lives.

How grounded are you in your faith? Are you firm enough to be strong in the face of the new religions paraded before you each day? Let me say something important—**Never say that you could not be moved. If you do, you are opening yourself to a big attack. Satan loves a challenge!** There is only one way to protect yourself from this attack, and that is to be <u>fully grounded in the Word</u>, learning all God teaches on false doctrines, false prophets and temptations of the enemy. When false teachers and prophets begin to speak of their own beliefs, you need to be prepared to refute their teachings and defend your own. Christians are so ill-equipped to explain why they believe what they believe. We need to come into agreement to work on educating ourselves.

Lord, help me to dig into, feast upon and memorize Your Word. It truly is a "lamp unto my feet and a light unto my path." I do not want to fall for the false doctrines of the enemy. Amen.

May 8th <u>House Building</u> *(Matthew 7:26-27)*

*"Everyone who hears these words of Mine and does not act
on them will be like a foolish man who built his house on the
sand. The rain fell, and the floods came, and the winds blew and
slammed against that house; and it fell—and great was its fall."*

We tend to think that the new houses we build will stand forever. Some things have improved tremendously over the years; but the basics of building have been cheapened or hurried. Hand-hewn beams for walls and rafters are replaced with less than great quality—2 x 4's and pre-made trusses. The interior finishes like trims, flooring, cabinetry and plumbing are all more modern, but actually less strong and dense than in the past. Houses like these will require more repair than older homes. The house God is building has an entirely different foundation made up of faith, hope,

173

love, service, prayer, worship, obedience, good fruits and forgiveness. When we build His House by acting on these foundational elements, His House will be a place of impact where ministry will happen, love will be spoken, and healing for souls will take place. If we begin to cheapen the ministry done here, God will remove His blessings and we will fail.

I talked to a woman shortly before His House opened. She is an avowed atheist who had recently buried her husband who died a long cancer death. In our conversation, she was encouraging me about the store. She made the following statement: "If a person walks into a store that says Christian or Bible over its doors, and they are ignored or treated unkindly, they walk out emptier than when they walked in the door." She was talking from personal experience. Probably, she went looking for encouragement after her husband died...and was ignored! Shame on whoever didn't minister to her needs! I get so mad about this I could just spit! The doors of every Christian business should be closed if they are not there to minister to those who walk into them. That woman may never again come to the point where she would hear the truth of the Gospel. Whose head is her blood on? We are taught in Scripture that if we don't tell others, and they die in their unconfessed sin, we are responsible for their lack of salvation. **As for me and His House, we will serve the Lord.**

Lord, we are all called to minister. I confess to You that I have ignored opportunities You placed before me. There are likely times when I innocently missed a chance to tell others of Your love. Please quicken my spirit to know when these chances arise. Amen.

May 9th Spiritual Eyes *(Luke 24:45)*

Then He opened their minds to understand the Scriptures.

I have written many entries on studying and applying Scripture to the things in our lives. If you have tried to do so and still are having problems, do not give up! If I can understand them, anyone can! Did you read the verse above? God has to open your eyes and your mind to understand the messages of the Bible. He is waiting to open the minds of those who truly seek to know truth. I prayed for insight and discernment to understand the Scriptures; and the passion for His Word poured through me. Not only do I understand much (not all, because His ways are not our ways) of the Bible, but I also see things in the world through spiritual eyes. I see weather changes like I never have before. I see God's hand working in situations in my life and in the lives of others. I also see a hunger for a meaning to life in people I would never have thought to witness to (shame on me). God is working in awesome ways to bring new people into faith; but I wonder how much they grow once they get to a church? I also see people having their "ears tickled" with featherweight messages which never teach the hard truths of choosing between right and wrong. I see ill-equipped Christians who cannot defend their faith other than to say it makes them feel good. Jesus warned that real believers would be persecuted and blasphemed because of Him. If we aren't living those things, we don't know the whole story!

I see the teaching of the Scriptures which describe the events leading to the return of Christ being fulfilled left and right. We are hated because we are called a Christian nation. We are so far from being what we claim — no wonder America's enemies hate us! We are encouraging Israel to give of her (God ordained) land to keep middle east peace. We are allowing the innocent unborn to be openly murdered every day. These are all signs that we are living in the end times. Open your Bible and ask God to reveal these truths to you. As the time of Christ's return nears, we must look through Spiritual eyes to weigh all things against the Biblical teachings. If it was wrong a few thousand years ago, it is still wrong today. It does not matter if society says it's okay. Society cannot save us from eternal damnation.

Lord, our shallow walk will not be enough to withstand the tests of the devil. Give us a deeper hunger. Open my eyes to see things in the light of Your truth. May I weigh every single thing against the truths in Your Word. Amen.

May 10th <u>Suffering</u> *(Romans 8:28)*

And we know that God causes all things to work together for good to those who love God, to those who are called according to His purpose.

We have all been in situations we felt powerless to control and have believed there was no possible way good could come of them. Mary and Martha felt the same way when their brother Lazarus died. They were very honest with Jesus about how they felt. Remember, they both told Jesus that their brother *would not have died if He had come sooner.* Actually, Jesus said, *"This sickness is not to end in death, but for the glory of God, so that the Son of God may be glorified by it."* How could Jesus ignore the call of His dear friends and actually tarry two days longer before going to them? How could this possibly *"work together for good to those who love God?"* I know I use this saying repeatedly, but *His ways are not our ways.* Mary and Martha were looking at the reality of a dying brother who probably took care of them. Jesus could have stopped Lazarus's suffering and prevented his death. Why didn't He do it? The real reason is that we would not know the story if it ended any other way. We need the miracle of this resurrection in order to see hope beyond our current circumstances. Jesus knew that without the miracle of a restored life, credit for the healing would have gone to someone else. Don't we do that? We pray for healing and then thank the doctors for bringing it. Jesus knew… and that is exactly why He stayed away.

I can honestly say that the greatest benefit from my suffering has been that it has made me stronger and has grown my faith. Each time I let the Lord guide and direct me I have come out stronger. I also am more able to help others who deal with the same situations. I know the pain of death of a loved one. I know what being broke feels like. I know what losing a job I depended on feels like. I know *"all things work together for the good of those who love the Lord and are called according to His purpose."* I know *"no weapon formed against me shall prosper."* I know *"I am more than a conqueror in Christ Jesus."*

Father, how grateful I am that I never have to weather storms alone. I can rest in the confidence that You will never leave or forsake me. You will calm the stormy seas and You will bring peace in the most trying of circumstances. You are my ever-present hope and my strength. Amen.

May 11ᵗʰ Redeemed *(Isaiah 53:5-6)*

He was <u>pierced</u> through for our transgressions, He was <u>crushed</u> for our iniquities; the <u>chastening</u> for our well-being fell upon Him, and by His <u>scourging</u> we are healed. All of us like sheep have gone astray, each of us has turned to his own way; but the LORD has caused the <u>iniquity of us all to fall on</u> Him.

Sometimes we find a verse which absolutely makes us realize how grateful we are for the sacrifice of Christ. That must have happened when I wrote the following journal entry: "Lord, how can I ever thank You enough for the Cross? I can never repay Your sacrifice on my behalf with money, work or word. I can never explain what Your obedience and suffering for someone who didn't care about You at all for the first 38 years of her life means. The sins of my past left me bruised and battered, scarred and torn, afraid and hardened. You broke through the rock hard veneer I had around my heart and began 11 years ago to soften and prepare the rocky soil to receive seeds of faith. I am ever grateful." Have you ever realized how unfair Jesus was treated in order to ensure our reconciliation with God? Jesus was <u>pierced</u> when a Roman soldier was commanded to verify His death. At the piercing, water (holiness) and blood (humanity) flowed from His side. He was <u>crushed</u>—beaten almost beyond recognition. He received the <u>chastening</u> we deserved for our sins, even though He was sinless. He was <u>scourged</u>—beaten with a multi-tipped leather whip that was fitted with bits of bone and wood to dig into the flesh. He carried the weight of the world's sins upon His shoulders.

I know this is not a pleasant passage to read. It wasn't a pleasant set of circumstances to live! Think about the person you dislike most in the world. (Okay, I know we are to love everyone... but surely there is someone who is not your favorite, or who has hurt you very much.) Can you even begin to imagine yourself suffering like described above for that person to have eternal life? The first time I watched the "Passion of the Christ" movie, I watched closely until the scourging scene began. I had to look away from the violence and hatred in that scene. I kept thinking that as bad as the movie was, it was so much worse for Jesus. The camera could not catch the emotional strain of betrayal and abandonment. It couldn't fully portray the grief at leaving His mother, His best friend and His disciples. No film could capture the horror of momentary separation from God the Father.

Lord, I know what hard hearts feel like! I know what it takes to crack them. I know hopelessness and despair. Touch hearts like You touched mine, Lord. Amen.

May 12th <u>Gail: Stepping out in Strength</u> *(Philippians 4: 13)*

I can do all things through Him who strengthens me.

$\mathcal{G}$od brings specific people into our lives *"for such a time as this."* Gail is one of those people. The first time I met Gail, I didn't like her. Fortunately for me, first impressions didn't last and we became dear friends. Gail was raised on the family farm and learned a great work ethic at the hands of her parents. As an adult, she began to play sports, especially softball; and she took a job in the city we live in. Shortly after we became friends, Gail took a fall off her front porch and began having numbness and tingling in her legs. She thought this was a symptom of the fall. Gail was diagnosed with MS (Multiple Sclerosis). Faith carried her through that difficult period of adjustment. One day Gail's friend, Jocelyn, who owns a salon in New York, cut the hair of a new customer named Tom. Their conversation turned to family. Tom commented that he wasn't married. Jocelyn told him she had a woman for him, but she lived in Michigan. He said he wouldn't close a door God may have opened. Tom and Gail were to meet the weekend following the terrorist attacks of September 11, 2001. Because of border closings, Gail didn't go. Tom wouldn't have been able to spend time with her because his father died that week. Gail sent a sympathy card... Tom sent flowers... she called him... he called her... she told him she had MS... he told her he didn't care... she went there... he came here... and on July 13, 2002, she walked down the aisle and up to the altar to marry the man God sent to her!

Does God direct paths? Gail longed for a man to love her, but when she decided God was enough He gave her the desire of her heart. Gail has never given up. She has taken an early medical retirement, purchased a speedy "Amigo" to ride on and remains involved with friends and family events. She and Tom go camping in the summer and travel several times a year to visit his family in New York. Every step is a struggle, but every step is a victory. MS doesn't stop Gail from fighting. I have to say that if I have a sore throat I think the world has come to an end! If my back hurts I am unbearable to live with. We need to learn from Gail's determination.

Father, there are many Gail's in the world. They have severe handi-caps which cripple their physical mobility, but their spirits move on and their faith in You proves that they can truly 'do all things' because 'You give them strength.' Amen.

May 13th <u>Heavenly Body</u> *(I John 3:2)*

*Beloved, now we are children of God, and it has not appeared
as yet what we will be. We know that when He appears
we will be like Him, because we will see Him just as He is.*

$\mathcal{I}$ really give little thought to my after death body. I think about seeing Jesus when I get to Heaven. I think about the beauty of all the voices raised in praise—singing their New Song all in one language—His Language. Bodies will be different, in that they will not be diseased or weak. Bones will be strong; eyes will see clearly; knees and hips won't need to be replaced; teeth will not decay; and cancer will be no more. Bodies will no longer suffer physical abuse, drug addictions, fleshly lusts, or even fatigue. I also think about crip-pled bodies being healed. Several friends with debilitating diseases will be free to run. I love to think about the healings Jesus performed, which are detailed throughout the Gospel accounts. I have written before that Jesus had to have been almost magnetic with kindness and charisma for people to leave everything to follow Him. If that is the case, imagine what His reaction would have been as He brought healing to total strangers. I picture Jesus opening the eyes of blind souls who react in glee and amazement as they see the things others just take for granted. I see Jesus watching the cripple stand up and carry his pallet away. I imagine Him stopping the hemorrhage of the woman who fought the crowds to come to Him for healing. These people longed for healed bodies...and Jesus met their deepest long-ings. I picture His excitement, His tears, His hugs and handshakes. I picture Him looking Heavenward, thanking His Father for allowing Him to bring these gifts to His people.

The people Jesus healed received a taste of what we will receive with our heavenly bodies. They already have that which we long for. I have no idea what my heavenly body will look like—actually, anything would be an improvement! I am more excited about watching those who have not had health here, as they get their first taste of real life there! We need to share the Gospel with those who are suffering here; so they can look forward to their reward in Heaven.

Jesus, I will run to You with open arms when the doors of Heaven are folded back to receive me. Help me to tell those who don't run now that they can run in the day of my Lord. Mostly, I just want to see what caused so many to forsake home and family to follow You. Amen.

May 14th <u>Judging Others</u> *(Galatians 6:1-2)*

Brethren, even if anyone is caught in any trespass, you who are spiritual restore such a one in a spirit of gentleness; each one looking to yourself, so that you too will not be tempted. Bear one another's burdens, and thereby fulfill the law of Christ.

I remember years ago of hearing an uncomfortable phrase: "The Church eats its own." I have watched that happen over and over. The one place where forgiveness and restoration should happen is often the place where those who have fallen are shunned and forced out. They are made to feel filthy and unworthy of being with the "holy people." What a joke this is! Those same holy people need to read Scripture, follow Jesus' examples and look in the mirror. When I think I am better than anyone else, I need to remember that pride in itself is a sin against God. We are to confront sin in love, forgive sin in love, and not continue to dwell on that sin in judgment.

It is so easy to judge others. An old Indian adage says to never judge another "until you walk a mile in his moccasins." Why do we so like to find fault, criticize, tear down and "share about" others. The clear answer is that if we can talk someone else down, we think we look better. The reality is that we end up looking bad. I have talked recently with someone about believing everything she sees on television or in print. Accusations can be made, which later prove to be completely unfounded. My friend Karen's story, as told in an April entry, proves this to be true. We need to verify and then confront in a Biblical manner—with a spirit of gentleness—and restore the guilty one to good standing. We are absolutely commanded not to judge the person, but to always judge the <u>sin</u>. Remember, we all deserve to be judged as we judge others.

Who am I to criticize any person—because I have been forgiven for my past sins! Jesus doesn't lord them over my head and keep me at arm's length! I will strive to do the same, Lord. Amen.

May 15th   <u>God's Glory</u>   *(2 Corinthians 4:6)*

For God, who said, "Light shall shine out of darkness," is the One who has shone in our hearts to give the Light of the knowledge of the glory of God in the face of Christ.

God is all about light and <u>never</u> about darkness. That light shines on us and once we believe in who He is; we are filled with that same light. He is glorified in the life and embodiment of Jesus. Everything we see Jesus do, speak or teach is God's way. We see things through earthly, human eyes right now. There is much we cannot possibly understand. On that day when we meet with our Jesus, we will see everything clearly and be absolutely thrilled we believed in that which we could not see. Every day, with every struggle, every prayer filled moment, every time He answers our needs; we are being transformed into His image. He is our 'be all, our end all, and our all-in-all'—and we need to be like Him. This entry makes me think about Simeon whose story is described in the second chapter of the gospel of <u>Luke </u>as follows: *"And there was a man in Jerusalem whose name was Simeon; and this man was righteous and devout, looking for the consolation of Israel; and the Holy Spirit was upon him. And Simeon blessed them and said to Mary His mother, 'Behold, this Child is appointed for the fall and rise of many in Israel, and for a sign to be opposed..."* Simeon spent his entire life looking for the coming Messiah. When he laid his eyes upon the baby Jesus his spirit knew his questions had been answered. He also was warning Mary and Joseph, while Christ was still an infant, that he would be opposed. Simeon followed those words by telling God he was ready to die... his waiting was now over.

Have you ever seen or felt the glory of God move? There is no mistaking when it happens. I have felt it several times in my personal prayer time; two of which led to the opening of <u>His House</u> and the writing of this book! I have seen Him move in a church setting four or five times. Every time that has happened, the person in the pulpit has had to cast their agenda out the door and give God full reign in His house. If you want to see the Lord move, be quiet before Him and willing to move as He directs.

Lord, I want to see what Simeon saw through his own eyes. I long to see Your face, Your glory, and Your arms outstretched to receive me. Calm me to listen for Your words and to watch for You to move. Amen.

May 16th <u>Painful Pruning</u> *(John 15:1-2)*

"I am the true vine, and My Father is the vinedresser.
"Every branch in Me that does not bear fruit, He takes away;
and every branch that bears fruit He prunes it so that it
may bear more fruit."

*P*eter is a great example of someone who was pruned by Jesus, the vinedresser. Peter was rash, impulsive, easily defeated and prone to outbursts. He also denied Christ three times during His trial. Peter needed a lot of pruning because God had big, big plans for his future! After Peter was humbled and convicted of his rash impulses, he became the head of the early Christian church. I hate being pruned! But, I also see children who hate being disciplined or told "no." In most circumstances the discipline is for their own good. When I am pruned or cut back my Father is removing the dead branches (those which are not producing good fruit of right living). The branches, which don't produce fruit, sap the energy and nourishment from the rest. I have been pruned in many ways. No more soap operas; reckless spending; wasteful use of my time; judging, criticizing and faultfinding of others. The pruning hurts bad; but I always come out stronger, more focused, more disciplined, and more ready to be who the Father wants me to be as I walk the earth carrying His Name.

Here come the hard questions! What areas of your life need to be pruned? I am not asking what you will allow to be pruned; but what needs to be pruned? What things waste your time? What things keep you from being in God's word and being effective in His kingdom? I can remember when I finally realized I had to give up soap operas! Dan, his daughter, my son and I all fast forwarded through three and one half hours of soaps every night. We were like vultures around the living room, feeding on the garbage on daytime television. Think of the free time we had once we stopped! I had hours to spend in Bible study every day. I had time to share the Gospel. I had time to pray. I was pruned of that which was unnecessary; and I was given the gift of time!

Father, I know there are things in my life which keep me from being fully effective for You. I trust that the pruning is for my own good, because I trust fully in You. Amen.

May 17th <u>Seeking God</u> *(Luke 11:9-10)*

"So I say to you, ask, and it will be given to you; seek,
and you will find; knock, and it will be opened to you.
For everyone who asks, receives; and he who seeks, finds;
and to him who knocks, it will be opened."

I always believed in God and accepted Jesus... in my mind. Once I opened the Word I began to know God in a more meaningful way. I began to seek after Him not knowing that for 38 years he had been "seeking" after me. In hindsight, I remember the heart tugs and the yearning for more meaning and purpose. The Lord was at work trying to get me to acknowledge Him, His authority, and His sacrifice on my behalf. When I did begin to seek Him the floodgates opened and the passion I had withheld or ignored for years poured forth. I began to see, not through "eyes dimmed," but through "eyes wide open." I was so excited I literally couldn't stop talking about my faith. The most amazing part is that this fire, love and passion were always there hidden beneath the false desires of my heart. There is a huge difference between knowing *about* Jesus and *knowing* Jesus. We are called the bride of Christ. Picture a woman when she first meets the man she is to one day marry. She doesn't want to know *about* him... she wants to know *him*. She is going to spend the rest of her life with him, so casual information is not enough! The same applies in our walk with Christ. We should be seeking to know every thing we can learn about Him. We cannot have a chat over coffee, so we need to read His "last will and testament" where He reveals all of His plans and wishes for us.

Are you a seeker? Has He been a knocker whom you have been ignoring? You will never find the peace and deep abiding faith you need if you don't take the step into a new realm. He is life itself. He is all we truly need—because money, things, people and careers can never save us. Prepare to meet the 'bridegroom' with whom you will spend eternity. You will not regret the choice.

Lord, You have actively sought me, and I have run as fast as possible in the other direction. Now I turn to face You, to find You. Reveal all truth of who You are. I want to see through eyes wide open. Amen.

May 18th   The Sweet Word   *(Ezekiel 3:1-2)*

Then He said to me, "Son of man, eat what you find;
eat this scroll, and go, speak to the house of Israel."
So I opened my mouth, and He fed me this scroll.

have taught on this story of Ezekiel where he is told to eat the scroll which is written front and back of the sins, condemnation and coming woes of Israel. I love the word picture of God saying, *"Feast upon My word and then go and proclaim to the people what I tell you. Then their sin will be defined, and they will turn from it."* Ezekiel did as he was instructed, ate the scroll and found it to be very sweet—like honey on his tongue. He was then sent to tell the people what it said. God has always raised up prophets, apostles, and teachers to study and proclaim His truths. Their job is to define sin in order for people to understand their need for a Savior. Truth be told, people have always rejected these words. To accept them and apply them would mean life changes; and most of us reject the idea of change. I am like Ezekiel. I hunger and feed upon the Word. I glean from it until my needs and curiosities are satisfied. It is sweet, like honey to my mouth. Some days it is like a cool, refreshing, invigorating drink of water.

Instruction books are rarely read. Think about the number of people who are unable to set their VCR to tape a television program. Think of putting a bicycle, a piece of furniture, or a craft project together. Most manuals are left unopened and unused. I have a license plate on my car which reads, "IF ALL ELSE FAILS, READ THE INSTRUCTIONS." The picture in the background is an open Bible, but I have had numerous people tell me they never open an instruction manual. They aren't realizing what the inscription truly means. Do you open the "Instruction Manual" in order to receive God's directions, cautions and promises? Try it; the taste is sweet. Dwell upon promises like, *"He who created you will not slumber..."* Without this foundation, we can never be an Ezekiel—one sent to change the hearts of the lost.

———————

Father, I love Your Word. It is the constant comfort, counsel, and love from You, Lord. Amen.

May 19th <u>Jesus Wept</u> *(John 11:33-35)*

When Jesus therefore saw her weeping, and the Jews who came
with her also weeping, He was deeply moved in spirit and
was troubled, and said, "Where have you laid him?"
They said to Him, "Lord, come and see." Jesus wept.

"*Jesus wept*" has always been one of my favorite verses. I love to encourage others during grief, illness, tragedy or loss by telling them that nothing they feel is foreign to the Lord our God. We are wonderfully blessed to not serve a stone idol. Instead we serve a risen, tortured, beaten, blasphemed and persecuted Savior! When I grieve the loss of someone I love, I think of Jesus at Lazarus's grave. When I am not satisfied with my little house, I think of a Lord "with nowhere to lay His head." When I worry about money, health and family, I think of His words telling me that *"my Lord shall supply all my needs,"* as He does the tiny sparrows. There is nothing, absolutely nothing, which Jesus hasn't felt. That is why God had to come to us in flesh. Because of Jesus walking the earth, being tempted, feeling pain and being rejected, God knows exactly how we feel.

———————

Are you grieving the loss of someone you loved? Maybe your grief is the death of a dream resulting from divorce, job loss or family separation. My prayer is that you are comforted to know that Jesus understands your pain and hears your cries to Him. Jesus felt Mary's pain at the Cross. He felt Peter's pain after his betrayal. He felt the fear and shame of the adulterous woman. Surely, He feels your loss. He alone can bring you hope. He gave Mary the promise of being mother to John. He restored Peter and made him the "Rock" of the early Christian church. He liberated the adulterous woman by telling her to *go and sin no more!* Trust Him for your hope at the end of the darkness you are facing.

Jesus, You are awesome. You are compassionate. You understand my every need, my grief, and my sense of hopelessness. You are my all in all. Amen.

May 20th <u>God's Kind of Greatness</u> *(Mark 9:34-35)*

But they kept silent, for on the way they had discussed with one another which of them was the greatest. Sitting down, He called the twelve and said to them, "If anyone wants to be first, he shall be last of all and servant of all."

*W*hat we see as "great" in this world carries no value in God's eyes… unless the great we see is a "great servant" of God. God resists the proud and welcomes the humble with open arms and grace because of humility. To be Christ like, we must be willing to be blasphemed, persecuted, wrongly accused, battered, judged, sentenced and ready to die for our faith. When we do that we are exalted by God, not by man, and are given our riches in the heavenly realm. Wisdom isn't all book smarts. Wisdom is life experiences, the study of the Scriptures, the things we learn from our elders and the speaking to our hearts by the Holy Spirit. We will never know the value of righteousness, humility, sacrifice, selflessness and love until we look in Jesus' eyes and see what those characteristics really look like. Some of the "greatest" people I know are servants of God. These are the humble servants who clean the church, prepare meals for the needy, visit the shut-ins, teach the Sunday school classes and wear out their knees praying for the needs of others. The apostles discussed who was greatest; but Jesus explained if this was their focus, then not one of them was truly great.

We are all familiar with people who think they are great. These people have no sense of humility. They believe the world revolves around them. In nearly every case the meaningful impact they make on the world is questionable. Picture Hollywood's stars and see the self obsession surrounding them. They have a powerful influence on the minds of our young people. The influence is rarely good and can actually lead the innocent to emulate lifestyles contrary to that which we have taught them. Unfortunately, we are given very few media hyped examples of people who serve God, meet the needs of others and live lives of eternal purpose. Who do you see as great in your circle of friends and family? What needs to change in your life in order for you to be a great servant?

Lord, I have allowed my focus on entertainers and celebrities to influence my life. I need a refocus... in order to see that which is truly important. You were a servant, and there was no shame in that. Make me a willing and obedient servant. Amen.

May 21ˢᵗ Trees *(Psalms 92:12-13)*

The righteous man will flourish like the palm tree; He will grow like a cedar in Lebanon. Planted in the house of the LORD, They will flourish in the courts of our God. They will still yield fruit in old age; They shall be full of sap and very green.

I think first of the roots of the towering elm tree digging ever deeper into the soil for nutrients and for stability. Likewise, believers need to dig deeper the same way, so that their faith roots keep them fertilized, nourished and grounded when the winds of life blow. Trees show their age when growth rings are examined. Each year's ring makes the tree stronger and more productive. We age the same way, but our years in Christ should show us to be strong and productive Christians. A tree has a bark outer layer to protect the tender inside "flesh" of the tree. We are to wear the spiritual armor of God on our outside to protect ourselves from attack. Then we will be tender and gentle, strong and solid on the inside. Trees reach to the sky, straining to touch the very face of God. We should do the same—ever reaching, ever striving, and ever seeking for more of God's love.

When the strong winds blow, the tree, unless there is a problem of disease or infestation, moves ever so gently from the trunk up. Weak branches may break off and leaves may fly, but the deeply buried roots will hold the tree firmly in its place. Without that grounding, trees would be flying through the air every time the wind blows. How deeply are you grounded in the word of God and the truths of your faith? When life's winds blow, are you firm in your faith, or prone to fly away... giving up and grabbing onto something new for meaning in your life? Reread the promise at the top of this entry. Nothing else will ever offer you the same stability as faith in the living God.

Father God, I need more grounding in the truths of Your teachings. I have allowed myself to be blown off course and carried away on the winds of change. I am sorry; and I ask for Your Spirit as my guide to keep me focused and intent upon my purpose in You. Amen.

May 22ⁿᵈ <u>Every Knee Shall Bow</u> *(Philippians 2:9-11)*

For this reason also, God highly exalted Him, and bestowed on Him the name which is above every name, so that at the name of Jesus EVERY KNEE WILL BOW, of those who are in heaven and on earth and under the earth, and that every tongue will confess that Jesus Christ is Lord, to the glory of God the Father.

*J*n response to the above Scripture verse, I wrote in January of 2006: "I look forward to the awesome excitement which those who know Him will feel in the moment they realize what is happening to them. I can't wait to see His eyes, touch His chest where His heart beats, and fall at His feet like the woman with the alabaster box. A popular contemporary Christian song probably best describes the mix of emotions we will feel when we first see Jesus. "Will I be able to speak one single word?" On the other side of this thought, so many people will not understand the appearance of the Lord. They will cringe in fear, cry out in anger, speak forth in anguish, or be bent over in regret and realization." As I read this passage, I pictured an endless sea of people of every possible nationality and language. They are standing to see His face and then falling to their knees as they cry out, "Jesus. Yes, it is Jesus! We worship Your holy Name." For some of them those words will come too late. These are the ones who heard of His grace, His salvation, and are regretting their denials. They are realizing their money, notoriety and careers really mean nothing. The things they spent their entire lives seeking are gone. Make no mistake; **every knee** will bow to Christ.

All of us know people who do not know Jesus. Some of them have heard the Gospel shared and have refused to believe or accept it. Some know about Him, but have never come to a relationship place with Christ. Yet, there are some who have never heard the truth of our need for salvation and have no idea about why Christians are secure in their beliefs. We must tell them. Imagine looking across the sea of people and seeing people you failed to share Christ with. We will answer for the missed opportunities to share the Gospel.

Lord, I long for that day and want to tell as many people as possible about You, Your Word, Your promises and Your eventual return. Be my strength. Amen.

May 23ʳᵈ <u>Grace</u> *(1 John 2:1-2)*

My little children, I am writing these things to you so that
you may not sin. And if anyone sins, we have an Advocate
with the Father, Jesus Christ the righteous; and He Himself
is the propitiation for our sins; and not for ours only,
but also for those of the whole world.

*G*race is defined as "unearned, unmerited favor." That means we don't receive it by doing good works, and that we truly do not deserve it. Maybe the word picture (parable) below will help you to better understand the concept of grace:

———————

As I prepared to stand in judgment for my life choices, I was given a seat at the defense table. I saw the "prosecutor," a most evil looking person; and then I looked to my left, and there sat my lawyer... a kind, quiet and gentle man... whose appearance seemed familiar to me. There appeared the judge in full flowing robes. He commanded an awesome presence as he moved across the room. The prosecutor rose and said, "My name is Satan and I am here to show you why this man belongs in hell." He spoke of lies I'd told, things I'd stolen, and when I'd cheated others. I was so embarrassed that I couldn't look at anyone. As upset as I was at Satan for telling all these things about me, I was also upset at my lawyer who sat there silently, not offering any form of defense at all. Satan finished and said, "This man belongs in hell! He is guilty of all I have charged him with, and there is not a person who can prove otherwise." When it was his turn, my lawyer got up and started walking toward the bench. I realized why he seemed so familiar. This was Jesus representing me, my Lord and my Savior. He turned to address the court. "Satan was correct in saying this man has sinned. I won't deny any of these allegations; and yes, the wages of sin is death." Jesus took a deep breath, turned to his Father with outstretched arms and proclaimed, "However, I died on the cross so that he might have eternal life, and he has accepted me as his Savior. He is mine. This man is not to be given justice, but mercy." Jesus sat down, looked at his Father and replied, "There is nothing else that needs to be done. I've done it all." The judge lifted his mighty hand and slammed the gavel down. "This man is free! The penalty for his sin has already been paid in full. Case dismissed."

———————

Father, the parable says it all. I am glad You don't judge me like I have judged others. How blessed am I to know that Your Son died for my sins and shortcomings. Help me to not condemn anyone, but help me to never condone sin. Amen.

May 24ᵗʰ <u>Death's Door</u> *(Revelation 14:13)*

And I heard a voice from heaven, saying, "Write, 'Blessed are the dead who die in the Lord from now on!' "Yes," says the Spirit, "so that they may rest from their labors, for their deeds follow with them."

As a child I was terrified of death, funerals and cemeteries. I believe this began when I attended the funeral of a friend of my grandparents who was not a believer and didn't want his hands positioned in any way that might resemble prayer, so his arms were at his sides instead. For years (until I was a married adult) I dreamed of him rising up out of the casket, stiff armed like Bela Lugosi in a horror movie. These things no longer cause me fear. Maybe the change came with age, but mostly I remember my Grandpa dying with us in the room... and there was no struggle or fear. He simply went to sleep while holding my cousin's hand. After losing so many others I loved and spending a great deal of time near their caskets, I do not fear death. I fear the legacy I leave more than the separation of death from this life. I am always baffled by Christians who are afraid to die. Yes, we would hate to leave those we so dearly love, but we will wake up in a new body seeing the One who so dearly loved us. I don't know about you, but I cannot wait for *"rest from their labors."* Thanks be to Jesus that at the end of this life the labor and struggle which began in the Garden of Eden will be over... retirement from strife forever!

Are you afraid of death? Look deep at your fear. What exactly are you afraid of? We need to pin down the source of the fear, pray for revelation in that area of our lives, and begin to fill our spirits with the promise Scriptures for eternal life. Jesus told His disciples He was leaving to go and prepare a place for them, and then He would return to take them there. That promise is for us, too. He is preparing a place where no tears will fall. I am ready to go... are you?

As a Christian, it is important for me to seek and love You, lift Your Name, touch hearts and leave a lasting legacy. I am working on that. Show me what You need me to do, Lord Jesus. Amen.

May 25ᵗʰ Worship and Praise *(Psalms 95:1-2)*

O come, let us sing for joy to the LORD, Let us shout joyfully to the rock of our salvation. Let us come before His presence with thanksgiving. Let us shout joyfully to Him with psalms.

Jesus, Jesus—You give my life such hope;
Jesus, Jesus—that is why I can cope;
You fill my heart with songs of praise;
I'll serve You, Lord, through all my days.
Jesus, Jesus—You're my joy, my peace, my hope.

Jesus, Jesus—You have set this captive free;
Jesus, Jesus—Others' eyes can't help but see
The truth You teach, the love You give—
Draw them near, Lord—let them live.
Come, Lord Jesus; and we will worship Thee.

Worship is a very personal form of praise and of giving thanks. Thanksgiving escapes the prayers of many of us;

we are too busy bringing our laundry list before the Throne. What do you have to give thanks for? Do your eyes see, your lungs breathe, and your feet walk? Do you have a roof over your head, a car to get you where you need to go, and clothes to wear? Do you have an income, a friend, or a loving family? Do you have a church to attend, a Bible to read, and a voice to sing with? Why do we struggle with praise? Think about this. You prepare a great meal for your family... pineapple glazed ham, mashed potatoes with real gravy, deviled eggs, a crispy salad with scratch dressing, warm rolls...and your family sits to eat. They gobble their favorites and then scatter without one word of thanks for your work. How happy are you? I'll bet you are excited to cook for them again tomorrow! How must God feel when we take every blessing for granted?!

O' Father, I am so guilty of this very thing. I fail to come into Your presence with thanksgiving pouring from my lips. Because of this, my worship is not as sincere as it could be. Amen.

May 26th <u>Pleasing God</u> *(Hebrews 11:6)*

And without faith it is impossible to please Him, for he
who comes to God must believe that He is and that
He is a rewarder of those who seek Him.

*P*ure faith, not lip service, pleases God. He knows the difference. Those who live in righteousness instead of in flesh are pleasing to him. When we seek to fellowship with Him, we bring Him pleasure. He created us to seek Him. Willingness to suffer for our obedience pleases God, as does showing patience during that suffering. Gentle, quiet and kind spirits are pleasing to God. Praises offered on His behalf please Him. Believers who order or prioritize their steps along His paths please him. All who are willing to sacrifice for His sake please Him. We are called to service; and that call can require us to sacrifice of our time, money, sleep, and our physical comforts.

If we can only please God through having faith as the above Scripture reads, we must realize that pretend faith will never please Him. Faith produces good fruits in the lives of a Christian. Look at the teaching above and see some faith fruits. Fellowship, seeking Him, obedience, gentleness, sincere praises and sacrifice are all the resulting actions from having faith. How do you measure up in these areas? What is your priority—pleasing God or pleasing yourself? Being a person of faith doesn't stop us from living our lives in a faithless world; it merely strengthens us in our day-to-day battles. The fruits of our faith show others what serving Christ means.

Thank You, Lord, for these gentle reminders of what You are pleased by. Help me to be obedient in all areas of my life. May my words, thoughts and deeds reveal to the world that You live in my heart. Amen.

May 27th <u>Word of Truth</u> *(John 19:35)*

And he who has seen has testified, and his testimony is true; and he knows that he is telling the truth, so that you also may believe.

*P*eople often say that the Bible is a book written by a bunch of men. My response is that they are absolutely right. If I were dying and wanted to leave a legacy to my heirs, but was too weak to write, couldn't I commission those around me to write my words? Couldn't I dictate my thoughts, desires and teachings for Brent, Tyler and Hailey? Would these words be less mine because I had someone write them for me? If it is "just a book written by a bunch of men," where is the "book of Billy Graham?" Surely the greatest evangelist of our time would be entitled! Why has the writing of the Bible stopped and never been added to? For example, if I found a letter by one of my Grandma's childhood friends which talked about her, I would believe the words simply because that person walked, talked, and spent time with her, and watched how she lived her life. The fact that Matthew and John were two of Jesus' apostles who walked with Him and watched Him teach, feed, heal and forgive... would lead me to believe the accounts they have written. The letters Paul wrote to the churches in Rome, Corinth and Philippi were copied by hand and dispersed to the small Christian congregations throughout the cities. Those letters, because God saw fit to preserve them, make up the bulk of the New Testament. God saw to their preservation so each of us could feed upon their ageless truths today.

Very few Christians are equipped to defend the Word of God against the attacks and insinuations of the people who would refute it as truth. Why are we so ill-equipped? One problem is the lack of apologetics teaching in the modern church. Programs and special events take precedent. The church is not fully to blame though. Believers need to take some form of responsibility for their own personal faith growth. If I waited for someone to teach me the things of the Bible, I would still be waiting. Make an effort to learn more about the Bible, its teachings and its defense.

Father God, I fall very far short in being able to explain to others the basis for my beliefs and Christian ethics. I need to apply more time and energy to this part of my faith walk. Open my eyes, ears and heart to receive Your truths. Amen.

May 28th Spiritual Thirst *(Psalms 42:1-2)*

As the deer pants for the water brooks, So my soul pants for You, O God. My soul thirsts for God, for the living God; When shall I come and appear before God?

*B*efore I came to faith, I was a very outgoing friendly person who sought approval in any way I could get it. I drank from a flowing fountain of sins. I always sought love, and I was willing to do anything to get it. None of the things I sought after ever satisfied my burning thirst for love. When I first opened the Word and began to read, I was so challenged and excited. Then I went to church and couldn't get enough of the teachings. I was amazed that others didn't seem as excited and blown away as I was about grace. I think that is a problem in the church. We have lost our thirst, passion, thrill and excitement for our Lord. Excited and passionate new believers are a must in any congregation. They are contagious and bring sparks of life to all they come in contact with. I know myself enough to know that if I walked away today from my daily time in the Bible I would soon drift away altogether. Once that happened, it would be hard to go back. I keep my thirst quenched with daily time set apart for the Lord. I know what thirst is; I know that only Christ satisfies the longing of my dry, thirsty soul!

Relationships require commitment; especially a personal relationship with God. King David talked about his soul panting after the things of God! How long, if ever, has it been since you panted after Him? Have you ever been thirsty? I don't mean a little thirsty, but the kind of thirst you can feel deep in your throat. The thirst burns and consumes your every thought. Think about that deep, cold drink of clear, clean water. Our thirst for Christ should be like that. Nothing else can satisfy... no hobby, no person, no money and no false doctrines. He alone removes the spiritual thirst of our hearts.

Living, loving God, I long to know You more. I haven't thirsted after You like I should. I have been too distracted. May the passion of Your Spirit burn within me—drawing me ever closer to You. Amen.

May 29th Spiritual Life *(John 6:63)*

"It is the Spirit who gives life; the flesh profits nothing; the words that I have spoken to you are spirit and are life."

*P*hysical life for people is manifested at conception and gives our souls a vehicle to carry them through the earthly number of days we are given. Our flesh is of no value, except to provide that carriage. It will die when we die and return to dust. Spiritual life is in our hearts from the moment of birth. It quickens us to hunger for meaning and to seek something or someone higher than we are. When we hear, receive and accept the Gospel of Christ, His Holy Spirit fills our fleshly vehicle and we begin to walk in love and in opposition to the fleshly world. Life begins at that moment (NEW BIRTH) not life as we had before, but life centered around and focused on our God. Our lives change, are refocused, and are reprioritized when spiritual life becomes who we are.

Jesus had a visitor who came to Him in the dark of night for teaching. Nicodemus was a powerful Jewish leader who sensed in his spirit that the things Jesus spoke of were true. He was eager to learn until Jesus told him he must be born again! Nicodemus challenged the thought, thinking that Christ meant the physical act of birth from the point of conception. He knew that was impossible. Jesus told him this was a spiritual rebirth—a change from the inside out. Are you confused by the NEW BIRTH concept? One basic explanation is that the physical body has a spirit within. New birth is when that spirit unites with God's Spirit and gives the believer a new life… one set apart for the Lord.

I want new birth in You, Jesus. I may not understand everything… like Nicodemus… but, I am ready to learn and trust You to only do what is best for me in my life. Birth Your Spirit within me. Amen.

May 30th Repentance *(James 4:17)*

*Therefore, to one who knows the right thing to do
and does not do it, to him it is sin.*

*T*his verse from James says it all. Before sin is defined we may have a slight excuse that we didn't know right from wrong. Each of us is born with an innate knowledge between right and wrong. The only exception to this is one born with a serious mental disorder. God's teaching reveals the ways He has ordained for His children to walk. Once we have had the definition and clear lines, we are acting on our own when we knowingly disobey God's words. I have done this many times by acting on impulse, speaking words I know are wrong, failing to witness, or allowing circumstances around me to dictate my actions (instead of allowing the conviction of the Spirit to be my guide). When I do these things I am instantly convicted and called to repentance. Herod Antipas, the Roman leader in the area of Galilee, is a great example of someone who knows what is right and does what is wrong. The account of his life is told in the sixth chapter of the gospel of Mark. Herod likes to go and listen to the teachings of John the Baptist, in spite of the fact that John tells him that he is living with his brother's wife and it is unlawful. Herod has John beheaded in order to please his wife and stepdaughter, and to fulfill a rash promise he made. Scripture tells us he was greatly distressed at what he had done. Herod knew he was living in sin, was hungry for the conviction John's word brought, and was caught in a trap of his own making.

This may seem to be a foolish question. Have you ever done something wrong, in spite of great conviction by the Holy Spirit? Most of us have. Are we really so different from Herod? We sit under teaching which tells us the moral absolutes of God's Holy Word... then we bow to peer pressure, to fleshly temptation, and to political correctness. Remember the truth of 1 Corinthians 10: 13: *"No temptation has seized you, except what is common to man; God is faithful... when you are tempted He will provide a way out."*

Thank You for always giving me a way out of my sin, Lord. Just as Herod could have reneged on his word to kill John the Baptist, I could take the right escape out of the temptations and messes I get caught up in. Amen.

May 31ˢᵗ Belonging *(I Corinthians 6:19-20)*

Do you not know that your body is a temple of the Holy Spirit
who is in you, whom you have from God, and that you are
not your own? For you have been bought with a price;
therefore glorify God in your body.

The first Bible story that comes to my mind from reading the verse above is of Jesus telling the parable of The Prodigal Son in Luke 15. It tells of a son who wants freedom from the "bondage" of serving under his wealthy father. He requests his share of the coming inheritance; and unfortunately for him, his father gives him what he asks for! The young man leaves and wastes his money on riotous living and prostitutes. He soon finds himself slopping pigs and longing for a taste of the scraps he is feeding them. He decides to return to his father as a servant. His father welcomes him, restoring him to son status. I am not so different from that Prodigal Son. I spent thirty-eight years seeking to belong somewhere. I acted in very ungodly and unladylike ways. Today when I even have the urge to act like that, I am convicted by God's Spirit and am instantly stopped. That shows me that He cares about everything in my life, and wants me to walk rightly before Him, I am blessed! I am chosen. I belong.

Why did the Prodigal Son use his body to fulfill his vulgar needs? Because he didn't realize that it was a *"temple of the Holy Spirit."* I did the same thing as he did. Had I known what I know now, I would never have acted in the shameful ways of my past. Have you also dishonored your temple body? Come to the Cross of Jesus to have those sins forgiven. Begin today to walk in the knowledge that you carry the Spirit of the living God inside of your soul! I would be remiss if I didn't mention here that we need to tell our children this truth. They are being persuaded by their counselors, teachers, role models, and the entertainment community that they must have sex to fit in. This reduces them to nothing more than animals that cannot control the lusts of their flesh. Tell them! Please tell them that they can be pure in a vile world!

Father, You created my body to carry my spirit and Your Spirit to a lost world. Help me to deny the lusts of my flesh, confess past sins and repent of them. I will run the other way. I must; I am Your holy temple. Amen.

June 1st The Divided Baby *(1 Kings 3:25)*

The king said, "Divide the living child in two, and give half to the one and half to the other."

When Solomon asked God for wisdom rather than riches, lots of heirs or long life, God gave him the ability to discern truth between arguing parties. The story in 1st Kings, Chapter 3 shows us this very clearly. Two women (referred to as harlots) come before the king. One tells him they live together in the same house and gave birth to their sons just three days apart. The other woman's child died in the night because she lay upon it. She switched the babies. The speaking woman wakened to nurse the baby and found the dead child beside her. She looked at the baby and realized he was not the infant she birthed just days before. An argument ensued with both women claiming the living child as hers. Solomon, knowing he has to discern which woman truly is the mother of the child, calls for a sword to be brought to him. He tells his servant to cut the living child in half and divide it between the women! The mother of the dead child says, *"He shall be neither mine nor yours: divide him!"* The woman who truly bore the child tells King Solomon to give the baby to the other woman. She would rather protect her child... a sign of real love. Solomon realizes the second woman is willing for the baby to be divided, and thus she cannot be the birth mother. The story ends with all of Israel being in awe of the wisdom God gave their king.

Would you have ever thought to call for the sword? I wouldn't, because I am more emotion driven. The wisdom of Solomon is

Godlike wisdom. God knows all truth and will reveal what is done in darkness. He knew who this child belonged to and gave Solomon the discernment needed. We see the heart of the woman who would rather have the baby die and be divided, and we don't like her one bit. We see the heart of the woman who truly gave birth to the baby, caring more for the child than for her own longings. This story may seem far fetched, but we face situations like this every day. In the business world, we claw our way to the top and do almost anything to stay there. In divorce situations, we force our children to choose sides. We need a dose of Solomon's wisdom.

Father God, I long for the wisdom of King Solomon. I want it not to lord it over others, but that all of my judgments might be based on wisdom and not emotions. Thank You that what was done in darkness—by the woman who switched the babies—was revealed in light. Amen.

June 2ⁿᵈ Powerful Words (Psalms 19:14)

Let the words of my mouth and the meditation of my heart be acceptable in Your sight, O Lord, my rock and my Redeemer.

*Y*ears ago, I remember talking about the words I heard Christians speaking, which were negative and divisive. The man I was talking with asked me if Jesus was in the corner. I didn't understand these words and questioned him as to their meaning. He said to picture Jesus sitting on a stool in the corner of every room you walked into. He would overhear our conversations, watch our reactions, and see how we interact with others. I tried that exercise and was convicted within ten minutes. I talk back to the television all the time... and being a political junkie... don't usually show the love Jesus would want me to toward those whose politics I disagree with! I decided to try it for just one day at the office... I failed the test! I tried it at home one night. I would not have wanted Jesus to hear my ornery words to Dan. I could actually feel myself striving to speak and the Holy Spirit working to shut me up! You may be better with your words; try the test and find out. The Psalmist writes in the verse above that he wants not only his words, but his thoughts to be acceptable to God. You might say that you cannot control your thoughts. We have the power to cast wrong thoughts out of our minds in the name of Jesus Christ. As an example: *"In the name of Jesus Christ, I rebuke this thought about pornography. I want to do all things in a pleasing way Lord. Be my strength."* We have the ability to focus our thoughts on things which are good, pure, lovely and holy.

How are your words? How are your thoughts? Is this an area you need help with? Ask the Lord to fill your mouth and mind with thoughts acceptable to Him. The easiest way I know to do this is to know Scripture verses you can call up when wrong thoughts come to mind. One example is Philippians 4:13 *"I can do all things through Christ who gives me strength."*

Jesus, I need the strong presence of Your Holy Spirit in order for me to better reflect You to the world. I want my words and my thoughts, as well as my deeds, to be acceptable to You. May I use Your strong name to rebuke the thoughts and to avoid the words of my flesh. I am Your child... please guide me as I seek to change. Amen.

June 3rd To Die is Gain *(Philippians 1:21)*

For to me, to live is Christ and to die is gain.

I remember the first time I heard this verse at a Bible Study just weeks into my new relationship with Christ. I came home and asked Dan what he thought it meant. Neither of us could understand how dying could be gain. Paul is writing to the church of Philippi while in prison in Rome. Why is he in prison...for preaching the Gospel of Jesus Christ! He is writing to tell his fellow believers that if he lives... he lives to serve Christ, and if he dies, he gains Heaven and the Presence of his Savior. We must understand those who are without faith in Christ, who make a decision to reject Him, have no hope after this life ends. Paul would have one day had that lack of hope. But, on the Road to Damascus he found Christ (or Christ found him!) Paul didn't want to die, but he knew that death to further the Gospel was worth the sacrifice. The Bible gives us many other examples of people like Paul who were willing to die for the God of Israel. Daniel refused to stop praying and was cast into the lions' den. God shut the mouths of the lions and spared His prayer warrior. Stephen, the first Christian to die for the cause of Christ, made sure he told who Jesus really was before being stoned to death. Joshua walked into foreign lands and into the face of mighty armies armed with only God. Each of these men saw death not as an end of life but instead as the beginning of real life. We can hold so tight to life here that we never long for life in Heaven.

In America we have little comprehension of the sacrifices believers throughout the world deal with every day. Missionaries live in rugged surroundings with meager provisions and often with threat of death. Their purpose to spread the Gospel is greater than their love of this fleeting life. Look at yourself. Does death hold fear for you? If you are a Christian, that should not be the case. Of course we all hate the thoughts of leaving our loved ones. Why not work even harder to make sure they spend eternity with you in glory? Do you think *"to die is gain?"*

Father, I confess that I haven't lived my life in a way which would make death feel like gain. I am pretty absorbed with the things of this earth... and fail to offer my whole life—with no regard of what that means to You. I want Paul's fire and his willingness to be an offering for the furtherance of Your kingdom. Father, give me that holy boldness. Amen.

June 4th   Esther: Preparing to Meet the King   *(Esther 2:4)*

"Then let the young lady who pleases the king be queen in place of Vashti." And the matter pleased the king, and he did accordingly.

*E*sther's story takes place in the land of Persia (modern day Iran) approximately 480 years before the birth of Christ. Ahasuerus is the king of Persia and is looking for a woman to replace the former queen who was dethroned because she refused to be paraded before him and his drinking buddies after a seven day long party! The king sends messengers throughout the kingdom to gather beautiful virgins who will be prepared for one night with the king. Preparations can take up to twelve months as their skin and hair are made perfect and as they are taught proper etiquette for their meeting with the leader of their nation. During those twelve months the virgins lived in a harem. On the night of their visit to the king, they would take all of their personal belongings with the hope he would choose them and move them into the palace. If not, they would move to another harem where they would live for the rest of their life. They could never marry another man after "belonging" to the king. Esther prepares for her meeting, telling no one of her Jewish heritage, and finally, goes to meet Ahasuerus. He chooses Esther as his queen... and prepares a great banquet to celebrate his lovely new wife. Esther's cousin, Mordecai, who has raised the young orphan girl, cautions her to remain silent about her Jewish lineage until the time is right.

Surely the ritual of selecting the most beautiful of the Persian virgins is distasteful to us. We must realize the time period this story is set in and that most marriages were arranged in that day. In many parts of the world they still are. Esther is a Jewish girl whose family chose to remain in Persia after Israel was freed from Persian control. As an orphan of little means, her only hope is to be chosen to be among those in the king's harem where she will be provided for the rest of her life. Mordecai's warning to remain silent about being a Jew will be lauded... in God's perfect timing.

Father, may I learn the lessons You wove throughout Your word, even when they are distasteful to my moral beliefs. Esther was lovely and was chosen by her king. I, too, am lovely, and was chosen by my King Jesus. May I be found pure and righteous in His eyes. Help me to always be ready... for such a time... Amen.

June 5ᵗʰ   Esther: A Plot is Revealed   *(Esther 3:6)*

But he disdained to lay hands on Mordecai alone, for they had told him who the people of Mordecai were; therefore Haman sought to destroy all the Jews, the people of Mordecai, who were throughout the whole kingdom of Ahasuerus.

Our story continues with Mordecai watching near the palace gates for word or a view of Esther. He overhears plotting against the king, gets word into the palace, and the plot is averted. Haman, a servant of Ahasuerus, is promoted into a place of great authority... and then the pride sets in! He commands everyone to bow to him as he enters the gate. Mordecai absolutely refuses to bow before him causing burning hatred between these two men. After repeated confrontations, Haman decides to get revenge on Mordecai's insubordination. He discovers Mordecai's Jewish heritage and plots to eradicate the entire Jewish population in Persia. Ahasuerus, not knowing of the heritage of his beloved Esther, believes Haman when he says *"there is a certain people scattered and dispersed among the peoples... who do not observe the king's laws."* The king agrees to Haman's plan and uses his signet (signature) ring to seal their edict in wax. Haman has finally bested the Jew who has caused him such anger and frustration. Word is sent throughout the kingdom into each province that the Jews are to be slain on the thirteenth day of the twelfth month. All of their belongings are to be seized as plunder. Mordecai, at great risk to himself and knowing he is putting Esther into danger, goes and tells her of Haman's plan to annihilate the Jewish population.

What is it about power? Haman was probably a nice guy until he was given authority. Most of us have seen this happen before when one of our friends or family members gains some degree of prestige or authority. The change can come quickly or be a subtle metamorphosis. Only a truly humble person can handle power and not let it handle them. Mordecai, on the other hand, is a humble man. He could have tried to gain entrance into the palace on the shirttails of his cousin. Instead, he hears of the plan Haman has devised and determines to do whatever is necessary to save his people.

Father, help me to never let power or authority go to my head and change my heart. Help me to remain humble and ready at all times to give an accounting for my actions. Give me a Mordecai heart and insulation from the Haman's of this world, who have a hatred for You and Your children. I will never bow to anyone but my King Jesus. Amen.

June 6ᵗʰ   Esther: For Such a Time as This   *(Esther 4:14)*

"For if you remain silent at this time, relief and deliverance will arise for the Jews from another place and you and your father's house will perish. And who knows whether you have not attained royalty for such a time as this?"

*E*sther has a decision to make... a decision which could cost her life! Esther, though she is Queen of Persia, is under this same law as the rest of the King's subjects. She can only come to the king when he summons her. If he refuses to hear her, she can be killed. She asks the Jewish population to pray and fast for her, and she does the same. Finally, Esther comes to her king who extends the golden scepter to her. He asks what she wants to speak about and she says she would like for Haman to be brought in. Esther requests that she,

Ahasuerus, and Haman have a special banquet the next day. Haman, full of pride and thinking he is going to get a promotion, prepares to leave the palace. He comes face to face with Mordecai, who refuses to bow to him. He then goes home and tells his family the good news of his coming banquet and promotion and of his anger at Mordecai. His wife suggests that he build a high gallows and hang Mordecai. That night, the king cannot sleep and finds in his reading Mordecai foiled an attempt on his life and was never rewarded. Haman is called the next day and asked what should happen to a man the king wants to honor. Thinking the honoree is himself, he plans an elaborate parade with the focus on the one the king seeks to praise. Ahasuerus tells him to do exactly as he has said... to honor MORDECAI!!! At the banquet Esther reveals her Jewish heritage, confronts Haman's plan to destroy her people, and the king orders him hanged on the gallows he built for Mordecai. The word is sent throughout Persia to not slay the Jews on the designated day. Good triumphs over evil.

If you were to ask most of my Bible Study class what my favorite Scripture is, they would tell you, *"For such a time as this..."* This book carries that Scripture as its title. Many of us never fulfill that purpose because we fail to seek God's divine plan. Esther became the Queen of Persia to save her people. Mordecai became a thorn in Haman's side to reveal his character. I became a writer to teach you these truths. We all have a purpose; what is yours?

Father God, for such a time as this, You have chosen me to be Your light in a dark world. Help me to seek to know, know, and know Your purpose for my life. Give me the strength and determination of Esther and Mordecai. Amen.

June 7th Elijah: Fed by Ravens *(1 Kings 17:4)*

"It shall be that you will drink of the brook,
and I have commanded the ravens to provide for you there."

*M*ost of us have a hard time acknowledging that God is our provider and all things come from Him. We believe that our good work, smart thinking, and elbow grease provide for our shelter and housing. God, who knit us together, gave us our ability to work and our ability to think. Contrary to popular teaching, you were created and are not the product of some cosmic explosion! Elijah is a prophet, one who reveals God's words to His children. He finds out in the verse above how God expects us to trust His provision. God tells him to go out of his homeland, to find the Brook of Cherith, and to wait for further word to come to him there. God is protecting Elijah, who has recently told Ahab, the King of Israel, a severe drought is coming on his land. Ahab seeks to "kill the messenger." You see, God has seen Ahab's sin and how he is leading his nation astray. God also tells Elijah not to worry about food; because He has commanded the ravens to feed him! Elijah does exactly as he is commanded. The ravens bring him *"bread and meat in the morning and bread and meat in the evening."* The fresh water of the brook provided all the drinking water Elijah required. God provided for his every need... and then dried up the brook when it was time for Elijah to move on to his next God ordained appointment.

God is our faithful provider. Think about your life. What are some things you know He has provided for you? In my life, He has unquestionably provided five jobs, suitable housing, strength in times of testing, a Christian bookstore and the ability to teach and write. I take nothing for granted; and believe there are no "coincidences" when it comes to the things I listed. What can you learn from Elijah? Step out in faith? Trust God in all circumstances? Go willingly where He leads you? Are you ready to step out in faith? I have and have been absolutely blessed with His goodness and provision. It is so fun to sit back, relax and let Him drive the vehicle of your life.

Father God, You are faithful, just, kind, generous, and eternal. You were there for Elijah and will be there for me. You sent the ravens with bread and meat; and sent me Your Son, the bread of life to meet my every need. Amen.

June 8th   Elijah: the Widow of Zarephath   *(1 Kings 17:12)*

But she said, "As the LORD your God lives, I have no bread, only a handful of flour in the bowl and a little oil in the jar; and behold, I am gathering a few sticks that I may go in and prepare for me and my son that we may eat it and die."

*E*lijah is out of water. The Brook of Cherith has dried up and God is moving His prophet. God's promise is that a widow has been commanded to provide for his needs. Elijah heads to Zarephath and, as he enters the city gate, he sees a widow gathering sticks and asks her for a small jar of water to drink. As she walked away, he asked her if she had a bite of bread for him. The verse above is her response. The sticks she gathers are to start a fire to bake the little flour into bread. After that is gone, she and her son will die from starvation. What must she have thought when Elijah tells her to prepare the bread for him to eat instead! Elijah prophesies God's word to her saying the oil and the flour will never run out until the day He sends rain upon the land. She feeds him, feeds her son, feeds herself… and the bowl never empties. Her son becomes very ill; and the distraught widow is angry with Elijah, thinking he somehow brought this upon her home. He takes the boy to his room, lays him on the bed, and lays himself upon him. Three times he asks the Lord to breathe the breath of life back into the boy. The Scripture tells us the Lord heard the cry of Elijah and returned life to the child. Elijah carries him back downstairs to his mother. She tells the man of God, *"Now I know you are a man of God and that the word of the Lord in your mouth is truth."*

The widow in this story has to come to a place of trust, a place most of us hope to never come to. She has to choose between feeding her child, feeding herself or feeding a stranger. How strong must the

211

draw of the Holy Spirit have been in her life for her to make the sacrifice she made? How we react in times of testing is revealed in how she reacted to her child's illness, blaming Elijah, and thinking he might have caused it. She figured if he was really a "man of God" he could have prevented the illness in the first place. How like us to blame someone—even God—when difficulties come into our lives.

Holy God, I doubt that I would have offered the last bit of food to Elijah. I am too self-absorbed to think good could come of such a sacrifice. Help me to have a wise and discerning spirit so I will hear Your voice when something like this happens in my life. Give me the generous spirit of this widow. Amen.

June 9th   Elijah: Meeting with Obadiah   *(1 Kings 18:9)*

He said, "What sin have I committed, that you are giving your servant into the hand of Ahab to put me to death?"

$\mathcal{E}$ lijah, like most of the other prophets of God, has been moved out of Israel. Jezebel, wife of King Ahab, has previously ordered all prophets killed for the words they have spoken against her evil ways and idol worship. Elijah returns to Samaria and encounters Obadiah, a servant of the king. Obadiah recognizes Elijah immediately as God's prophet and falls at his feet in reverence. Elijah tells him to go to King Ahab and tell him, "Elijah is here." Obadiah would rather do anything than fulfill that request. When Jezebel commanded the killing of the prophets, Obadiah hid one hundred of them in caves. Now he is being sent to tell the king the most despised of all God's prophets wants to meet him face to face. The above verse shows exactly how Obadiah feels. Elijah gives him his word that he will not flee and will meet with the king. Obadiah does as told with great fear. Ahab greets Elijah with, *"Is this you, you troubler of Israel?"* Elijah refutes his words by telling him Ahab himself is the one who has caused great trouble in Israel by leading his people away from the Laws of God. Ahab will answer for that and for worshipping the idol Baal along with his wife. Obadiah's life is spared because of his obedience.

Elijah is a brave man to come before the king who is waiting for the chance to kill him. We can understand Ahab's hatred for the prophet. None of us would want to have someone tell us what the consequences of our actions will be. Obadiah likely wonders if it was worth it to hide the 100 prophets, cover his tracks, and then be sent to the king to announce the arrival of his enemy. How would you like to be in this situation? Think of a time when you had to tell someone the things they were doing were wrong. Did they like it? Were they angry for your intervention? Now you know how Obadiah felt!

Jehovah God, I can feel Obadiah's fear as I read this story. I wouldn't want to do what he was asked. On the other hand, Elijah's obedience proved that God was still in control; and Obadiah's faithfulness was to be rewarded. Help me be brave and bold as I confront people with the truths You give to me regarding the things in their lives. Amen.

June 10th <u>Elijah: Prophets of Baal</u> *(1 Kings 18:24)*

"Then you can call on the name of your god, and I will call on the name of the Lord, and the God who answers by fire, He is God."

This is my favorite Elijah story and I think you will enjoy it, too. Elijah tells King Ahab to gather nine hundred and fifty of the prophets of the gods he and Jezebel worship and to meet him at Mount Carmel. Elijah tells the people it is time for them to make a decision about which God is really worth serving and reminds them they cannot serve two gods. He calls for two oxen to be pieced and placed over wood. The prophets of Baal and Asherah are called upon to pray for their god to light the fire under the ox. They called and called for fire... and nothing happened. Elijah mocks them and says maybe their god is gone away on a journey or is napping and doesn't hear them. They started to call out again... no response. The false prophets began to cut their skin with swords and lances until blood gushed out! This went on until evening with no response from their gods. Elijah calls the people near, and takes twelve stones for each of the twelve tribes of Israel. A trench is dug around the base of the altar, wood is placed over it, and the second ox is laid upon it. He then has them fill the trench with water, soak the wood, and soak the altar. Three times he has this done. He calls upon the God of Israel speaking aloud so that all may hear him tell God today the people shall know He alone is God. God sent the fire raining down from Heaven and the fire destroys the wet wood; the oxen are burned; and the water in the trench evaporates! The people fall on their faces in fear of the Lord.

Don't you love it! In a world where false prophets are every-where—on television, in our movies, and even in our churches—God still reigns! The false prophets could cut themselves to bits; their stone idols could do nothing to bring fire to the dry wood. Why? They are of no value or ability. They are worth no more than the material they are made of. Elijah's God is the living God of Israel and could do anything he asked. After the fire came down, all of the false prophets were slain. Unfortunately, there are always more where they came from.

Oh, Father God in Heaven, You are all I need. False gods and false prophets have no part in my life. You alone created me, gave me life, and guide my paths. You will prove Yourself faithful to those who are faithful to You. Your word cautions against false prophets; keep me ever mindful of the difference between Your prophets and them. Amen.

June 11th <u>Trap of the Evil Man</u> *(John 18:25)*

He who leads the upright astray in an evil way will
himself fall into his own pit, but the blameless will inherit good.

*W*hy does it seem that people who act in ungodly ways get ahead further and faster than those of us who walk in obedience to the Lord? Why do CEO's of huge companies succeed in stealing from the people who provide for their huge salaries? This doesn't seem fair to us, but we must remember every thought, word and deed will be accounted for at judgment day. Jeroboam, the first king of northern Israel after the nation divided, is a perfect example of someone who did everything contrary to God, seemed to succeed and reap the benefits, but left a horrible legacy. Repeatedly throughout the Old Testament books of Kings and Chronicles, we find the memory of Jeroboam and his leadership impact. 2 Kings 15:9 reads, *"He did evil in the sight of the LORD, as his fathers had done; he did not depart from the sins of <u>Jeroboam</u> the son of Nebat, which he made Israel to sin."* What a legacy! The people, without proper leadership, were easily led away from the ways of God and into a life of sin. Jeroboam led them astray and the terrible references still blemish his name thousands of years later. Our actions do have an impact on our lives, our peers, and our placement for all of eternity. One other truth on the apparent success of unethical people comes to my mind. These people have to be looking constantly over their shoulder, waiting for their dealings to be revealed. Remember always that what is done in darkness will be revealed in light. The evil man will fall into the pit he digs for himself.

Do you ever feel like you are beating your head against the proverbial wall to make a business succeed? Do your co-workers avoid their work yet get all the praise? Do you serve others, pay your tithes, and struggle to make ends meet, while others serve no one but themselves and have money for fancy toys, vacations, and luxuries? Remember the legacy you are leaving for your peers to see. Remember, the Lord knows who is honoring Him. Remember, your reward is in Heaven where thieves cannot steal it. Trust Him with your faithfulness; for He is always faithful.

Father God, I confess that I have been envious of others who seem to have great success in spite of less than ethical practices. I want Your approval more than I want to gain anything in a way which would shine a bad light on Your name. I know where my reward is... and it may never be here on this earth. Amen.

June 12th   Hardened to God's Reproach   *(Proverbs 29:1)*

*A man who hardens his neck after much reproof
will suddenly be broken beyond remedy.*

*H*ave you ever met someone with a hardened heart to the things of faith? Their heart is hard because of bad childhood memories from a church situation or emotional injury from an adult faith confrontation. Some simply believe all Christians to be hypocrites, which is the best excuse around to not participate in the work of the kingdom. People like this sap the strength out of our witness, don't they? I was one of them! Yes, fifteen years ago I wanted nothing to do with Jesus. I believed in God; and would have told you I was a Christian if you had asked me. I just didn't want to "get religious." I had no idea of the difference between religion and faith. There is a huge difference! I had the hardened neck mentioned in the verse above. I hated conviction and was much convicted of the sin in my life. I just wasn't sorry enough to do something about it. The verse also says the hard necked one will suddenly be *broken beyond remedy.* Now that is a scary thought! What does someone *broken beyond remedy* look like? I looked like everyone else in the world. I looked busy. I looked happy. I looked well fed. I looked like I didn't have a care in the world. But the way I looked and the way I really was were two different things. I was empty. I was spiritually bankrupt. I wanted unconditional love. I wanted help with the burdens in my life. I wanted meaning beyond my next leather purse.

216

Could God soften my stiff neck and my hard heart enough to make a difference?

There are stiff-necked and hard hearted people all around us? You may be one yourself! You may have decided to allow "religion" to seep into the cracks. What you need is "relationship" instead. Your smooth veneer can fool some people, maybe most people; but God sees through that veneer. He is looking at your hard heart. He is rubbing your stiff neck and waiting for you to drop the wall of defenses you have built. Let the fortified walls around your heart be broken. He can change it all; but you must trust Him to do it.

Father God, I know people who need You in their lives. I need more of You in mine. Please show me through the power of the Holy Spirit how to break these walls. Help me not to judge others who have their hearts hardened. They are hurting and afraid of what relinquishing control might mean. Amen.

June 13ᵗʰ <u>Worship in Truth</u> *(John 4:23-24)*

But an hour is coming, and now is, when the true worshipers will worship the Father in spirit and truth; for such people the Father seeks to be His worshipers. "God is spirit and those who worship Him must worship in spirit and truth."

I have always wanted to know more about the role of the Holy Spirit in the life of Christians. More traditional denominations don't emphasize the Spirit like the Pentecostal or Charismatic churches do. As I began to search the Scriptures, I found the above verse…and it completely caught my attention. Let's break it down and study it further. *"But an hour is coming, and now is…"* makes us realize that there truly is a coming day when we will stand before the throne of God and worship Him for who He is and His Son for the picture of holiness He gave us in His walk upon this earth. Look closer... the verse says the hour or day *now is.* Today is the day we are to worship God... not some ambiguous day in the far distant future! Let's read further, *"true worshipers will worship the Father in spirit and truth; for such people the Father seeks to be His worshipers."* We are to worship in *spirit and truth,* but what does that mean? God seeks those who will fully worship Him. These worshippers aren't worried about the people around them, the quality of the music, or the choice of songs. They commune with the One who gave them life itself! This should make you excited! God is telling you to let loose and really abandon restraints...

When we see someone worship this way; we have one of two reactions. The first is to think they have stepped over the line between dignity and lunacy. We are suspicious to know if their worship is contrived or real. We don't understand the freedom of that kind of soul baring transparency. We are called to be dignified and respectful in our worship; but He wants our worship—not our religion! The second reaction we might have to abandoned worship is a hunger in our hearts to know that kind of relationship. Think about this... when you walk into the room where a favorite child is, do you want them to come to you like a little soldier or with running excited abandon, wrapping their arms around your legs, and not wanting to let go? We are that child... God is that adult; and He wants that passion from us!

I want to worship like this. I confess that I have hindrances and even fears which keep me from that abandon. Please join my spirit with Your Holy Spirit, that He might teach me how to release the strongholds, which are holding me back. You are my Abba (Daddy) Father, and I want to run into Your Presence. Amen.

June 14th   He First Loved Us   *(1 John 4:19)*

We love, because He first loved us.

*H*ow is your love walk? Do you love easily, without reservation, and hesitation? How does your love walk compare with the example of Jesus' love as He walked the earth during His three year ministry? Jesus put His needs aside in order to serve those He loved more than life itself. Few of us could honestly say the same. We love our families, our church families, our co-workers, and our neighbors. We especially love those who love us. Jesus teaches us that we are to go the extra mile and love those who hate us, persecute us, and blaspheme our names! OUCH! Now, how is your love walk? Some people just rub us the wrong way. They make us uncomfortable or uneasy. They find fault with everything we do. They are unlovable! None of these truths give us the freedom to not love them! We are told to *love, because He first loved us.* Do you think Jesus wanted to share the last supper and the first holy communion with Judas Iscariot, who would betray Him just hours later? Do you think He wanted to not address the adultery of the woman cast at His feet by the Jewish leaders? Do you think Jesus didn't know how Zacchaeus, the turncoat tax collector, was hurting His people? Jesus knew all about these people and their sins; but that did not stop Him from loving them. This is one example of how Jesus' teachings revolutionized the world.

Let me ask you again, how is your love walk? Would you have shared that meal with Judas? Most of us cannot even sit at a family event with family members we don't like. How would you look at the woman caught in the act of adultery? How do you act around people who live lifestyles contrary to yours? Do you judge them and condemn them to the "beyond help" file? What about Zacchaeus? Do you judge those who cheat, steal, and betray their own people? We are to <u>always</u> judge sin. However, we are to <u>never</u> judge the sinner. Hard truths aren't they? Those sins will be judged by the only One qualified to judge them. Our job is to simply walk in love.

Lord, I confess that my love walk has not been what You command. I have been judgmental, critical, and self-serving. I seem to have forgotten that I do not deserve the love You give me. I need Your help in this area of my faith walk. Help me love as You loved and to strive daily to love even those whom I deem unlovable. Amen.

June 15th <u>Thank You, Lord</u> *(Jude 1:24)*

Now to Him who is able to keep you from stumbling and to make you stand in the presence of His glory blameless with great joy...

*W*hy did I spend the beginning of my life doing inappropriate things with my words, thoughts, and actions? I felt the deep need to seek someone to love me. A journal entry from January 2006 includes this prayer of thanks: "Thank You, Father, for cleansing me from the vulgarity which poured from my lips like Scripture does today. I believe part of the reason I did that was due to my seeking love. I spoke vulgarity in nearly every sentence for many years. Thank You, Father, for cleansing me from my overflowing pride. I confess that I still deal with this issue, but I am learning to walk in more humility. I am a work in progress and will still need Your reminders from time to time, especially when the store becomes a success. Help me to keep my eyes on Jesus, my heart in tune to the Holy Spirit, and help me realize that all I have comes from You." Simple, heartfelt thanks, from a heart of great gratitude.

Are you good at saying "thank you" to those who bring blessings to your life? I think it is a lost art in the impersonal society we live in today. Words of thanks really cost us very little, so why are they so hard to speak? Maybe knowing where I came from makes me quicker to praise and thank God. There is a Bible story where someone who owes a little is given mercy. Then, someone who owes a lot also has debt forgiven. The one forgiven little is selfish in forgiving those who owe money to him. The one who is forgiven much loves much. That love translates to forgiving others. I am that one...much forgiven! I could spend all day, every day, saying thanks for all I have been forgiven. The reason most of us fail to walk in full gratitude is because we think we aren't bad enough to need grace. We need to make a better effort toward being grateful. Let us look deeply at the gratitude we must carry in our hearts toward Christ and His sacrifice for us.

———————————

Lord, I know that I have failed to say "thank You" for all You have done in my life. Father, please forgive this shortcoming and renew my relationship to right standing. Thank You for life itself. Amen.

June 16ᵗʰ   I Called; He Heard   *(2 Samuel 22:7)*

In my distress I called upon the LORD, Yes, I cried to my God; and from His temple He heard my voice and my cry for help came into His ears.

*D*o you remember the first time you called out to God during a time of need or suffering in your life? Did you feel His presence? Did He answer the cry? The Bible is full of characters that called upon the Name of God and heard His response. One of my favorite Bible stories is of King Hezekiah of Judah in Chapter 20 of 2 Kings. Hezekiah, who is critically ill, receives a word from God, sent through the prophet Isaiah; telling him to get his affairs in order for he is going to die. Hezekiah lies upon his bed facing the wall and cries out with tears and words reminding God of how he has faithfully served Him and led Judah righteously throughout his reign. Before Isaiah has even left the King's palace the word of God tells him to return to Hezekiah and say, *Thus says the LORD, the God of your father David, "I have heard your prayer, I have seen your tears; behold, I will heal you. On the third day you shall go up to the house of the LORD."* He continues by telling the king he will live for fifteen more years, and God will use Hezekiah to defend Jerusalem from the King of Assyria. A poultice is placed upon Hezekiah's boil and healing comes. Hezekiah, instead of fully trusting God's word through Isaiah, asks for a sign that indeed his life will be extended. He requests that the shadow on the sundial move back ten steps. He knows that the clock will always advance in hours... and needs to clearly see God's promise. The shadow moves back and Hezekiah lives an additional fifteen years.

Hezekiah called out and had an almost immediate response. Why doesn't it always work that way? Why didn't my prayers work when Dan was losing his job along with over twenty-six years of seniority? Why doesn't it work every time we pray for health or recovery? Why doesn't it work when we pray over prodigal children? I cannot explain these things to you. I only know this: prayers contrary to God's will not be honored by a holy God. How would I ever have known that Dan's job loss would lead to us becoming Christians? How would I know that his job loss would lead us on the path we have walked for twelve years... a path which led me to write this book to help you grow your faith? God is awesome!

Oh, Father God, how I wish my prayers were always in line with the plans You have made for my life? In hindsight, some of the best things of my life have happened when You didn't answer my prayers. The disappointments have long since turned to blessings. I will learn to trust that You always know what is best for me and for my future. Amen.

June 17th Judas Iscariot: Betrayer *(Luke 22:3-4)*

Satan entered into Judas who was called Iscariot, belonging to the number of the twelve. And he went away and discussed with the chief priests and officers how he might betray Him to them.

Today, we look at Judas Iscariot and the events of his walk with Jesus as one of His twelve closest friends. Scripture doesn't reveal nuggets of Judas' childhood where we might capture a glimpse of the decisions he made in his short adult life. We aren't told of how he was called into Jesus' circle or how he fit in among them. We do know from small references that Judas was the treasurer for Jesus and His followers...and that he was stealing from the money bag. He accused the woman who anointed Jesus' head and feet with costly oil of wasting the money which could have been used to feed the poor. Somehow, we are left with the impression that Judas himself was the poor one not being fed! Maybe the best glimpse we get of Judas' character is his visit to those who despised Jesus and his disclosure of his Master's location for the price of a common household slave. Judas, like many of the other apostles, wanted Jesus to be a great military leader or a mighty insurrectionist who would overthrow the government system. Maybe he thought this would cause Jesus to make a bold first move toward that eventuality. Whatever the reason, Judas betrayed Jesus. Just hours after sharing the "bread and body of Christ" during the last supper, Judas kissed Jesus on the cheek—a prearranged signal for Jewish officials to arrest Him—and betrayed the best friend he had ever known.

We can accept foolishness like Samson's or being doubtful like Thomas, but we cannot understand betrayal—especially betrayal leading to the death of Jesus. Judas opened himself up to the enemy of his soul through his fleshly desires. Judas had a choice to betray Jesus or not. Yes, it did set into motion the events leading to our salvation. It was part of God's plan; still, Judas made the decision to betray. The burden of that betrayal was so heavy Judas hung himself. The tragedy of his story is that JESUS WOULD HAVE FORGIVEN HIS BETRAYAL HAD HE ONLY ASKED!

Jesus, my betrayals may not seem as severe as Judas' were, but my sins, just like his, sent You to Calvary. It is easy for me to judge him without ever looking into the mirror and seeing my own sin revealed. You surely would have forgiven him and restored him to good standing had he only asked. Judas didn't have to die separated from You. Thank You, Lord Jesus that I received forgiveness before something led to my death. Amen.

June 18th   Job Doors: Home Interiors   *(Proverbs 3:5-6)*

Trust in the LORD with all your heart *and do not lean on your own understanding. In all your ways acknowledge Him, and He will make your paths straight.*

*T*his entry, as well as the next three, is part of my testimony of how God directs our paths and leads us down roads we never thought to travel. My hope is that you will see God's provision for my job needs and realize that He cares for your needs just as He does mine. This story begins approximately 14 years ago, long before I accepted Christ as my personal Lord and Savior. As I shared lunch with a group of local business women, who had been volunteers for my previous job, I told them that I was leaving my position. They asked what I was going to do. A voice spoke out saying, "I am going to sell Home Interiors." I remember turning around to see who had spoken these words, only to find several women looking at me. I realized I had spoken them! Where did those words come from? I hadn't given any thought to that kind of work. My first instinct was to rescind the words and tell them I had no idea where the idea had come from. Two of the women volunteered to host home shows for me. I found myself agreeing—and I hadn't even contacted the company to see what working for them entailed! Years before, I had a Home Interiors representative who was Christian; and I didn't like her because she was "churchy." I left the luncheon with the thought that if she still was in the phonebook I would call her. If not, the whole thing was a fluke. Unfortunately for me (or so I thought), her name was in there. She remembered me, and when I jokingly told her what had happened, she said she would be to my house in thirty minutes. I was being SO set up by God! I had no idea Home Interiors was a <u>Christian</u> company, founded by a wonderful <u>Christian</u> woman, and was currently being run by her wonderful <u>Christian</u> heirs! I had no idea my unit manager would be a <u>Christian,</u> that most of the displayers in my unit would be <u>Christians,</u> and that my branch manager would be a fine <u>Christian</u> woman. I hope by now you can see how God was setting me up for a fall...a fall into the loving arms of Jesus.

I continued to fight the "threat" of Christianity in my life. I was terrified of what I would have to give up. Little did I know that the woman I called that day to inquire about this company had prayed for my salvation every time she left my house years and years before this encounter. God is **awesome**!

Jesus, how can I ever doubt Your provision in my life? Amen.

June 19th <u>Job Doors: The Home Furnishings Store</u>
(Proverbs 3:5-6)

*Trust in the LORD with all your heart and **do not lean on your own understanding.** In all your ways acknowledge Him, and He will make your paths straight.*

I loved my job with Home Interiors, but being gone at night was wearing on me. Dan and I agreed that I needed to find something closer to home. Shortly we found out Dan was losing his job of 26 years. Here was my husband devastated by job loss; and all I could think about was that I wanted a new sofa! Upon our return from a few days with my parents, we found a local furniture store flyer promoting a Spring Sofa Sale! Our friends who owned the store were very busy; and by the time the female owner got to us I had selected a sofa and found fabric swatches for two coordinating chairs. She asked who helped me; and I said she was busy so I helped myself! She said, "We need your services. Are you looking for a job?" We left that day with new furniture ordered, with old friends revisited, and with a whole new job to begin the following week. Little did we know that these friends would have a profound impact on our lives. The owner had been my Mary Kay consultant years before when I was a single mother and living a very ungodly lifestyle. She was forever inviting me to Christian Women's functions, which I would act interested in and then never attend. The last thing I wanted to be was a "holy roller" like her. I figured that I could do this job without being **preached at**. I found out that the name "The Carpenter's Corner" was because the

Carpenter of life had provided for this business after the male owner had lost a job in Ohio. I figured wrong. I didn't get **preached at** but witnessed to by people who lived their faith openly and conducted their business according to Christian principles. One Saturday they invited us to go with them to church the next day. I was preparing my well rehearsed decline when Dan said, "Yes, we could go with you." I turned and looked at him like he had grown two more heads! We had been avoiding church attendance throughout our married life. He must have lost his mind! We agreed to meet them at the church for the regular service the next morning.

That visit led to a twelve year love affair with my Lord Jesus. On February 14, 1996, I gave my heart to Christ and have had a burning hunger for the Word of God... isn't He **unbelievable**?

Jesus, how awesome are Your ways and the power of Your direction! Thank You for using others to lead me home to You. Amen.

June 20ᵗʰ Job Doors: The Bookstore *(Proverbs 3:5-6)*

*Trust in the LORD with all your heart and do not lean on your own understanding. **In all your ways acknowledge Him, and He will make your paths straight.***

After five years at the Carpenter's Corner, I began to develop problems from being on my feet for long days. I left the store, enjoyed a quiet Christmas, and took a part-time job at a downtown sandwich shop. I soon realized my heart wasn't at that job. I missed the ministry I had for the previous five years. Curiosity has always been one of my weak spots, and curiosity about what was happening at the local Christian bookstore was keeping me awake nights. I went to talk to the owner about the price and what the sale included. She told me I was too late because she had just signed a purchase agreement with local buyers. She asked if I would be willing to work for the new owners. I left her with my name and address and she said she would pass it on to them. Later that evening, I received a call from a former customer from the furniture store who told me that she and her husband were buying the bookstore. God never fails to amaze me with His imaginative and inventive ways of entwining people in my past and using them to re-invent my future! I agreed to interview — and spent the night praying that this would be a match that the Lord would use in mighty ways in His service to the Owosso communities spiritual needs. I was hired the next day for a higher wage than I had requested. I knew, without a doubt, that this was God's plan for my life. I rolled up my sleeves, put on my imagination cap, and set out to prove my worth to my employers and to my Lord. The next eighteen months were the most fulfilling and exhausting of my life. I learned that there is no such thing as a "routine day" in a small customer focused Christian bookstore. I found one real truth: the greatest gift that you can offer to another human being is a listening ear.

The ministry opportunities at the bookstore are a whole book unto themselves. Can't you just picture God looking down from Heaven, waving His finger to open these job doors? Do you understand more clearly why I trust Him to direct my paths? My God is a "**supernatural**" God!

Jesus, how could anyone doubt after hearing this testimony? You are absolutely, unconditionally, and ultimately the most awesome God! Amen.

June 21ˢᵗ <u>Job Doors: Northside Realty</u> *(Proverbs 3:5-6)*

*Trust in the LORD with all your heart and do not lean on your own understanding. In all your ways acknowledge Him, and **He will make your paths straight.***

*E*ighteen months later, I faced a difficult job market for someone my age and with a less than svelte figure! One day while painting, I listened to a T.V. evangelist speak on the fact that God doesn't answer prayers—rather He answers the faith that brings the prayers to Him. I was rolling the paint on the walls as the tears rolled down my cheeks, and I talked to God. I told Him I was stepping out in faith and trusting Him to show me what to do. I also informed Him that I was going to go the next day and make a deposit on nail schooling unless He showed me a reason not to. I'm sure that He chuckled as I told Him I had a deadline. **Twenty minutes later the telephone rang**. A voice from my past, Roger Snyder, a family friend was on the line. He said he didn't know if I would ever consider leaving my job at the bookstore, but that he and his wife, Bonnie, would love to have me come to work for them in their new real estate office. I was so quiet that he must have thought I had hung up on him. Actually I was thanking the Lord for at least making me feel worthwhile again. Dan and I talked about the job and discussed what I would need for wages. I figured that a brand new business probably didn't even have a typewriter, let alone a computer, or fax machine. All of this was great for me because I knew absolutely NOTHING about being a secretary! I was trying not to get my hopes too high because when they saw my secretarial skills they would laugh me out of the building! I walked in the door and there were three private offices, a huge secretarial workspace, a computer, and yes (oh, no), a fax machine! They showed me around and talked to me like I already had the job. We talked honestly about the fact that I knew nothing about the skills needed to manage an office. When the interview turned to wages, Bonnie told me she hated to talk money, but offered me—**to the exact penny**—what Dan and I had discussed. I hesitated, thanked God again, and accepted the job. I have been at Northside Realty for over five years now. Thankfully, God let Roger remember my work ethic as a teenager; which led to a job 25 years later! My God is a **Faithful** God!

Jesus, how could anyone doubt that You are Lord of the details?
Amen.

June 22ⁿᵈ **Mary Magdalene: Healed** *(Mark 16:9)*

... He first appeared to Mary Magdalene,
from whom He had cast out seven demons.

Mary Magdalene is a character with so many layers and who was used powerfully in the Gospel accounts. She knew the absolute power of Jesus to transform souls...that is why I love to become Mary's character in live drama. I read between the few lines of Scripture regarding her, put myself in her shoes and bring her passion and story to life. Mary was born in Magdala, a Galilean trading center known as a corrupt city because it was a slave and sinful merchandise trade hub. Knowing her birth place helps us to understand in part why she was looking for a life changing message. When I portray Mary, I have her hearing of this new teacher (Jesus) who is talking of grace, love, and release from sins. She is afraid to meet Him, but is inexplicably drawn to seek Him out. Mary listens from a distance, knowing full well that the people with Jesus will condemn her for her life choices. I have Mary turning to leave as the day draws to a close only to feel a magnetic drawing, which causes her to turn back toward Christ... and to see Him looking directly at her. I talk of Peter, the impulsive apostle, trying to stop Jesus from talking to her "because of the sort of woman she is." Jesus doesn't care about her past, but walks directly toward her to give her a future. After they meet one another, I have Jesus invite her to meet His mother—who in turn asks her to work with her to prepare meals. I picture Mary as she pours out her heart to Jesus, telling Him of the demons which haunt her. We have no idea what her demons were; but they don't really matter because we all have our own, don't we? Mary's redemption at the hand of Jesus reveals why she would later stand at His trial, His crucifixion, and be the first to know of His resurrection.

What do you have in common with Mary Magdalene? What are your personal "demons?" Divorce, unconfessed sin, child molestation, unforgiveness or abortion... none of them matter to Jesus. He longs to remove the bondage these "demons" hold over you. Mary knew people would judge her, yet she was drawn to seek Jesus. Have you felt the same pulling at your spirit? There is nothing too big for His grace to cover.

———————————

Lord Jesus, I know that I carry my own hidden "demons," and they keep me from opening my heart fully to You. Mary's story gives me hope for a new start. Please show me where that new hope begins and how I can break the shackles of my past to begin anew. Amen.

June 23rd   Mary Magdalene: Vicki's Interpretation
(John 19:25)

…But standing by the cross of Jesus were His mother, and His mother's sister, Mary the wife of Clopas, and Mary Magdalene.

*I*n my character portrayal of Mary Magdalene, I keep the relationship between her and Peter somewhat tumultuous and difficult. Peter, being another of my favorite characters, is rash and impulsive. I can just picture him being distrustful of Mary's conversion. I also picture Mary, who has been used and abused her whole life, reacting to his macho garbage in a less than apologetic way. However, they have a common friend in Jesus and a common mission to share the Gospel. She has watched the deaf ears opened, the blind eyes uncovered, and the lame as they take their first steps. She has watched Jesus forgive an adulterous woman, restore life to a widow's child, and call out Zacchaeus, a traitor to the Jewish people, asking for food, and lodging at his house. She watched the Jewish leaders try to trap Him, the rich young ruler refuse to give up his wealth, and His own brothers act like He was insane. Mary Magdalene has seen it all! She is sold out to serve Him as Lord. That is why, when all the others scatter during Jesus' arrest and trial, she is there. I portray her as running through the crowd of people who are shouting for Him to be crucified. She is looking for His closest friends… "Where are they? Surely they couldn't have abandoned Him at this time when He needs them so badly!!" Mary is frantic, "This cannot be happening," she cries. Suddenly she sees Peter off in the distance. She runs to ask him to help Jesus... just in time to hear him deny ever knowing Him! Mary runs to the officials shouting, "Ask me. Ask me. I will tell you about this Man! I will never deny Him; because He didn't deny me!" Mary is inconsolable as she watches the One who gave her life led away to be crucified. What she wouldn't give to have one more chance to sit at His feet.

Can you feel Mary's anger and frustration? Can you imagine what Jesus felt? His closest friends have betrayed Him, abandoned Him, and denied knowing Him. Think how He feels when we don't speak up to defend His name when it is being blasphemed. Think of how He feels when we don't give of our time to get to know Him more intimately! Are you more like the fleeing apostles, or the Christ focused Mary?

Jesus, I have let You down as surely as Your apostles did. I have failed to tell others of Your life changing part in my life. I have not fought for the things of God because I have bowed to political correctness. Give me Mary's kind of boldness. Amen.

June 24th Mary Magdalene: First to see Jesus *(John 20:1)*

*Now on the first day of the week Mary Magdalene came
early to the tomb, while it was still dark, and saw
the stone already taken away from the tomb.*

Mary followed Jesus as He carried His cross on the road to Golgotha's hill. She wanted to give Him a drink, wipe the blood from his brow—even try to help Him carry His burden. With each step, her anger grows. "Why is this happening? Why do they hate Him so?" The questions never stop, and neither do her frustrations with Jesus' friends. Mary, His mother, doesn't deserve to feel the anguish, which is apparent on her face as she watches the spikes pounded into the wrists and feet of her beloved Son. The women watch in horror as Jesus hangs between Heaven and earth, between life and death, between earthly mother and Heavenly Father. Mary Magdalene sees what she has always seen—Jesus putting the needs of others before His own. He fights for every breath, yet asks John His beloved friend to care for His mother. He asks her to care for John knowing she will need a new purpose. Jesus breathes His last breath as Mary's hope dies on that cross. Because it is nearing time for the Sabbath rest, Jesus is wrapped in temporary grave clothes and sealed into a borrowed tomb. That night, Mary Magdalene relives every painful moment. On the morning after the Sabbath, she goes to the tomb to prepare Jesus' body with herbs and proper grave clothes; but the stone is rolled away! Jesus is gone! "They must have stolen His body! I must find Him… I owe Him this last act of service…" Mary is so grieved she runs out of the tomb and smack into the chest of the gardener! She beats on his chest shouting, "Where is He? Where is His body? Help me to find Him… I owe Him my very life!" The gardener speaks her name, "Shhhh, don't cry Mary." She recognizes the way He says her name! Suddenly she realizes it is Him… it is Jesus… He's alive! She grabs Him afraid to let go lest He leave her again. He chuckles, "Mary, I can't breathe! Don't hold too tightly to Me in this flesh. Go, Mary, and tell the others… I am alive!"

This is obviously my interpretation of what happened at the cross and at the opened tomb. She watched it all. She stayed when everyone else fled and was rewarded for her faithfulness. Mary was the first one to carry the full Gospel of Jesus' resurrection to the world.

Jesus, may I carry Your Gospel as passionately and thankfully as Mary. May I realize exactly what my redemption cost You. May Your Holy Spirit remind me of this message whenever I begin to take my faith for granted. Amen.

June 25th <u>Solomon: Give Me Wisdom</u> *(1 Kings 3:9)*

*"So give Your servant an understanding heart to judge
Your people to discern between good and evil. For who
is able to judge this great people of Yours?"*

*T*oday, we begin a study on the life of Solomon, King of Israel—reputedly the wisest man who ever lived. Solomon is the son of King David. He has inherited the kingdom of his father who was at war during his entire reign. God has promised Solomon peace in his lifetime as long as he walks in God's righteous way. The verse at the top of the page is Solomon's response to a question posed by God. He has been given the choice of great riches, long life, many heirs, or a powerful and influential kingdom. Solomon chooses godly wisdom instead of all the other offerings. Solomon knows that with real wisdom he will be the best king possible in a nation ravaged by war. God promises he will not only have great wisdom but all the things he did not choose. Wisdom, unless put into action, is useless. Wisdom guides and directs us, but does not necessarily keep us from sin. Solomon put his wisdom to work and had a blessed time of growth and abundance. Israel, under his wise direction, lived in peace and safety without threat from the enemies who had fought against his father. Riches increased as did military power. Scripture tells us Solomon's wisdom surpassed the wisdom of all the sons of the east. In his lifetime he spoke 3,000 proverbs (short teachings of wisdom) and wrote over 1,000 songs! Leaders came from all over the nations to hear the wisdom of God's wise king.

What would have been your response to God's question of your greatest wish? Be honest? The humble answer of godly wisdom sounds great, but would you really not choose riches or long life? Solomon was wise enough to know that leadership required insight, character, and integrity. Money can destroy all three! I have seen a lot of rich fools! I have seen poor (by the world's standard) people who are extremely wise and are used mightily in the kingdom of God. Which would you choose to emulate?

233

Father God, I want to seek that which You most want me to be and to have. I am tempted by riches, covetous of long life and crave popularity. I need to think of what I want my legacy to be. "A wise Christian who influenced lives in a positive way" would be a great epitaph on a cemetery monument. It would be much better than "she had great wealth and lousy integrity." Help me to always choose Your will as my own. Amen.

June 26th   Solomon: A Slow Drift from Grace   *(1 Kings 3:1)*

Then Solomon formed a marriage alliance with Pharaoh king of Egypt, and took Pharaoh's daughter and brought her to the city of David until he had finished building his own house and the house of the Lord and the wall around Jerusalem.

*A*ll of the wisdom in the world cannot keep us from being "common sense stupid!" Solomon, by marrying an Egyptian princess, has broken one of God's commands for His people not to intermarry with the nations around them. Why would God command this? Because keeping the bloodline of Israel is vital to the eventual birth of the promised Messiah. Another truth is that unequally yoked marriages rarely succeed. In the entry for April 25th, I elaborated on why unequal yoking causes a dilution of commitment to God. Solomon built altars for his wife to worship foreign gods. That started a complete drift away from the truths of Solomon's wisdom. In Chapter Eleven, we find that Solomon has seven hundred wives, three hundred concubines (mistresses), and a heart turned away to worship the gods of these women. Solomon, the man with more godly wisdom than any man before or since, has turned away from God to worship at the altar of the flesh. All the good things he did were overshadowed by his drift away. He built and dedicated the temple of God… the first permanent house of worship since Israel arrived years before in the promised land. He carried the Ark Of The Covenant containing Moses' staff, a sampling of the manna from Heaven, and the stone tablets of the ten commandments. He did all of these things right; but the most important thing was forsaken.

Solomon's fall away from faith began as a slow drift. He didn't wake up one day and decide to disobey God. It started with an unholy marriage alliance, which seemed relatively harmless. Soon he was marrying women from all the surrounding nations. The worship of their gods likely seemed harmless at first... just a little compromise. Isn't that how our drift begins? Skipping a few church services, not paying our tithes, avoiding Bible reading, using a few cuss words, slipping back into our former lifestyles... that is how drift happens; and it always separates us from God's grace.

Abba Father, may I come to You in heartfelt sorrow for the things I have done which have caused me to drift from You. I have tried to walk by my own wisdom... and have paid the price for doing so. Receive me, reconnect with me, and restore me to Your good grace. Amen.

June 27th <u>Solomon: Consequence of Sin</u> *(1 Kings 11:11)*

So the Lord said to Solomon, "Because you have done this;
and you have not kept My covenant and My statutes, which
I have commanded you, I will surely tear the kingdom from you,
and will give it to your servant."

*W*hen will we learn that sin always has consequences? Sometimes the repercussions are immediate and the price of sin is quickly paid. Other times the consequences are so long reaching they affect others for years or even generations to come. Read the passage above again. Can you realize how angry God is to tell Solomon the kingdom promised to his ancestors hundreds of years before is to be snatched out of the hands of his heir? Solomon's son,

Rehoboam, follows him as King over the nation of Israel. Reho is a foolish young man who seeks advice from wise elders, which he disregards. He then seeks guidance from young men, spoiled rich children like him, who tell him to treat his people even worse than his father did. Great advice, if you don't want your populace to respect your leadership! Through all of this a young man—a former servant of Solomon—is raised up as a leader of the people. His name is Jeroboam, and he says all the right things to get the loyalty of northern Israel. The people, having no voice in the way they will be treated, return to their homes, and sever loyalty with Rehoboam. The former glorious kingdom of David and Solomon divides into two differing factions with separate governments. Rehoboam retains control of southern Israel (home of the tribes of Judah and Benjamin), which becomes known as Judah. Jeroboam becomes the King of Samaria, northern Israel and the remaining tribes of that nation.

Have you ever done what Rehoboam did? Have you received sound advice from someone you can trust, only to follow foolish advice from someone else? Most of us will seek to go to someone who will agree with us, "tickle our ears"; rather than with someone who might challenge our bad ideas. Follow through with these hard consequences had to cost God a lot. His plan to give His chosen people a land where they could be safe has been destroyed by their disobedience. Our sin always causes God pain.

Father, I need to admit to You that I have sought "ear tickling" advice from others, rather than Scriptural advice from Your word and Your Holy Spirit. Sometimes I am afraid You will advise me to do things I would rather not do...like obey...or forgive...or give...or apologize. Help me to seek Your direction, not that of those who don't have my best interest at heart. Amen.

June 28ᵗʰ G.P.S.: Joshua and Jonah *(Joshua 6:2)*

*The Lord said to Joshua, "See, I have given Jericho
into your hand, with its king and the valiant warriors."*

I was listening to a television commercial about automobile
GPS systems. I commented to the TV that I have a **GPS** of
my own, it is **God's Protective Steering**! Several Old Testament
characters come to my mind in relation to this protective guidance.
First, let's look at Joshua, the man chosen to fill the mighty shoes
of Moses! Joshua has led the Hebrew people across the border
and into the promised land. The above verse shows God directing
him that he is to take Jericho, a fortress in this new land. That
wouldn't be so bad if they weren't attacking a walled city with
guards posted everywhere. Even that isn't as bad as how God tells
him to proceed! Joshua is instructed to take the people and march
once around the city each of the next six days... in silence! On
the seventh day, they are to march seven times around the city
and the priests, on cue, are to blow their trumpets as the people
shout as loud as they can! What kind of crazy plan is that! It is
GPS! They marched, blew and hollered; and the walls fell down!
Jonah's story is almost as crazy! He is told to go to the city of
Nineveh, a people Jonah absolutely detests, and warn them to turn
from their evil ways or be destroyed. Jonah would rather drown.
That is almost what happens when he gets thrown over the side of
a ship he boards to try to hide from God's mission for him. You
can't hide from God... fool! Only God in His **Protective Steering**
could cause a whale to swallow a drowning Jonah as he descended
into the pit of hell! How great was **God's Protective Steering** in
the case of these two men!

How willing are you to follow God's direction even when
everyone else will think you have finally gone off the deep end?
Joshua knew the men of Jericho were laughing as they circled
that city for six days. They must have really had a chuckle as the
people circled the impenetrable wall on the seventh day... until

the walls came tumbling down and the city was captured! What about Jonah... trying to run from God? Are you really so different? God's plans will be accomplished whether you want them to or not. It was God's will to save Nineveh... so Jonah's rebellion was worthless.

Father God, Your ways are definitely not my ways! I would rather have You just knock the wall down than make me look foolish circling it. But, I also know that I learn powerful lessons from obeying Your commands. Jonah had to learn the hard way... help me not go to that extreme. Amen.

June 29th   G.P.S.: Hosea and Hannah   *(Hosea 1:2)*

When the Lord first spoke through Hosea, the Lord said to Hosea, "Go take to yourself a wife of harlotry and have children of harlotry...".

*T*oday is our second day looking at pictures of how God used **GPS: God's Protective Steering** to direct the lives of His children. This first story is a little hard to explain... but here goes! Hosea is a prophet, used to giving God's word to others. Imagine his shock when the Holy God of Israel tells him to marry a prostitute! Even worse, he is told to have children with her! What can God be thinking? Hosea probably bought a box of Q-tips to make sure he was hearing right! He obeys God, marries Gomer, and brings her home. He learns to love her; but she cannot trust. Gomer leaves her home and returns to harlotry. Time and time again, God sends Hosea after her. What could God have been doing in this situation? Maybe His **GPS** was broken! Think about Hannah, the humble woman who wanted nothing more than to give birth to a child. She makes a covenant promise with her Lord that if He would give her a son she would dedicate him into God's service for his entire life. We have to wonder if she really believed she would conceive. She did and kept her promise. Her little son, Samuel, became the protégé of the priest

Eli; and was used to anoint David, the future King of Israel. God was sure using His **GPS** to steer Samuel in the right direction... but what about that Hosea/Gomer thing?

Okay, the **GPS** of the Lord wasn't broken or malfunctioning when He sent Hosea to Gomer. Look closely, this story is a parable. Parables are word pictures used to teach a moral lesson. Hosea is Jesus and we are the sinning Gomer, who continue to go back toward the sin we wallowed in before we knew Him in the first place. We are so unsure of certain grace that we are drawn back to the very thing which hurts us most. **God's Protective Steering** was directing Hosea to show Gomer unconditional love. In the same vein, He was orchestrating Hannah's child to be pivotal in the history of His chosen people. Does God still use **GPS** today? Think about that.

Father God, I confess that I judged Gomer, thought Hosea crazy, and doubted Your plan. I forgot that You are always in control and always have a perfect design for our lives. Help me to run from sin like Gomer, love unconditionally like Hosea, and keep my promises like Hannah. Only then can You use me like You did Samuel. Amen.

June 30th G.P.S.: God Still Works Today *(Proverbs 16:9)*

The mind of man plans his way, but the Lord directs his steps.

*H*ave you ever met a young couple who have it so together they make you feel like they need to mentor you rather than vice versa? My son, Brent, came to know Christ during his junior year of high school. He was dating a sweet young Christian woman who was a great witness to him. Today, she is one half of the couple I opened this entry with. She was attending the University of Michigan in the engineering program, where she met another engineering student who was a fellow Christian. The two of them married, graduated from college and were all set to make a ton of money…until Christ called them into full time ministry! With much prayer and the blessing of their families, this dynamic duo followed **GPS: God's Protective Steering** and became on campus leaders for Campus Crusade for Christ. No cushy, high paying jobs and fancy homes for them. Instead, they rely on monthly financial support to pay their bills as they devote every waking minute to sharing the Gospel of Christ on college campuses. Another one of the young people who was instrumental in Brent coming to Christ was Guy, a dedicated young Christian who spent numerous nights sleeping on the hardwood floor beside Brent's bed and telling him about salvation. Later, as a college student, Guy would work summers at youth camps as a counselor. He would come to the store where I worked and tell me about the ministry opportunities there. Guy is now a married father who recently left his well paying local job to go back to his first job love. He and his wife are working as athletic directors at a Christian youth camp. What an awesome atmosphere that will be to raise their children in. **GPS: God's Protective Steering** was clearly directing these two young couples.

Imagine in the unkind world we live in, where people kick and claw their way to the top, two young couples who in spite of education, difficulties, and derision by their peers, chose to work for God instead of man! What if that same thing happened to your child after you paid for years of very costly education? **GPS: God's Protective Steering** can only work when we are flexible and dedicated to His purpose more than our needs. Most of us have a hard time opening the Bible for daily study, let alone following the call on our hearts.

I admire the courage of these young people, Lord. How amazing they are. You surely are using **GPS: God's Protective Steering** *in our world today. Help my "receiver" to be tuned in to Your "transmitter." I walk into the unknown trusting You to steer my footsteps. Amen.*

July 1ˢᵗ <u>The Fear of the Lord</u> *(Proverbs 9:10)*

The fear of the Lord is the beginning of wisdom and
the knowledge of the Holy One is understanding.

The proverb above tells us that fearing the Lord is the beginning of real wisdom. Does that mean we are to be afraid of
God? Does it mean He is some powerful bully sitting in Heaven
waiting for us to fail so He can bop us? No. Fear in this context
is reverence, awe, or respect for the One who controls the entire
world! I love to do woodworking using power tools. We found out
years ago how dangerous a radial arm saw can be. Dan was cutting
a board and was standing off to the side instead of the end where
he usually stood. The saw blade bucked and the narrow strip he
was cutting shot straight back and through the basement wall! Had
he been where he usually was, the piece of wood could have gone
right into the flesh of his abdomen. Believe me; I learned respect
for radial arm saws that day. Was I afraid of it? No. I was aware of
the danger of working casually around it. The same goes for my
relationship with God. I want to be in right standing with Him, not
because I am afraid of Him; but because I love Him and respect
Him. The rest of the proverb tells us that real understanding is the
knowledge of the Holy One. How do we get that knowledge? We
only gain it through time in God's holy Word, in listening, prayer
and in reverent worship.

There are many people with tons of costly education. Does that
make them wiser than a Christian who has been schooled in the Word
of God? Does the college education equip someone to handle life
situations in a better way? If I am facing a huge difficulty in my life
and need a comforter or encourager, I would choose a Scripturally-
literate Christian over an educated, book smart scholar any day.
When my spirit is wounded I need Spirit food not education food. I
am surely not saying that Christians cannot be educated, or that the
educated cannot be Christians. Godly advice and godly counsel can
never be outdone by mere intelligence. Unfortunately, we place far

too much emphasis on formal education and far too little on Biblical education.

Father, may I never value education, which can be a most wonderful asset, more than the wisdom I gain from time in Your Word. You hold the keys to real education and real wisdom... the kind of wisdom which teaches me how to walk in Your truths. Amen.

July 2nd <u>Where Were They?</u> *(Matthew 26:31)*

Then Jesus said to them, "You will all fall away because of Me this night, for it is written, 'I will strike down the shepherd and the sheep of the flock shall be scattered.'"

Jesus had predicted the scattering of His disciples at the time of His arrest and trial. Where was everyone else? Where was the woman He had shown mercy to when caught in adultery? Where was Zacchaeus? Where was the healed man whose friends lowered him through the roof to receive Jesus' touch? What about the woman healed from thirteen years of blood hemorrhage? Where was blind Bartimaeus? Was no one grateful enough to dare face what was happening to the One who had touched them in love? How quickly we forget the wonder of where we used to be and where we are now because of the sacrifice of Jesus. If someone gives us a birthday gift; we thank them and send a thank you card. Here we see someone who restored sight, gave movement to the lame, and blew the breath of life into the dead. Where were His thanks? Where was the loyalty to Him? How it must have hurt Jesus to realize that so few valued Him enough to stand with Him. I may be overreacting... maybe they were there in the shadows, not moving in too close. It would seem that at least one of the Gospel writers would have mentioned it. I guess it doesn't really surprise me after all. I have seen too many examples of "fair weather friends" scattering when the going gets tough.

How do you feel about Jesus' friends not sticking close to Him in His hardest times? Would He have done the same to Thomas, James, Andrew, or Thaddeus if they had been arrested? He was a "friend who stuck closer than a brother." He was the "Good Shepherd" who defended His flock. Think of what a smile, a shed tear, or a shout to stop His trial would have meant to Jesus. The amazing thing is that He forgave every one of them from the cross. Jesus was forsaken by most of the people He knew best, but He was never out of the sight of the One Who sent Him to do that job. His Mother and His Heavenly Father were both there.

Sweet Jesus, I never want to take for granted exactly what my salvation cost You. I'll never know exactly what You felt when everyone abandoned You. I can only imagine how I would feel in the same situation. Your unconditional and forgiving love is beyond my limited comprehension. Amen.

July 3rd Mary's Pain *(John 19:26-27)*

When Jesus then saw His mother and the disciple whom He loved standing nearby, He said to His mother, "Woman behold your son!" Then he said to the disciple, "Behold your mother!" From that hour, the disciple took her into his own household.

*T*hankfully, most of us will outlive our children and never have to watch them suffer or die. In most cases, mothers have an inborn instinct to support and shelter their children. Imagine how Mary must have felt as she watched the sham trial of her beloved son. I have to wonder just how much information the angel disclosed to her at the time she was first told that she was chosen to be the mother of the Messiah. Did she know that His life would be just thirty-three years long? Would she have said yes to Gabriel if she knew how Jesus would suffer? Would she wish away their time together, in order to not have to watch His crucifixion? I have to believe that God gave her only the necessary amount of information, much like

He does us. When our children are conceived we never think of future health concerns, unexplainable accidents or the heartbreaks they may face. We step into parenthood with only the best of intentions, trusting God to provide and protect our offspring. Sometimes things go terribly wrong. Mary knew Jesus had to die; she just didn't want it to happen so soon. Imagine the kind of son He must have been. He treated others with so much love... imagine how He would treat the woman who gave Him life! Mary did exactly what she had to do...she stayed within His vision, silently weeping heartbroken tears. She was there if He needed to look at her for reassurance. No matter the personal cost to her, Mary had to watch every moment of the horrible end to her son's life. God's inborn instinct reigned in this mother's heart.

Can you imagine what Mary felt? If your child suffers with long term illness, you have a degree of relief to see the suffering end. Mary probably did the same, wishing the end of Jesus' suffering would come quickly. We can all learn from the strength of this woman, selected by God and faithful to her calling. She didn't beg Jesus to not move forward in the events leading to the end. Mary is a picture of grace and dignity.

Father, You chose Mary's womb to carry Your Messiah into the world. She was faithful in her service and loyal to the end. Lord, help me to be a person who keeps my word, follows through, and perseveres in spite of tragedy. Her legacy is a great example for mothers in today's world. Amen.

July 4th Not by My Might *(Zechariah 4:6)*

'Not by might, nor by power,
but by My Spirit,' says the Lord of hosts.

*H*ow many of us can't wait to take credit for our successes and can't wait to pass the blame for our failures? We are always prepared to tell everyone how we worked our way to the top, wrote the great historical novel, lived our lives righteously before the Lord, or made our fortune by the sweat of our brow. How often do we tell people, "God has blessed me with a business head and I thank Him for my success?" Scripture tells us that *"every good and perfect gift comes from the Lord."* Without His provision we couldn't see, let alone write a book. Without His gifts we wouldn't be able to succeed in business, design engineering miracles, or build assembly lines. I am the first one to tell people I have been given the gifts of teaching, speaking, and writing. I have taken full credit for these things in the past. Owning our bookstore has changed that for me. We are not located in the heart of the business district. Therefore, we get limited drop-in traffic. We have had to rely on God sending business to His House. I have always been successful in my endeavors. His House has humbled me. Now I truly know that the store's success is *not by my might, not by my power...* but only by the guidance, provision, and Spirit of God. Actually, humble isn't as bad as I thought it would be.

If I could give Christians one piece of advice: it would be to remain humble when God sends successes and blessings into your life. We must not take His provision for granted. He can withhold just as easily as He can give. Earlier lessons on King David and King Solomon prove that. Is it really so difficult to acknowledge the power He is in your life? Many people will never profess faith for this very reason. Pride reigns in the heart of a soul controlled by the enemy. Satan would rather have you do anything than acknowledge your need for Your Creator. The enemy of our souls comes to kill, steal, and destroy. Don't give him the victory.

Without You, I have no power, might, or success, Lord. Help me to rebuke the subtle influences of the enemy. From this day forward, I give You authority. I thank You for my gifts and abilities, and I welcome Your perfect will for my life. Amen.

July 5th Aunt Sue's Letter *(John 4:37-38)*

For in this the saying is true, "One sows and another reaps."
I sent you to reap that for which you have not labored;
others have labored, and you have entered into their labors.

*P*lease read these excerpts from a letter I wrote to my aunt as she was dying from lung cancer. "On Thursday, the Lord spoke to me and told me to come and see you. I prayed all the way there and asked Him what He wanted me to say to you. I promised Him that I would speak with a HOLY BOLDNESS about the fact that you need to be right with Him. My prayer is that everyone in my family would know the peace of Christ as they take their dying breath. This is the only assurance of eternal life with Him, life that is free of suffering and illness. I avoided His call on my heart for years before I realized that obedience to Him actually brought me freedom. I am freed because I no longer am tempted to do the things that I spent time doing. I'm far from perfect; but I am forgiven for EVERYTHING I have ever done. I had spent all of my life trying to find someone to love me unconditionally; and finally realized that no person can do that. You look at a shortened life as something to regret or fear; I see it as the fact that likely you will get to see my Jesus before I do! It is easy for me to sound really righteous and tell you that God is in control. I have no idea how I would handle the illness that you are dealing with, but my prayer is for the strength that He gives to His saints that allows them to continue to praise His name as they face the end of earthly life. If I knew that someone I loved was hungry, I would feed them. If I sensed their thirst, I would give them water. When I see that they need guidance, love, direction, hope, faith, and peace; I can only give them the source of all of those things, JESUS CHRIST! I feel at peace now that I have shared this with you. I no longer have to feel regret for my failure on Friday. I should have spoken because everyone else in that hospital room needs this, too!"

This letter was the tool I used to share the Gospel of salvation with my aunt. I included the steps to new life in Christ; and never received a response. After her funeral, I was talking with her daughter about a visit from her pastor to Aunt Sue's bedside shortly before her death. I told Linda I had sent a letter to her telling her about salvation. Linda told me she had read the letter… which led her mother to Christ!

Lord, when You tell me to witness, may I do as told. When I fail in my mission, please provide me another means to achieve the same goal. Help me to know that unresponsive responses never mean Your Word has fallen on deaf ears. Amen.

July 6th No Respecter of Persons *(2 Chronicles 19:7)*

Wherefore now let the fear of the LORD be upon you; take heed and do it: for there is no iniquity with the LORD our God, nor respect of persons, nor taking of gifts. KJV

The verse above is taken from the Old Testament book of 2nd Chronicles. In the passage prior to this; we read that Jehoshaphat, King of Judah, is bringing judges into the land to judge in the different provinces. The rule of the Law of God is to be strictly adhered to. The King is telling the judges to *"be very careful what you do, for the Lord our God will have no part in unrighteousness or partiality or the taking of bribes."* He is commanding honesty, fairness, and impartiality of those who will have final say in all disputes in his land. The Scripture verse also tells us that God is no respecter of persons. He doesn't care how much money you have, what family you were born into, or what you do for a living. God's children are all part of His creation and He loves them all the same. How wonderful it would be if our legal system were based on the moral rules as well as the Biblical Law of God. No bought off judges, no money hungry attorneys, no loopholes for criminals to escape through. God is a just and fair God. His laws are not crooked. We are the ones who bend them.

Do you get frustrated when you see the laws of our land twisted and bent until they are nearly unrecognizable? Is it possible to keep yourself from showing partiality and favoritism? Unfortunately, we base our beliefs on the prejudices of our lives. Money, pedigree, and career choice are all parts of how people are given worth in our society. God is not a respecter of persons. He flat out does not care about these things. He looks at the heart, sees the need, and heals the hurts. We need to be more like Him in our interpersonal relationships. Let us agree to begin today to do just that.

Lord Jesus, You never cared who came to You... the children, the handicapped, the poverty stricken, or the turncoat tax collector. Help me to drop my prejudices that I may show everyone compassion and love. Amen.

July 7th <u>Reverence for the Bible</u> *(Psalms 119:99)*

I have more insight than all my teachers,
For Your testimonies are my meditation.

My early morning time with the Lord is when I am rejuvenated. I am fresh from sleep, the house is quiet, and the phone isn't likely to ring at 5:00 a.m. Even when Brent still lived at home, I made this a priority. Why? My morning time with the Lord sets the tone for my day. I read a devotional, write a journal entry, turn off the light, and pray. I usually do this with a candle or the fireplace lit, which helps me to focus, and be less distracted. After those things I open my Bible, gently and reverently touch its pages, and ask for wisdom and understanding. I begin to read and usually read two or three chapters per day. On weekends or non-work days, I read as much as I can. I finish one book before moving on to another. Some people read from both the New and Old Testaments each day to read through in a year. This is not one of my favorite reading plans. I would rather read one verse each day and really understand and apply it to my life, than to read fast and have little or no recall of my reading. As I read, I stop and mark key words or verses using colored pencils or Bible highlighters. Some have said it is wrong to write in or mark in a Bible; because it is God's Holy Word. My initial response is that I revere the Word so much that I want to absorb every word I can. God would not be happy for me to have a very revered and unread Bible on the shelf.

Have you learned more about the Bible since starting this devotional? Now would be a great time to begin reading a chapter or two each day. I would recommend beginning in the Gospel books of Matthew or John. These are accounts of Jesus' birth, life, teaching, ministry, trial, death, and resurrection. Don't let unpronounceable names stop you. They are not important; but the teaching, promises, and insights are. Please try this. Christ wants to communicate with you. He will not force Himself on you. I will pray today for everyone who is reading this entry. I will ask God to give you wisdom and understanding.

Lord Jesus, speak to me. I quiet myself before You. Please help me to understand what I will read today. Please show me how to apply it to my life. Open my eyes, ears and hearts. Amen.

July 8ᵗʰ Stepping out in Faith *(Matthew 17:20)*

"..truly I say to you, if you have faith the size of a mustard seed, you will say to this mountain, 'Move from here to there,' and it will move; and nothing will be impossible to you."

Stepping out of our comfort zone is something most of us are reluctant. My friend, Janet, is one of the brave ones among us. Janet had been at her prior position for ten years. She liked her job and was great at it, but sometimes God has a bigger plan for our lives. About a month before this writing, Janet told me she was leaving her job—and her guaranteed wages and benefits—to step out into a new career. I believe God breathes a dream into each of us. I spoke before about the fact that God usually gives us gifts and passions leading to that dream. Janet has long been determined to be debt free in her personal finances. She also has a heart to teach others how to achieve the same freedom from debt's bondage. Janet's previous job was in the Real Estate field. She was privy to the huge number of foreclosures in our area. Janet talked repeatedly about the lack of education in the area of finances. In God's perfect timing, He brought a man into Janet's life who shared her passion and her desire to help others. Janet has stepped into that man's company and will be a great blessing to those who need a mortgage officer who truly cares about their needs. She is a woman of deep faith who has held firm in her commitment to marriage, parenting and service to the kingdom. I admire her spunk, her determination and her willingness to obey the movement of God in her life.

Are you willing to be moved where God moves you? I remember thinking I could never marry a minister because of how they are moved from church to church and congregation to congregation. I am a homebody who most generally hates change. Janet had a dream born in her heart, and *'for such a time as this'* God moved her to the place she can best be used. I challenge you to listen and watch for the direction and movements of the Holy Spirit. If God moves you, He will provide for your needs.

Father God, I confess that I hate change. I am not comfortable leaving that which is comfortable to me. I also fear making a mistake and thinking it is Your will for me. Show me Your clear direction. Amen.

July 9th   Book Smarts/Bible Smarts   *(1 Corinthians 3:18)*

Let no man deceive himself. If any man among you

thinks that he is wise in this age, he must become foolish,
so that he may become wise.

When I come face to face with a nonbeliever or even an athiest, who fully denies believing in God at all, I need to remember to not get angry. I must not get mouthy or act out in ways which reflect poorly on my faith. My negative, critical, or judgemental reaction can serve to further separate that doubter from the One who seeks to bring him into a saving grace. There is a huge difference in book smarts, common sense, and godly wisdom. Book smarts rarely help us to interact with others. Common sense helps us to make logical decisions affecting our lives. But, godly wisdom helps us to walk in God's paths, His plans, and His grace. Call me a 'religious fool,' but I long to walk in His grace all my days. We must remember that we will rarely ever change a nonbeliever's mind by our words. Only the Holy Spirit can do that. Instead, we need to allow our actions to serve as our witness. One thing I do tell those who challenge my faith or the validity of the Bible is that they have every right to believe what they believe; however, their belief does not make truth untrue.

There are a lot of educated fools and a lot of very wise uneducated men in the world. We must be patient to speak without getting defensive. We are also called to be equipped enough to defend our faith and its Bible. Have you dealt with this kind of confrontation in your faith walk? How did you hold up in the face of the challenge? Let's commit ourselves to patience, diligence, and hunger to share through our actions.

Father God, I allow myself to be shut down in the face of challenges to my faith. I feel ill-equipped to deflect the barbs of those who hate that which I believe. Open my eyes, close my mouth, and let Your light shine. Amen.

July 10th <u>On Holy Ground</u> *(Exodus 3:5)*

Then He said, "Do not come near here; remove your sandals from your feet, for the place on which you are standing is holy ground."

Moses, God's chosen one to deliver the Hebrew people from Egyptian bondage, has climbed Mount Horeb with his flock of sheep. Off in the distance, he sees a burning bush. He goes closer to investigate what might have caused the flames and is fascinated that the bush does not burn up. Imagine his shock when a voice from Heaven calls out, "Moses, Moses." In spite of his fear, Moses realizes that this is God; the God of his people and of his ancestors Abraham, Isaac, and Jacob. God tells him to remove his sandals because the place he stands upon is holy ground. Moses obeys and hides his face. Hebrews know they cannot look upon the face of God and live! God begins to tell him He has heard the cries of the Hebrew slaves, who are in bondage, and under the heavy yoke of Pharaoh, King of Egypt. God then tells him that he will be the tool God will use to bring His children out of Egypt and into a promised land—a land flowing with milk and honey. Moses advises God to send someone more eloquent, a better speaker to Pharaoh. God will not change His mind. Moses is in for a big adventure!

Moses feels fully unqualified to do the job God is sending him to do! Have you ever felt the same? Most of us hate to do anything which takes us out of our comfort zone. I didn't know how to be a secretary, but God called me to the Real Estate company. I didn't know how to open a business, but God did! I knew nothing about publishing a book, but God showed me. What is it you feel unqualified to do? You will never know what amazing things God can do with your life… until you step off the comfortable path, check out the burning bushes He puts in your way, and listen for His commands. Take off those shoes; you're bound for holy ground!

Lord, I feel unqualified, insecure, and afraid, but I know that You will never send me anywhere You don't equip me to go. I step off the beaten path and onto Your road less traveled. Amen.

July 11th <u>Parents Choosing Favorites</u> *(Genesis 25:28)*

*Now Isaac loved Esau, because he had a taste
for game, but Rebekah loved Jacob.*

saac and Rebekah will never win the "Best Bible Parents" award. Jacob and Esau are very different sons. Esau is a hairy hunter who is adored by his father because of the savory food his wild game yields. Rebekah loves her pampered son, Jacob and despises the fact that he, being the younger brother, will not inherit his father's birthright. Isaac knows he is nearing death and asks Esau to hunt game and make his some of his favorite food. After that, he will grant Esau his blessings and birthright. Rebekah overhears and begins to scheme against her older son and her husband. She prepares savory stew, wraps the bare flesh of Jacob with lambskin and dresses him in his brother's clothes. She sends him to his blind father to feed him the food. Isaac questions who he really is but ends up bestowing the family blessing on Jacob. When Esau returns, he realizes his mother and brother have betrayed him. He knows a blessing once given cannot be rescinded! He vows to kill his brother as soon as their father has died. Rebekah sends Jacob away to protect him from Esau's anger. Isaac dies and Rebekah is left with the son she betrayed and without the one she loved most. Rebekah pays a huge price for her partiality and deceit.

This story is literally as old as the hills! Did your parents play the favorites game? I have only one son, so I never had to worry about this. What do you think about Rebekah and her part in this? Jacob could have refused to participate—Esau could have not threatened—Isaac could have tried harder to challenge his younger son. There was a lot at stake. The oldest son stood to inherit a double portion of the estate. No wonder Esau was so distraught; every promise for his future was stolen. What lesson do you learn from this story? Choosing favorites always leaves hurt feelings.

Father God, help me to be fair and impartial in my dealings with children, friends and family members. You call us to love one another. Help me to model that love every day of my life. Amen.

July 12th Thy Kingdom Come *(Luke 22:29-30)*

… and just as My Father has granted Me a kingdom, I grant you that you may eat and drink at My table in My kingdom, and you will sit on thrones judging the twelve tribes of Israel.

In the here and now, we are tied to the world because we here in it and must work in conjunction with it. Scripture tells us we are to be "**in** the world but not **of** the world." We are to be a witness here but are not to seek or act upon the things of this evil world. Christians are not to be separated from everyone else; how could we fill the commission to *"go into all the world making disciples of all men?"* One day, we will reign in a very different world. When we reign, it will be with Jesus beside us. We will have authority over the evil of the world; and Jesus will be our Model for justice. In that Kingdom, there will be no darkness—only light and peace. How I look forward to a day when there will be no divorce, fighting, hatred, war, cancer, colostomies, suffering, child abuse, promiscuity, drug addictions, alcoholism, gambling, persecution. In that day real peace will reign, love will be acted out, and righteousness will be rewarded. Believers will reign there with the One who strengthened us enough to survive today! We need to act like survivors!

How connected are you to the world? That may seem like a foolish question because we live, love, and breathe in the here and now. Think about how the things of this life work to keep us from looking in hope toward our eternal life. Recreation supersedes worship. Television supersedes conversation. Filthy novels supersede time in God's Word. Busyness supersedes the business of Kingdom building. I am not saying that television, recreation, reading, or busyness is wrong. They are only wrong if they keep us from doing what our Lord commands us to do. My advice to you today is to not get so consumed by this world, that you do not look forward to the next one, which will last for all of eternity.

Lord, the things of this world have come between You and me. I have allowed this to happen. I confess the sin, repent, and turn from it. I ask the guidance and counsel of the Holy Spirit to help me to remain focused and looking ever forward to the day I will reign forever with You in Your holy kingdom. Amen.

July 13th Unanswered Prayers *(Isaiah 55:8-9)*

*"For My thoughts are not your thoughts, Nor are your ways
My ways," declares the LORD. For as the heavens are higher
than the earth. So are My ways higher than your ways
and My thoughts than your thoughts."*

I always remember being taught that God always answer prayers. Sometimes the answer is "yes," sometimes an emphatic "no," and sometimes it is "wait." We hate the "no's" and "waits." Each of us wants our prayer requests answered with a quick "yes." God's Word also says to remember that the Lord will never say "yes" to something which is contrary to His plans for us or His righteousness. Many times we look back at unanswered prayers and realize that He did us a favor by not granting them. He knew what tomorrow held and how our paths were going to turn. We must realize the truth of the Scripture at the top of this entry. His ways are not the same as ours... thank God! His thoughts are not the same as our thoughts... thank God! He is God. And no matter what the world says, He is still in control.

Think about young children. What answer do they always want to hear? Of course they want a quick and decisive "yes" no matter what they ask. As their parent, friend, or teacher our job is to always weigh their wants and requests against what is best for them in the long run. Our Heavenly Father has that same responsibility. He knows the goal He has for our lives. We make many choices along that path without consulting Him at all. However, when we do come to Him with a prayer request, He has to decide whether to allow us to walk further from Him, or to deny a request, and subtly draw us back. Would you expect any less from the One who knit you together and knows the number of hairs on your head? Trust Him with your requests. He only wants the best for you.

Jesus, Thank You for having my best interest at heart, for answering my prayers in Your way, and in your perfect timing… and for hearing me at all! I confess past disappointments because of unanswered or denied prayer requests. I know Your plans are for my well being. Amen.

July 14th Face of God *(Job 19:25-26)*

"As for me, I know that my Redeemer lives, and at the last He will take His stand on the earth. Even after my skin is destroyed, yet from my flesh I shall see God."

The promise that after all the praying, worshipping, studying, teaching, seeking, finding, loving, and serving I have done, is that I will see the face of God and touch the hem of Jesus' robe! I am glad that on the day when every tongue confesses and every knee bows I will not be caught in the horrible realization that I saw You for the first time and denied You every time before. My earnest prayer is "come, Lord Jesus, while my grandchildren and nieces and nephews are still young. Come before the moral decay of society further destroys all good, purity, innocence. Jesus, let me see Your face—the sure and steady light at the end of my long difficult journey." For years, I prayed to see the face of Jesus. I thought it would make my focus easier in prayer and worship. I read an application in the Life Application Bible stating that once we become familiar with some-thing, we begin to take it for granted. Much like when we first meet the person we will eventually marry, and we cannot stop looking forward to their face. After twenty years of marriage, kids and work... are we as excited each time we see that face? Would Jesus' face become so commonplace and familiar we would take it for granted?

Come, let us agree to seek hard after the face of our Lord, to pray about the day we will first see it, and seek to do everything in our power to honor His Name. His Presence will be the only light in the new kingdom of God. There will be no need for sun, moon and stars... because *Jesus is the light of the world.* Begin today to picture in your mind what Heaven might look, sound, smell, and feel like. May these thoughts help you to enter a deeper place of prayer.

Jesus, I do long to see Your face. I long to walk with You all my days. My desire is that You would come soon and take me and those I love out of this vile world. I realize it will happen in Your time frame, not mine. Come, Lord Jesus. Amen.

July 15th   Rachel's Strength   *(Proverbs 31:25)*

Strength and dignity are her clothing; and she smiles at the future.

Let me introduce you to my dear friend, Rachel. When I grow up, I want to be just like her! Rachel is one of the most caring, kind, and genuine people I know. She is always ready to help someone in need, to reach out to hurting strangers and to counsel with those who have lost a loved one. Rachel knows the pain of loss because she buried her fifteen-year-old son several years ago after he died in a tragic horse accident while vacationing with friends. The hurt and questions were overwhelming as they faced this horrible loss; but her faith never waivered. Rachel knew her son loved Jesus and was going to a wonderful new home, but she longed to hold him again and tell him she loved him. I bet Kevin knew exactly how his mother felt about him... because Rachel exudes love! Many people would take this tragedy and turn inward, burying themselves into a cocoon of sorrow. Rachel turned her grief outward and began to minister to other mothers who lost children. She "fed the multitudes" at Thanksgiving dinners, started a small group in her home, befriended the elderly in our church, and continued to minister to others. When I grow up I want to be like Rachel; because she truly lives the "Jesus with skin on" Gospel.

Rachel is a rare gem in this ugly world. She is a servant and has a wonderful hunger for the Word of God. She is a dedicated mother, wife, and grandma. We can all learn from her example. When we hurt, we need to turn outward toward others, not inward toward bitterness. Have you faced a similar tragedy? How did you handle yourself? I am certainly not saying for us not to grieve. God gave us healing tears. Remember, *"Jesus wept"* at the tomb of His friend, so He understands our grief. Death is not the final chapter in the life of a Christian. It is merely the step into forever life with the Lord. Rachel knows she will see her handsome son and have the chance to tell him, "I love you, Kevin." She *"smiles at that future."*

Lord, thank You for healing tears. May I be strong in my losses knowing You are in full control of my tomorrows and my forever! I anxiously await the day I will see my loved ones again. Amen.

July 16th Noah: God's Fool *(Genesis 6:18)*

"I will establish My covenant with you; and you shall enter the ark— you and your sons and your wife, and your sons' wives with you."

*T*oday, we begin a study on great Bible characters who could easily have earned the title "God's Fool." These heroes were called to forsake home, family, and pride to walk the path God laid out for them. Scripture tells us God regretted ever creating man because of their sinful ways and faithfulness. The following verse tells us why Noah would be spared, *"... Noah found favor in the eyes of the Lord."* God told Noah He was going to eradicate man from the face of the earth by sending a great flood. Noah and his family alone would be spared. God gave Noah very specific instructions for a boat (ark) to be made of gopher wood, covered with pitch, and containing rooms or pens. The ark was to be 450 feet long, 75 feet wide and 45 feet high. All of this sounds great... except Noah lived hundreds of miles from the nearest body of water in a land where rain was a rarity! Noah had two choices: doubt and ignore God's command or suffer the ridicule he was certain to get from those who would watch the ark being made. We have to wonder what Noah's own family thought. He must have had a great reputation as father and husband for his family to follow what seemed his lead of foolishness. Noah chose obedience, built the ark, filled it with God's creatures, and closed the door behind his family. Surely he heard the insults hurled as the door closed... until the rain fell and didn't stop falling... for days.

Noah looked like a fool as he built, filled, and entered the ark. God knew he was trustworthy. Would you be willing to be considered a "fool" in order to follow the Lord's commands? Have you ever been called to do anything like this? Many times in the last twelve years, I have had to do things totally contrary to my family and friends' ideas of right. His House and this book are two examples. Why would anyone, with a good job, take on a new business during a horrible time in Michigan's economy? God said to do it! Why would someone with that business and another job take on the very labor intensive work of writing this book? God said to!

Lord, my spirit is willing to follow You, but my flesh tends to be very weak. Make me strong in the face of ridicule. Amen.

July 17ᵗʰ   Moses: God's Fool   *(Exodus 5:22)*

Then Moses returned to the Lord and said, "O Lord, why have You brought harm to this people? Why did You ever send me?"

*W*e met Moses a few days ago in the Holy Ground lesson. Fast forward through this series of events. Moses has gone to Pharaoh several times asking for the release of the Hebrew slaves. He has been used of God to bring ten plagues upon Egypt... neat things like frogs, flies, and bloody water... He has protected the people from the plague of death, led them out of Egypt to the Red Sea, been chased by the Egyptian army, had the Red Sea parted, led the slaves to freedom on dry ground, and watched the enemy drown as the waters flowed back into the sea bed. After all of that, you would surely think he is their hero... kind of like a Hebrew "Superman" or something. Instead, he listens to them whine about everything! "We want bread. It was better in Egypt." So, God sends manna the bread of Heaven. "We want meat!" God sends quail from Heaven. "We want more water. Did you bring us out here to kill us?" God sends water from the rock. If I were Moses, I would have answered that last question with a hearty "YES, and I love being treated like your whipping boy, too!" Why did Moses put up with them? He is a fool for God! Remember, Moses talked to God, watched Him carve out the dry land from the Red Sea, and saw His finger write the Ten Commandments. He knows God. God knows him. He is proud to be God's fool!

This lesson is meant to be funny, but can you imagine how frustrated Moses was? Read the book of Exodus... it will frustrate you, too! No matter what the people did, Moses was dedicated to seeing them into the land God prepared for them. Have you ever worked in ministry, or even at a regular job, and faced the criticism of others? It hurts, doesn't it? Moses listened to it for nearly fifty years. The lesson here is for us to be very careful with our criticism and fault-finding of others. Let's think about the age old *"do unto others as you would have them do unto you"* rule!

Father, I confess that I have been quick to challenge those in positions of leadership. May I learn to be gentle and kind instead of harsh and critical. Make me a fool like Moses. Amen.

July 18th Joshua: God's Fool *(Joshua 6:10)*

But Joshua commanded the people, saying, "You shall not shout nor let your voice be heard nor let a word proceed out of your mouth, until the day I tell you, "Shout!" Then you shall shout!"

Joshua was certainly another "Fool for God." He had seen overt proof of God's faithfulness; and he was ready to step out in faith no matter how foolish the world thought he was. Joshua had watched the Red Sea part for Moses, the will of Pharaoh be broken, and the Hebrews protected as they walked forty years in the wilderness. He had seen mighty men fall, weak men flourish, and food fall from Heaven. Why would he doubt God's ability as they came up against the mighty walls of Jericho? *"Walk (you and all the people) around the walls of the city in silence for six straight days."* God's command seemed ludicrous! They would be the laughing stock of the nations! "On day seven, circle the city seven times... and at a signal have the horns blow, the people shout, and the noise level rise to deafening." This is even worse! But...the walls came down, the enemy was defeated and Jericho became a city of God! What looked like folly to others was as clear as day to Joshua, who's God had never failed him.

Sometimes God asks us to follow a certain path or do a specific thing, which others simply cannot understand. Forgive an enemy, give your last dollar to someone in need, write a book and open a bookstore. Others may think we are crazy; and they are right. We are crazy enough to follow the *"still small voice in our spirit"* and trust God to lead us down safe paths. Obedience by faith, instead

261

of running with the crowd, is what we are set apart to do. Joshua's enemies had a good laugh each time he marched his people around the fortified, indestructible wall. God had the last laugh, when the walls tumbled down. I dare you to be a Joshua.

Father, sometimes I want to be obedient, but I fear what others will say about me. I confess the truth… that is pride! Make me a fool like Joshua. You have never let me down either. Amen.

July 19th Esther: God's Fool *(Esther 2:20)*

Esther had not yet made known her kindred or her people, even as Mordecai had commanded her; for Esther did what Mordecai told her as she had done when under his care.

Today we meet Esther, the Queen of Persia, and clearly another "Fool for God." Let me tell you about this heroic Bible character. Esther is the orphaned daughter of a Jewish family who is being raised by her cousin, Mordecai. King Ahasuerus has a lovely wife, who refuses to be paraded before his drunken guests after a week long celebration. Queen Vashti knows full well what this refusal will cost her. She is deposed as queen and the search for her replacement ensues. The King's agents go throughout the kingdom gathering the beautiful young virgins who begin a rigorous beauty regimen to make themselves presentable for one night with the King. Esther waits patiently for her time…and finds favor before King Ahasuerus. She is his new queen but he has no idea she is a Jew! God has placed Esther in a particular place and at a particular time *"for such a time as this."* Esther is later used to save the entire Jewish race from the eradication planned by the evil Haman. In God's perfect time, her nationality is revealed, but only after Esther risks her life to save her people. Why would she be willing to go before the King… she is a "Fool for God."

When Esther entered the presence of King Ahasuerus, she knew she could be put to death. In Persian protocol, no one—not even a queen—could go before the King without being summoned. Esther, and the entire Jewish population in Persia, prayed and fasted for three days before she acted. God heard the prayers, opened King Ahasuerus's heart to receive her, and used her obedience to protect His chosen people. How strong would you be on behalf of other Christians if something like this was required of you? Do you tend to be more self focused or more others focused? Esther was selfless; and others would likely consider her foolish.

My Heavenly Father, You used Esther to save her people and could use me in Your kingdom work if I would get past my fears. Give me a God centered, risk taking kind of heart. Amen.

July 20th   Ruth: God's Fool   *(Ruth 1:16)*

But Ruth said, "Do not urge me to leave you or turn back from following you; for where you go, I will go, and where you lodge, I will lodge. Your people shall be my people, and your God, my God."

*D*o you know someone who is totally committed to service and is faithful to a fault? Ruth is the picture of that description. She is the daughter-in-law of Naomi and is living in the land of Moab. Naomi has heard there is food in Israel; and because of her family being there she decides to return home. She tells both of her son's widows she is leaving and they should return to their families to marry again and have children. Ruth refuses to leave Naomi and makes the plea we read at the top of this page. Ruth, because of her commitment to Naomi, does not take her own needs into consideration. They travel to Israel and Naomi is welcomed back into her family. Ruth, however, is from the land of Moab... an enemy nation of Israel. Hebrew law commands land owners to leave the corners of their fields unharvested in order for the poor to glean (pick) what is left to feed their families. Ruth becomes a hardworking gleaner who catches the eye of Boaz, a wealthy relative of Naomi. Ruth's work ethic, her dedication to Naomi and her godly disposition lead to her marriage to Boaz. King David is born to their family four generations later. God rewards faithfulness.

Ruth's actions spoke more than her words could ever do. Others noticed her godly qualities. Ruth was a "Fool for God," who knew that He deemed *obedience better than sacrifice.* Her vows to the family of her husband didn't end with his death. Would you be willing to forsake your family, home, and safety to care for someone you had no obligation to? Would you go to a land you knew would not welcome you? We can learn a lot from Ruth. Fools like her are rare in our world today.

My Heavenly Father, Ruth is everything I am not! Help me, through the work of the Holy Spirit to be less self absorbed and more in tune with the needs of others. Amen.

July 21ˢᵗ   Joseph: God's Fool   *(Genesis 39:18)*

Then she spoke to him with these words, "The Hebrew slave, whom you brought to us, came in to me to make sport of me; and as I raised my voice and screamed, he left his garment beside me and fled outside."

*O*h my! Reread the passage above. Joseph, who you first met in the series on "Building a Dream," has been accused by his employer's wife of sexual assault. Unfortunately, sometimes things done in innocence lead to false accusations. Joseph finds himself being hauled off to prison... minus his clothes! Potiphar, his overseer, takes his naughty wife's word over that of the man who has served him with honor and loyalty. Joseph, who is definitely a "Fool for God" finds himself in prison... just exactly where God can use him! Then, through a twisted turn of events, he ends up second in command to Pharaoh, the King of Egypt. Scripture tells us that God blessed everything Joseph put his hand to. Why is that? God had a plan, and Joseph was willing to follow along. Maybe Joseph could have fought harder against the accusations waged against him; but he knew from prior experience that "God's ways are not our ways." Joseph was up for God's challenge... are you?

We have studied this series of people who could (likely would) be called fools by the world's standards. Ruth, Joseph, Moses, Noah, Esther, and Joshua were obedient and committed to their faith. Joseph had been sold into bondage by his jealous brothers, thrown in prison several times, and separated from the father he adored. He never let those things stop him. Joseph was determined to persevere because he knew God had a plan! Think again about these characters. Each is a great role model in a world where we need godly examples.

Lord, I would have whined and pitched a fit if I had been in Joseph's shoes. False accusations, even for Your cause, scare me. Help me to trust in Your provision, Your plan, and Your pathways. Amen.

July 22nd Rough Waters *(Matthew 14:29)*

And He said, "Come!" And Peter got out of the boat,
and walked on the water and came toward Jesus.

Peter has long been one of my personal favorite characters in Scripture. Maybe because he is impulsive and rash like I am! In this story, the apostles are in a boat crossing the Sea of Galilee. They have been with Jesus as He fed the five thousand with a few loaves and fishes. As the day came to an end, Jesus sends the disciples ahead to the other side. Jesus personally sees to the sendoff of His followers and then takes Himself away for quiet prayer with His Father. Later, on the sea, the boat of the apostles is tossed about by wind and waves. Jesus comes walking, in the dark of the night, upon the rough seas. When they see His figure, they cry out in fear thinking He is a ghost. Jesus tells them, *"Take courage, it is I; do not be afraid."* Peter, in his own impulsive way, asks Jesus to allow him to walk on water, too. Jesus tells him to come. Peter steps out of the boat and is actually walking atop the surface... until he looks at the winds, the waves, and the rolling of the boat. Suddenly, he takes his eyes off Jesus, looks at his circumstances, and begins to sink! In fear, he cries out to his Lord, and Jesus reaches out His hand, catches hold of Peter and helps him back into the boat. Jesus says to him, *"Ye have little faith."* The waters were rough, the storm was rolling, but Jesus was still in charge.

I have heard teaching from two different aspects in regards to this passage of Scripture. One side is that Peter was a showoff who wanted to impress the others, thus asking to walk on the water. His sinking was allowed to humble him. On the other hand, Peter was the one brave soul who stepped out of the boat, in the midst of a terrible storm. None of the others volunteered to give it a try! How willing are you to step out of the storms of your life, which are causing a tossing and turning keeping you from having any degree of peace? You have to step out of the boat in order for Jesus to take your hand and keep you from drowning in troubled waters. Peter may have been impulsive; but he was also willing to try something new!

Jesus, I would likely have stayed in the boat and been too afraid to step out like Peter. I allow the storms of my life to keep me from finding real peace. I always see the wind and waves. Help me, Lord. Amen.

July 23ʳᵈ   Peace Be Still   (Mark 4:39)

And He got up and rebuked the wind and said to the sea, "Hush, be still." And the wind died down and became perfectly calm.

*H*ere we have a similar situation to that in yesterday's lesson. In this passage, Jesus is asleep in the bottom of the boat as He and His disciples are crossing the Sea of Galilee after a day of teaching. A storm begins to roll the waters, which lie 680 feet below sea level and are surrounded by hills. Winds across the land intensify over the body of water causing sudden unexpected storms. The disciples, most of whom are seasoned fisherman, are afraid of this sudden tempest. Jesus sleeps peacefully, as they try to keep the boat afloat. As the storm worsens, they think they are about to die. The boat is filling with water and they awaken Jesus and ask Him how He can sleep—when they are all about to die! Jesus stands up and rebukes the storm... the winds cease to blow... the waves calm... and His friends look at Him in utter disbelief. "Why are you afraid? Do you still have no faith?" He asks them. Remember, they have seen demons cast out, leprosy healed, lame men walking, and blind eyes opened! Yes, where is their faith? They still don't fully understand who Jesus is or the power He holds. They will see many more miracles... and still have doubts.

Our grandson has stayed overnight with us weekly since he was a newborn and slept in the bedroom his daddy used as a child. We had a picture of Jesus in the boat with the disciples at just the moment when the waters are calmed. From the time Tyler first learned to talk, we had a routine of stopping on the staircase where I would point to the picture and his little voice would say, *"Peace, be still."* Are the storms of your life overflowing your faith bucket? Do you feel like you are perishing in them? Do you need a little dose of *"Peace, be still"* in your life? Call on the Lord. He may not remove the storm, but He will hold your hand as you walk through it. Do you have doubts? Don't worry, so did His closest friends.

Jesus, please remove the storms, which are washing over me and making me feel like there is no hope. Lord, if they cannot be calmed, then please hold my hand and lead me through them. Amen.

July 24ᵗʰ <u>Askers/Seekers</u> *(Hosea 10:12)*

Sow with a view to righteousness, reap in accordance with kindness; break up your fallow ground, for it is time to seek the Lord until He comes to rain righteousness on you.

The Scripture verse above is a great word picture comparing our faith walk with common gardening tasks. I remember a story my dad used to tell where a woman comes to a gardener with a particularly "green thumb" and tells him how wonderful the garden is and how God created such a lovely masterpiece. The gardener has finally listened to all he can take and replies, "Why yes, He created a lovely, lovely garden, but you should have seen it when He had it all on His own!" The gardener worked hard to make the things in his garden grow, bloom, and produce. The Master Gardener needs us to work to produce good fruits from the garden of blessings He gives His children. We are to "sow" righteousness, "reap" in all kindness, "break up" the hard clumps in our hearts, which keep us from being fertile soil, and after all these things are done, He will "rain" His blessings down upon us. Put on those gardening gloves... time to work!

How much righteousness have you sown lately? How much "unrighteousness" have you sown? Are you treating others with kindness and reaping it in return? What about your seeking of the Lord? Are you so hungry for the seeds of His Word that the soil in your heart is loose and ready for the seed to be planted? I can promise you that the "Son" will never shine on your garden until you begin to work according to His ways. We all want to skip some of the steps... especially pulling all those weeds; but the distractions of this life will always choke out the blooms.

Holy Spirit, please teach me to sow, reap, plow, and wait patiently upon Your harvest in my life. I long to bloom where I am planted but sometimes let "sin weeds" distract me. I am Yours. Amen.

July 25th <u>Your First Love</u> *(Revelation 2:4)*

"But I have this against you, that you have left your first love."

The following entry was written on February 14, 2007. "Sweet Jesus today is my 11th anniversary since I officially gave my heart to You in that garage sale chair at the Oliver Street house. This verse (the same as above) makes me think about the first moment I knew that I loved You. As I sat in that chair, prayed the prayer to receive Your grace, and began a new walk in my life, I had no idea what our future together would hold. I think back to how You have guided me through job changes, parenting problems, three immediate family deaths, many extended family deaths, church changes, two great visions, the opening of His House, and the births of our grandchildren, my teaching ministry and now the writing of this devotional book. It has surely been a great journey and You have directed my paths every step of the way." As you can see, Jesus is my first love. This kind of love is not like a high school crush or even the love between a husband and wife. It is pure, holy, faithful, and constant love. The verse above is written to the early Christian church in Ephesus. They were doing a lot right; but they had allowed their eyes to wander away from their first love—the Gospel of Christ. Jesus has to be first, or He will always take second chair to other things in our lives.

Our first love usually sticks in our mind, even if the relationship didn't last. We remember the eye contacts, the words spoken and the love letters sent and received. Do you remember when you first really fell in love with Jesus? I don't mean a casual once a week relationship. I mean when He became first in line for your time, your thoughts, and your focus. If you haven't yet experienced this, it is not too late. His spoken words were written and preserved *"for such a time as this."* Today is your day to read His love letter, hear Him tell you how much you mean to Him. I'll bet your first love would never have died on that cross for you! *"Seek first the kingdom of God and all these things shall be added unto you."*

Jesus, I have forgotten what the first passion and excitement I felt for You was like. Business and busyness have clouded my vision. Make it new in my heart again that I might burn with a holy fire for You. Amen.

July 26th Jonah Running 'from' God *(Jonah 1:3)*

But Jonah rose up to flee to Tarshish
from the presence of the Lord...

Jonah's story teaches us it is always easier to obey God's commands than to pay the price of disobedience. Jonah is one of God's prophets. Through prophets God speaks warnings, blessings, and commands to His people. He is told to go to Nineveh and cry against the city's wickedness, telling them to repent or face destruction. Jonah hates the Ninevites, so he decides to flee and hide from God (BIG MISTAKE!) Jonah boards a ship, which is tossed in a horrible storm. Through a process of elimination, the captain deems Jonah to be the one who brought this unexpected storm upon the waters. Jonah confesses that he is running from God, and then tells them to throw him overboard. The other sailors gladly oblige; and just as he is about to drown...a giant fish is sent to swallow him! Ummmm... bet it smelled great in there! Jonah repents in the belly of the whale and is regurgitated onto dry land. Imagine the stories he can tell his grandchildren! God sent the fish *"for such a time as this,"* but what about those blasted Ninevites?

Ever tried to run from God? Here's a word of wisdom... it will never happen! He sees all, hears all, smells all, and made all. You may as well do as He commands, because one way or another His plans will happen. At least Jonah gets credit for offering himself to be thrown overboard for the sake of his fellow sailors. He realized his sin had put others in danger. They were the innocent bystanders.

Have you ever been endangered by someone else's choices? It isn't pleasant is it? Hopefully, three days in the belly of the fish has changed Jonah's attitude. We'll see tomorrow.

Jesus, I know it doesn't work when I try to run from You and Your commands to me. Hopefully, You can get my attention in a way far less drastic than You used on Jonah. Give me an obedient heart. Amen.

July 27ᵗʰ Jonah Running 'for' God *(Jonah 3:2)*

"Arise, go to Nineveh the great city and proclaim to it the proclamation which I am going to tell you."

$\int$ ome people are so grateful for their redemption they never fall back into their old ways. Others have a hard time changing; and Jonah is one of those men. We pick up Jonah's story as God is giving him a second chance to do what he was sent to do in the first place. God doesn't berate him, remind him of his past failures, or give up on him. Jonah, grudgingly, goes to proclaim God's warnings to Nineveh. Inwardly he hopes they will ignore the warnings and be destroyed! Instead, they heed the warnings, repent of their sins, and cry out to God. Yes! Jonah has done his job! Sadly, he sits upon a hill overlooking the city pouting and feeling sorry for himself. At times like this, I think God must have wanted to send him back into the water... or back in with the fish guts! Jonah forgets much too quickly how he was pardoned. He foolishly thinks he alone deserves grace. How grateful I am that Jonah is not the God who judges me.

I remember years ago when I worked at the Christian bookstore and a high school friend came in. She stood on the mat inside the door and said in shock, "Vicki, what are you doing here?" I looked at her and asked the same. We knew one another when Christ certainly wasn't the central focus of our lives. She didn't look at me and say,

"God, Vicki doesn't deserve Your grace." No, as a believer, she was thrilled to see me in such a place. Jonah should have been grateful for God's mercy and wanted that same mercy shared with others. My prayer is that we learn from Jonah's faults and welcome anyone and everyone into the kingdom of God.

Lord, may I never think I deserve mercy and others don't. Jonah couldn't understand the concept of grace; and it kept him from every fully knowing and serving You. Amen.

July 28th   God of Comfort   *(2 Corinthians 1:3-4)*

Blessed be the God and Father of our Lord Jesus Christ,
the Father of mercies and God of all comfort, who comforts us
in all our affliction so that we will be able to comfort those
who are in any affliction with the comfort with which we
ourselves are comforted by God.

The Scripture verse for this lesson is written by the Apostle Paul who is writing to the church at Corinth. He is teaching that affliction is a natural part of life—even for believers. He is assuring them that though they are afflicted, God is with them. Many times I hear people say things like, "Why do bad things happen to Christians? Where is their protection by the God they serve?" Someone asked why anyone would believe in Christ, when believers will suffer like everyone else. We must realize that just because we follow Christ we are not immune to the illness, perils, evil, and death in this world. If we were, we would have no testimony before others regarding the strength we have been given in the face of hardship. Christ says, *"Peace I leave with you; My peace I give to you; not as the **world** gives do I give to you. Do not let your heart be troubled, nor let it be fearful."* Notice, this peace in the face of storms is not peace like the world gives peace; it is inner peace and the knowledge that after these struggles... peace forever!

I have felt the pain of grief—and been carried through it. I have watched Christians bury their loved ones—and watched God carry them through. I have watched Christians die—without fear because they knew where they were going after their last breath. Peace like that can never come from this world. We will never be taken out of the world; but how we approach these difficulties will be more witness of our faith than our words ever will. Where does your peace come from? Do you place your faith in money, people, fame, or material possessions? Think about these truths.

Lord, I am asking You to come and be my comfort in all afflictions. I need to trust that You are always faithful...in all places and in all situations. This world is surely not a place conducive to peace. Amen.

July 29th <u>They are Getting It!</u> *(Acts 26:18)*

*"...**open** their **eyes** so that they may turn from darkness to light and from the dominion of Satan to God; that they may receive forgiveness of sins and an inheritance among those who have been sanctified by faith in Me."*

I am writing this entry on Friday morning, sitting at His House, thinking about my relationship with God; and I am so excited I could spit! I have been a Bible teacher since shortly after I became a Christian. At this time, I teach at His House on Thursday evenings to a mixed bag of ages and denominational backgrounds. My "Seekers" are taught the Word of God and its' application to their lives. There are days I feel like I need to lighten up the messages, but every time I think that, God speaks another hard lesson for me to teach. Last week, I read about Jehoshaphat, King of Judah, and the importance of the teaching of the Law. I followed a cross reference to a parallel passage in Nehemiah, where the Law was read and the people began to grieve because of how far they were from God's ideal. I was so excited about the lesson…and the excitement was contagious! We talked about the absolute "whys" of our need for the Bible. We shared with one another… and the lights were coming on in their eyes! God was working, through my personal study, and teaching, to finally get them to understand how vitally important personal time in the Word is. They were as excited as I was! "They were Getting It!"

Some who are reading this passage were part of that class last night. For all others, I can only tell you that dedicated time in the Word, with prayer for wisdom and understanding, will open your eyes to God's hidden truths and His messages to you. I know I harp on this a lot. There is a reason for it. A wise believer once told me, "Someday we might not be able to hold the Word in our hands; therefore, we need to have it hidden in our hearts." I have not forgotten those words. They are my purpose for being at His House, teaching, and personal study. I want the Word—the pure Word of God. I also want that for others… thus I teach.

Father God, give me open eyes, receptive ears, and a discerning heart to really understand Your Scriptures. I want what the "Seekers" are finding. I am hungry… feed me, Lord. Amen.

July 30th Salvation is Near Us *(Romans 13:11)*

Do this, knowing the time, that it is already the hour for you to awaken from sleep; for now salvation is nearer to us than when we believed.

What does the line, "*now salvation is nearer to us than when we believed*" mean? One truth about Scripture is that each of us can read a verse, and depending on the situations of our life, interpret it in a different way. I have read verses and could swear it wasn't in the Bible the last time I read it. I think surely I would remember it if I had read it. No, it wasn't applicable in my situation when I read it before. Today, as I read the above verse and picture what *"near salvation"* looks like, I believe it means Christ's return is imminent. This week, I have talked to people regarding three marriages in distress, several people who are very ill, home sellers who cannot move their property in a difficult Michigan market, and people whose children are out of control. We, as a nation, are a mess! Young people are killing others without remorse, parents are aborting their unborn to meet their "personal choices," and careers are more important than families. I truly believe the end of this age is near. I don't say this to frighten you, but to make you aware of just how near our salvation—revealed in Christ's appearance—is. Notice the warning about our need to awaken from our sleep. That is a "heads up" caution! Our lost loved ones need to be ready.

If you are a born-again Christian, you are closer today than you were yesterday to the return of Jesus. Each minute, hour, and day brings us closer to the day we will see Jesus face to face whether in death or in His return for His church. Are you ready? Are your loved ones? God will not be mocked forever. He moved in the days of Noah, and He will move in our days. The Lord cannot look upon sin for He is a Holy God. Only through sincere faith and heartfelt repentance can we be taken home.

Father God, the times are evil and that evil reigns in the hearts of men. We are living in a world just like the one during the time of the great flood. Use us to make a difference as we wait for Your salvation to draw near. Amen.

July 31ˢᵗ <u>My Friend Marna</u> *(Psalms 119:160)*

The sum of Your word is truth, and every one of
Your righteous ordinances is everlasting.

*M*arna makes me laugh! She also makes me want to pull my hair out by the roots sometimes! This sweet friend came to the real estate office in the fall of 2005 and shortly thereafter, began asking faith questions. In God's great timing, her daughter had gone to church with a friend and had questions her mother couldn't answer. In talking to Marna about the children's program at our church, I informed her of my adult class. Several weeks later, I gave Marna a study Bible and she began to attend my class. Marna is a curious woman and looks at most things through challenging eyes. She is a "show me" kind of person. She came to a personal relationship with Christ during a class on sharing the Gospel. Marna has a hard edge... from years of self-preservation. She also has a tender, kind, and serving heart which led her to encourage me to open His House, and to this day she continues to volunteer there one morning each week. She is absolute proof that *"for such a time as this"* God puts people into our lives.

Are there people who challenge your faith or ask a lot of questions? Before you decide they are beyond hope... remember Marna's story. She did not raise her children in church and still struggles against the things she feels she is being kept from doing because she is a Christian. She challenges everything; and that makes her a good learner. If Marna ever focuses all her energy... and there is an abundance of it... into kingdom work, she will change the world for Christ. I was a challenger, doubter, persecutor, and blasphemer. Today, I am the owner of a Christian store and am writing a devotional book for you to read. God will use those He created with unique gifts... in His perfect timing!

Jesus, I know there are people I feel can never be beneficial in the work of Your kingdom. I also know You have plan for each one who will turn to You and offer their service. Remove my need to judge... give me a heart of Christ-like compassion. Amen.

August 1st   Israel: God's Chosen People   *(Exodus 3:7-8)*

The LORD said, "I have surely seen the affliction of My people
who are in Egypt, and have given heed to their cry because of
their taskmasters, for I am aware of their sufferings. So I have
come down to deliver them from the power of the Egyptians,
and to bring them up from that land to a good and spacious land,
to a land flowing with milk and honey."

oday, we begin a series of lessons on the nation of Israel. Before you lay the book down because you hate history and do not understand Middle East politics, open your mind to hear basic Bible teaching on this subject. Israel is identified throughout Scripture as "God's Chosen People." Let me begin by stating that the rest of us are not "unchosen people." Before time began, God created each of us and chose us. The "chosen" designation means simply they were the race to bring the Word of God and the Messiah into the world. When Adam and Eve sinned in the Garden of Eden, the need for a Redeemer was born. In the book of Genesis, God told Abraham to leave his home to go to a new land; which God would show him. God gave this fledgling group His law (the Ten Commandments). He used Moses to free them from Egyptian bondage, and He used Joshua to lead them in to the Promised Land. He defeated mighty armies before them and brought them to a land of plenty. The nation of Israel we know today is very different than this wandering tribe of nomads following after the commands of an invisible God.

Being "chosen" by God is a great blessing. That was especially true when He used His chosen people to write down and painstakingly preserve the Old Testament portion of the Bible. God spoke into the hearts of His prophets, apostles, and historians telling them exactly what needed to be recorded for future validation. Much of the rest of the world despises Israel because of it claims to prime land in the Middle East. Many enemies have strived to eradicate this nation, but God has a plan to preserve His people. If I told you that you were chosen before the foundations of the world to serve God, what would you think? Never forget that truth for you were chosen, just as surely as they were.

———————————

Lord, I love the thought of being chosen and loved. Lord, those in the nation of Israel are our brothers and sisters. We all serve the same Father God. Today I lift my prayers on behalf of Your children, Israel. Amen

August 2nd Israel: Delivered from Egypt *(Exodus 3:12)*

And He said, "Certainly I will be with you, and this shall be the sign to you that it is I who have sent you: when you have brought the people out of Egypt, you shall worship God at this mountain."

Today, we find the Hebrew people in bondage in the land of Egypt. Moses is the man God has chosen to deliver His children from Pharaoh's hand. Moses tries to get God to send another person citing his poor speech as an excuse. Moses goes repeatedly to Pharaoh, who refuses to obey God's command to free the Hebrew slaves. After repeated plagues, including the death of Pharaoh's son, the people are allowed to leave. They cross the Red Sea on dry land, move into the wilderness, and prepare to go into the land God promised them. Then the whining began—and it never stopped! Moses had the patience of a saint! Several times when the people were grumbling against God, He threatened to wipe them out and start over. Moses always interceded for his people. After Moses died, Joshua led the people into the land God had kept them out of for forty years until the whining generation was gone. Repeatedly, God told the Hebrews: *"If you will walk in My statutes, obey My laws and walk in My commandments; then I will be your God and you will be My people."* Joshua led them into the land, into mighty battles, and into the territories set aside for each of the twelve tribes of Israel. Finally, Israel was home.

———————————

One of the final plagues God sent upon Egypt was the death plague where all firstborn of man and beast was to die. He made provision for His people in order to protect them. The blood of a lamb was to be painted on the side posts and the top piece of the door to the Hebrew homes. Wherever this blood was seen, the death angel would pass by. Pharaoh lost his own child, but not one Hebrew died. God used the blood of a pure, unblemished lamb to save His people from Egyptian bondage. He used the blood of a pure, spotless Jesus to save us from sin's bondage. Have you thanked Him recently for His sacrifice of shed blood on your behalf?

Jesus, You have stayed the hand of the death angel. At the moment of my last earthly breath, I will come immediately into Your presence. Thank You for Your shed blood, which saves me! Amen.

August 3rd   Israel: A Nation Divided   *(Judges 21:25)*

In those days there was no kind in Israel;
everyone did what was right in his own eyes.

Anarchy is a term for a system of government with no law and no oversight. Anarchy reigned in Israel. They asked God for a king and He told them they didn't need a king, but to simply keep their eyes on Him. Finally, He relented; and Saul became king. He was a poor leader and was replaced at death with David, a shepherd known as *"a man after God's own heart."* Just two generations later, Israel fulfilled the words of the prophets and became a divided nation. The north was Israel (or Samaria) and the south was Judah (hence the name "Jew"). Each portion of the land was ruled separately. The northern kingdom had not one righteous king. Judah, the home of Jerusalem, had several godly kings dispersed among its bad ones. During these days, Israel began to forsake God's laws, forsake worship and offering and began to intermarry with the people in the nations around them. Watered down Jewish heritage led to watered down and divided loyalties. God's prophets had spoken that *"a house divided can not stand."* Those prophets were right; Israel was in for a fall.

I have written before of the disintegration of America's moral standard in the 1960's when the family first began to be broken down. Since then, we have plummeted headlong into sin and near anarchy. Israel did the same. Instead of one nation; they became divided, distracted, and despised by the nations around them. They flaunted their sin, mocked God's prophets, and served idols of other nations. King Solomon, the last king of the unified Israel said, *"... there is nothing new under the sun."* He was right. We, in our nation today, are living in a similar immoral, Godless society with each person doing what is right in his own eyes.

Heavenly Father, America is a divided nation, not so much by boundaries but by moral issues. Our homes and families are divided. Our children are raising themselves with no regard for moral absolutes. We need Your healing hand upon us. Amen.

August 4th Israel: Scattered *(2 Kings 17:7)*

Now this came about because the sons of Israel had sinned
against the Lord their God, who had brought them up
from the land of Egypt from under that hand of
Pharaoh... and they had feared other gods....

The divided nation of Israel has come to its breaking point. The northern kingdom, under the rule of Hoshea, is taken captive by the King of Assyria. God allows this because the people have rejected His laws, followed foreign gods, killed His prophets, practiced sorcery and witchcraft, and sold their souls into sins bondage. The small remnant left in Israel was soon overtaken by aliens invading their land from Babylon. Israel was scattered into other nations. Judah was still free, but was rushing headlong into the same sin as the north. A few years later, they too were invaded by the Assyrian army and scattered. God had sent prophets to His people for generations warning them to repent and turn to Him. The *house divided could not stand.* Thousands of years later, Israel returned to their homeland; and in 1948 officially became a recognized state. The hatred of the nations around them has deep roots. While Israel was scattered, surrounding nations moved in and began to use her land. Today, she is a despised and embattled state with many nations in the eastern region openly stating they want her gone. Israel will never be entirely lost. God promised Abraham thousands of years ago that his seed would become a great nation. He promised King David an heir always on the throne. If you take nothing else from these lessons remember this. God gave the land to His children—others may try to take it away—but it will always belong to the seed of Abraham.

Some of this may seem boring to you. Let me say this, the knowledge of Israel's history and heritage is vital in your understanding the books of the Bible. The Old Testament teaches us the history and is lush with promises God made about the land He had chosen for them. Don't discount this type of teaching. It is even more applicable today, in the light of the wars in the Middle East, than it was years ago. Ask God to help you understand this.

Heavenly Father, I am not a great historian, but I do know that You want me to understand these things so I can intelligently discuss them with others. I am praying for my brothers and sisters in Israel. Amen.

August 5ᵗʰ Doing Spiritual Laundry *(Isaiah 1:16)*

*"Wash yourselves, make yourselves clean; remove
the evil of your deeds from My sight, cease to do evil."*

*L*ife is full of teachable lessons. The entry I had planned for this day was not coming together; and I was struggling with the words. I took a break and went to fold a load of laundry…and then it hit me. "I will write about spiritual cleansing using laundry names! Yep, they will love it!" I haven't lost my mind…take a laundry aisle journey with me. Sometimes life gets dirty, nasty smelling from all of the unclean things in our world. At times like this, a long "soak" in the Word of God is just what the Doctor recommended. He advises you to look at the big "spots," the spills, and slops of your recent days. Turn on some music — worship music that is; and begin to "Shout" the enemy's assaults away. Don't let the "Tide" carry you into the lake of hopelessness. What you need most is a "Snuggle" with a "Downy" soft blanket, a cup of hot "Cheer," and a Word from God to put the "Bounce" back in your step. Do you realize that the enemy of your soul longs to control this "Era" of your life? Don't give in. Instead, "hang" him out to "dry" and let Jesus, the living "Dynamo," place you right back into His "fold." Now that wasn't so painful, was it?

Though this is good for a chuckle, there is truly teaching here. The world is seeking in every way to distract and destroy the peace of believers. We can make a decision to allow this in our lives, or we can "shout" those attacks away with the Word of God. Did you realize that *the Word is sharper than a double edged sword* and can be used to rebuke the enemy? Tell him, *"No weapon formed against me will prosper, because I am a blood bought child of the living God and am more than a conqueror though Christ who gives me strength."* Come on, use the Word, fight the battles, and get your Spiritual Laundry ready to wear!

Holy Spirit, I do need to choose this day whom I will serve. I need to be shown how to make this committed decision every day. Wash me and I will be whiter than snow. Amen.

August 6ᵗʰ <u>Salvation: Why We Need It</u> *(John 3:16)*

For God so loved the world, that He gave His only begotten Son,
that whoever believes in Him shall not perish, but have eternal life.

*W*hether you are already a Christian saved by the power of Jesus or a seeker longing to find what the term salvation means; these lessons are written to bring you into a deeper walk with Jesus Christ. Why is being born again necessary? Jesus addressed this question in John 3:3-7. Nicodemus, a Jewish leader, came to Christ, under cover of darkness for teaching. Nicodemus asked what the new birth meant. *"Jesus answered and said to him, 'Truly, truly, I say to you, unless one is born again he cannot see the kingdom of God.'" Nicodemus said to Him, 'How can a man be born when he is old? He cannot enter a second time into his mother's womb and be born, can he?' Jesus answered, 'Truly, truly, I say to you, unless one is born of water and the Spirit he cannot enter into the kingdom of God. That which is born of the flesh is flesh, and that which is born of the Spirit is spirit. Do not be amazed that I said to you, 'You must be born again.'"* If you did not fully hear what Jesus was saying, reread these words again. Jesus is emphatic about the fact that the rebirth experience is essential to entering the kingdom of Heaven. This one passage refutes the world's teachings that everyone will go to Heaven, or that a loving God would not send good people to hell. God sends no one to hell (eternal separation) from Him; but we <u>must</u> <u>choose</u> where we will spend eternity. We must be born again, not as in our first birth (water birth) into the world, but into our spiritual birth into God's world.

What you are reading may be absolutely life changing as to the direction you will walk in the future. Let me ask you a few questions. Do you live to serve yourself and your own needs? Have you ever truly asked Jesus to come into your heart and direct your paths? Do you feel empty, purposeless, or spiritually hungry? Be honest with yourself; you may fool others, but God knows your heart. Are you ready to renew your commitment to Christ or to begin anew with Him in charge of your life? Stop now and pray for the Holy Spirit to open your eyes to His truths.

Holy Spirit, I hunger for a purpose and meaning, which my life lacks. I live for myself... and feel dead inside. Open my ears, eyes, and mind to receive the truths You will reveal to my spirit in these lessons. Amen.

August 7th <u>Salvation: Admission of Sin</u> *(Romans 3:23)*

...for all have sinned and fall short of the glory of God...

Today, we look at the first of the ABC's of salvation in Christ: A=Admit you are a sinner, B=Believe who Christ is and the power He has to change you, and C=Confess your sins and confess His Name. One of the first sermons I ever heard nearly caused me to leave the church. The Pastor said all people in the pews were sinners and needed the salvation of Christ. Who did he think he was, calling me a sinner? I didn't steal openly, hate my parents, or kill others... so I was a good person. Compared to Ted Bundy and Jeffrey Dahmer... I was an angel! I began to read the Bible and realized that the Ten Commandments were a series of life guideposts. I began to understand what sin is and the effect it has in our lives. Sin is <u>anything</u> contrary to God's perfect will. <u>All sin separates us from God</u>. Yes, my gossip or lying is just as despicable in His eyes as were the murders of the men I mentioned above. God is holy and cannot be part of any evil. Sin is born with us. If you doubt the inherent sin nature of man, give two toddlers one toy to play with! We have placed human standards about which sin is worst; but let me say again... all <u>sin separates us from God</u>. What can bring sinners back into right standing with a holy God? Is there hope for sinners to not sin? Will we always be separated from Him? There is hope. Read Romans 6:11&14. *"Even so consider yourselves to be dead to sin, but alive to God in Christ Jesus... For sin shall not be master over you, for you are not under law but under grace."* There is hope through a personal relationship with Jesus Christ!

Are you having a hard time absorbing the truth that you are a sinner? That truth is contrary to everything we hold dear. We never want to admit we are lacking in any aspect of our lives. Truth sometimes hurts; and if you are hurting because of this passage, the Holy Spirit is showing you the things which need to be revealed in order for you to come into saving knowledge of Jesus Christ. Go ahead, admit you are a sinner; once you do; reconstructive surgery on your spiritual life can begin.

Holy Spirit, it hurts me to confess that yes, I am a sinner. I always thought I was "good enough" to get to Heaven on my own merit. Reveal all of my sins to me... I hold nothing back. Amen.

August 8ᵗʰ Salvation: Believe in Christ *(Romans 5:8)*

But God demonstrates His own love toward us, in that while we were yet sinners, Christ died for us.

You are moving toward a heart changing, life changing new understanding of the emptiness you feel in your life. Today, we look at the 'B' portion of the plan of salvation. B=Believe in whom Christ is and the power He has to change you. You have learned that we are all sinners. Let me teach you about my Jesus. God created man to walk in intimacy and fellowship with Him. There was no life expectancy charts in the days of creation...man was to live eternally with God. When sin entered the Garden of Eden, all that changed. Sin brought death; and death brought eternal separation from God. He needed a solution to reconcile His children to Him. Throughout the Old Testament, God's prophets talked about a "Messiah," a "Redeemer" who would be used to cleanse man from his sin. This Redeemer had to be perfect and sinless, a spotless lamb. He could not be born of the union of a woman and a man—for that union produced the sin filled children of the evil world. God sent His Holy Spirit upon a virgin girl named Mary. Her son was born in humble circumstances and was revealed first to the shepherds. He is the Shepherd who would lead us, the blemished flock, back to God. Jesus lived for thirty-three years, taught, healed the sick, challenged the concept of religion verses relationship, cast out demons, and loved everyone. He did exactly what His Father sent Him to do. Jesus was falsely accused, tried, and crucified. He hung on a sinner's cross between Heaven and earth and as 1 Peter 2:24 says: *"and He Himself bore our sins in His body on the Cross, so that we might die to sin and live to righteousness; for by His wounds you were healed."* Three days later, Jesus was raised from the dead, appeared to hundreds of people in His resurrected body, and went to sit at the right hand of God. This is a picture of our resurrection to eternal life.

Jesus died on that sinner's cross to give us eternal life. That sacrifice must be acknowledged as part of the plan for our salvation. Do you believe what is written here? It is all taught directly from the pages of the Bible. If you were the only one on earth, He would do the same… just for you. That is love, the kind of love we have never known. If you are feeling empty and purposeless, it is because you need that love.

Holy Spirit, now I have a better picture of exactly who Jesus was and what His purpose on earth was. He was sent here to save me! He was sent here to save everyone who will call upon His name. Praise be to God! Amen.

August 9th Salvation: Confession *(Romans 10:9-10)*

"…if you confess with your mouth Jesus as Lord, and believe in your heart that God raised Him from the dead, you will be saved;

for with the heart a person believes, resulting in righteousness,
and with the mouth he confesses, resulting in salvation."

*T*oday, is the final day in our ABC's of Salvation teachings. You have heard why salvation is necessary, the truth of the inherent sin nature of man, and the Scriptural basis for who Christ is. I do not pretend to be an expert in theology. I am an expert in the difference Christ can make in a life. I walked for thirty-eight years my way. I have walked for twelve years His way…and there is no comparison. My prayer is a burning passion has been ignited in your heart from these passages. You may want to stop now, pray for the power of the Holy Spirit and reread the three previous entries. Don't rush this step. A commitment to Christ should always be a life changing decision. The final step in new birth in Christ is to C=Confess your sins and confess His Name. Most people think confession means only to speak out what you have done wrong. We also confess our belief in something. Today's Scripture verse tells us that we must confess with our mouth that Jesus is Lord. Do you believe who He is? Are you willing to allow Him to be Lord in your life? If you aren't willing for that, He cannot make life changes in you. Do you believe in His resurrection? He is waiting for you to call out to Him. Here is a sample prayer for you to use as you take these steps to salvation in Christ: *"Jesus, I am a sinner. I have tried to do things my way and to live my life by my own standards. I confess those sins and ask You to take them away from me. I believe You are God's Son sent from Heaven to redeem a lost world. I believe You died for me and were resurrected into eternal life. Your resurrection is my resurrection. Today, I receive my salvation, my 'new birth.' I receive Your Spirit into my spirit that I may walk in newness of life. Amen."*

If you prayed this prayer for the first time, you are part of the family of God. Go tell someone about your decision. That will make it very real in your life. Speak to God in prayer—simple conversation. Get yourself into a Bible and begin to walk a new life!

Holy Spirit, I have made this confession of faith. Please help me to be strong in the face of temptation to return to my old ways. Help me to understand the Bible and the things of God. Amen.

August 10ᵗʰ   Elijah Tests God *(2 Kings 1:10)*

Elijah replied to the captain of fifty, "If I am a man of God, let fire come down from Heaven and consume you and your fifty." Then fire came down from Heaven and consumed him and his fifty.

*E*lijah is one of the Bible's most interesting characters. He is a prophet of God, a messenger sent to share God's word with His people. Most would call him eccentric and colorful; I would call him honest. Elijah was never afraid to speak what God told him to...and he paid dearly for that honesty. This entry is set during the reign of King Ahaziah of Samaria (northern Israel). The king has fallen and been severely injured. He wants to know if he is going to die, so he sends messengers to inquire from Baal—a foreign god—for word on his healing. At the same time, God sends an angel to Elijah and tells him to meet the messengers and ask them why they are seeking from Baal. He is to ask them, "Is there not a God in Samaria?" He is then to tell them to relay God's word that the King will surely die. Elijah obeys, meets the messengers, and gives them the word. The King is furious that they didn't continue on to seek Baal, and he sends those fifty plus fifty more to confront Elijah and bring him back to face him. Elijah, in order to prove he is truly a "man of God" makes the statement in today's verse. There are times when God will use a series of circumstances to prove to the lost that He is indeed God... fire from Heaven was one of those actions.

Are you bold in your witness or afraid of what others may think of your words about Christ? God used Elijah in a mighty way because he was willing to be used. The King of Samaria had a proven heritage of God's faithfulness to his people to fall back on.

Remember though, there were no righteous kings in the northern kingdom. Ahaziah sought a stone idol instead of a living God. Do you do the same? Maybe you seek direction from friends, parents, or your Pastor... before you seek from God and His word. He will never tell you a lie or placate you. By the way, Ahaziah died just as God said and those who witnessed Elijah's words saw truth!

Father, I do what Ahaziah did by seeking advice and direction from man before I do from You. I have been wrong. Forgive me, restore me, and show me how to find Your truths. This is new to me. Amen.

August 11th Elijah Passes the Mantle *(1 Kings 19:19b)*

...and Elijah passed by him and cast his mantle on him.

Think about great leaders and the shoes left to be filled by those who succeed them in their positions. I think of Abraham Lincoln, Billy Graham and Ronald Reagan. Regardless of politics, great leaders are great leaders. They set a powerful example for all who follow after them. Long before Jesus became our greatest leader, God raised up prophets to speak His words and lead His people. Yesterday, we met Elijah who was truly a great prophet. God had used Elijah to fulfill his purpose and was preparing to take him home to his reward. But, first a successor had to be found. Elisha is chosen and begins to walk with Elijah in order to be groomed by him. In a series of three conversations, Elijah asks his protégé if he understands that God is going to take his mentor away today. Each time, Elisha answers that he understands fully. The two men stand beside the Jordan River, which has divided by the touching of Elijah's mantle. Elijah asks, *"What do you want from me before I go?"* Elisha, knowing his shoes will be hard to fill, responds that he would like a double portion of Elijah's spirit to fall upon him. Elijah says it is a big request, which will only be answered if Elisha actually sees him taken to Heaven. Suddenly, a chariot of fire appears in the heavens and Elijah is carried to it upon a whirlwind. Elisha mourns the loss of his friend but knows the work of the kingdom must go on. He picks up Elijah's mantle, touches the Jordan River, and as the water parts...he walks on to fill the shoes of his beloved master.

Have you ever had to fill in for or succeed someone in a position where you felt incompetent? Imagine how Elisha feels. Everyone knows the kind of man he is to follow. "Can I measure up? Will they listen to me? I am not nearly as capable as he was?" All of these are the thoughts and fears we face at a time of change. But, God had big plans for Elisha. He also has big plans for you. Remember Philippians 4:13? *"I can do all things through Christ who strengthens me."* If what you want to do is in God's will, you will not fail. If it isn't in His will, He will surely show you. Go ahead and fill those big shoes... step out in faith.

Lord, I feel incompetent compared to Your great teachers, preachers, and service workers. But, I do trust that You have a plan for me. Mold me, shape me, and use me for Your purpose. Amen.

August 12ᵗʰ Elisha: The Woman and the Oil *(2 Kings 4:3)*

Then he said, "Go, borrow vessels at large for yourself from all your neighbors, even empty vessels; do not get a few."

*E*lisha has certainly filled Elijah's shoes. Today, we meet the widow of one of God's prophets who cries out to Elisha in her deep moment of need, *"My husband is dead and the creditor has come to take my two children to be his slaves."* Elisha asks if she has anything at all to repay the creditors. She tells him she has nothing but a small jar of oil. Elisha speaks the verse above to her. He then tells her to take the empty vessels (don't you love how he told her to get lots of them, not a few) and to go into her house and close the door. She is to begin pouring from her jar into the empty vessels, setting each one aside as it is filled. She does exactly as told and fills every vessel until there are none left. At that moment, the oil stopped coming from her jar! She runs to tell Elisha. "Go sell the oil, pay your debtor, and live off the rest of the money," he tells her. The number of vessels she gathered in faith determined the amount of blessing God could pour out for her.

The Bible is full of these little "sermonettes" or life lessons. How often do you limit God's pouring out of blessings by not having a vessel big enough to hold His abundance? Recently in a discussion about this book, I said I would never get rich or famous from it; but I wanted to sell enough to pay for the initial publishing investment. A friend silenced me with one of those "shame on you" looks. She told me not to bind God's hand with my faithless words. Ouch! How many times have I done just that? "I just need $300 in sales per week to make ends meet," or "We need ten more folding chairs because the "Seekers" class will never get bigger than that." Shame on me is right! I need endless sales so I can minister to the needs of others. I need hundreds of chairs because that means hundreds of people are hungering for the Word of God. We must not limit His desire to bless us.

Lord, I will try to stop handicapping the blessings You want to pour out upon my life. I think little, maybe because I am afraid of being disappointed. You have never failed me yet. Amen.

August 13th Elisha: The Shunammite Woman *(2 Kings 4:16)*

*Then he said, "At this season next year you will embrace a son."
And she said, "No, my lord, O man of God,
do no lie to your maidservant."*

In Elisha's travels he encountered a prominent woman in Shunem who prepared him a meal. She and her husband prepared a room for him, so when he was in Shunem he would have a place to stay. Elisha, looking for a way to repay her kindness, asks what he could do for her. She tells him she is fine and just wishes she had a son because her husband is getting old and soon she will be alone. *"At this season next year you will embrace a son,"* says Elisha. The woman chastises him for an apparent attempt at consolation. The woman then conceives and bares a son. Years later, the child goes to see his father in the field and has a horrible pain in his head. He is brought to his mother and dies in her arms. The distraught woman lays her son on the bed of Elisha and sends and goes with her servant to find him. She falls at Elisha's feet and cries out her heart. *"I told you not to deceive me. Why did you send a son just to take him away?"* Elisha hastens to her home, goes into the room where the child lays, and lays upon him breathing life back into his lungs. He then called the mother and told her to take up her son. Her faith in Elisha as God's servant restored her son to life.

The kindness of the Shunammite woman and her husband was repaid by a loving God who gave her the desire of her heart. Why, then, would God allow her son to die? "His ways are not our ways." I can never speak for God. I do know the Shunammite woman would never again take her son for granted, his health for granted, God for granted...get the picture? Others would have seen what was going on. They also watched life restored at the hand of the "man of God." How many of them turned from other gods or idols because of the miracle seen here? We must remember this...all life comes from God. All blessings come from God. Who are we to challenge when it is time for the blessing to return to the Blesser?

Oh Father, I forget that all things come from Your hand. I take the good things of my life for granted and then cry out against You when they leave my hands. Help me to remember blessings are from the Blesser. Amen.

August 14th <u>Samson: So Strong</u> *(Judges 14:5-6)*

Then Samson went down to Timnah...and behold, a young lion came roaring toward him. The Spirit of the Lord came upon him mightily, so that he tore him as one tears a young goat through...

*T*ucked into the pages of the book of Judges is one of my favorite stories in the Bible. Samson is a strange blend of wisdom and foolishness, strength and weakness, success and failure. Samson was set apart for service to God from the moment of his birth. The verse above shows the physical strength this mighty man was born with. Samson never told his parents about the encounter with the lion. He was on his way to meet a Philistine woman who he wanted to marry—contrary to his parent's wishes and God's commands. He was attracted to the woman, and on his way to get her; he stopped to look at the lion's carcass. There he found a bee's nest, and he took of the honey and ate it. During a feast, Samson made a riddle with the young men, *"Out of the eater came something to eat, out of the strong came something sweet."* He gave them three days to figure out the riddle. His future wife was coerced into telling them the answer. When Samson found out that he had been tricked into revealing it to her, he replied *"If you hadn't plowed with my heifer, you wouldn't have found the answer."* Samson, in anger and revenge, went out and burned their crops. When caught; he freed himself, took the jawbone of a donkey, and killed a thousand men. Samson was a strong warrior... with a foolish weakness for women!

Samson exhibits the same disease many of us do. It is the "I disease" and its primary symptom is the "I wants." "I want a Philistine woman. I want to eat honey from a dead animal, even if it is contrary to Jewish clean laws. I want revenge." Do you understand what I am writing about? Samson had everything going for him... and was never satisfied. Because of his foolishness, he was ineffectual for the Lord. Samson was betrayed because he set himself up for the fall.

Father God, Samson disobeyed Your laws to satisfy the desires of his flesh. I have surely done the same. May I curb my anger, temper my need for revenge, and walk in obedience only to You. Amen.

August 15th   Samson: So Weak   *(Judges 16:19)*

She made him sleep on her knee, and called for a man and had him shave off the seven locks of his hair. Then she began to afflict him, and his strength left him.

*S*amson is a picture of what is wrong in our society today. We are self absorbed and self focused. We want it and want it now! We have little regard for the teachings and ways of God. Is someone like Samson still able to be used by God? Let's take a look. After Samson's battle with the Philistines, he falls in love with Delilah... just the name sounds like trouble to me! God has given Samson amazing strength and everyone wants to know how to take it from him. Delilah is persuaded, for a fistful of dollars, to use her feminine wiles to entice an admission from Samson. She asks him over and over again where his strength is from—and Samson keeps telling her little fibs. *"Bind me with new cords, or new ropes, or weave my locks of hair together..."* Each thing he tells her she does and then calls the Philistines to get him while he's weak. Each time, Samson is not weakened, gets away from the enemy, and then listens to her whine about his being dishonest with her! Hello, Samson! Is anybody home in that head of yours? Finally, he honestly tells her that cutting his hair will render him useless. She betrays him again, he is captured by the Philistines, has his eyes gouged out, and is used to grind meal in the prison. All is hopeless... until his hair starts to grow back! Samson, in his one final act on God's behalf, causes the wealthy Philistine leaders to be crushed in a building whose support pillars he destroys. In a crushing death, Samson serves God.

We may marvel at the foolishness of Samson. Is he so different from us really? How many of us keep going back to the things which bring us down in our lives? Think about bad relationships, gambling, wasteful spending, drugs, alcohol... we try to quit or get free and turn around and walk right back in to where we were. Samson wasn't using his God-given wisdom; he was using his passion driven foolishness. We must not forget God still used this "broken pot" to fulfill His purpose with the Philistines. He can still use you... even in your weakened state. Call on Him.

Lord, it is easy for me to judge and condemn Samson. He was weak... and so am I. How do I control my flesh in order for You to use the wisdom You gave me? I need to be rooted in Your word first. Help me, Lord. Amen.

August 16th Ahab and the Vineyard *(1 Kings 21:16)*

When Ahab heard that Naboth was dead, Ahab arose to go down to the vineyard of Naboth the Jezreelite, to take possession of it.

Have you ever met a spoiled brat? Let me introduce you to Ahab, King of Israel. Ahab is looking out the window of his palace and sees a vineyard nearby, which he covets to use as a vegetable garden. He offers to buy it from its owner, Naboth. Property division in Israel is done according to tribe and family, and Naboth says he would never sell the land he inherited. Ahab goes into his room, turns to the wall, refuses to eat, and pouts! His nasty wife, Jezebel, asks what is wrong. She tells him she will get the vineyard for him. Jezebel has Naboth arrested and falsely accused by two witnesses for blasphemy against Ahab and God. Naboth is tried and his false accusers speak against him. He is taken outside the city and stoned to death. Jezebel tells Ahab the vineyard is all his. He is elated until Elijah, the prophet, confronts him for his part in the death of Naboth. God's word to Ahab is, *"In the place where the dogs licked up the blood of Naboth the dogs will lick up your blood."* King Ahab got the vineyard, but he also got what God spoke. We read in the next chapter that Ahab is wounded in battle, lies dying in his chariot, and dies that day. His blood is washed out of the chariots and the dogs lap up the bloody water. What a legacy this evil king left for himself.

What Ahab didn't think of, Jezebel did! What a pair these two were! Ahab obviously was not used to being told that he couldn't have something. Here is a tough word... we are raising a generation of Ahab's. Our children think the world revolves around them. We are mistakenly convinced that telling them "No" will damage their fragile psyches. We are failing our children as sure as Jezebel failed the moral test when she had Nabob falsely accused. God's word encourages discipline. It tells us that we will discipline and correct... because we love. Have you created little Ahab's?

Lord, I have a hard time knowing how to discipline myself and my children. Love requires discipline, but I need the teaching of the Holy Spirit to make necessary changes in me. I do not want to be like Ahab or raise children like him. Amen.

August 17Th <u>On Death</u> *(2 Timothy 4:6-8)*

For I am already being poured out as a drink offering,
and the time of my departure has come. I have fought the good
fight, I have finished the course, I have kept the faith; in the future
there is laid up for me the crown of righteousness, which the Lord,
the righteous Judge, will award to me on that day; and not only
to me, but also to all who have loved His appearing.

If 2007 were to be my last year, I would speak privately to all members of my family and share my faith. I would love my children, husband and grandchildren to distraction. I would seek the Word of God in a whole new way. I would share it with others. I would worry less about a clean house, more about good friendships. I would tell people what they mean to me. I would run in the rain, walk in the sun, and open my eyes to the glory of all God's creation around me. My prayer life would deepen, my worship would be more passionate, and my life would be lived as it should be. I would prepare a eulogy to speak to those at my funeral telling of why I died with hope and how they can do the same. Can you imagine the impact of the voice of the deceased telling survivors they need to get right with the Lord!

Why do we wait until we are old or near death to really live? Think about some of the great Bible heroes and their deaths. Moses would love to have lived long enough to walk into the Promised Land. Peter surely didn't want to be crucified upside down! Stephen didn't want to be stoned; and I am sure Jesus didn't want to die at thirty-three years of age. There is one difference between the deaths of these men and the deaths of many today. Each of them lived their dream! They lived to die for that which they believed in no matter what the cost. Think about the recorded messages they could have left! Stephen would say, "Forgive everyone who hurt you—they didn't know what they were doing." Moses would tell you it is easier to walk by the Law of God than it is to walk against it. Peter would say it was all worth it because he was forgiven for denying his Lord. Think about your legacy. Think about how you would live if 2007 were your last year.

Lord, help me to live each day as if it were my last. Help me to be a witness for You every day You give me breath. Amen.

August 18th   True & False Prophets 1   *(2 Corinthians 11:13)*

For such men are false apostles, deceitful workers, disguising themselves as servants of righteousness, whose end will be according to their deeds.

$\mathcal{O}$ ne of my teaching priorities is training my students how to discern the difference between true and false prophets. Throughout Scripture we are cautioned about this very real problem. There have always been false prophets. The unfortunate truth is that some of them are in Christian churches. False prophets speak to the ears of the listeners. Scripture tells us people want their ears to be "tickled" and will go wherever that will happen. A lack of hard teaching about the moral absolutes is leading to a weak body of Christian believers with a shallow faith, which will never stand the onslaught of the enemy. Recently, a friend said she had attended a "mega church" on vacation. She said there was not one word of Scripture, not one traditional hymn of faith, and not one word which would cause anyone to be challenged. We are getting the music, the programs, and the fellowship part down pat. What about the teaching of the hard truths and moral absolutes of God's Word? A false prophet will say anything is okay in the church body. He will tell us Biblical teachings which are outdated and must be challenged. He will tell us that we need to "dumb down" the message in order to be inclusive to everyone. These things are flat out contrary to Gods words. He addresses this in the verse at the top of this page. They are *"disguising themselves as servants of righteousness, whose end will be according to their deeds."* God help those who are not teaching truth.

Do you want your "ears tickled?" It is like years of believing in Santa Claus only to find out your parents were lying to you all along. It is like finding the stash of molars and incisors the 'tooth fairy' collected in your mother's jewelry box. Picture this: You stand before God and have to explain why you listened to false teachings, didn't weigh them against the Word, and even taught them to others. God help you. We must stop listening to false prophets who will fill our heads with garbage about being "enlightened."

Lord, give me discernment and wisdom to weigh all things against Your truths. Quicken my spirit to understand what false teachers are speaking. Amen.

August 19ᵗʰ   <u>True & False Prophets 2</u>   *(1 Kings 22:14)*

But Micaiah said, "As the Lord lives,
what the Lord says to me, that I shall speak."

*T*oday's teaching is a great word picture of what I spoke about yesterday. Two kings, Jehoshaphat from Judah and Ahab of Israel, have met together to see if they can join forces against a common enemy. Ahab calls his prophets together and asks them if they should proceed. The prophets tell them, *"Go up, for the Lord will give them into your hand."* Jehoshaphat, one of the righteous kings of the southern kingdom, senses that these are not true prophets of God. He questions Ahab to find if there are any other prophets to inquire of God's words. Ahab says, *"There is yet one man... but I hate him... because he does not prophesy good concerning me."* Jehoshaphat calls for the prophet Micaiah. The messenger sent for the prophet tells him, *"Please let your word be like the word of them and speak favorably."* Micaiah responds, *"As the Lord lives, what the Lord says to me, that I shall speak."* He comes before the kings and sarcastically tells Ahab to go forth and God will give over his enemies. Ahab senses the sarcasm and challenges the prophet. Micaiah tells him he sees Israel scattered on the mountains like sheep without a shepherd. He continues to tell of a vision where an evil spirit volunteers to go and convince Ahab to go into a battle where he will be defeated. Ahab has the prophet jailed and dies, as prophesied in the battle.

———————————

As I was typing this entry, I thought about parents who tell their children not to do something because it will bring trouble into their lives. The child, like King Ahab, goes ahead and does what was cautioned against. The outcome is as the parent warned, and all that's left to say is, "I told you so." The difference here is that Ahab is an adult, but he had no desire for truth... just for "ear tickling!" Watch yourself! You may think you want that which requires no change in your life, but God wants you to hear His true words. Are you ready to listen to Him?

———————————

299

Jesus, "ear tickling" sounds great to my flesh. Truth sounds harsh and costly. I need to be willing to pay the price of hearing Your words for my life. Amen.

August 20th <u>Church Rites: Baby Dedication</u> *(1 Samuel 1:28)*

"So I have also dedicated him to the Lord; as long as he lives he is dedicated to the Lord."

For the next six days, we are going to review why we celebrate specific church rites and what they mean in our spiritual lives. We begin with baby dedications. The story surrounding the above verse involves Hannah and her husband Elkanah. Hannah is one of Elkanah's two wives...the barren one. She grieves each month as she realizes she has not conceived and is constantly reminded of her barren state by the other wife. In a culture where motherhood is the main purpose of women, she is ashamed and grieved. Her grief is so overwhelming and her prayers so earnest that Eli the priest thinks she is drunk in the temple! Once Hannah explains the reason for her tears, Eli sends her away telling her God had heard her prayers and would grant her the desire of her heart. Hannah conceives and gives birth to Samuel, her precious son. Keeping a promise she had made, Hannah dedicates Samuel into the Lord's hands. She took her child to Eli and left him to be groomed for kingdom work. Why do we dedicate babies to the Lord in the modern church? This rite involves a dedication of the child to serve the Lord and a commitment by the church family to be positive role models and counselors in the life of the child. In most Protestant denominations, this is done in the place of a baby baptism, as a means of putting the child in God's hands until they reach the age of accountability and can make an informed decision to serve Christ.

Baby dedications involve responsibility on the part of all involved. They are a precursor to adult decisions for salvation through profession of faith in Christ. The parents recognize the truth that God gave them the child, knit him together in the womb, and ultimately is who that baby will answer to as an adult. Our grandson was never dedicated as a baby. However, I lay my hand upon his head and pray over him nearly every week dedicating him into the service of the Lord. It is never too late to do this.

Jesus, babies are a gift from Heaven and the world will do its best to steal them away. Help me to dedicate the children I know into Your hands to receive Your hedge of protection. Use me in the life of a child. Amen.

August 21ˢᵗ   Church Rites: Holy Communion   *(Luke 22:19)*

When He had taken some bread and given thanks, He broke it and gave it to them saying, "This is My body which is given for you; do this in remembrance of Me."

Holy Communion is a ritual set in place as Jesus shared His last meal with His disciples before being arrested, tried, and crucified. As they partook of this Passover meal, they were commemorating the provision God made for His children when they escaped slavery in Egypt. Their departure came so quickly, they didn't have time to allow their bread to rise. The Passover is also known as the Feast of Unleavened Bread. During this meal, Jesus took the cup of wine, gave thanks to the Father for it, and called it to represent His shed blood. That blood, which would mere hours later, flow down the Cross, washes us clean. He took a piece of unleavened bread, broke it, and passed it to the others at the table stating, *"This is My body which is given for you."* That body would be abused and offered up so that we could know for certain that our eternity with God in Heaven was sealed. When we partake of Communion in our church services, we are to do so in full remembrance of Jesus' sacrifice on our behalf. We are to remember the cleansing power of His shed blood. We must dwell upon the price He paid for our sins. We are to never take Communion lightly or

301

with irreverence. It is one of the most solemn church rites and is a reverent reminder of what real love is. Think about this before you partake.

In Chapter 11 of 1 Corinthians, we find precautions of how we are to be in our attitudes as we share in Holy Communion. We learn that we are not to take of the elements if we have anything against another. We are to go and make it right with our brother; and then come once we are in accordance with God's Word before we partake. This is a reverent and intimate interchange between our spirit and the Holy Spirit. No matter who is around you; stop and reflect on what you are doing as you use these elements. Have you taken Holy Communion in less than ideal situations? Start from this day to make a new effort to honor and glorify the Lord.

Holy Spirit, this is new teaching to me. I confess that I have taken the elements of Communion without full reverence. Close my ears and eyes to that which is around me and help me to focus on You. Amen.

August 22nd <u>Church Rites: Tithe & Offering</u> *(Malachi 3:10)*

"Bring the whole tithe into the storehouse, so that there
may be food in My house, and test Me now in this,"
says the Lord of Hosts, "if I will not open for you the window
of Heaven and pour out for you a blessing..."

ithing is likely one of the least understood forms of worship in the church. Read the verse again. We learn several things from it: bring it all in, it provides for God's house, it opens the windows of Heaven, and blessings pour out from there. The word tithe comes from a word meaning "tenth." God's laws, as given in the Old Testament books of Exodus, Leviticus, Numbers, and Deuteronomy, teach us about this principle which acknowledges that all things come from God. We are to give Him back the first tenth of our earnings, harvest, gifts, and talents. The tenth we offer is used to provide for those in service in the house of God. It provides for the needs of the congregation, the needs of the poor, and for the missionaries the church supports. Notice the part of the verse stating we are to *"test Me now in this, if I will not open for you the window of heaven and pour out for you a blessing."* He has blessings for us. Our faith in offering the tithe unlatches the window so the blessings can pour forth. We don't give because of the blessings. We give because we realize that all we have is from Him in the first place.

When you think of ways to worship God, do you think of tithing? Most of us feel worship is singing, praying, or giving glory to God in a physical way. Tithes and offerings (gifts above and beyond the first tenth) are also forms of worship. How can we better acknowledge the deity and glory of God than to offer Him a small share of ourselves? Are you a tither? If so, has your faithfulness been rewarded by God's blessings? If not, follow the last portion of the Scripture and test Him in this one form of worship.

Father God, I do not have an abundance of wealth, but I offer You that first share. I worship You with thought, word, and deed. Amen.

August 23rd   Church Rites: Baptism   *(Romans 6:4)*

Therefore we have been buried with Him through baptism into death, so that as Christ was raised from the dead through the glory of the Father, so we too might walk in newness of life.

*B*aptism is not the same as salvation. There are likely many baptized people who have never prayed to receive Christ into their hearts. So why do people participate in the rite of baptism? We need to look at what this ritual actually represents. Look at the verse above. Baptism is a picture of the burial and resurrection of Christ. Just as he was buried for three days and arose to newness of life in Heaven, we who call upon His name are "buried" in baptismal waters and "resurrected" from them to new life. If baptism doesn't save us, why do it? The baptism ceremony is an outward profession of an inward faith. Some will be baptized with full emersion; fully reenacting the burial and resurrection. Others will have the living water sprinkled upon their head. Whichever is chosen, the outcome is the same. The baptized one is making a heart commitment, old sin is washed away, and new life starts. Combined with the prayer of salvation, the believer is ready to walk in fullness of life in Christ. Just yesterday, I heard a great word picture of baptism. I wear a wedding ring. It does not make me married to Dan, but it is a reminder of that marriage. If I take it off and go after attention of other men, I am still married just ring-less. The ring (like the baptism) doesn't make the commitment. What it does is mark me as belonging to my husband for others to know I am not free.

Have you been baptized? When I was in high school, my parents were going to be baptized, and told my brother and me we were going to get baptized along with them. At that age, all I was concerned about was how bad my hair would look wet and what would the boys in church think of me! The baptism ceremony did not change my heart. I walked many years in sin afterwards. However, a seed was sown deep in my spirit. Years later that seed would be fertilized, watered, and would begin to grow. The baptism didn't save me...but it did mark me for Christ. If you have not been baptized, seek a place for that ceremony, make your outward faith commitment, give your heart to Christ... and walk in resurrected life.

I love the picture of belonging to You and being resurrected into newness of life, Jesus. I have walked in lukewarm faith; today I am ready to make a new commitment to a deeper walk. Amen.

August 24ᵗʰ   Church Rites: Weddings *(Ephesians 5:31)*

For this reason a man shall leave his father and mother and shall be joined to his wife, and the two shall become one flesh.

Why do people get married? If half of all first marriages end in divorce, why bother? The clear answer to these questions is that God ordained marriage. Read the verse again. Marriage between a man and a woman was created in the Garden of Eden, when God took of Adam's ribs to create his "helpmate." Now, let's look at why the marriage vows are spoken in a church setting. The "until death do us part" words are a covenant (a promise) made before God and witnesses. A marriage ceremony performed by a minister as a representative (agent) of God is similar to a spoken contract between two parties. Marriage vows represent the union of two individuals into one united body. When that union of two is completed, an amazing thing happens. God joins His Spirit with the spirits of the husband and wife to form a tightly *interwoven three strand cord.* Scripture tells us that *cord is not easily broken.* Unfortunately, most people are much more interested in the wedding festivities than they are in the marriage—which will require work each day of its existence.

Why do marriages fail at such an alarming rate? There are several reasons, but one of the most cautioned against in Scripture is an unequally yoked marriage. God's laws forbade His people to intermarry with the nations around them. Why… is it because God is prejudiced? No, He understood the principle of divided loyalty. When a believer marries someone without the same faith, they are drawn away from a full commitment to Christ. In our society, we hear that marriage can be between any two people who love one another and want to commit themselves to the relationship. God set the example for marriage, and no political group or special interest lobby can change that. Marriage between a man and a woman is a picture of the relationship between Christ and His bride (we, the church.) Pray for your marriage and the marriages of others around you. The enemy is bent on ruining this union.

Lord Jesus, I see marriages failing all around me. Help me to be an encourager to those who are in difficult circumstances. I do believe You ordained marriage between a man and a woman. Help me to stand for that truth in a politically correct society. Amen.

August 25th   Church Rites: Altar Calls   *(Luke 15:7)*

…there shall be more joy in Heaven over one sinner who repents than over ninety-nine righteous persons who need no repentance.

*W*here have the altar calls gone from today's churches? I believe they have gone the same way as the real Bible teaching which convicts the sinner. We need to look closely at why altar calls are necessary. In the early days of the American church, traveling ministers went from place to place and held tent revivals. These men spoke the hard words of Scripture and allowed their listeners to realize how far their sin set them apart from God. Once the spirits were convicted, the parishoners were called forward to confess and repent of their sins, commit their lives to Christ, and to find the restoration they so needed. We have removed most of these steps in our "Christian Entertainment Centers" where sin is never defined, people are encouraged to "get right with the Lord" from their comfortable pew, and life changes are rarely made. My personal opinion is that every service should have an altar call… whether there are responses or not. I also believe we need to define exactly what keeps us from being "right with the Lord" or we will never have real realization of our need for grace.

Altar calls are humbling. Most of us, if we are honest, hate to be humbled. That is why they are so necessary. Only when we come to the end of ourselves and humble our pride before God, will we be usable in His kingdom. 1 John 2:16 speaks directly to this situation. *"For all that is in the world, the lust of the flesh and the lust of the eyes and the boastful pride of life, is not from the Father, but is from the world."* There is little sincere repentance without full transparency before God. If you happen to be in a church where altar calls are used, and you feel the prodding of the Holy Spirit, please follow His leading. It may be the turning point in your faith walk.

Lord Jesus, I am guilty of worrying more about what others will think than I am about what You are speaking to my heart. I need Your convicting Spirit and Your gentle restoration through grace. Amen.

August 26th   <u>Rehoboam: Bad Advice</u>   *(1 Kings 12:13)*

The king answered the people harshly, for he forsook the advice of the elder which they had given him.

*B*ad advice is bad no matter who gives it to us. Rehoboam is the unwise son of King Solomon. He has inherited the southern kingdom of Israel and is deciding how he will reign. He seeks the advice of his father's elders. They tell him to honor the requests of his subjects for a lighter work load; and they in turn will honor and respect their new king. Good advice, right? Not if you are trying to impress the young hot shots you hang around with. Rehoboam tells them of the requests by the people, and they tell him to tell them to quit whining or he will double their workload! They tell him to say he is more of a man than his father was. Bad advice, right? Guess which one he choses? Right! He tells them he will increase their work load and they know exactly where they stand. The people go home, meet together, and choose a leader. Rehoboam's foolish decision brings about the division of Israel into two kingdoms with two rulers and with enmity between them. Bad advice comes to no good.

Did you ever get some really bad advice? Did you follow it? We must always look deep to see the motives of the ones who advise us. Friends who have bad marriage relationships might encourage us to give up on ours. Parents who have raised their own irresponsible children may give you parenting tips. Sometimes the bad advice is not intended to cause us harm, but it does just that in our particular situation. Seek God's advice. He will never steer you wrong because He has your best interest at heart.

———————————

Jesus, I have taken lots of bad advice from people who didn't have my best interest at heart. Show me how to seek Your counsel through Your word and focused prayer. Amen.

August 27th <u>Divided Nation</u> *(1 Kings 12:20)*

It came about when all Israel heard that Jeroboam had returned, that they sent and called him to the assembly and made him king over all Israel.

*R*emember the bad advice Rehoboam acted upon yesterday? His folly led to a divided Israel with him ruling the southern kingdom and with Jeroboam ruling the north, which was called Samaria. Rehoboam, trying to save face, gathers the military aged men and prepares to go to war against the northern kingdom. This is a situation similar to America's Civil War where a nation divided and warred within its boundaries. God sends word through the prophet Shemaiah to stop the preparation for battle. At least this time, Rehoboam listens to the advice and returns home to rule over less than half of the land God ordained for Israel. The division affected Israel's ability to fight against its enemies for years to come. No united front, no military back up, and no national patriotism. A modern picture of this is in Korea, where the north and south are divided by the DMZ (Demilitarized Zone). North Korea is ruled by a crazy dictator and South Korea has a democratic form of government. Scripture tells us in Luke 11:17 *"Any* *kingdom divided against itself is laid waste; and a house divided against itself falls."*

America is not divided into two territories like the above examples. We are; however, divided in our moral, ethical, and political beliefs. Our nation is divided almost equally in half. Does it hurt us? We are powerless in our standing within the rest of the world. They see our infighting and moral lapses, our divided loyalties, and look at us as weak and easy targets. Like Israel, a nation divided is unable to protect itself. Pray for our nation.

Father, our nation is divided by moral issues and political differences. Our children stand to inherit these problems. Give us wise leaders, not foolish ones like Rehoboam. Amen.

August 28ᵗʰ   Jeroboam: Idolatry   *(1 Kings 12:28)*

So the king consulted, and made two golden calves, and he said to them, "It is too much for you to go up to Jerusalem; behold your gods, O Israel, that brought you up from the land of Egypt."

*I*f Rehoboam was a foolish leader, that must mean that Jeroboam, King of Israel, is a better one... right? Let's find out. Jeroboam has built himself a home in the north and all appears to be well. He wants it to stay that way. We must understand that the center for worship in Israel is in Jerusalem, which is the southern portion of the kingdom. The people, according to their laws, are to go to Jerusalem several times a year for festivals and feasts. Jeroboam is smart enough to realize that loyalty to a newly divided north can be shattered if the people worship in the temple with their Hebrew brothers. He must stop that from happening. Jeroboam, who has been handed this kingship by God, turns fully from His laws and builds golden calves (idols), and puts them in two northern cities to make it "convenient" for the worshippers. He tops that off by appointing priests *"from among all the people who were not the sons of Levi."* Are you seeing a problem? Soon thereafter, this "sham" religion had little in common with the laws of God.

Do you see how vital good leadership is? I hate to harp on one topic, but this is vitally important. We must keep the true teachings of God in our contemporary services. Some would say, "We live under grace, so the Law is obsolete." Yes, we do live under grace. Does that mean *"Thou shalt not kill"* is obsolete? Is it okay to commit adultery, steal and dishonor the Sabbath? Understand this…we cannot pick and choose which portions of Scripture are important. Without all of the parts of the Biblical picture, we are missing the full message. Programs and music are no substitute for the truth… period.

Father, we are cutting You out of our church services. We are building temples filled with everything You warned us against. Lord, help us. Amen.

August 29th <u>Bless Evil Men?</u> *(Ecclesiastes 2:26)*

To the man who pleases him, God gives wisdom, knowledge and happiness, but to the sinner he gives the task of gathering and storing up wealth to hand it over to the one who pleases God. NIV

*I*n my recent study of Kings and Chronicles, I have read dozens of times these words: "____ did that which was evil in the eyes of the Lord." Or, " _____ did that which was right in the eyes of the Lord, seeking His laws, serving only the God of Israel, and not worshipping the idols of the nations around them." After the latter description, a list of blessings are ususally highlighted. Why does God sometimes seem to allow evil people to succeed and become very wealthy? At the same time, some very dedicated believers struggle from paycheck to paycheck. It doesn't seem fair does it? Maybe the "stored up wealth" spoken of in the Scripture above is for our heavenly home! I know we all want the walk here to be easier, but maybe He knows we would begin to dismiss him, just as the other men of this world do. Without great riches, we must trust Him for our provision. We must be satisfied with godly wisdom and knowledge.

Think of situations you are familiar with where Christians suffer with health issues, with financial problems, and with family issues. Do you question why God would allow these things? Does it make you question His love and loyalty? Do you truly believe God has your best interest at heart? I do not speak for God, only from personal experience. Every time I have faced this kind of situation, I came out stronger and more faithful than prior to the testing. Dan and I live a relatively quiet life. We are home bodies and enjoy silence. There was a time when my son was in high school when Dan's daughter came to live with us. Our quiet home became a war zone with slamming doors, dueling stereos, and nasty words. Dan and I wanted to move out and leave them to battle one another! If we hadn't worked together every day, our family could have been destroyed. Instead, we prayed and sought God as new Christians; and He brought us through. We became stronger in our time of testing. Hopefully, God would say we *"did that which was right in the eyes of the Lord."*

Lord, I see what I feel is injustice toward believers in this world, but I trust You to work all things together for the good of those who love the Lord and are called according to Your purpose. Amen.

August 30th Naaman the Leper *(2 Kings 5:14)*

So he went down and dipped himself seven times in the Jordan, according to the word of the man of God; and his flesh was restored like the flesh of a little child and he was clean.

*N*aaman is the captain of the Aramean army and was highly respected by those in leadership. He was given victory in battle, but Naaman was a leper. Leprosy was the most feared diseases in Bible times. It is like AIDS today, in that there is no cure; and was highly contagious. A young Jewish girl serves Naaman's wife. The girl tells her mistress that if Naaman went to the prophet Elisha, he could be healed of the disease. The king of Aram sent a letter with Naaman, gaining him access to Israel. The king of Israel thinks the king of Aram is trying to bring trouble upon him by bringing someone who asks for an impossible cure. Elisha hears of this and tells the king he would like to meet with this leper. Naaman comes to Elisha, who tells him to go and wash seven times in the Jordan River and he will be clean. Naaman was furious! He thought Elisha was making a fool of him by making the healing so simple. He wanted a great fanfare, a waving of hands over him, and a miraculous cure. His servants ask him, *"had the prophet told you to do some great thing, would you not have done it?"* They challenge him to follow Elisha's plan. When he does, his flesh is restored, clean and like the skin of a little child.

God used this little girl of faith to achieve a purpose which would sow seeds into the entire Aramean kingdom. Naaman wanted reverence and awe from Elisha. Instead, he was given simple directions for healing. Have you ever given someone common sense advice to better their marriage or to work on their parenting skills, only to have them seek answers from those who do not speak from God's word? I have friends who I speak to all the time about their poor marital and parenting situations. I encourage them with Scripture... and the words fall on deaf ears. We aren't so different from Naaman. We want television talk shows to fix the problems in our lives. The real answers lie in the pages of the Bible.

Lord, most of my advisors do not speak Your Word; and Your Word is what I most need for the situations in my life. Open my eyes to where my answers lie within the pages of the Bible. Amen.

August 31ˢᵗ   <u>Children of God</u> *(1 John 3:1)*

See how great a love the Father has bestowed on us, that we would be called children of God; and such we are. For this reason the world does not know us, because it did not know Him.

*A*re you a child of God? Do you look or act any differently from those in the world who do not call themselves Christians? What does it mean to be called *"children of God"* in a world which is contrary to everything that means? I confess I have struggled with trying to fit in with friends and family yet trying to keep myself set apart as a child of God. When I write these entries, it is not that I am holding my godliness over your head. Believe me, I struggle as hard as or maybe even harder than others do. I know people who are inherently nice people... and I am not one of them! How can God then call me His child? He knows my heart and knows the person I want to be. If you were to meet me today, you would get to know who I am at this point in my life. God, on the other hand, knows who He made me to be. He knows my yesterdays, my today, and all my tomorrows. He knows what I have been through and what I will go through. Because of that truth, He calls me His child. No one else knows the Vicki in my spirit, the struggles, and the frustrations. You may see me as a teacher, a business owner and an author. He sees me as a broken clay pot willing to be used to achieve His purpose on this earth. I am surely, His Child!

How do others see you? How do you see yourself? Do you see the markings of God on your thoughts, your words, your actions, and your relationships? Jeremiah 29:11 tells us *"For I know the plans that I have for you, declares the LORD, plans for welfare and not for calamity to give you a future and a hope."* You are not alone... because you belong to Him. Ask Him to help you feel like a "child of God."

313

Lord, the world has beaten me down to the point I had forgotten I belong to You first! I am excited to have this reminder brought before me. Today, I begin to walk as a child of the living God. Amen.

September 1ˢᵗ <u>Your Appointed Position</u> *(Acts 22:10)*

"And I said, 'What shall I do, Lord?' And the Lord said to me, 'Get up and go on into Damascus, and there you will be told of all that has been appointed for you to do.'"

*D*o you think God has a specific plan for your life? Remember Jeremiah 29: 11 from yesterday's lesson? *"For I know the plans that I have for you,"* declares the LORD, *"plans for welfare and not for calamity to give you a future and a hope."* Look closely... He has plans for you, not for evil but for a future with hope! That should make you smile! God's plan for you is not the same as His plan for me. We have each been given different gifts and graces. I am a writer, a teacher, and a public speaker. Friends of mine would rather have their teeth pulled out without anesthesia than speak in front of a group. Does that mean my gifts are better than theirs? Absolutely not! I would love to be as creative as Bonnie, as disciplined as Janet, and as much a servant as Geri. I would love to type as fast as Gail, be a nurse like Karen, and be as encouraging as Esther. I can work to develop skills; but I cannot change who I inherently am. Maybe we need to walk on that Damascus Road—the path God takes us down where He can get our attention—just like Paul did in the verse above. Once there, away from the foolishness of this world, He can show us the plans He has for our lives.

What gifts has God given to you? Are you using them to serve your own purpose or the purpose He has set out before you? These are important questions because they help us understand why He made us the way He did. If you have a heart to teach, you can teach in the church. If you have the gift of music, it can be used to share hope with others. If you are willing, you can follow the plans He has set before you.

_____

Lord, maybe I need to walk on that Damascus Road to where You would have me be and serve in Your kingdom. I will need to step out in faith; please hold my hand, Lord. Amen.

September 2ⁿᵈ Nothing can Separate Us *(Romans 8:38-39)*

For I am convinced that neither death, nor life, nor angels,
nor principalities, nor things present, nor things to come, nor
powers, nor height, nor depth, nor any other created thing,
will be able to separate us from the love of God,
which is in Christ Jesus our Lord.

What if I tell you that there is absolutely nothing that can separate you from Christ? He will never abandon you, divorce you, pull Himself away from you, or forsake you. Even governments, persecutors, and municipal powers cannot separate you from your Messiah. There is actually only one way for you to be estranged from Him; and that is for you to move. If you don't feel as close to Christ as you once did, who moved? *He is the same yesterday, today, and forever.* He does not change, but we sure do. We get too busy to pray, too tied up in relationships to spend time in His Word, or too busy working to fellowship with His people on Sundays. We move away and then expect Him to be waiting when we decide to come back into a relationship with Him. The amazing thing is that even in those situations, Jesus is waiting. He is a gentleman and will wait patiently for us to wake up and realize our need for Him.

_____

What separates you from Jesus? If you answered your own movement, this entry was written just for you. Let's be honest with ourselves. Paul, the writer of the book of Romans, warns us in today's

Scripture that *"powers"* will try to separate us from our faith. What are *"powers"* which could do this? You must realize that the enemy of your soul, Satan, will go to any length to divide you from your Savior. However, we give him way too much credit for moving us, when in all actuality we make poor decisions. My encouragement to you is to not allow yourself, your circumstances, or any *"power"* to move you from God.

I have moved and have no one to blame for my distance. You never change, Jesus. May I get back into step with You today—before another moment passes. Amen.

September 3ʳᵈ <u>Fatherhood</u> *(Numbers 23:19)*

"God is not a man, that He should lie, nor a son of man,
that He should repent; has He said, and will He not do it?
Or has He spoken, and will He not make it good?

*W*hen I think of God as my Abba Father (loving Daddy), I realize he is involved and is concerned about everything in my life. He, unlike earthly fathers, never leaves, never lies, never abandons, never forsakes, and never sees suffering without being moved by mercy. The greatest truth I see is that He sacrificed in a way I can't imagine an earthly father sacrificing. Earthly fathers sacrifice their children for material things, jobs, hobbies, activities, and sexual wanderings. God sacrificed only once; but that sacrifice cost him everything. He had to watch his Son on that cross, broken, bleeding, and humiliated. How grateful I am, that the same Father God would do this again, even if I were the only person on earth. God, as Father, is the perfect combination of justice, love, impartiality, and compassion. He never sins; therefore, He never needs to say I am sorry. He always keeps His promises. We can only wish that more earthly fathers would model their fathering skills after the God of Heaven.

Did you grow up with a good father example? I have listened to people on both sides. One dear friend had a wonderful childhood with a large family and a Pastor father who made time for each of his children as well as his flock. Another friend had a father who left her mother to raise all of the children alone with little money and no support. Yet another friend was the victim of sexual abuse at the hand of her father. She would rather he had left than stay and cause the nightmare she lived. No matter what your father was like, your Father is caring and loving. He is waiting to bring you peace, give you blessings, and lead you *"beside still waters."* People who have had a rough time comprehending God's love, in most cases have had a poor example of father love. If you know someone who is a good father… tell them… they need to hear it.

My Heavenly Father, You are the perfect model of fatherhood, and I thank You for all You have taught me. So many I know need You in their lives. Help me to be Your instrument to lead them. Amen.

September 4th   <u>Captured Thought</u>   *(2 Corinthians 10:5)*

We are destroying speculations and every lofty thing raised up against the knowledge of God, and we are taking every thought captive to the obedience of Christ.

For all of the people who say they cannot stop obsessing about things like money, food, drugs, sexual lusts…they need to read the above verse and claim it as their own. Friends and I are fasting the four Tuesdays of Lent; and I obsess twice as much about food when I can't have any! I absolutely know that I can live days and days without food…if you seen me you would fully understand. Obedience to Christ means not putting anything in a position of prominence before Him in our lives. How do I do that? How do you do that? Here are some answers found in Philippians 4: 8 *"Finally, brethren, **whatever is true, whatever is honorable, whatever is right, whatever is pure, whatever is lovely, whatever is of*** *good repute, if there is any excellence and if anything worthy of praise, dwell on these things."* We need to think about good things, pure things, honorable things, and the Word of God. We are given the name of Jesus Christ to use against the tools of the enemy. We must rebuke bad thoughts. Here is an example: "In the strong name of Jesus Christ, I claim freedom from these thoughts. I do not need _____ more than I need Him. Get behind me, Satan!"

What do you obsess about? You need freedom in your life. As long as the food (drugs, alcohol, pornography...) controls you, you will never know peace or joy. Are you ready for freedom? Memorize some promise verses. Use them and Christ's name to rebuke wrong thoughts. Today can be the first day of the rest of your life.

---

*Lord, I **choose** today to give You control over all the distractions in my life. They have kept me from being fully Yours. No More! In the strong name of Jesus Christ, I am celebrating victory. Amen.*

September 5th <u>Law Brings Great Peace</u> *(Psalms 119:165)*

*Those who love Your law have great peace,
and nothing causes them to stumble.*

*L*et's look at laws and rules and the effect they play in our lives. We will use two families as our word picture. Family One has no set rules. The children are disrespectful to one another and to their parents. They are allowed to decide for themselves their study, television, play, and bed schedules. The parents do not enfore obedience at home, which results in disobedience at school and in public places. This lack of discipline effects every element of their lives. Family Two has set rules...set by mature parents who care about their children's safety, future, and relationships. Their children have set bedtimes, mealtimes, chores, and scheduled homework sessions. Disobedience is addressed, the children are loved, and they are welcomed wherever they go. These cases would have seemed extreme fifty years ago. Today, our society has many more Family One's than Two's. When did the change come? It began when we started dumbing down the family system and making our children think they are the center of the world. This lack of discipline has led to the vulgar society we live in. Personal responsibility and public propriety are rare qualities.

Reread the verse. Being attentive to the rules brings peace and keeps us from falling into sin. Great translation isn't it? When we know the difference between right and wrong and walk in right pathways, our homes, our families, our communities, and our country are better places. I have little patience for undisciplined children. Usually, I want to paddle their parents! This problem is as old as the days of Moses, when God gave the Ten Commandments. He knew humans needed laws in order for them to live without chaos. Life without chaos equals peace and safety.

Father, I am the first to admit I resist rules and balk at them. I now understand laws are for my own good. May I begin today to learn and apply Your laws to my life. Amen.

September 6ᵗʰ The Prodigal Son *(Luke 15:32)*

We had to celebrate and rejoice, for this brother of yours was dead and has begun to live, and was lost and has been found.

*I*n the parable of the Prodigal Son, a man has two sons and the younger one decides he wants freedom from his father's rules. He wants freedom to make his own choices. Does this remind you of yesterday's entry? He wants his inheritance to take with him. He leaves, without a look back at how he is hurting those who love him, and wastes every penny on "riotous living." Soon, he finds himself friendless because the money is gone. He takes a job slopping pigs, something absolutely contrary to the Jewish laws he grew up under. He is so impoverished and desperate, he wants to eat some of the pig's food. In a moment of realization, he decides to return home; not as a son but as a slave. His father never stopped watching for his son to return and seeing him coming down the road, he runs to meet his prodigal child. He clothes him in fine clothes, places the family ring upon his finger, and orders the choicest calf to be prepared for a celebration. The older son is furious. He has served his father without fail and never had such a celebration. He feels betrayed and separated. His father tells him that he will still have the same inheritance—it was always his—but his brother, who was lost to them, is now found.

This parable represents many things in our minds. My thought is this. The father is, of course, Father God. The older son is the life-long believer who serves in the kingdom his entire life. The young son is the recently converted Christian who the senior believers decide do not deserve forgiveness from Christ. The young prodigal has to come to the end of self, realize he is incapable of restoring himself, and humble himself enough to come to God as a servant. Think about this... are you the young prodigal who came home to ask forgiveness of the Father? I am that person. Are you the one who has served Christ your entire life—without fanfare—and have a hard time looking upon those who seem quite undignified in their faith walk? We must drop the pretenses, reach out to one another, and behold the joy of the Father.

Father God, Your mercy is forever and for whoever calls out to You. I am grateful for my own salvation and will rejoice with all others who find it, too. Stop my judging heart that I might please You each day. Amen.

September 7th **All in the Name of Christ** *(Colossians 3:16-17)*

*Let the word of Christ richly dwell within you, with all wisdom
teaching and admonishing one another with psalms and hymns
and spiritual songs, singing with thankfulness in your hearts to
God. Whatever you do in word or deed, do all in the name of the
Lord Jesus, giving thanks through Him to God the Father.*

et's look first at the last sentence of today's Scripture verse:
"*Whatever you do in word or deed, do all in the name of the
Lord Jesus, giving thanks through Him to God the Father.*" Few of
us could ever say everything we do is to the ultimate glory of Jesus.
When I think of the events of this week, I realize several times I said
or did things which would not glorify the Name of Christ. Bragging,
judging, and criticizing are just a few things I get caught up in. The
power of the tongue destroys; destruction not only to those we speak
against but also to the witness we have for Christ. What about giving
thanks? Are you good at that? Not me! I have to admit I kind of like
the martyr thing I have going on... "I work so many hours per week I
don't have enough money to do that." or "I don't know why I can't lose
weight—I only had four cookies today." Once again, pity parties for
Vicki alone! Do I thank Him for both of my jobs? Do I tell Him daily
how blessed I am to have His House to minister to others' spiritual
needs? Do I thank Him for a healthy (though tubby) body? No, No,
and No! Read the first sentence again. Does the Word dwell so richly
in your spirit that you use it to teach, admonish, and encourage?

Yes, here is another one of those "You need to be reading the
Bible" entries. Some of us, like little children, do not know what is
best for us. I speak only from experience... the Word of God is life
changing! When we have it in us, we are able to use it to comfort
a friend, encourage a stranger, and challenge a sin. Only then are
we doing everything in the name of the Lord Jesus. What greater
praise can there be to God, the Father, than for us to use His Word
to minister to the hearts of His children? We need more praising,
worshipping, thanking... and less worldly words.

Lord, my words have not been such as would be worthy of Your name. I need a whole new vocabulary… teach me to speak "Jesus." Stop any words from my mouth, which do not reflect on You. Amen.

September 8th <u>Afflicted</u> *(2 Corinthians 4:7-9)*

But we have this treasure in earthen vessels, so that the surpassing greatness of the power will be of God and not from ourselves; we are afflicted in every way, but not crushed; perplexed, but not despairing; persecuted, but not forsaken; struck down, but not destroyed…

*W*hy would God use flawed, broken earthen vessels like us to carry the important message of salvation to the world? He knows the human touch and the human experience is priceless in showing the lost how to relate to a holy God. Our common faults and failures make us realize how much we need Christ. If we were perfect, how could we model the picture of grace to the world? There have been many times when I had reservations about sharing my personal testimony, which I am very ashamed of. But, that same testimony, coupled with the proof of Christ's change in my life, give me a surefire witness to lost souls. Why does He use cracked pots or broken vessels? Because only then can the *"surpassing greatness of the power… be of God and not from ourselves."* Cracked pots should not be proud pots or boastful pots… simply grateful pots! Those pots face affliction and crushing; but once repaired at the hand of the Potter, they can never be destroyed!

Okay, Cracked Pot, how are you allowing God to use you in His plans? Do you have a testimony? Has your life changed since meeting Christ—tell someone. Have you come through testing and been stronger for it—encourage someone else. You do not have to know all the answers and all of the technical terms about Christianity;

you simply have to have a heart for the lost! Remember, they are broken earthen vessels who need the restorative touch of the Potter in order for their lives to be forever changed. Don't waste another minute. They need to hear your testimony.

Spirit of the Living God, embolden me to tell others of the difference You have made in my life. My testimony of Your restoration in my life can help another. Please show me who that person is. Amen.

September 9th   Stephen, Chosen by God   *(Acts 6:8)*

And Stephen, full of grace and power, was performing great wonders and signs among the people.

*W*ouldn't you love to be called *"full of grace and power"* by God? Stephen was a disciple of Jesus Christ who was part of the food distribution program of the early Christian church. The Apostles were passionately sharing the gospel and didn't have time to feed the widows and the poor. They chose seven men *"of good reputation, full of the Spirit and of wisdom"* to put in charge of the feeding. Stephen, as we read in the verse, is performing wonders and signs. The church is growing rapidly… and as it has throughout history, it's met with stiff resistance. False witnesses were enlisted to accuse Stephen of blasphemy against the Law of Moses and against God. He is arrested and taken before the Jewish Council. In that meeting, Scripture tells us *"all who were sitting in the Council saw his face like the face of an angel."* Stephen, when asked if the accusations were true, begins a thorough history of the Hebrew nation from the time of God's appearance to Abraham, through the reign of King David, and right on through the crucifixion of Jesus Christ. What a powerful speaker!

What would keep God from calling you *"full of grace and power?"* Stephen knew how to defend his faith because he knew

323

the history behind it. Remember, there were no Bibles as we know them during this period. The history had to be memorized in order for it to be taught to future generations. How would you handle the false accusations if they were hurled at you, blackening your name and reputation? Stephen didn't lash out. Instead, he tried to diffuse their agitation and anger. He spoke of what they had in common—their Jewish heritage. Tomorrow, we find out if his plan worked.

Lord, "full of grace and power" doesn't describe me. Stephen was a servant but also a great teacher. Lord, I know I need to be prepared at all times to defend my faith. Please teach me how to not lash out at false accusations. Amen.

September 10th   Stephen Sees God   *(Acts 7:56)*

...and he said, "Behold, I see the heavens opened up and the Son of Man standing at the right hand of God."

*W*e finish our study of Stephen—the First Christian Martyr—in today's entry. Stephen is a great orator and an educated historian. He is doing well in diffusing the anger of the Jewish Council until he reminds them that they have a history of killing God's prophets whenever they speak truth contrary to the leaderships practices. *"They killled those who had previously announced the coming of the Righteous One, whose betrayers and murderers you have now become."* Ouch! Now Stephen is stepping on toes! He is accusing the Jewish leaders of killing Christ's prophets and then of killing Christ Himself! Somehow, I don't think they will take this lightly. The men begin to shout insults at him, gnashing their teeth in anger. *"But being full of the Holy Spirit, he gazed intently into heaven and saw the glory of God, and Jesus standing at the right hand of God."* He tells them what he sees as they rush at him, drive him out of the city and stone him. In his dying breath, he asks God to forgive his killers. All this is watched by a Jewish Pharisee named Saul... later to be the Apostle Paul! The man who oversaw the killing of the first Christian Martyr would later become the writer of much of the Bible's New Testament! His ways are beyond us!

Stephen may have been able to temper the anger of the Jewish leaders, but he refused to "sugar-coat" the truth. He knew he was going to die, and his willingness to sacrifice his life for the further-ance of the gospel of Christ sowed seeds in the heart of Saul. Jesus watched what was happening from His Heavenly home, encour-aging Stephen's spirit through His Spirit, and welcomed his loyal child home. This should encourage all believers as they prepare to face the end of earthly life... He is waiting.

Father, I confess that I doubt I could ever be as strong as Stephen. I want to be that sure of my future after this life ends. Please help me to be the strongest person I can be and to face death with faith. Amen.

September 11th America Under Attack *(Ezekiel 19:7)*

"He destroyed their fortified towers and laid waste their cities; and the land and its fullness were appalled because of the sound of his roaring."

September 11, 2001 is a day that American adults will always remember. The horrifying pictures of commercial airliners flying into the World Trade Center's towers will haunt us forever. I will never forget the fear of that morning. Dan and I had been studying about Christians being *"salt and light"* in their world. When he called me from work to ask what was going on, all I could do was cry and tell him to start *"salting"* in earnest. I remember my anger at the inhumane waste of innocent lives on airplanes, in buildings, and answering the calls to service through police and fire departments. Why does something like this happen? There are many reasons, but the fundamental truth is that America is despised as the "Great Satan." We are seen as a people who claim to be Christians and act totally the opposite to Christ's teachings. We claim to be moral and are fully immoral. The rest of the world loves our money… and hates our form of government. They especially despise the fact that America stands with her sister nation, Israel. We are a prime target, too comfortable in our "soft" lives and open to the attack of those who despise us. Why did it happen? Hatred is the clearest answer. That kind of hatred always leads to death.

Do you remember the day of these attacks? I am sickened to think of the fear of the passengers on the four planes which crashed. I kept thinking about how many people thought they would get to faith "some day" when life was less busy… and died apart from God. We must all be aware that none of us know when our last breath will come. We must not put off sharing our faith with others… God forbid that one person die apart from the Lord when we had a chance to witness.

Lord, we cannot understand the evil within the heart of a man, which would cause him to commit such a horrific act. I do know this… I do not want to die apart from You. I do not want to see someone I love die not knowing You either. Give me words… Amen.

September 12th   America Turns to Faith   *(2 Chronicles 7:14)*

If My people who are called by My name humble themselves and pray and seek My face and turn from their wicked ways, then I will hear from heaven, will forgive their sin and will heal their land.

$\mathcal{I}$ always find it odd that people turn to God when events like the September 11, 2001 terrorist attacks happen. If I were not a believer, I would think watching the horror of that day would cause me to doubt God… not draw nearer to Him. Maybe events like this make us more aware of our own mortality and that there must be more to life than what we live each day. The first Sunday after the attacks our church was filled to capacity. The children's department had parents lining the walls who were apprehensive about being apart from their children. People were realizing how important their families were. They were seeking truth, seeking patriotism, and seeking companionship. During all of this, I heard a local pastor stating that these were "temporary commitments," and life would soon return to the pre-September 11th ways. I felt he was being unreasonably cynical. I was wrong. By the third week after the attacks, there were plenty of parking spaces, plenty of seats in the pews and fewer children in church. Our sense of patriotism was still strong, but our search for the real meaning of life waned. I am not saying lives were not changed for Christ during that tumultuous time; but many people went back to the lives they lived before the attacks.

I remember talking to a friend the day after the attacks, she told me she had lived and worked in New York City for ten years and never (NEVER) heard one person mention God, faith, or church. She grieved for the dead, who died without knowing Christ. She did have one friend she kept in touch with who "for some unexplainable reason" was late for her job at the World Trade Center on the morning of September 11. That woman was asking pointed questions as to why her life was spared. Even in the darkest days in America, God was at work. Remember, when people are facing hard times, they are ready for your gentle witness... not forceful pushing... but gentle witness.

Father, May my commitment to You be full fledged and never half-hearted or lukewarm. I need You in my life every day... not just when times get hard. Amen.

September 13th <u>America Forgets</u> *(Deuteronomy 32:28-29)*

For they are a nation lacking in counsel, and there is no
understanding in them. Would that they were wise,
that they understood this, that they would discern their future!

*A*merica too quickly forgot the horror of the terrorist attacks on September 11, 2001. We forgot how to be kind, how to be patriotic, and how to be a land united. We instead became a *house divided*, which Scripture assures us will lead to our fall. The two party system of our government quickly went back to dividing the population. Unfortunately, politics overwhelmed rational thought and we began the infighting and animosity again. Even worse is the problem directly addressed by the verse for today's entry. We are a nation which rejects godly counsel, Biblical understanding, and true wisdom. The small spark of faith and unity ignited by the tragedy was gone. Just a few months later, we couldn't say "Merry Christmas" in our shopping centers, we were being challenged to not say "One nation under God" when we said the pledge of allegiance and American athiests wanted "In God we Trust" off our currency. America needs to wake up! Let me say this, not to cause fear but to make everyone aware of the state of our nation. We can remove prayer from our schools, God from our public places, and morality from our government. We also remove the hedge of protection promised by God in yesterday's verse. Reread it!

You may wonder how you can fight—here I go on my rampage! Tell people "MERRY CHRISTMAS" because you are a Christian. Stand up for your faith to the "squeaky wheel" which is getting all the attention in this nation. Why do the "athiests and agnostics" get all the media coverage? Talk about what has happened since September 11th, how we have turned from our faith. Then, on a personal note... get yourself working in the kingdom of God. Turn outside of your own needs to help or encourage someone else. Live as you were commanded: *"Love the Lord your God with all your heart; and love your neighbor as yourself!"*

I tend to run hot and cold in my commitments. How could I expect my nation to do any differently. Yes, we have forgotten the horror of that day. Yes, we have forgotten how faith helped us through those hard times. Yes, we have become a divided people. Help us, Father. Amen.

September 14th <u>Secret Christians</u> *(John 3:2)*

...this man came to Jesus by night and said to Him, "Rabbi, we know that You have come from God as a teacher; for no one can do these signs that You do unless God is with him."

The speaker in the above verse is Nicodemus, who we first me in the August 6th devotional. Nicodemus is a man of the Pharisees and a ruler of the Jews. He stands to lose his leadership position, his reputation, his place of respect in the Synagogue, his friendships, and maybe his family by seeking Christ. Notice in the above verse *"this man came to Jesus by night."* He is hungry for truth, but he isn't quite committed enough to admit publicly his faith in who Jesus is. See what he says, *"We know that You have come from God as a teacher; for no one can do these signs that You do unless God is with him."* Let me ask you this. If you hunger for truth, believe Christ is truth and know he came from God... why do you sneak to learn more? Well, many people attend church on Sundays and never tell another soul what they heard or learned while there. They might even sneak in a little Bible reading, as long as no one knows! Are we really so different from Nicodemus? How overt are we about our faith?

Did you know that Jesus was buried in a borrowed tomb? Another Jewish leader, who was a secret follower of Christ, buried Him in his tomb. Read with me: *"After these things, Joseph of Arimathea, being a disciple of Jesus, <u>but a secret one for fear of the Jews</u>, asked Pilate that he might take away the body of Jesus; and Pilate granted* *permission. So he came and took away His body."* Doesn't this make you wonder how many other men in the Jewish faith were really hidden followers of Christ? Are you a secret Christian? What causes you to not be bold in your faith? Joseph had to step out—reveal his real beliefs to the leadership—when he asked for Jesus' body. What will it take for you?

I am not as bold as I should be about my personal relationship with You, Lord. I have always thought faith was a private thing. I see though, I can never be Your witness if I don't open my mouth. Amen.

September 15th <u>Iron Sharpens Iron</u> *(Proverbs 27:17)*

Iron sharpens iron, so one man sharpens another.

What do you picture when you think of iron sharpening iron? I see two pieces of metal, rubbing against one another, removing anything which causes friction, and leaving them brilliantly bright. Have you ever tried to cut with a dull knife or unsharpened scissors? Have you ever worked with an unproductive person? That person needs his skills and work habits honed in order for him to be useful. This Scripture tells us that one man can sharpen or hone another. How does that happen? Our daily interactions can either sharpen us or make us dull and useless. Who do you spend your time with? What do you spend your time doing? These are hard words, but I am going to say them anyway. You may have to give up the company of those who dull you and make you ineffectual. You may have to give up habits and time wasters like television, sports, hobbies, and video games. Who can sharpen us? God can through time with Him in His word. Mentors can teach and hone the wisdom of a child of God. Friends who speak truth and light into you will sharpen you; those who speak garbage will dumb you down.

Sometimes challenges by those who believe differently or who are seeking truth sharpen us. My friend, Marna, challenged me to dig deep into the Bible in order for me to answer the questions she asked. At our Seekers class, we sharpen one another as we share our experiences and our varied understanding of the Word of God. I hone and sharpen them as I teach directly from the Bible. They sharpen me as they ask questions and cause me to dig deep into my mind to recall specific Scriptures and Bible truths. My prayer is this book is sharpening you, making you more God focused and hungry to learn. Who dulls you? What might you need to give up which is dumbing you down? Give this serious thought today, and then put what the Holy Spirit reveals to you to work.

I long to be sharp and well honed in order for me to be useful and effective in Your kingdom, Father God. Please reveal anyone or anything which prevents that from happening. Reveal truth to my spirit. Amen.

September 16th   <u>Solomon: Seeking</u>   *(Song of Songs 3:1-2)*

On my bed night after night I sought him Whom my soul loves; I sought him but did not find him. 'I must arise now and go about the city; in the streets and in the squares I must seek him whom my soul loves.' I sought him but did not find him.

Tucked into the pages of the Old Testament is a love story. It is a story which could be written about the relationship between a man and woman in the intimacy of marriage. This story is so much more though. It is a picture of Jesus and His bride, the Christian church. It is a glimpse of how intimately we are to know the One who would sacrifice everything for the one He loves. The woman in the story, as we read in the beginning of the verse above is seeking pure, unselfish, and fulfilling love. That kind of love is spirit love not lust of the flesh; and there is surely a difference. The woman has likely looked for love in money, people, and things, but none of them satisfied heart deep "soul love." She has looked and never found the thing she longs for most in her life. Once she stops looking for love in other things, she will turn around—look deep within—and there will be the One who created her, who knows her more intimately than any man will ever know her. She will see Jesus, the lover of her soul...and in that day she will find that which has been the desire of her heart.

Are you a Seeker like the woman in today's verse? Luke 11:10 tells us *"For everyone who asks, receives; and he who seeks, finds; and to him who knocks, it will be opened."* If you earnestly and honestly seek after the things of God, He promises you will find them. If you knock on the door of Scripture, He will open that door and allow you to come in and see the things hidden there for those who come to Him in faith. Think of the abandon she exhibits as she runs around looking for her love. She doesn't care what others think or how many have let her down... she is seeking a deep and abiding relationship. Run hard after the things of God.

Father, I am asking, seeking, and knocking for You to enter my heart and be the love of my life. Please hear my pleas and my callings. Come unto me, Lord Jesus. Amen.

September 17th <u>Dan: Alcoholic</u> *(Deuteronomy 21:20)*

"They shall say to the elders of his city, 'This son of ours is stubborn and rebellious, he will not obey us, he is a glutton and a drunkard.'"

Sometimes, even when we are doing things totally contrary to what God has planned for us, He is working to draw us to Him. I met Dan in a bar. I found out he had been married twice before; so when he started asking me out, I told him we needed to just be friends. Dan was the most likeable guy, but he had a bad drinking problem. He was never an obnoxious drunk—more of a sad drunk. Vietnam haunted him. So did the early deaths of both of his parents. We finally began to date, but Dan's out of control drinking pushed me to the limit. We parted ways, but on Easter Sunday, April 21, 1984; my parents forced me to go and get Dan, who was in his house with no electricity, running water, or food. The house was being foreclosed on, he was losing his job... he had hit bottom. I brought him to my apartment where he called his doctor and asked to be checked in to the stress center of our local hospital. I dropped Dan off there early on that Monday with every intention of never dealing with him or his alcohol problems again.

Neither of us really knew the Lord. If we had, we wouldn't have met at the bar in the first place. Many times when I share Dan's story with others, they think I sound harsh. I told him at the hospital that he was "on his own." He had hurt me in every way possible. Why? Because I cared about him, and he didn't care about himself. Dan had hit bottom, but he took others down with him. During the second week of his time in the hospital, a nurse called and asked me to come and visit Dan. She said part of their recovery is to make things right with those they have hurt during their addiction. Reluctantly, I went, and it was the first time I saw Dan with clear eyes and clear skin. I was glad for him, but never believed he wouldn't drink again. Do you have a "Dan" in your life? Are you a Dan? Do you have an addiction which hinders you from being who God wants you to be?

Father, I know people—like Dan—who are trapped in addictive lifestyles and need help. I confess I do not want to be around them, but I must realize You love them; and because of that truth, I must too. Amen.

September 18th   <u>Dan: Dry Alcoholic</u>   *(Isaiah 61:1)*

The Spirit of the Lord GOD is upon me, because the LORD
has anointed me to bring good news to the afflicted;
He has sent me to bind up the brokenhearted, to proclaim
liberty to captives and freedom to prisoners.

I have no idea how Dan and I went from the stress unit to dating. Somehow, it just happened! After he had been sober for a few months, he asked me to marry him. I fully expected him to drink again, so I told him to ask me again after he was sober for a year. He did, and on July 2, 1985 we were married. We started with very little because Dan had filed bankruptcy. Before we even acknowledged God's existence, He was doing amazing things in our lives. We purchased a horrible house, in a great neighborhood, when one loan officer agreed to "give us a chance." We began to renovate that home and ended up living there for nineteen years. Each time an unexpected challenge came up, I was certain he would drink...he didn't. Dan lost his job at a local battery plant at the end of 1994. I was sure he would drink because of the stress... he didn't. We faced the hardship of raising battling teenagers... and he didn't drink. We worked together every day at a furniture store for two years...and he didn't drink. Dan has now been sober for twenty-three years... what an amazing God we serve!

Those who did not know Dan and me in the early days of our relationship cannot believe some of the stories I tell. My husband is a wonderful man of God, a devoted husband, a dedicated father, and a doting grandfather. My family would disown me and keep him if they could! Before we had a shared faith, Dan had his "Damascus Road" experience like Paul, the Apostle. His life was changed completely and irrevocably. Do you see nothing and no one is beyond God's scope of change? I wish I had video tape of Dan and I before 1985. You would understand that God can take the two neediest people in town, allow us to make foolish choices which ultimately separate us from Him, pick us up—dust us off—

and wash us clean. If He can change these two hearts... He can change anyone.

Lord, Dan and Vicki were given a new start, a second chance. There is hope for those I love who are trapped in wrong lifestyles. Use me as an instrument of change in the lives of these people. Reflect You in me. Amen.

September 19th <u>Dan: Man of God</u> *(Romans 6:4)*

Therefore we have been buried with Him through baptism into death, so that as Christ was raised from the dead through the glory of the Father, so we too might walk in newness of life.

People think Dan never gets a chance to talk because I do enough for both of us! That is not true... well, at least partially not true. Dan is my best friend. He is my cheerleader, my partner, my encourager, and... he does dishes and buys groceries! (Okay, now I know he is the perfect man!) More than all of those things, is the fact that Dan and I made the journey from rejected to redeemed together. Neither of us wanted a thing to do with "religious people," so of course we didn't go to church. Sown seeds get watered and fertilized, and because we worked together they were being sown in both of us. Finally, in 1995 we walked into a church, found a new family, found a Savior, found the Bible, and found out there is no greater joy than growing together in Christ. I teach, he is there. I write, he helps. I work at His House, he relieves me. I have visions, he never questions. If I could wish one thing for my friends and family, it is that they could be married to their best friend, their prayer partner, and the one who truly is their other half.

I hope you have learned something from these passages besides Dan's story. This is a clear picture of the redemption process. Dan was, by all accounts, beyond hope. But, Jesus is hope. Dan was living a life which made him have little value in society's eyes. But, Jesus gave him value when He knit him together. Dan was a sinner. Jesus paid the price for each of those sins. Dan was as handicapped as Blind Bartimaeus, but Jesus stopped, stood him up, fixed his problems, and sent him on with new vision. I have fallen in love with my husband again as I wrote this series. Remember, no one is beyond hope.

The redemptive work in this lost sinner's life gives me hope. I have my own handicaps, though some don't show on the outside. Jesus, I want full and complete restoration. Begin Your work in me. Amen.

September 20th   Armor of God: Struggle
(Ephesians 6:12-13)

For our struggle is not against flesh and blood, but against the rulers, against the powers, against the world forces of this darkness, against the spiritual forces of wickedness in the heavenly places. Therefore, take up the full armor of God, so that you will be able to resist in the evil day, and having done everything, to stand firm.

Today, we begin a series on the Spiritual Armor we are told to wear as Christians in battle against the forces of evil. Too many people fail to understand the impact spiritual warfare can have on our lives and our faith walks. Look closely at the passage again. *"For our struggle is not against flesh and blood."* Most of the marriages struggling to survive, most of the parenting problems, and most of the workplace battles are spiritual struggles. These struggles manifest themselves into conflicts with other people, but they stem from the real battle between good and evil in the heart of man. This is especially true in our society today where the world is telling us everything is okay as long as it makes us feel good. No! Forces of darkness want us to believe that: but God's Word speaks absolutely contrary to these rationales. We are to *"take up the full armor of God, so that you will be able to resist in the evil day."* Today is surely the evil day... how do we stand firm?

Think about where you have seen spiritual struggles. I quickly think of marriages of people I know where one person is a believer and is in a constant battle with their spouse. The believer refuses to compromise, and the unsaved spouse rebukes the witness of the believer. This is a clear-cut spiritual struggle. The forces of darkness will do everything to cause fights and divisions. When there is division..the house is sure to fall. Satan has a firm hand hold on the collar of the nonbeliever and isn't going to be a gentleman and give up the fight. The Christian must stand firm and never cede ground to the enemy.

Holy Spirit, I know spiritual warfare is going on all around me. The powers of darkness are heavy and evil. I will need to learn how to stand against these attacks. Amen.

September 21ˢᵗ Armor of God: Truth *(Ephesians 6:14)*

*Stand firm therefore, having **girded your loins with truth**, and having put on the breastplate of righteousness.*

*T*he verse above tells us to stand firm by girding our loins with truth. This would be like putting on a wide belt wrapping around the lower back and abdomen. Picture a rock solid cumberband around your vital organs, made of God's pure truth. In a secular humanistic society, where people are told they each have their own internal moral compass, truth is called relative. I searched the Scriptures to find a suitable definition of truth. Here are a few verses: *The sum of your word is truth* (Psalm 119:160); *...Who may dwell on Your holy hill? He who walks with integrity, and works righteousness, and speaks truth in his heart.* (Psalm 15:1-2) and finally, *I am the way, the truth and the life.* (John 14:6). Another verse tells us that truth *will set us free.* The truth of God's diety, provision, and love helps us to walk in honesty and integrity. This is true even as the evil of this world rages around us.

Going into any kind of battle without truth's protection is foolish. If you are being falsely accused, the truth will exonnerate you. If you are being challenged about being a "foolish blind Christian," the truth of your faith will speak louder than words. If you think your marriage cannot be saved, the truth of honored wedding vows will protect you. If you have to choose between telling a lie or being honest, the truth is always liberating. God's word is truth...no matter what it's detractors say. *For such a time as this...* God wanted me to feed His truth into you... that is the truth.

Guide me in full truth, Jesus. I long to be free from the burden of lies, half truths, and apologies. You are truth... You have set me free. Show me where to tell others about this loin girding truth. Amen.

September 22nd   Armor of God: Righteousness
(Ephesians 6:14)

*Stand firm therefore, having girded your loins with truth, and having **put on the breastplate of righteousness**.*

Cover your heart and your lungs with the next item in the spiritual armor of God. Today, we look at the breastplate of righteousness. If your heart is right and holy, *no weapon formed against you will prosper.* The heart pumps blood throughout the entire body. If it is pumping impurities, the body will cease to live. When we go into the battle with anything but the pure righteousness of our Lord, we are setting ourselves up for sure failure. God's Word is full of promises for those who walk in righteous paths. *For the Lord God is a sun and shield; the Lord bestows favor and honor; no good thing does He withhold from those whose walk is blameless.* (Psalm 84: 1 NIV) Did you break the verse down? He is our shield. He is the giver of favor and honor. He gives those things without question to those who walk blamelessly before Him! These are powerful truths and should give all of us the desire to wear that righteous breastplate everyday.

I have heard for years the saying that there are no guilty men in prisons. Each one proclaims his innocence, says he was set up, and assures us that he doesn't deserve to be behind bars. Somehow, I don't believe that everyone in the prison system is innocent. We all view sin as whatever others are doing; but never what we ourselves are doing. God's righteous breastplate will never cover an insincere and evil heart. He will not bestow favor on those who are trying to disguise evil. Wear your pure and righteous ways proudly but never in pride. Without Christ, none is able to be called righteous.

Lord, I have been guilty of judging others and lording my "godliness" over them. I am sorry. Pride in any form is a sin. I want to walk wearing Your righteousness every day. Amen.

September 23rd   <u>Armor of God: Gospel Clad Feet</u>
(Ephesians 6:15)

*...and having **shod your feet with the preparation of the Gospel of Peace.***

*T*he world is aching for peace. I talk to people every day whose lives are in constant turmoil and who need hope. Real hope and real peace come from only one source; and that source is the Gospel message of Christ's redemption for the sinner. One of the greatest deficiencies in the body of Christ is the lack of trained and willing witnesses. How can we have this huge body of believers and have so few equipped to share their faith with the lost? Churches are not making disciples in their congregations. Programs are never a substitute for one on one mentoring and teaching believers how to simply and effectively share the Bible verses which show a lost soul how to find Jesus. The feet, shod in the Gospel are willing to walk to wherever God sends them. This part of the spiritual armor requires action and preparation. Are you ready?

The enemy loves to make us believe the Gospel is too difficult for non-clergy to use. As long as we are afraid to tell others... we are rendered powerless to change lives. Satan is indeed a clever enemy who knows, if he makes us feel unqualified, he can control the spread of the good news of salvation. He has forgotton one thing. *We are more than conquerors in Christ!* God's plan will come to fulfillment in spite of the roadblocks put before us. One other very real truth is that we are a lazy people who think someone else will do kingdom work and we can simply be "good citizens" of God's holy church. It is not always the enemy who silences our witness...and we are giving him far too much credit. We must not credit his work when reality is that we are too self-focused to go and tell others about Jesus. You are a "blood-bought child of the Living God," and you need to tell others that!

Lord, this takes me out of my comfort zone and into unknown territory. I do want others to know You as I do. Please show me how to be equipped and prepared to share the Gospel of Christ with the lost. Amen.

September 24th   <u>Armor of God: Faith</u>   *(Ephesians 6:16)*

*...in addition to all, **taking up the shield of faith** with which you will be able to extinguish all the flaming arrows of the evil one.*

*J*ust yesterday, I had a friend ask me how to "get faith" or get more faith than she already has. This woman is a lifelong

Christian and has been active in her church her whole adult life. Only one thing is missing... she has never been taught on what faith is, how it comes, and why it is rewarded. Today, we are going to focus on the shield of faith...which makes us able to ward off the attacks of the enemy. Let me begin by saying Satan hates faith because it snatches us out of his hand and puts our feet firmly on God's paths. Hebrews 11:6 tells us *"without faith it is impossible to please Him, for he who comes to God must believe that He is and that He is a rewarder of those who seek Him."* Please don't rush over these verses. God is ready to speak to you, but you must listen. It is impossible to please God without faith! All of your church work will get you nowhere with Him. Faith believes in something your eyes cannot see. It requires no faith at all for you to believe I wrote this book; because, you are holding it in your hand... obviously someone wrote it. Faith was the impetus, which moved me from a vision about *"For Such a Time as This..."* to stepping out and actually putting the words on paper. Faith is what makes me believe it will be paid for, published, distributed, sold, opened and will be a blessing to you!

If we cannot please God without faith... and faith is believing in things we cannot see... how do we obtain faith? *"Faith comes by hearing, and hearing by the word of Christ."* (Romans 10:17) Where does faith come from? Only by hearing the WORD OF GOD! As a Bible teacher, this gets me so excited I could dance! The answer to my friend's honest question is that she can only gain faith by hearing and understanding the Word! Once we have that Word in us, it is readily on our lips to ward off (rebuke) the assaults of the enemy! How is your "Faith Shield?" Are you ready to make it tougher, polish it up, and put it to the test? Get in the Word of God, ask Him to help you to understand and grow that faith bank account.

Faith teaching is new to me, Lord. I am not certain how to grow my faith, but I trust You—in faith—to open my eyes to all truth. Only then will I be able to deflect the enemies arrows. I am excited to get started, Lord. Amen.

September 25th   Armor of God: Salvation & Word
(Ephesians 6:17)

*And **take the helmet of salvation**, and **the sword of the Spirit**, which is the word of God.*

𝒲e have a lot to cover in this final entry on the Armor of God. To review: we have talked about spiritual warfare, girding ourselves with truth, wearing righteousness, carrying the Gospel on willing feet, and using the sheild of our faith to ward off the attacks of the enemy. Today, we add head protection and a mighty sword. The helmet of salvation is a covering which protects our minds and our thoughts. When properly worn, it wards off the mental battles which Satan loves to play with God's children. Here's an example: you commit to reading your Bible faithfully every morning. The commitment is kept for several days, but the enemy starts telling you that you're wasting time because you will never understand it and are too old to memorize it. His mental assault convinces you... and you break the promise to God. Satan wins! The helmet of salvation is your sheild against those thoughts. How do you deflect them? You use the sword of the Spirit of God...His Word! **The very thing Satan is keeping you from is the thing which will beat him every time!** Do you think He doesn't know that? Of course he does... that is why he fights your Bible time.

When we are saved and are reborn in our spirits, we become new creations in Christ. We are able to wear His name, learn from His word, and rebuke the enemy's advances using a combination of the two. Nothing pleases God more than to hear you use Scripture to rebuke. Read Hebrews 4:12, *"For the **word** of God is living and active and sharper than any two-edged **sword**... and able to judge the thoughts and intentions of the heart."* Does that help you to understand how powerful Scripture is? It is alive, it is active, it is sharp, it helps us to discern between soul (our emotions and our thoughts) and spirit (the innermost part of us which relates to God) truths, and it helps us to judge our own hearts. Are you getting more excited about the Bible and its authority? My earnest prayer is that your spirit is on fire for His Word.

May I hunger so much for Your Word, that nothing else can satisfy the desires of my heart. Jesus, I want this sword to be ready for battle and I will surely wear the helmet of salvation to foil the plots of the enemy as he wages war with my mind. Amen.

September 26th   Politically Correct: Schools   *(Mark 10:14)*

*"Permit the children to come to Me; do not hinder them;
for the kingdom of God belongs to such as these."*

Jesus loved children. I picture Him sitting and listening intently to their words, taking time to really hear them. The verse for this entry is His response to the disciples trying to get people to stop bringing children for Him to touch and bless. The disciples weren't being mean. They realized how tired and overwhelmed He must be after long days of healing and teaching. Jesus stopped them by saying, *"…whoever does not receive the kingdom of God like a child will not enter it at all."* What? We must come to Him like children… open, seeking, simple understanding, and honest! That puts things in new perspective…He wants simple—pure—humble faith! He isn't impressed with our wisdom and book smarts! He wants a teachable spirit. Do you have one? Are you trying to make faith too difficult?

A member of my 'Seekers' class told me last week that her children's teacher couldn't correct and mark their classwork with red pen because it was "too harsh" on them! She said the teacher has to use "cheerful colors" like blue or green. Let me tell you this—I had papers marked with red for years and I suffer no long-range problems because of it…other than visions which lead me to do totally unexpected things like open bookstores and write books! What is going on in our schools? This is political correctness gone way too far. We cannot say "Merry Christmas" because we might offend someone of another faith. Our grandson was told he couldn't bring pens, pencils, or "special school supplies" to class because everyone has to have the same thing! Give me a break. Let me tell you what our children really need. THEY NEED JESUS… PERIOD! They need to be able to pray in school. They need to be able to talk about their church and Sunday School activities. They need to know that someone cares about their eternal souls… not the kinds of clothes they wear. We are a nation of political correctness… and it is destroying us.

Lord, You were never politically correct. You called the children to You. We will soon be a nation without any Christian witnesses in our schools. It is time for Your people to fight back. Enable us, Lord. Amen.

September 27th   Politically Correct: Government
(Psalms 33:12)

Blessed is the nation whose God is the LORD,
the people whom He has chosen for His own inheritance.

*L*et me tell you that I was raised to be aware of our form of government and am a news junkie. I am fed up with the cries from the few, ruling over the majority in America. A few want prayer removed from our schools… and it happens. A few want the unborn to be sacrificed for the "choice" of the mother… and it happens. A few want the Ten Commandments removed from courthouses... and it happens. Where is the church while all this is happening? This nation's entire legal system was established on the Law of God! There is no historical proof of a need for separation of church and state. Our founding fathers spoke only of having no state-sponsored church, which would be mandatory and government controlled. God, through Moses, gave us the laws for moral failures, violent actions, and restitution. God's law said, "Do not murder, steal, lie or commit adultery." Those "sins" are all addressed in American law. If the "Political Correct Police" have their way, we will soon have no legal system to protect us. What a shame... God has blessed America...and we curse ourselves!

God cautioned Israel to not intermarry and intermingle with the nations around them. He knew such actions would pull His people away from the blessings He had prepared for them. The same holds true for America. Yes, we are a nation of immigrants and a land where dreams can come true. We are being destroyed by a politically correct sense of inclusiveness and tolerance. America was blessed, because it walked with God, carried His principles, and stood with His children, Israel. America has lost the respect of people around the world and in our own country. Our lips are sealed, our hands are tied and we are no longer the "shining city on a hill." The church of Jesus Christ needs to stand up and be counted.

Father God, You instituted government. You set up the system of judges and leaders. You taught us how to direct a military. You advised us on how to teach our children. You cautioned us what serving the gods of other nations would cost us. Father, only You can change America. Amen.

September 28th Politically Correct: Church *(James 1:27)*

Pure and undefiled religion in the sight of our God and Father is this: to visit orphans and widows in their distress and to keep oneself unstained by the world.

*H*ow much does the church of today reflect the Scripture verse for this entry? During the days of the early church; the widows, orphans, and aliens (strangers in the land) were the central focus for the church's activity. I do believe that most congregations take care of their own by providing funeral dinners, getting food to the shut-ins and the elderly, and caring for the sick. My observation is that we need to reach outside the four walls of our buildings and tend to the needs of the "lost" more than the "found" within our fellowship. Several years ago, our church was sponsoring Red Cross food pantries in our community. A truck full of surplus food would be loaded and driven to our location where the less fortunate in our community could come and get food for free. I can never express to you the blessings we received during these gatherings. We were able to talk to, love on, and encourage those who would likely never enter the doors of the local church. They had needs, and their needs were being met. What we didn't realize before hand was our deep needs to serve were being met at the same time.

The church has become politically correct in the sense that we do not "insinuate ourselves" into our communities. We are safe in our warm and comfortable buildings while a world of needs are hovering right outside our doors. Look again at the verse above. We are to keep ourselves unstained by the world around us... not acting like they do. This does not tell us to ignore the needs of that world. Why do we think the mission field is only in lands across the sea? The first month His House was open, a very inebriated man came in to talk on his way home from the local bar. He needed the Spirit of God, not the spirits in a beer bottle. The mission field is right where you are. Roll up your sleeves and get to work.

Holy Spirit, I have been too comfortable for too long. I need Your nudge to move outside the areas I am familiar with and into areas where You can use me. I am all Yours; just show me where to be Your hands. Amen.

September 29th <u>Mocking God</u>   *(Galatians 6:7-8)*

Do not be deceived, God is not mocked; for whatever a man sows,
this he will also reap. For the one who sows to his own flesh
will from the flesh reap corruption, but the one who sows
to the Spirit will from the Spirit reap eternal life.

*G*od will not be mocked! Those words should send shivers up the spine of everyone who hears them. Here are a few groups who need to hear this message loud and clear. HOLLYWOOD: *God will not be mocked!* POLITICAL LEADERS: *God will not be mocked!* EDUCATIONAL LEADERS: *God will not be mocked!* FALSE PROPHETS: *God will not be mocked!* "EAR TICKLING" CHURCHES: *God will not be mocked!* LUKEWARM CHRISTIANS: *God will not be mocked!* Do you get the picture here? Read the verse again, s-l-o-w-l-y. What you sow… you reap. If you sow immorality—you reap a nation without morals. If you sow false doctrines—you reap a weakened church. If you sow fear—you reap fear. If you sow Christ—you reap godly followers. If you sow love—you reap a compassionate nation. If you sow the teachings of the Holy Spirit—you reap a better life here and eternal life in Heaven. The mocking of God by those who are "educated or wise" will reap perilous results.

Israel had a proven history of mocking God even after He delivered them from Egypt, provided for them for forty years in the wilderness, defeated mighty enemies before them, and delivered them into their land. They tried to disguise sin by calling it other names… does that sound familiar? What do the words *God will not be mocked!* mean to you? Do you see the mocking in our world? Do you hear that we must accept that all gods are the same as our God? Do you see His Name mocked in movies, music, and school? God has put up with this long enough. He never refrained from allowing Israel to be disciplined. They reaped what they sowed. So will we.

347

Father God, I have reaped the benefits and the disciplines for the things I have sown in my life. I want to sow only righteousness from this time forward. I see how You are mocked in our world today. Strengthen me to never do the same. Amen.

September 30th <u>Rejecting God</u> *(Hebrews 4:6-7)*

Therefore, since it remains for some to enter it, and those who formerly had good news preached to them failed to enter because of disobedience, He again fixes a certain day..."TODAY IF YOU HEAR HIS VOICE, DO NOT HARDEN YOUR HEARTS."

I had a hardened heart for the first thirty-five years of my life. I rejected the witness of believers, made fun of Christians, and knew I didn't need to be "religious" in order to have a good life. I was wrong. The verse for today's devotional is worth reading again and again. It tells us there are those who have heard the Gospel message and have ignored it. Those in disobedience will not enter the gates of Heaven. If you don't like this word, don't blame me. God spoke it! He is giving you another chance to listen. Most who read this book are already believers. However, if you are reading it as a "seeker," today is another chance to listen to His call on your heart. *"TODAY IF YOU HEAR HIS VOICE, DO NOT HARDEN YOUR HEARTS."* I have lost loved ones who heard the message and rejected it. I have lost loved ones who knew Jesus and looked forward to new life with Him. The second losses are so much easier to face.

Let me say this... God loves you. He loves you so much He was willing to die for your sins. He is waiting patiently for you to acknowledge who He is and how much you need Him in your life. If you started reading this book after August 6th, please go back and read the entries for four days beginning there. God is calling you to come to a relationship with Him, to His peace, to His provision, and to His protection. My hardened heart began to change in the fall of 1995. It softened one layer at a time, until God could move in and take up residence. Prior to that, I could have died separated from Him forever. He wouldn't have kept us apart; but my decision to ignore Him would have. Don't let another day pass... call Him.

Father, hardened hearts are everywhere. The world is telling us we need only ourselves. No wonder we are so empty. Jesus, break down the walls which separate us from You. Amen.

October 1ˢᵗ Doubting "Roger" *(Ezekiel 36:26)*

"Moreover, I will give you a new heart and put a new spirit within you; and I will remove the heart of stone from your flesh and give you a heart of flesh."

Some people just need to see things with their eyes before they will fully believe or understand them. Thomas was one of those people. The story is told in the 20ᵗʰ Chapter of John's gospel. Jesus has been tried, crucified, and buried. The hope of the Apostles died with Him, and now they are hiding in fear of being arrested as followers of Christ. Each of them is dealing with their own emotional struggles, knowing full well they had let the Lord down by not being there for Him in His arrest and crucifixion. Fear reigns, but is erased when Jesus appears to them behind their locked doors. Jesus commissions them with, *"...as the Father has sent Me, I also send you."* Thomas is absent during this encounter and doesn't believe the words of his friends. He says, *"Unless I see in His hands the imprint of the nails, and put my finger into the place of the nails, and put my hand into His side, I will not believe."* Jesus understands the rational doubt of a dear friend; and eight days later appears and allows Thomas to touch the nail scarred hands. Now, Thomas believes and will be used by His God.

My boss at the real estate company is a lot like Thomas. Roger has a degree of faith, but he is a "show me" kind of guy. We have great talks about faith and God, yet he still believes that God is not heavily involved in the events of our everyday lives. Roger says, "God gave me a brain and certain abilities and then expects me to go out and use them." One thing he cannot doubt or question is the ways he has watched God work in my life during the last five years. Roger was directed by God to call me to his new company. He watched the events following the vision for His House. He has seen lives changed during times of teaching and events in the office. Now, he has watched this book come together. God is showing Roger His Presence. Roger just wants to see His face. Don't give up on the doubters in your life... they are often God's most powerful tools! He just needs to remove those *"hearts of stone."*

Lord, I know many people like Thomas and Roger. They need proof and will chalk much up to "circumstances" and "coincidences." Open the eyes of their hearts, Lord. They want to see You. Amen.

October 2nd Bonnie's Beauty *(Ecclesiastes 4:9-10)*

Two are better than one because they have a good return
for their labor. For if either of them falls, the one will
lift up his companion. But, woe to the one who falls
when there is not another to lift him up.

Barnabas, a Christian in the early church of Jerusalem, is a great role model for us to look up to. He was a great encourager to Peter and Paul as they worked to build a body of believers and equip them to go forth and evangelize with the Gospel. Paul, because of his former actions against the church, is not quickly welcomed into the circle of believers. Barnabas worked hard to change that. He met with Paul and convinced the others that his conversion was true; and that Paul was now a passionate and determined believer intent on spreading the good news of Christ to all men, not just the Jews. Barnabas was part of Paul's first missionary team. He is known to us today as a quiet, influential supporter of those who carried Jesus to Israel and into the Gentile world. Barnabas was a willing cheerleader and team player. We all need a Barnabas in our lives.

I would like you to meet Bonnie. She is a great encourager. Bonnie has grown greatly in her faith walk over the last several years. She is a dedicated Christian, family woman, and friend. She has a close circle of long-term friends who all work together on projects from interior decorating to home renovations. Bonnie is a team player who would be the first to pick up a fallen friend as in the Scripture for today's entry. She cheered me on through the opening of His House, is encouraging me in the writing of this book, and attends the 'Seekers' class every week. Bonnie is much like Barnabas... an encourager to everyone. Do you know a Bonnie? Do you have a great friend who is always ready to dig in and help? If you have a friend like that, thank them. If you need a friend like that, look for one who sticks closer than a brother.

Father, true friends are hard to find. Some days, I wonder if they even exist. Thank You for the examples of Barnabas and Bonnie. I need to be the kind of friend they model. God bless my friends. Amen.

October 3rd Hezekiah's Faith (*2 Kings 18:5*)

He trusted in the Lord, the God of Israel; so that after him there was none like him among all the kings of Judah...

Hezekiah was one of the few godly kings to ever lead Judah. Scripture tells us wherever he went he prospered and was victorious in battle. The kings of Assyria continually threatened to invade Judah and were paid a tribute to ward off their attacks. Hezekiah hadn't paid this because he was so blessed by God who had His hand upon him. Sennecherib, the new Assyrian king, besieged some of Judah's cities and asked Hezekiah where the tribute money was. King Hezekiah stripped the gold and silver from the House of the Lord in order to ward off a full attack. The Assyrian king challenged Hezekiah telling him that his faith in the God of Israel was misplaced. Sennecherib reminded him of the mighty nations which had fallen before his army. Hezekiah remained strong in his faith, sought God in earnest prayer, and was encouraged by the prophet Isaiah. God encouraged Hezekiah that Sennecherib's blasphemy was against Him, and that He would have the last word. He did!

Hezekiah was a man faithful to his Lord and was rewarded for that faith. Sennecherib was relying on his own might, his stone idols, and his past successes. He didn't realize how powerful the God of Israel was. Jesus, hundreds of years later, would tell His followers they would be hated... not for who they were; but for "whose" they were! The world hates the Jesus who reigns in us making us different from them. Have you faced any form of persecution for your faith? Have you lost friends or family members because you "changed" when you became a believer? Remember this, God's people have always been...and will always be... persecuted. We must be willing to suffer for our faith. Anything worth having requires effort... and this faith is surely worth our effort.

Jesus, I know there are many people who do not understand my faith and the change it brought in my life. Some are persecutors, but more importantly, some are curious seekers who are watching to see if my change is permanent and real. Strengthen me to remain strong. Amen.

October 4th <u>Witchcraft</u> *(Deuteronomy 18:9-11)*

"When you enter the land which the LORD your God gives you, you shall not learn to imitate the detestable things of those nations. There shall not be found among you anyone who makes his son or his daughter pass through the fire, one who uses divination,

*one who practices witchcraft, or one who interprets omens,
or a sorcerer, or one who casts a spell, or a medium,
or a spiritist, or one who calls up the dead."*

*W*hich part of the command above don't we understand? No divinations, witchcraft, channeling, sorcery, spells, mediums, or calling up the dead... PERIOD! One of the greatest hypocrisies I see in the church is that we do not run kicking and screaming from things like the Harry Potter books, psychic readings, horoscopes and necromancy, which is calling up the dead. We cannot talk about Jesus in the public forum, but must be "tolerant and open minded of other religions" including Wicca and other occult practices. God's word (read it again if you must) explicitly warns us against the influences of these things in our lives. Subtle and seductive are the works of the enemy to make that which is evil look harmless or even good. The Harry Potter books are a great example. "They are just fiction and no child will believe in casting spells and curses," is the lame excuse I have heard from dozens of people about reading these books themselves and allowing their children to read them "because it is improving their reading skills." Lord, help us...we are blind fools being led by our enemy!

Some of you are hating these words. That is fine... because God wants them spoken knowing full well they will be rejected... just as the prophets in the Old Testament were. The enemy cannot enslave born-again Christians against their will. We open the doors wide for his admittance when we seek the things of darkness. The above Scripture is completed with these words: *"For whoever does these things is detestable to the LORD... You shall be blameless before the LORD your God."*

Jesus, I have taken lightly and even acted inappropriately on these things. Open my eyes to all truth. Strengthen me to be bold enough to speak out against false teachings and witchcraft. Amen.

October 5ᵗʰ <u>Psychics</u> *(Acts 8:9)*

Now there was a man named Simon, who formerly was practicing magic in the city and astonishing the people of Samaria, claiming to be someone great; and they all, from smallest to greatest, were giving attention to him, saying, "This man is what is called the Great Power of God."

oday, we continue our look at the occult and the part it plays in our society. I very much believe that there are psychics, astrologists, and mediums who are endued with supernatural powers. The problem lies in where the powers come from. We, as Christians, need to be aware that:

* Psychics are not "harmless entertainment"
* 70 million Americans believe it is possible to talk with the dead
* Television and movie producers make psychic practices attractive
* "900" numbers make billions of dollars each year
* Occult marketing is designed to prey upon societies' weakest.

Psychics use a proven formula of asking leading (cold) questions; using a system of probabilites. Example: (Someone you know died, correct?) They watch or listen carefully for the clients reactions and lead them into the story—making themselves look clairvoyant. Most psychics have an accuracy rate of 13-15%. Question: if they are truly psychic and can see all things, why don't they win the lottery every day?

Some psychics or mediums will tell their listeners "their psychic powers are gifts from God." Let us look to Scripture for the fallacy in that statement. *"Do not turn to mediums or spiritists; do not seek them out to be defiled by them. I am the LORD your God."* We are to test every spirit in order to see if it is truly of God. If you know someone who is seeking readings from a psychic or a medium to interact with the dead, you must speak truth into their lives. They may hate the message; but we are called to speak out against these things.

––––––––––

Everything not of You is against You, Lord. There are no grey areas in the area of sorcery, psychics, or witchcraft. Lord, help me to pray against these forces of evil. Amen.

October 6th <u>Supplied Needs</u> *(Philippians 4:19)*

My God shall supply all your needs according to
His riches in glory in Christ Jesus...

*D*o you believe the verse for this lesson? Read it again..He <u>shall</u> supply <u>all </u>your needs... not some, not part of them, not maybe... but shall! After an incident last week, I can testify. When the vision for this book occurred, I knew God was going to have to do some amazing works for it to happen. Just as the vision for His House, this would require money...money Dan and I didn't have. I was praising God as I drove home on Wednesday, thanking Him for some unexpected free advertising, when He spoke to my spirit saying, "I've got your back." Needless to say, every hair on my body stood on end as I replied, "Yes, You always do." The next day, my Seekers' class sowed seed into our ministry through financial gifts in cards. With money I had been "squirreling away" since the vision, we had $600 toward my initial $1,150 publishing fee. Late that evening, as Dan put the money in our safe, he found a bank envelope with ten, $100 bills! Yes, $1,000 in a safe, which was empty when checked before Christmas! This is not a lie. If we had known the money was there, we would have paid off credit card debt before. He truly *will supply all our needs.*

––––––––––

Why was the money there, and how did it get there? I cannot answer either question. I don't know why these things happen to us... except when He gives me a vision, I act on what He shows me. This isn't magic or some kind of a fluke. God has plans for all of us;

and I believe He shows them to us in visions, dreams, and mental pictures. I also believe most people ignore them; because they might require stepping out of a comfort zone. Has God given you a vision? Did He birth a dream in your heart? I have said before and will say again you will never know what He can do until you step out in faith. Only then can He provide for all your needs.

Lord, I have been reluctant to step out in faith. Man has let me down so many times; but You are "not a man that You should lie." Breathe Your dream into my heart and I will seek to obey Your plan. Amen.

October 7th <u>Distracted Visionary</u> *(2 Kings 12:4-5)*

Then Joash said to the priests, "All the money of the sacred things which is brought into the house of the Lord, in current money, both the money of each man's assessment and all the money which any man's heart prompts him to bring into the house of the Lord, let the priests take it for themselves, each from his acquaintance; and they shall repair the damages of the house wherever any damage may be found.

*J*oash, one of the few good kings in Judah, collected money to do the necessary repairs on the temple in Jerusalem. Somehow, disrepair was everywhere and no one had noticed. Joash collected the money, delegated the work, and then failed to follow through to make sure the work was done. Twenty-three years later, he noticed! Where was his mind, his awareness as he visited the temple at least once a week for those twenty-three years? How could he have not seen that the stoneworkers weren't doing their jobs? How could obvious construction problems, which weren't being repaired be overlooked? Joash was visionary enough to see the needs, yet distracted enough to ignore lack of progress. What good did the money do except to line the pockets of those contractors selected to do the work? Without follow-through, our giftings are useless.

How is your "follow-through" on the things you are assigned to do? Do you have a good reputation as someone who completes the tasks put before you? Good intentions are useless unless they are seen to completion. Yesterday, we talked about God's visions and His provisions for the works He has planned for us. If I hadn't followed through with the vision for His House, He wouldn't entrust *"For Such a Time as This..."* to me. Each of us needs to pray for "stick-to-it-iveness" in order for us to be useful in kingdom work.

Lord, Your Spirit is convicting me as I read this passage. I am guilty of not following through with everything You give me to do. I start excited and end up distracted. Give me focus and commitment. Amen.

October 8th Positively Negative *(Numbers 12:1)*

Then Miriam and Aaron spoke against Moses because of the Cushite woman whom he had married....

*M*iriam and Aaron are the brother and sister of Moses, God's chosen one to lead His children out of bondage in Egypt. Aaron was there when the plagues were challenging Pharaoh. They were spared during the Passover, watched the Red Sea part for their passage on dry land, and witnessed the waters flow back in to drown the Egyptian army. They sinned while Moses was on the mountain getting the Ten Commandments; by making the golden calf and inciting the people to worship it. Now, in the passage above, they are grumbling against their brother. The Cushite wife isn't the problem... their jealousy of Moses is! Neither Aaron nor Miriam looked deep into themselves to really see what their problem was. They were feigning "constructive criticism," when in all truth, they were trying to undermine his authority. Unfortunately for them, Moses' authority came from God... who sent a seven day case of leprosy to wake Miriam up!

Are you a murmurer or a grumbler? Do you like to spread negativity in the area around you? God gives explicit words regarding things God will never sanction. Proverbs 6:19 says the Lord hates, *"A false witness who utters lies, and one who spreads strife among brothers."* He doesn't take gossip any more lightly than murder or adultery! Ouch! That one hits home. Moses was walking with God. Jealousy led his siblings to try to undermine him. God wasn't happy then; and He isn't happy now. Our job as Christians is to diffuse, not incite, gossip. When we approach the gossip fire, we need to **bring water not gasoline**.

Father God, I have sinned against You and Your laws. My tongue has been unkind, divisive, and unbridled. Please help me to stop before I speak words which are contrary to Your teachings. Amen.

October 9th   <u>Josiah and Athaliah</u>   *(2 Kings 11:1)*

When Athaliah the mother of Ahaziah saw that her son was dead, she rose and destroyed all the royal offspring.

*A*thaliah is one nasty woman! Her son, the King of Judah, has been murdered. The "poor grieving mother" kills all of the other royal siblings... to insure her own seat upon the throne. Only one child, Josiah, survives and is hidden for six years. When the child is seven, the chief priest reveals to the army that there is someone surviving who has authority to the throne. Under full guard, Josiah is brought into the temple, where the king's crown is placed upon his head. The people begin to celebrate, clapping their hands, and shouting, *"long live the king."* Athaliah hears the noise and comes to the temple to see what the celebration is about. She tears her clothes and hurls accusations of treason at the leaders and the child king. Jehoiada, the priest, commands that she be taken outside the city gates and killed. Athaliah's evil was justly repaid with likewise treatment. And the vile idols she served were destroyed along with her.

We have heard our whole lives "what goes around comes around." Athaliah found that out the hard way. She was power hungry and was left powerless in the face of God's justice. Athaliah killed innocent people, but God needed to preserve the bloodline of David in order for the Messiah to be born as promised. We may think we are in control, but God has a plan. Look at the circumstances of your life. Do you see God's hand and plan for you? Ask Him to reveal it to you. Wouldn't that be better than trying to fight insurmountable battles like Athaliah did?

Father, Athaliah did everything the wrong way. She shed innocent blood, brought idols into the temple, and tried to reign through fear not finesse. I want to live my life in a way pleasing unto You. Help me to grow in You, today. Amen.

October 10th   <u>Josiah: Finds the Law</u>   *(2 Kings 22:11)*

When the king heard the words of the book of the law,
he tore his clothes.

Josiah was made King of Judah at the amazingly young age of eight! He had wise counselors and is described as doing *"right in the sight of the Lord... nor did he turn aside to the right or the left."* During his eighteenth year, he commanded the high priest to count the money in the temple and then have repairs made as necessary. As he was doing that, Hilkiah, the high priest finds the book of the Law. Word is sent to Josiah that the work has ensued and of the finding of "a book." The scribe begins to read it to the young king and *"when the king heard the words of the book of the Law, he tore his clothes"* in obvious alarm. He immediately sends for the priests and prophets; sending them to seek God's word on what he was to do. God tells them He has been forsaken as the people of Israel have served other gods. To King Josiah He says, *"...because your heart was tender and you humbled yourself before the Lord when you heard what I spoke against this place... I have heard you... I will gather you to your fathers... and your eyes will not see all the evil which I will bring..."*

Josiah had all of Judah's elders brought to Jerusalem and he read all the words of the book of the Law. He then made a covenant to fully walk in God's ways. The people entered into the covenant. Every vessel used to worship other gods was removed and destroyed. Josiah heard the Law and was absolutely convicted. Even though he was a righteous king, he realized he and his people were far from God. Josiah kept his promise to God. Have you? Are you convicted by what you read in the Bible? If you read it and are not convicted, you need to read on a deeper level.

Father, I would love to be described as doing right in Your sight and never turning right or left from Your ways. I have a long way to go and am ready to begin today. Convict and challenge me. Amen.

October 11ᵗʰ Temptations Escape *(1 Corinthians 10:13)*

There hath no temptation taken you but such as is common to man: but God is faithful, who will not suffer you to be tempted above that ye are able; but will with **the temptation also make a way to escape...KJV**

Throughout Scripture, we see how men were tempted and how they resisted or fell into the temptations. David, the future king of Israel, had many opportunities to slay his enemy, King Saul. His friend, Abishai, was there each time, telling David to *"attack him, for surely God put him here for you to slay him."* David refused to do that because he revered the anointing of God on King Saul. Surely there were times Noah, the ark builder, was tempted to stop work on the boat—just to escape the ridicule of those around him. Instead, he kept his eyes on God. I would imagine Queen Esther would rather do just about anything than walk uninvited into the King's court—and risk death. She ignored the temptation because she knew *"for such a time as this"* she had been chosen. Daniel was a Babylonian prisoner who could easily have broken his pattern of praying openly to the God of Israel several times each day. He, instead, obeyed God's command and was thrown into the lion's den. Surely, he was tempted; but he never followed temptation's path.

Scripture is also full of examples of those who did fall into the trap of temptation and paid the price for disobedience. Absalom died for coveting his father's position. Amnon died for raping his sister. Joseph's brothers faced famine for selling him into slavery. Jesus was tempted to deny God and follow Satan; but He was obedient all the way to the Cross. How do you hold up in the face of serious temptation? Are you a Noah or an Absalom? Are you strong and disciplined enough to resist the tempting and to seek that means of escape? Ask God to help you gain control over things which tempt you.

Lord, I am strong in some areas but vulnerable and weak in others. I need Your fortitude and discipline in all areas of my life. Each day, may I look fully unto You for those things. Amen.

October 12th   Life Lessons: Chicken Coop   (*Deuteronomy 34:8*)

*So the sons of Israel wept for Moses
in the plains of Moab thirty days...*

*L*ife lessons are the things I learned while living in the various homes of my childhood. The first home I remember is referred to in our family as the "chicken coop." The house was less than 800 square feet and six of us lived there! I learned so much during my years in the "chicken coop," and I became a "mature" kindergartener while "roosting" there. I loved every minute of the days

I spent in school that first year. But, one thing I clearly remember was the impact of the sudden death of President John F. Kennedy on November 22, 1963 in Dallas, Texas. The recollection of the heaviness over our little house as my parents grieved the loss of their President has never left me. The people of Israel took thirty days to grieve the death of their great leader, Moses, who sacrificed everything on their behalf. He left his nation, faced the ridicule of Pharaoh, led a multitude of whiners for forty years in the wildnerness, and was unable to step his feet on the soil of the land God promised His people. Moses did what he did because he was a leader. President Kennedy died a leader. How rarely it is for us to acknowledge or thank those in leadership positions over us...until after they are gone. My life lesson from the "chicken coop" house is the importance of honoring leaders.

We are called to honor those who are in positions of authority. This truth applies to municpal (local) leaders, government leaders on all levels, those in charge of our work places, and those in authority positions of our churches. Romans 13:2-3 addresses this issue. *"Therefore whoever resists authority has opposed the ordinance of God; and they who have opposed will receive condemnation upon themselves. For rulers are not a cause of fear for good behavior, but for evil. Do you want to have no fear of authority? Do what is good and you will have praise from the same."* We need not fear authority, unless we are doing wrong. We are called to pray for and respect those in leadership positions... whether we agree with their actions or not.

Father, You set the system of leadership and told us to pray for those in authority over us. I have been guilty, just like those in Moses' day, of criticizing those who lead our nation. Help me to be grateful for those You have placed in authority over me. Amen.

October 13th   Life Lessons: Farmhouse   *(Psalms 68:6)*

God makes a home for the lonely; He leads out the prisoners into prosperity. Only the rebellious dwell in a parched land.

*Y*esterday, we learned about honoring leaders. Today, I want to tell you about the lesson I learned during the years at our farmhouse. My mother was a stay-at-home parent when we were young... how could she do anything else... she was ALWAYS pregnant! Dad came home one day and said he bought us a bigger house, a farmhouse in Oakley. I will never forget the day we first went to see it. Mom had all four of us in the car. We drove down this country road and found the mailbox. Unfortunately, all we could see of the house was the top of the second story and the dilapidated roof. The weeds in the yard had obviously not been cut for years...and that was the best feature! There was no indoor toilet, partial electric wiring, old wood siding nailed directly to the studs with no insulation, and walls drafty enough that when the wind blew, the kitchen cabinet doors flew open! My mom put the car in park, laid her head on the steering wheel, and cried. Dad, with a grin on his face, told her it had "potential!" From swinging on the barn ropes, to food fights in the kitchen; and from family card games to chasing the neighbor's cows... we had fun there! My life lesson from the farmhouse was that people didn't care what the house looked like. They could just have a great time... adults acting like children.

I love to picture Jesus laughing and enjoying those He chose as His closest friends, those who came to Him for healing, and the children. He must have been magnetic for people to leave everything and follow after Him. I think He would have loved the farmhouse in Oakley. There were no pretentions there; and no one worried about messing up carpets, touching the walls, or using the outhouse! Where would Jesus like to visit? He wasn't a man of pretention. He was a healer, a friend, and a servant. Where do your priorities lie? What will people remember about your house? Is it a showplace or a home?

Lord, I have focused on things, which though not wrong keep me from focusing fully on You. I worry about food, clothes, furniture, and the opinions of others. I would rather run to You like an unencumbered child. Amen.

October 14ᵗʰ   Life Lessons: Modern Home *(Galatians 5:14)*

For the whole Law is fulfilled in one word, in the statement, "YOU SHALL LOVE YOUR NEIGHBOR AS YOURSELF."

After four years in the delapidated old farmhouse, my dad bought another house without my mother having any say! He told us it was a "newer, more modern ranch style home." Needless to say, after a "chicken coop" and a spooky farmhouse with an outdoor toilet; his word didn't hold much with Mom! When he pulled up in front of a lovely ranch with a two-car attached garage, Mom thought he was joking. He wasn't! We were moving to a home with a living room fireplace, three first floor bedrooms and a private lake in the back yard! We thought we had died and gone to Heaven, especially when the neighbors began to show up with cakes, cookies, casseroles, and "welcome to the neighborhood" gifts. I cannot imagine how much easier my Mother's life was during that two year period. On the farm, she did our washing with an old wringer washer on the back porch! Now, she had a first floor laundry with…that same wringer washer! Some things never change! I learned about "neighboring" while we lived there. The people there watched one anothers kids, helped with projects, took care of vacationer's homes, and welcomed new families with open arms. *"Loving your neighbor as yourself"* really can happen.

Our fancy new house wasn't what made the real difference in our lives when we moved into it. The neighboring and support of those on our road had great impact on us. Neighbors can change lives. When we lived in the "chicken coop," my sister, Shelly, was born and was a collicy baby. She cried constantly; and soon my mom was pregnant again! A woman in the house behind us would hear Shelly crying and come over to relieve Mom. When Jeanie was born, she was named after Jean, the woman who kept my mother sane until Shelly outgrew the collic. Are you a good neighbor? It is a lost art in some ways. As Christians we need to work on this.

Jesus, I get too busy to "neighbor" with those around me. I remember the story of the Good Samaritan who helped someone who was his nation's enemy. He didn't care because he saw a need and met it. Make me that kind of neighbor. Amen.

October 15th Life Lessons: House of Fire *(Psalms 39:3)*

My heart was hot within me, while I was musing the fire burned; then I spoke with my tongue.

*F*ire burns. That may seem like a foolish statement, but seeing the power of the flames burning your home is an unforgettable experience. We should have known that Dad would never be satisfied to stay in that new house. It didn't require enough physical discomfort to please him! Two years later, we were staying with my mother's sister and her family as work was done on another "dump" my Dad was fixing up to move us into. Carpet was being installed and we had to stay away because of the fumes of the flammable adhesive. On the way back to school after our lunch break, we could see huge black smoke clouds rising from the area of our house and the school directly across from it. Mom said it looked like the school was on fire. Shelly, who was a kindergartener, said: "Maybe it's our house." My mother told her not to say that because, "everything we own is tied up in that house." As we turned onto our street, we found it was our house; and one of the young men laying carpet was still in there. The other had run up the stairs and jumped out of the second story window. I will never forget the horror of watching the flames pour from the roof knowing there was someone inside. I learned fire burns hot, can kill and is not to be taken lightly.

We lost more than our house that day. We lost our innocence, our faith in a home being impenetrable, and my dad's health. He was out driving around as a timber buyer when he heard about the fire at his residence and there was one fatality. He was beside himself trying to figure out which one of us he had lost. His gastrointestinal health never fully recovered after shock. Today, when I see a fire truck with flashing lights and blaring sirens, I get a sick feeling in my gut. I remember us counting heads after the fire, to make sure we were all okay. That sure put the importance of family into perspective. Tell your family members you love them. We must keep them as a priority in our lives.

Father God, I am reminded of how important family is and of how hot fire burns. I ask Your hedge of protection around my family and my home. Thank You for perspective and reminders. Amen.

October 16th   Life Lessons: Trailer House   *(Psalms 42:1-2)*

As the deer pants for the water brooks, so my soul pants for You, O God. My soul thirsts for God, for the living God...

My final Life Lesson entry is not about a childhood home, but is instead about the 1963 two-bedroom house trailer my parents have lived in for the last twenty-four years. The trailer isn't much to look at. When we are all there, it is almost impossible to move around and get to the bathroom, which has a door that falls off the track every time you close it. The charm really isn't the trailer itself, but is the beautiful natural setting all around it. There are pine and birch trees all around, trails leading to additional lots beyond the woods and a peacefulness so contrary to our crazy life. We live in a small community, but it is a thriving metropolis compared to Fairview where my parents live. Sometimes, just sitting in a lawn chair and watching the pines move in the breeze is the perfect antidote to the craziness of life. The log home I wrote about in the February series is a mere hundred yards away; but my parents still live in the trailer! The log home is a dream; the house trailer is reality; and for right now, they love reality. I learned about enjoying nature from that place. I am closer to God there than I am anywhere else.

God speaks to us in the beauty of His creation... not necessarily in the beauty of our creations. We can make fancy homes with spotless floors and shiny clean windows; but they are not awe inspiring on a deep spiritual level. God speaks in the breeze, in the sunshine, in the first tulips of spring. He spoke to me in each home I lived in. He speaks in the people we share our lives with. Stop and think about your own life lessons from homes, neighbors, and specific instances throughout your years. I hope you have enjoyed my trip down memory lane... I sure have.

Holy Spirit, some of my memories are not so great, but many are awesome. Thank You for making me remember the events of my life, which have impacted who I am as an adult. Amen.

October 17th Sin in the Camp *(Numbers 32:23)*

But if you will not do so, behold, you have sinned against the Lord, and be sure your sin will find you out.

For a couple of months now my "Seekers'" lessons have continued to come back to the topic of "sin in the camp." These discussions began as a result of a local pastor openly sanctioning sin within his congregation. I have poured over Scripture for twelve years and have never found any teaching saying we are to accept any lifestyle or action in the name of inclusiveness. I fully understand the concept of "loving the sinner and hating the sin."

A few of my students were struggling to understand the difference between condemning sin and judging the sinner. Finally, after hours of teaching and examples of how God never tolerated evil practices, a word picture came to me. A pastor is a shepherd. His job is to lead, direct, and protect his flock (congregation.) If one little black sheep is allowed to wander off to places which put him in danger, his shepherd will soon find other little lambs following him. His responsibility is to stop the black sheep and its influence on the rest of the flock. In a church setting, one person living in apparent sin, without sanction by the pastor, will cause others to sin in a like manner. Their sin may not be exactly the same; but seeing sin condoned brings the "sin leavening" into the camp. Soon, the whole church will have lost its positive impact in a community. We are called to be holy people... period!

This may be another entry some of you do not like. I am not trying to be offensive in any way. God's Word, not mine, says *we are to be holy as He is holy*. It teaches us that sin is anything which separates us from Him. What is happening in these "inclusive" churches is people are coming there, continuing their lives of sin, and are being hoodwinked into believing they are right with God. Shame on the pastors who are not teaching truth. You may feel differently than me, but if I watched my pastor sanction sin I would be out the door in a flash. Think about it.

There is a very real difference in judging sin and judging a person. Lord, I need Your discernment and a holy boldness to speak up when I see tolerance of sin for the sake of political correctness. Amen.

October 18ᵗʰ   Moral Absolutes   *(1 Samuel 24:10)*

"Behold, this day your eyes have seen that the Lord had given you... into my hand in the cave... but my eye had pity on you... the Lord's anointed."

In today's entry, we find David fleeing from Saul; who knows David is to be his successor and that his own sin will bring his reign to an end. Saul hears that his enemy is hiding in the wilderness of Engedi. He gathers three thousand men to seek, find, and destroy David and his followers. A tired Saul goes into a cave to rest, totally unaware that David and his men are in the deeper rooms of the same cave! What are the odds of that? David's friends are convinced that God has delivered Saul right into their master's hands; and David should kill him and put an end to Saul's pursuit. David, *"a man after God's heart"* refuses to do so because Saul was God's choice to be King of Israel. Instead, David sneaks over and cuts a corner off Saul's robe! He leaves the cave, calls back to Saul, and tells him that he had opportunity to kill him. He assures him if that were his intent, he would have done so. Saul, instead of being grateful, accuses David of treating him like a dead dog! That's gratitude...

David was a man of moral absolutes. He believed Saul was God's chosen king of His favored nation and refused to do anything to change that. David may have looked like a fool... even a wimp, but he didn't care. He answered fully to God. Our world has a problem with moral absolutes. The secular humanists have told us that everything is okay... as long as it pleases us. Think about yourself in David's situation. Would you take the high ground like he did? We are commanded by Scripture to be morally pure... how do you measure up?

Lord, society tells me that anything goes; and Your word tells me just the opposite. I will need Your guidance, direction, and discretion as I seek to proclaim the truth of moral absolutes in a vulgar society. Amen.

October 19ᵗʰ   <u>Weigh All Against the Word</u>   *(Titus 1:9)*

*…holding fast the faithful word which is in accordance
with the teaching, so that he will be able both to exhort in
sound doctrine and to refute those who contradict.*

*H*ow do we figure out whether the opportunities in our lives
are from God or from a trap set by the enemy of our soul?
Sometimes, things look to be great blessings, which surely must be
from above. We must be wise and full of discernment in order to
not fall for fatal distractions. Let's look at some examples in this
entry. You and your spouse are looking for a new home. You are pre-
approved for a $120,000 mortgage, but you see a home for $145,000
which you absolutely fall in love with. A less than reputable lender
will get you the financing. Is this of God? Another example could
be the married man; new to the office, who is paying extra attention
to you. You could think God put him there… kind of like a birthday
present! Is it of God for you to have a personal relationship with him?
Finally, your best friend talks you into going on summer camping
trips, every Friday through Sunday evening for the months of July
and August. You have committed to teaching children's Sunday
School. Is it okay to change that commitment? The answers to these
may seem obvious; but how many of us fall into these traps?

———

Satan makes the most vile things look the most tempting. That
wonderful home, which you clearly cannot afford, is a carrot he
dangles before you to test your wisdom in handling finances. God's
word could speak to your dilemma, when He tells us not to *be either a
borrower or a lender.* I swear to you that the man in the office is not
a "birthday gift from God." He hates divorce and would never, never
condone adultery. It can be sugar-coated and called something else,
but the Bible says looking at someone with lust in your eyes is adultery. Finally, summer camping trips are great; but anything which
keeps you away from church for weeks and weeks in a row is not of
God. Scripture tells us to *not forsake gathering together* with other
believers. I challenge you to weigh all things against the Bible.

Father, I have been guilty of falling for things like the ones mentioned above. I know You would never condone things I see happening all the time. Show me how to apply and then act upon Your Word. Amen.

October 20th   <u>Brent and Dan</u>   *(Exodus 20:12)*

"Honor your father and your mother, that your days may be prolonged in the land which the LORD your God gives you."

*T*he Scripture for today's lesson is called the commandment with a promise. Read it again. Do you see the promise? If you honor your parents as you walk this earth, your life will be longer and better than if you don't. That promise seems vague until you begin to really think about its truth. Children who obey their parents and grow into respectful and productive adults will always have better lives. They will avoid the pitfalls of drugs, alcoholism, laziness, and self-absorption. My son, Brent, is no angel; but he honors Dan and me and respects us and our kingdom work. From the beginning of our relationship Brent and Dan cared for one another. Brent was too young to really remember the Dan who drank too much and caused such turmoil in our lives; and I am grateful for that. Brent remembers the man who never treated him as a "stepson," who taught him how to work and finish projects, and who was his constant coach and encourager. Dan and Brent both had birthdays during the week of this writing. Dan wrote a special note to his son; and Brent wrote that he hopes to be half the man his father is. Dan cried—because Brent sees how his father lives—as a Christian man—and honors him for it.

Noah's sons honored their father enough to risk ridicule from those who called all of them fools... until the flood grew and they alone survived. David's sons disrespected him and even tried to take his position... they died for it. Jesus honored His Father and His

371

mother... to the point of death on a cross. Now, He sits at the right hand of God receiving glory for his obedience. How good are you at honoring your mother and father. The verse doesn't say to only honor them if you agree with them. The commandments are without exception. You may not like what they do, but you're commanded to honor the position of parent.

Lord, I am quick to judge and condemn others for their parenting skills... or lack thereof. Help me to recall this commandment and to remember it is You who defined the family unit. Amen.

October 21ˢᵗ   <u>Brent and Faith</u>   *(Mark 16:15)*

He said to them, "Go into all the world and preach the gospel to all creation."

uring Brent's childhood, we were not Christians—actually we rejected anything whatsoever to do with faith. Had you asked Dan and me, we would have said we were going to Heaven because we were "good" people. Several times during those years, Brent would ask why we couldn't go to the church whose backyard butted up to our property. Each time we told him we didn't need to be "religious to be good people." Years later, when Dan and I became believers, we regretted every one of those comments. We were seeking the things of God; and Brent was seeking everything else. Then, God sent three young men: Jon, Mike, and Guy, into Brent's life. All three were passionate gospel sharing believers who began sharing their faith with Brent. Night after night, Dan and I would listen as their voices talked to Brent long into the night. Just a few months later, our son was baptized by these three young men and began to walk with Christ. He was active in youth activities and had a great circle of Christian friends. How we praised God for these young men who sought to fill the great commission...and to go into their own little world to witness to our son.

How good are you at sharing your faith? Maybe it has something to do with youth, but these young men couldn't be silenced. I am sure they faced persecution by some in their school, but that never stopped them. One of Jesus' last commands was for us to GO and PREACH to ALL. It is disappointing that so few Christians will ever truly share the gospel of Christ with a lost soul. Maybe, it is because we feel ill-equipped to do this. The young men I tell about here were heavy into the Word of God. They didn't wait until someone taught them how to witness. We need to take a lesson from them. Surely, Brent wasn't the only life they changed!

Jesus, I want to tell others about the difference You have made in my life, but I feel unsure and insecure. Give me the boldness of Guy, Jon, and Mike to change a life as they did when they witnessed to Brent. Amen.

October 22nd Brent as a Father *(Psalms 127:3)*

Behold, children are a gift of the LORD;
the fruit of the womb is a reward.

*B*rent is now a husband, the father of two small children, and has purchased his first home. I never imagined he would be as patient and loving as he is with his kids. I don't know why I am surprised, because he had Dan as his example. Tyler looks like a mini-Brent with big brown eyes and dark hair. Hailey looks exactly like her mommy, Sarah; and is petite and dainty. Brent's job affords him several months off during the winter, and he plays "Mr. Mom" very well. Just this week, Hailey spent a couple of days in the hospital... with her Daddy sleeping in the recliner next to her bed. He spent his twenty-seventh birthday there caring for his child... what a change that is from the teenager who thought of no one but himself! God has a way of growing us up—whether we like it or not. Life can pull us off course in our faith commitment, and that has happened with my son. I trust God to draw Brent back into a full faith walk. He is watching God work in our lives and knows how blessed we are. Brent is like many other young people, who think they will miss out on fun by walking a life dedicated to Christ. That's okay; God will always go after that one lost lamb and bring it back to the fold.

Brent realizes the sacrifices required to be a good parent. Now, he understands the times he was told that we couldn't or wouldn't afford something he wanted. God is working in his life, just as He is in the life of your child. Some of you are reading this and are blessed to have all of your children serving God. Others of you have wandering prodigals. And, yet, others have children who fully deny anything to do with the things of our faith. Don't stop praying for them. Remember this, our children are all gifts from God. Our children belonged to Him before they belong to us. We need to lift them daily back to His hands.

Jesus, so many people have children who are walking contrary to everything You call us to. It is easy to think they are beyond hope. You proved at the Cross no one is beyond hope. All of us have fallen short of the glory of God. Amen.

October 23rd Sarah: Longs for Child *(Genesis 18:10)*

He said, "I will surely return to you at this time next year; and behold, Sarah your wife will have a son." And Sarah was listening at the tent door behind him.

Sarah is one of the most fascinating women in Old Testament Scripture. Her whole sense of worth was destroyed by her inability to bear a child. Unfortunately, her desperation led her to take matters into her own hands; and she encouraged a union between her husband and her servant. Her own son was eventually born into turmoil and competition with a half brother born out of the covenant of marriage. Sarah didn't want to wait for God to act in her situation. We are a lot like that today. I have known several people who cannot carry a baby to term. Each of them, in their own way, is desperate to give birth to a child. Sarah's story isn't so different from these women's. This causes me to think about how timeless Scripture is. Thousands of years ago, women longed to have a child... some things never change; because God created us with that innate desire to nurture. Society can tell us there are more important things than being a parent... and jobs, money, and toys are great... but they are never a substitute for that which God ordained.

My daughter-in-law's name is Sarah, too. She is a natural born nurturer. Some things are not hereditary. Sarah hasn't had a great example of parenting in her life, and she is determined to break that generational curse. She and Brent began dating when Tyler was a toddler. She is today, and has always been, great with him. Ty used to tell us he was going to "gwow up and mawwy his Sawah." She and Brent share in their parenting duties and love their family, which is her lifelong dream. Sarah would love to have lots of kids. I don't know that it will happen that way, but I do know she will love each one she is given.

Lord, help me to accept the fact that not everyone who longs for a child will be able to bear one. There are always children around who need love. Use me to positively impact the life of one child. Amen.

October 24ᵗʰ   Let Us Pray   *(Matthew 6:6)*

...when you pray, go into your inner room, close your door and pray to your Father who is in secret, and your Father who sees what is done in secret will reward you.

*L*et's talk about prayer… public prayer. (There, that should have scared the daylights out of most of you!) My journal entry from February 26, 2007 reads as follows. "The extent of many believers' prayer life is a quick, 'Thanks for the cornflakes, Lord.' We pray before we eat, unless of course we are in a public place and would be embarrassed to have others see us bow our heads. Some of us do the quick, *'Now I lay me down to sleep…'* prayer, and never grow beyond that level. We need deep, fervent prayers. These kinds of prayers are focused, honest, open communication with God. Prayer is a dialogue…not a monologue. We are to pray, and we are to listen. Distracted prayer is probably of less value than the cereal and sleep ones I mentioned above. Why? We are attempting to fit God into the leftover spaces of our busy lives, rather than making Him the centerpiece of our existence. We can *'pray without ceasing'* all day long, but that never substitutes for focused *fervent prayers, which avail much!"*

What is the quality of your prayer life? Be honest; this is vitally important to how you will grow in your faith walk. My honest opinion is that a believer who never learns to pray will never mature in their relationship with Christ. In our marriage, friendships and workplaces, communication is vital. Marriage die because of lack of real dialogue. The same is true for friendships and parent/child relationships. Why would we think that a "personal relationship with Jesus Christ" would require any less? Dig through your Bible and find some Scripture prayers. Use them as models…and begin today to grow in this area. I will close with one today to use as a starting point.

Our Father, who is in Heaven, hallowed be Your name. Your kingdom come, Your will be done, on earth as it is in Heaven. Give us this day our daily bread. And forgive us our debts, as we also have forgiven our debtors. And do not lead us into temptation, but deliver us from evil. For Yours is the kingdom, and the power, and the glory forever. Amen.

October 25th   In the Furnace   *(Daniel 3:17)*

"If it be so, our God whom we serve is able to deliver us from the furnace of blazing fire; and He will deliver us out of your hand, O king."

hose blasted man-made idols get more people in trouble! In today's story, we find three Jewish men in captivity in Babylon during the reign of King Nebuchadnezzar. Neb has made a ninety foot tall statue of himself—no vanity there! The command goes out for every leader to come to the dedication of the statue. The three men are enlisted into the King's service and given new names of Shadrach, Meshach, and Abed-nego; and they are called to be part of this dedication ceremony. Warning goes out that anyone failing to bow to the statue will be cast into the fiery furnace. At the preset signal, all of the Babylonians bow to worship the idol... all except these three God fearing men who would rather die than bow. King Nebuchadnezzar orders them into the fire, which is to be turned up to seven times its normal temperature. They are cast in, bound, and tied as the King looks on. He sees a fourth man *"like the son of the gods"* walking about and not being burned in the furnace! Nebuchadnezzar sees this miracle and states, *"Blessed be the God of Shadrach, Meshach, and Abed-nego."*

This story has long been a favorite for children, but it truly holds much for us "big kids" to learn and apply, too. One of the basic commandments of God is for us to make and worship no idols... a law these Jewish men would surely know. They could have compromised in order to avoid the fire, but their commitment to their God was more important than their lives. Let me ask you a few questions. What would you do in the same situation? Would you bow do avoid suffering? Would you be willing to stand alone while everyone else bows? Would you deny the name of Christ to avoid persecution, suffering, or even death? Heavy questions require heavy self-examination. God will carry us through the fires, but only when we prove faithful.

Father God, I confess that I don't know how strong I could be in the face of what Shadrach, Meshach, and Abed-nego faced. I will need for You to grow my faith, strengthen my resolve, and fill me with the Presence of Your Holy Spirit. Amen.

October 26th <u>Testing of Jesus</u> *(Matthew 4:8-9)*

Again, the devil took Him to a very high mountain and showed Him all the kingdoms of the world and their glory; and he said to Him, "All these things I give You, if You fall down and worship me."

*T*oday, we will look at the testing of Jesus by Satan following His baptism by John the Baptist in the Jordan River. For forty days; the enemy tempted, tested, and challenged Jesus. The strength He exhibited there proved Jesus was the holy Son of God, who was able to withstand any temptation forced upon man. Jesus was weak with hunger, when Satan told Him to make the stones into bread. Jesus replied with the word of God, *"Man shall not live on bread alone, but on every word that proceeds out of the mouth of God."* Satan challenged Jesus to test God by throwing Himself off the pinnacle of the temple. Jesus again refuses and says, *"You shall not put the Lord your God to the test."* Finally, Satan offers Jesus all the kingdoms of the world, if He would only bow and worship him. Jesus again uses Scripture to rebuke this temptation, *"You shall worship the Lord your God and serve Him only."* Jesus withstood all the temptation Satan could bring. He is our example to follow.

I recommend for you to read this encounter in your Bible (Matthew 4:1-11). Notice this: Satan uses Scripture, which he twists to suit his needs. Jesus uses Scripture rightly; and those words are powerful enough to give Him strength to resist temptation. The offerings of the enemy were the very things Jesus might have needed in His testing... food, emotional security, and power or authority. Satan met his match in Jesus; because all these things already belonged to the Son of the God of Israel. We need to know the Word of God in order to be able to use it to diffuse the enemies assaults on our weak spots. How are you tempted? How strong are you to resist?

Lord, in my weak moments I am easily led astray. These weak times bring me shame, but I feel powerless to resist them. Lord, help me to find the verses I will need to rebuke the taunts of the one who despises my soul. Amen.

October 27th   Marta's Vision   *(Jeremiah 33:3)*

'Call to Me and I will answer you, and I will tell you great and mighty things, which you do not know.'

Marta is one of my "Seekers'" who came to class at the invitation of a friend. She is a single mother who has had struggles at her job with persecution because of her faith. Recently, she called and requested prayer about needing an open door for a new job. Read excerpts from a letter I received from Marta: "Hi Vicki, Do you remember a week ago after class when you were talking about the book you are writing. Tammy asked you how much they were going to be. You were explaining how you couldn't order as many as you would like to keep the cost down. I said to pray for the money. I wasn't sure that I wanted to tell you about the next part but after your story yesterday, I have to. I think I had my first vision. I saw you sitting in the middle of this long table, with the biggest smile on your face that I have ever seen, and you had piles of books on both sides of you. Behind you was a big sign that said *"For Such a Time as This."* A lot of people were around the tables but in front of you was someone taking a picture of you for a newspaper article. You were doing a book signing. I couldn't tell where this was at but I really believe that your book is going to be a big success. After that vision last week, when I got home I called my sister and told her that we needed to pray for Vicki to get a lot of money. I can't wait to see it happen. I can't wait to see my vision again as its happening. As always, I will keep praying for your success. Love you, Marta."

Marta wrote this to me following a story I shared of God's faithfulness in providing money for my publishing and a generous gift to pay off much of my His House debt. Marta could have been jealous of the gifts I received. Instead, she was home praying with her sister for me to "get a lot of money." Marta is a dear friend, a unwaivering supporter, and a hungry Bible student. I am blessed to call her my sister in Christ. Do you have a "Marta" in your life? She is an encourager and now a visionary. God will reward her for being obedient and responsive. Encourage the "persecuted Marta's" you know. Life is hard… oh, but our God is good!

Lord Jesus, You place people in our lives to encourage and support us. Today, I lift some of my encouragers to You. Bless them Lord. See to their every need. Make me an encourager to others… a godly cheerleader! Amen.

October 28th <u>Rob's Gift</u> *(Hebrews 13:5a)*

Make sure that your character is free from the love of money; being content with what you have…

I had a difficult time coming up with the appropriate verse to go along with Rob's story. Rob, my younger brother, was a computer genius before people even knew what computers were. Our father is a problem solver and a visionary who can figure out how to build or do just about anything, but he is a computer idiot! Rob began writing programming for computers during his high school years. He used to try to explain how computers worked… and would lose us after the "turn the computer on" line. God birthed a scientific brain into Rob, who in turn passed it on to both of his sons. My brother never wanted material things, but he loved family. He was a dedicated single father who was so proud of his sons, Jeremy and Sean, and his lovely daughter Jessica. Rob died in August of 2005 from diabetes related complications. His death was unexpected and tragic; especially because he never knew Jessica was expecting his first grandchild. Little Alexander Robert was born in April of 2006, and his grandpa would have been so proud. Rob's gift was computer science, but his legacy is love.

As I begin this series on my siblings, I am very emotional and convicted. I confess that I was not the sister I should have been to Rob—or to any of the others. Rob had a love and reverence for the natural creation of God's hands. He would talk about how awesome mountains were, how beautiful the landscapes of different areas were, and how much he loved the pines around Mom and Dad's property up north. He was in touch with God on a different level than me. I loved Rob and respected his amazing gift with computers more than I ever told him. Let me ask you this: do you have brothers or sisters you need to settle issues or simply catch up with? Has life taken you away from your family? The Bible is full of families divided by pride, money, jealousy, and differences. The God of reconciliation would never want us to be separated by death with healing words left unsaid.

Father, there are siblings, parents, friends, neighbors, and others whom I have lost contact with and whom I need to take time to reconnect to. I do not wish to leave this world with loving words left unsaid. Amen.

October 29th   <u>Shelly's Strength</u>   *(Matthew 5:4)*

Blessed are those who mourn, for they shall be comforted.

*S*helly seems nothing like the rest of us with her big blue eyes and her edgy sense of humor. She is the proverbial middle child. She is the type of woman who could have thirty kids and be happy as a clam—absolutely the opposite of her big sister Vicki! Shelly has known more suffering in her life than most of us will ever know in ours. She has buried two of her precious children; and the light has gone out in her eyes. Randie Renee, Shelly's oldest daughter died in 1996 at twelve years of age from asthma complications. She was a beautiful young lady. I call her 'God's prettiest angel.' Randie's death shook Shelly and our family to the core. Benjamin, Shelly's firstborn son, never recovered from the loss of his little sister. Shelly remarried and had two other children, but faced tragedy again when Benjamin died in 2003. Most of you reading this are wondering how a mother could survive these losses. I am her sister and wonder the same. She is strong and determined to care for her daughters, Lindsey and Carol and her son, Michael. Shelly grieves inside and never asks for help. She carries this hurt every day. She needs Jesus to help carry her burdened... and to help carry her.

Do you know someone who grieves like Shelly? That person needs your outreach and encouragement. When a family faces loss, everyone is around for the week of the funeral, maybe the week after that. Then the phone stops ringing and the knocks on the door cease. That is when the loss becomes so real and acute. 2 Corinthians 1:4 tells us Jesus *"comforts us in all our affliction so that we will be able to comfort those who are in any affliction..."* Shelly will learn to laugh again... with Jesus as healer.

Lord, thank You for comforting those who grieve and for carrying them through the darkest days. You understood loss. You wept at the loss of Your best friend. I am grateful to serve a God of compassion. Amen.

October 30ᵗʰ <u>**Jeanie's Drive**</u> *(Psalms 37:23)*

The steps of a man are established by the Lord, and He
delights in his way. When he falls, he will not be hurled headlong,
because the Lord is the One who holds his hand.

*M*y youngest sister could talk the ears off the cornstalks! She is funny, determined, and has a heart of gold. Jeanie was the first in our family to come into a saving knowledge of Jesus Christ. She witnessed from across the country… and I rejected every word. She is a Baptist living in Mormon country, and has raised her children in the church. Actually, we don't know one another as we should because she moved to Wyoming right after high school graduation and has lived there since. Jeanie is all about family and loves her times in Michigan to catch up and reconnect with everyone. She is dynamic and bossy—that makes her great at her job as manager in a large pizza chain. Jeanie's husband, Jerry, works deep in the mines of Wyoming… definitely not a job for the faint of heart! She has two grown children and a new grandson named Brayden. I admire my sister for how she strives to keep the Michigan connection alive in the busyness of her life. Family means everything to her, and that makes it worth the extra effort. God put her in Wyoming; and He will bring her back to Michigan in His perfect timing.

———————————

Jeanie lives far away from her family. You may know someone in the same situation. Ties can easily be broken when distance separates us. Extra effort is required…are you willing to put that effort forward? Our interpersonal relationships are never more important than when we have tragedy or deep need. Are you isolated or insulated from others? Do you have close friends and family members? Jesus is the *"friend who sticks closer than a brother."* Do you know Him? When Jeanie was far from home, she found Him to be a wonderful friend; and her witness, though ignored, sowed seeds deep into my spirit. Today, He is my friend, too.

———————————

Lord, I am not a great friend, and in some ways not a great family participant. These truths leave me feeling empty and alone. Please help me to study Your word on how to be active and vital in all of my relationships. Amen.

October 31ˢᵗ <u>Nathan's Place</u> *(Proverbs 17:17)*

A friend loves at all times, and a brother is born for adversity.

When I was a senior in high school, I found out that my mother was expecting! I was absolutely mortified! My parents were old people—in their mid thirties... what were they thinking? Nathan arrived in April of 1976 and our lives would never be the same again. He was a happy bouncing baby with four older brothers and sisters, you know—built in babysitters! He was very smart and very spoiled. Nathan attended a small Mennonite school in nearby Fairview. Nathan moved to Grand Rapids later, working in the computer field... and hating every minute of it. Several years ago, he quit that job and began to work as a brewer in a downtown pub. Yes, our little computer geek became a Brewmeister and found his niche. Each of us has a different gift. Nathan thought his was in the same field as Rob's, but his heart wasn't there. God breathes dreams, gifts, and abilities into each of us. Nathan and I may live entirely different kinds of lives; but we love and respect one another. The verse above talks about a *brother being born for adversity.* That doesn't mean siblings cannot agree or get along. A brother pulls together with his family when hard times come. This has proven out in our family losses and during the difficult times when our mother was very ill several years ago. In times of adversity, I choose Nathan as my partner to face challenges.

Age separated Nate and I for quite a few years. Now, he is closer to my age (ha, ha, little brother) and we find a lot more in common. My gift is teaching and speaking, writing and studying. Nathan's gifts are debating, gourmet cooking, brewing beer, and playing cards. We are different, but in our hearts we have a strong common bond—family. I am so grateful God did not make any of us five kids alike. We are all strong in different ways, live in different ways but all have a deep family connection.

Lord, thank You for making each person unique and original. That proves Your hand in our creation. It would have been easy to make mindless, personality-less cookie cutters. Instead, we are each created for our Creator... You are awesome. Amen.

November 1ˢᵗ   No Rich Foods   *(Daniel 1:8)*

But Daniel made up his mind that he would not defile himself with the king's choice food or with the wine which he drank...

aniel is a character from the Old Testament who is a man of great principle. He refuses to compromise the standards of a holy God, and today's entry chronicles one of his disciplined decisions. The King of Babylon has taken captive the young, good looking, and intelligent Jewish men and brought them to Babylon with the intention of grooming them to be great leaders in that foreign nation. Daniel is one of the chosen; and, the king very generously offers rich foods, fine wines, and special favors to these young men. Daniel refuses to partake in these foods, many of which are forbidden by Jewish clean/unclean laws. Accepting these foods and drinks would make him somehow beholden or dependent upon the King; and Daniel depended on God alone. He tells the commander that he will not eat the food. God will honor that, and Daniel will not be pale and unhealthy causing problems with the King. Daniel drinks water and eats vegetables only and grows in stamina and wisdom resulting in direct service under the King of Babylon.

Some in my "Seekers" class are participating in a Tuesday fast during the Lenten season. They are focusing on the Word and on

Prayer... and not on Snickers bars! One of them is diabetic and her husband was concerned. I told him that God would honor the fast. She has felt fine the two weeks of her commitment. Daniel and his friends refused the fat, rich foods laid before them. They were men of principle, and their obedience was honored by God who did not allow them to be weakened. Actually, their diet was healthier than the rich bounty laid before them. Are you good at sacrifice? Would you deny the things you knew were contrary to dietary laws and just dig in and pig out? Daniel refused to compromise, and in every way God rewarded his discipline.

Jesus, I cannot even refrain from chocolate and chips, let alone forsake a rich feast laid before me. I need discipline. I need to know the difference in appetite and hunger. I need to walk in obedience to You. Amen.

November 2nd   Mom and Me   *(Psalms 51:5)*

Behold, I was brought forth in iniquity, and in sin my mother conceived me, behold, You desire truth in the innermost being and in the hidden part You will make known wisdom.

*M*y mother is one of my best friends. After I was born, we were "single" for a while until she remarried and I was adopted. Mom grew up in a troubled family plagued with alcoholism, too many kids, and never enough money. She was the eldest daughter and became the caregiver for her six younger siblings. Probably because of how she was raised, my mother was never affectionate with us kids. We knew she loved us, but she didn't tell us or show us with hugs or kisses. As a child, I craved that missing outward display. In 1996, my Mother filled in books called "To my Daughter with Love" for each of us girls. In response to the question, 'What's most important to me about our friendship,' Mom wrote: *"That we have one! So many mothers and daughters never become friends. It took 39 years for my mother and me. I can still remember how* *good that felt. I guess we can tell each other how we feel about everything and we tend to think a lot alike... and we can share our love of God."* I waited my whole life for those words and others she wrote in my book. It is my greatest treasure and my written "hug" from **Mom.**

I find that the older generation is far less affectionate and open about their feelings than those who are my age. They were raised differently, and times have surely changed. My question for you today is—do you crave the affection of someone who does not find that sort of thing to be easy? There are some people who will never tell you they love you, or write a mushy card or letter. That does not mean they don't. Think about this. Jesus wrote us His love letter, outlining His dreams and plans for our lives, telling us of His love through word, thought, prayer, and deed. He holds nothing back. The New Testament is the written "hug" He sent to His children. Are you reading and rereading that letter? You should!

Words can be very cheap, and we tend to use them rashly. Your words are written down for us, preserved for our heritage and determine our eternity. How much more valuable are they than words with no cost? Amen.

November 3rd   Mom's Heart   *(Psalms 38:10)*

My heart throbs, my strength fails me; and the light of my eyes, even that has gone from me.

On June 15, 2003, I received a panicked call from my father saying Mom was in the hospital with an apparent heart attack. We grabbed our things and headed there to find her thrashing around because not only had she had the heart attack, she was given a drug she was highly allergic to. Two days later, Mom was laughing and eating regular food! We thought she had a miracle healing... we were wrong. Chest pains started again and she was transported to a Flint hospital for a routine cardiac catheterization. Dad, Jeanie, Nathan, and I were laughing in the waiting room when the surgeon ran in for permission for immediate surgery because, "Mrs. Walser is dying as we speak and there is no time to waste!" Each of us went into our own shells of fear, prayer, and brokenness. God spoke for me to read His Word. I didn't have my Bible with me, but found one under a stack of magazines. I began to pace the length of the room, reading verses out loud until He calmed my spirit. I gathered my family together and we began to pray. Mom survived that surgery, but later that night began to bleed from one of the bypasses. God performed miracle after miracle to keep her alive. You see, He wasn't finished with my mother... and neither were we. We no longer take her for granted.

My mother was never a particularly strong woman, but she serves a very strong God. He put the top five cardiac nurses on duty during the time of her second surgery... and they told us that never happens! Family began to gather at the hospital, encouraging us, and offering help wherever possible. I don't remember where this came from, but I read Mom this verse each day as she recovered in the hospital: *"Give me thy heart, says the Father above, No gift so precious to Him as our love; Softly He whispers, wherever thou art, Gratefully trust me and give me thy heart."* Tell your loved ones how much they mean to you... while you are able to. God gave you words, tears, and love... use all three.

Only a God with a big heart could do the amazing things You do in the lives of Your children. You are awesome; thank You, my Father. May Your hedge of protection be always upon me. Amen.

November 4th   At the Hospital: Jimmy   *(2 Timothy 4:5)*

But you, be sober in all things, endure hardship,
do the work of the evangelist, fulfill your ministry.

388

*T*here are two important stories of ministry opportunities we shared while Mom was in the hospital. One afternoon, we were sitting in the waiting room outside the CCU when a young woman burst through the doors wailing and crying, "No, No!" I automatically grabbed my cell phone (I do not know why) and walked to where she was. She told me her father was dying and she needed to call her sister to come. I dialed the number on my phone and talked to the woman at the other end. Once I handed the phone to the woman, I saw an elderly black woman come out crying and walk to a different window. I walked to her and asked if I could help her. She told me her husband, Jimmy, was dying. The other woman was her daughter. I laid hands on her and prayed, collected my phone, and returned to my sister, Shelly. Later, she and I were walking in to see Mom, when I spotted the elderly lady in a dark room. Shelly, unaware of what was going on, followed me in. I asked if the man in the bed was Jimmy and went to his bedside. I asked him if I could pray for him. He replied, "Yes, sister. Please do." I laid hands on Jimmy and prayed. He weakly thanked me and we left the room. Shelly was none too happy with me for "making her cry." I was none too happy with myself... because I didn't ask Jimmy if he knew Jesus.

When the spirit of conviction is upon me—or when I sense it is upon me—I get no peace. All night long I beat myself up for not sharing the Gospel of Christ with Jimmy. I just knew he was going to die apart from Christ and it was my fault. The next day, Jeanie asked why I was so quiet in Mom's room. I told her that I missed a huge opportunity to share my faith. She told me that minutes after I left, Jimmy's pastor and choir showed up. They had a regular hymn singing and praise shouting celebration as he was ushered into the arms of the Savior he served! Jeanie said, and so have many others, that if I needed to share Christ with Jimmy, I would have been directed to do so. Again, *His ways are not our ways...* thank God for that!

Lord, when You need me to speak out and share Your Gospel message, show me and speak through me. I can do nothing on my own. You direct my paths and ordain my encounters. Amen.

November 5th   At the Hospital: The Jar *(Galatians 6:10)*

Let us not lose heart in doing good, for in due time we will reap if we do not grow weary. So then, while we have opportunity, let us do good to all people, and especially to those who are of the household of faith.

After my mother was moved out of the Cardiac Care Unit and into recovery, I continued to go and visit with families there. I remembered how afraid and helpless we felt and sought to be an encourager to someone else. During one visit the room was full, but over in the corner sat a dignified elderly lady with a worn flannel hat. She looked so forlorn, I made my way over to her. She told me her patient's name was George, who was having quadruple bypass. I prayed with her and sat with her until she was allowed to go and see him. I assumed that George was her husband. I visited her for several days... and then lost track of her. I walked the halls of rehab looking for an elderly black man named George, but couldn't find him. The next week, a young boy stopped me as I came off the elevator, and asked if I was his "Grandma's angel." He said she had a gift for me. There she was, in George's room—but George was her fifty year old son. She hugged me, called me her angel, and then gave me a package wrapped in crinkled aluminum foil. The gift was an old Mason canning jar. She said to me, "I don't have anything nice to give you, but this is one of my favorite things. You look like someone who would love antiques." I have received many gifts, but never one as heartfelt as that jar.

This sweet lady in the tattered hat gave of the little she had. That reminds me of the story of the widow's mite in the Bible. Rich people were offering of their excess, but the widow put all she had into the offering box. Jesus honored her offering because no matter how small it was, it was a heart offering. My jar was a heart offering. I will likely never see her or George again this side of heaven, but I look forward to finding that hat on the head of a sweet hearted lady when I get to my eternal home. Little acts of kindness can mean so much in the life of another. May these stories be an encouragement for you to reach out to a stranger.

Jesus, thank You for teaching me how to give. You always looked for the "least of these" to serve. Lord, open my eyes for ministry opportunities. Direct my paths. Amen.

November 6ᵗʰ Sin No More *(Romans 11:32)*

*For God has shut up all in disobedience
so that He may show mercy to all.*

Are you glad Adam sinned in the Garden of Eden? We love to blame everything, especially the consequences of our sins and misdeeds on Adam and Eve. Sometimes, we flippantly say, "The devil made me do it!" Adam simply was the first to sin, the first to hide from God, the first to pass the buck, and the first to feel the pain separation from God brings upon us. Now, we have a choice whether to act contrary to God—or to join in the world's sin. Back to the, "are you glad Adam sinned" question. Would you ever know what real mercy is if you didn't realize how much you need it and how little you deserve it? If your child was never deathly ill, would you realize how important healing is? If you never have great financial struggles, will you appreciate the unexpected gift of money? If you haven't had to struggle in a difficult marriage, do you everyday appreciate the one you are married to? Dwell on these truths.

When someone's overt sin has gotten them into a hard situation, are you as willing to jump in and help them through the consequences? We love to pity the "innocent" victims and judge the "guilty" ones. God could feel the same way about us. He could say, "Vicki screwed up by not respecting Dan, and it is her fault their marriage is over. I wash my hands of the situation." Does He do that? No! *"If we confess our sins, He is faithful and just to forgive our sins and cleanse us from all unrighteousness."* (1 John 1:9) Once my sin is recognized, confessed, and repented, I am restored into His good graces. Thank God for His mercy beginning with Adam and Eve and continuing until the day He takes all of us to live with Him in Heaven.

Lord Jesus, help me to stop judging others and to realize how far my own sin removes me from full fellowship with You. Only through real grace am I restored and reinstated to right standing before a holy God. Amen.

November 7th Holiness *(Psalms 1:1-3)*

How blessed is the man who does not walk in the counsel of the wicked, nor stand in the path of sinner, nor sit in the seat of scoffers. But his delight is in the law of the Lord, and in His law he meditates day and night. He will be like a tree firmly planted by streams of water, which yields its fruit in its season and its leaf does not wither; and in whatever he does, he prospers.

I have heard people say that no one is holy or can ever be holy. I agree to a degree. We will never be holy as Christ is holy, for He was not born in sin as were the rest of us. We are called though to *"be holy as He is holy."* As I thought about how to approach this lesson, I found the verse above. Let's look at it one portion at a time. A holy man *does not walk in the counsel of the wicked, nor stand in the path of sinner.* He will seek to align himself with men of good repute and godly actions. A holy man avoids being with those who scoff at or reject the truth of the Gospel. God's men will *delight in the law of the Lord,* and will meditate on it day and night. Once he is firmly grounded in God's word, he will be *like a tree, firmly planted by the river* with deep roots, strong leaves, and an abundance of fruit in its season. Holy men are intentional men. They do not follow the breeze or act on every whim. They measure and weigh all things against the Word of God. Will becoming a holy child of God be easy? No! But the consequences of the alternative are deadly.

Striving to live a holy life is actually a great challenge. There is a freedom which comes when we instinctively know how to walk in righteous ways. I am in no way an expert in the teachings of the Bible, and I fail often to be who Jesus calls me to be. I still fight the fleshly lusts like pride, judging, and self-promotion. I know this to be true though: every minute I spend pouring over the Scriptures reinforces my inate sense of right and wrong. Most decisions make themselves based upon the teachings of God. We are blessed to have an "Owner's Manuel" to explain to us how to live in order to operate properly and at our full potential. Do you want to be holy? What will you need to sacrifice—or to begin to make habit of—in order for that to happen? A walk fully with Christ, led by the Holy Spirit, is the best commitment you will ever make.

Holy Spirit, I long to walk in the holiness God calls us to walk in. I, on my own, am incapable of this, but I, walking with You, can do all things because You are my strength. Amen.

November 8th Impact on a Child *(Isaiah 54:4)*

Fear not, for you will not be put to shame; and do not feel humiliated, for you will not be disgraced; but you will forget the shame of your youth...

Timothy was a favored disciple of the Apostle Paul and was taught the things of Christ by his mother Eunice and his grandmother Lois. The impact of the influence of godly women, who likely became believers at the teaching of Paul when he came to their home city of Lystra, cannot be overstated. Timothy carried the Gospel, and in spite of his youth, played a great part in the growth of the early church. As I thought about today's entry, I couldn't stop thinking of how much we adults influence the lives of the children God gives us to interact with in our lives. Two young women have started attending my "Seekers'" class at His House. I have known these girls since they were six and seven years old. They were like my own daughters and like sisters to Brent. All of the years I spent with them, I was not a Christian. Actually, I was the exact opposite of who I am today. We have lost touch over the last ten years; but they have known for some time that I am a believer and own the bookstore. Recently, Stacey—the older of the two—called me and said, "Shawnna needs you." She and her young husband had adopted a baby girl after years of miscarriages and disappointments, only to have the birth mother take the baby after five weeks. Shawnna was devastated, and her sister turned to someone who could help. How grateful I am to be used.

Even in my sinful past, God used me to influence Stacey and Shawnna in order that *"for such a time as this"* I might be used to strengthen them. These girls are hungry for the Word, are participating openly in class and are opening the door for me to have a positive impact on their children. Stacey has two children who come to class with her. Max, her son, hangs on every word of Bible teaching. I write this entry that you would realize how much impact the adult/child relationships in your life matter. God will use you just as He used me. Stop and think about a child you can begin to sow Christ into. Only in Heaven will you realize the impact.

Jesus, I have children in my sphere of influence who need to know about You. Lord, I am unsure of where to begin, but I will trust the work of the Holy Spirit to direct my words and hands. Amen.

November 9th <u>Search Me O' Lord</u> *(Psalms 51:12-13)*

Restore to me the joy of Your salvation and sustain me with a willing spirit. Then I will teach transgressors Your ways...

*K*ing David sinned against God when he committed adultery with the wife of Uriah. Most of us would say the sin was against Uriah and Bathsheba... and even against himself. David realized one ultimate truth...all sin is ultimately against God. Psalm 51 is David's cry for restoration between him and the God who called him *"a man after My heart."* David bares his soul in this humble Psalm where he states the following truths:

* The God of mercy is able to blot out our transgressions.
* He can cleanse us from <u>all</u> sin.
* Conviction for sin is ever before us.
* God is a blameless judge.
* God desires truth in our innermost being.
* He can restore joy and gladness.
* Those who are forgiven can teach others to forgive.
* Sacrifice is not as important as obedience.

David sinned. He felt the separation sin brought between him and God. He went to the throne of grace, seeking restoration from his Creator God.

We are all born into sin, and our inclination is to serve our flesh instead of serving a holy God. We can excuse sin or call it any name we want in order to rationalize our actions; but sin is sin. Like King David, we must long for restoration with the One who created us and loves us most. Our sin breaks His heart. Our sin affects others. In David's case, his sin led to the death of Uriah and the death of the baby he and Bathsheba conceived. Are you trying to hide current or past sin from God? He already knows your thoughts before you think them. Nothing done in darkness is hidden from Him. Come to him for the peace reconciliation will bring.

Father, I have sinned against You. I know that I need confession, restoration, and strength to not repeat this action. Only You, the Creator of my life, can change my heart. I open myself to You. Amen.

November 10th   <u>Jealousy and Envy</u>   *(Genesis 4:8)*

Cain told Abel his brother... and when they were in the field... Cain rose up against Abel his brother and killed him.

Where does jealousy come from? The Bible is full of stories of jealousy between brothers, between fathers and their sons... between leaders and those who want their positions. Cain and Abel are the sons of Adam and Eve, born after their parents were cast out from the Garden of Eden because of their sin. Cain is a farmer and Abel is a shepherd. When the offering is brought forward, Abel's offering is given higher regard; and the burning of jealousy began in the heart of the older brother. Cain plots and kills his brother. When God's voice asks Cain where his brother is, he responds with the well known reply, *"Am I my brother's keeper?"* God tells him his *brother's blood cries out from the ground.* Cain is cast out, away from God's generous provision to struggle for each crop, forever.

How are you about jealousy? The following is from a February, 2007 journal entry. "I would be an example of someone who gets jealous over someone elses material possessions, finances, and successes. If I were to admit it head on, get it out in the open, it would be better. Instead, I am prone to send little jealous barbs through words and inuendos. These are barbs I know hurt the other person... even though I speak them with a smile. Why do I get jealous? My pride! I want the best: a big bank account, a successful business, and a powerful ministry. If Jesus acted like I do, James and John would have been rendered ineffectual in kingdom building. Jesus was all for them "stealing His limelight!" Jealousy destroys our marriages, our families, our workplaces, and our churches." Are you prone to jealousy? Are you ready to change this attitude? Seek the things of God before jealousy destroys you like it did Cain.

Father, I am guilty of being jealous of the blessings others have. I forget to be grateful for the blessings in my own life. Lord, I need spiritual surgery to remove this ugly emotion from my heart. Amen.

November 11th My Friend Marilyn *(Isaiah 54:13)*

All your sons will be taught of the LORD;
and the well-being of your sons will be great.

*P*arenting is hard work...and there are many of you out there who feel like failures in that area of life. Learn lessons from Biblical parents who did a great job of parenting. I think of Hannah the mother of Samuel. She was blessed with the child she longed for her whole adult life, but then she relinquished control of her young son into God's hands. Elizabeth likely hated having her son, John the Baptist, go off and live in the wilderness as he was prepared for his ministry on behalf of Jesus. Instead of arguing, she entrusted her son and his mission into the hands of his Creator. Mary, the mother of Jesus watched her Son suffer and die. Undoubtedly she wanted to stop what was happening; but she entrusted her son into His Father's hands. Likely one of the hardest things a parent will ever do is to relinquish control and entrust their children into the hands of a loving God. We must never forget they belonged to Him before they were loaned to us.

Some people were born to be mothers, and my friend Marilyn is one of them. She is like a hen, clucking and nesting upon her chicks. I love her dearly, but would honestly tell her to let them little chicks test the waters themselves. Marilyn is a typical "I need to do everything for my kids" woman. Sometimes, I wish I were more of a Marilyn and less of a Vicki. I tend to let Brent make his own choices and face his own consequences. Some would call that indifference. I call it parenting with the outlook that I will not always be here to hold his hand. Unfortunately for us, children don't come with an owner's manual or a Parenting 101 class. Marilyn is a dedicated Christian with a heart full of love. She now has grandchildren to shower her affection on, and she certainly does that. How good are your parenting skills? Are you good at letting them fall down a few times, get some bruises, and learn?

Father, parenting is hard; we have learned this the hard way. Help me to make wise decisions. I lift this into Your very capable hands. Amen.

November 12th "Wright" Way to Love *(Ephesians 6:4)*

Fathers, do no provoke your children to anger;
but bring them up in the discipline and instruction of the Lord.

Have you ever heard of generational curses? On a basic level, these are habits, lifestyles, and sins passed down through the generations of a family. I pray curses from Tyler and Hailey all the time. I want Tyler to not inherit the anger so prevalent in his father's family. I pray for Hailey to have no drug or alcohol dependence and to be committed to sticking to her promises. My mother's parents raised their family on Wright Street on the wrong side of town. They were both alcoholics and their children bear the scars of that today. The generational curse of their alcohol addiction manifested itself in different forms in their children. Some are alcoholics, some are drug addicts, some are gamblers and some spend outrageously. The only way for these curses to be broken from the backs of the next generation is for intercessory prayers and faith in Jesus Christ to move into these homes. My grandparents were definitely not good parents; but they loved me without reservation or condition. No matter where I was or when I got there, they were ready to welcome me with open arms and spoil me rotten. Fortunately for me, they both had dry years before their deaths and I was able to get to know my real grandparents.

Generational curses fill the pages of the Bible. Adam and Eve fell to sin because they wanted to be like God. Their son Cain killed his brother in jealousy. David fell to sin because he longed for a woman who didn't belong to him. Amnon died for raping a sister who could never belong to him. Solomon was so wise that he thought God's rules didn't apply to him. His son Rehoboam thought the advice of godly leaders didn't apply to him. Generational curses must be broken if our children are to have healthy and happy lives. Divorce is a generational curse... as is promiscuity, unwed pregnancy, and lack of faith. We must pray against the spiritual forces that are bent on the destruction of our children.

Father, there are generational curses in my own family and in the families of many of my friends. I pray against these crippling and oppressive curses. Give me wisdom and discernment. Amen.

November 13th Father, Forgive Them *(Luke 23:34)*

But Jesus was saying, "Father, forgive them; for they do not know what they are doing."

Many of us have heard this request Jesus made from His cross, but have we really looked into what this says about Jesus and His ability to forgive? Jesus is suffering an agony most of us can not even imagine. Crucifixion is a slow suffocation where the victim must push up from his feet in order to take each breath. Jesus is fighting for breath; but He looks down upon the Jewish leaders, the Roman soldiers, and the people who turned so quickly to call for His crucifixion. He is watching the grief of His mother, the hopelessness in the eyes of Mary Magdalene and John and is hearing the jeers of the multitude—even those on the adjacent crosses. Jesus watches the Roman soldiers as they divide His garments by a casting of lots. He watches all of this... and unbelievably asks God to forgive them. He intercedes on behalf of His crucifiers saying they have no idea what they are doing. How can that be? He is not referring to the crucifixion itself, obviously they know about that practice. He means they have no idea of the implication of His death, and they are fulfilling the words of the prophets from centuries before. He means the temple curtain will be torn and a personal relationship with Him will be possible. He means His death and resurrection will be a picture of what all believers will face. He means they are causing an event, which will change the world forever!

We stuggle to forgive a spouse who forgets our birthday, a co-worker who cuts into our deals, or a brother who speaks against us. We have a hard time forgiving a child who fails us, a fellow believer who challenges us or an elected leader who goes astray. Jesus forgave those who nailed Him to a cross, placed a blasphemous sign above His head, divided His clothing, and hurled taunts at Him. What do you learn from these truths? Are you carrying grudges, anger, and unforgiveness? Do you realize how it paralizes you? It is time to forgive... only then will you be right with God.

Jesus, I have people whom I need to forgive, for their sakes as well as mine. You knew how difficult this would be. That is why You spent so much time teaching on it. I fall at Your feet... Help me to forgive. Amen.

November 14th That Which Satisfies Not *(Isaiah 55:1-2)*

"Ho! Every one who thirsts, come to the waters; and you who have no money come, buy and eat come, buy wine and milk without money and without cost. Why do you spend money for what is not

bread, and your wages for what does not satisfy? Listen carefully to Me, and eat what is good, and delight yourself in abundance."

*W*hy do we hunger and thirst for the things which will never make us happy? I have to confess that I have a purse fetish! Yes, I can smell a leather store from two miles away. The funny thing, is when I am looking for a new purse, I can never find one I like. If I am not on the hunt, I will find several. Does a new purse make me happy? Yes, for about an hour! Why do I buy them over and over when I know this to be true? The answer is that somewhere, deep in my spirit, is a longing for something which will satisfy my soul. Purses, cars, houses, clothes, books, cosmetic surgery, replacement spouses... will not meet those needs. The verse for this passage tells us to *eat what is good and delight yourself in the abundance* of God's provision. I have honestly found that Christ alone satisfies my soul. His Word is what I feast upon; and when I have trials, a purse has never filled my deepest needs. I can look and look for a perfect one... or I can look and look to THE PERFECT ONE.

Do you know someone who is never satisfied with what they have? I have watched numerous women about my age, who were abandoned like someone's cast of garbage, for a younger woman who would make their husband feel excited again. I have to wonder if those husbands ever find real joy...knowing full well that they may be cast off when they are "too old for fun." Working in the real estate business, I see people all the time who are longing to move up to a more expensive house. I also see the pages and pages of fore-closures in our local newspaper. They are often a direct result of our need for instant gratification. What is the deep longing and desire of your heart? I will pray for you as you read this entry and seek to fill the empty spaces.

Lord, I have tried to fill these heart deep needs with things and people. I am still empty. Show me how to fill them with Your Holy Spirit instead. Amen.

November 15ᵗʰ Reproach and Persecution *(Luke 6:22 KJV)*

*Blessed are ye, when men shall hate you, and when they shall
separate you from their company and shall reproach you,
and cast out your name as evil, for the Son of Man's sake.*

Persecution for Christ is very real. In our nation we realize very little real persecution like others around the world that are abused, tortured, and killed for the Name of Christ. We may get hurt feelings if our witness is rejected. We may become fringe members of a social group once we "get religious." The above verse tells us exactly what will happen to us for the sake of Christ. In our families we are judged; likewise in our neighborhoods, social groups, workplaces, and even in our closest circle of friends. People will not accept our testimony. They may reject us all together. Jesus tells us that when this happens, they are not rejecting us; they are rejecting Christ in us. Is the price too much too pay? Was Christ's death too much to pay? He was persecuted, blasphemed, spit upon, pierced with a crown of thorns, hung broken between two thieves, buried in a borrowed tomb, and abandoned by nearly every one of His closest friends. How does your persecution compare to that?

How persecuted do you feel after thinking about how Jesus suffered? I am writing this entry during Lent and have been rereading the Gospels from the triumphal entry of Christ when He returned to Jerusalem, through the ends of the books. This is a great reminder of the cost of real persecution. I have a hard word to say here, so don't run away without real thought. If you are not encountering any persecution, maybe you need to check the depth of your commitment and the strength of your witness. Also, you need to remember that no matter how much you care about the person(s) persecuting you, they do not have the power, means, or ability to save you! Hard truths—dwell on them.

Jesus, I need the constant reminder of how much You sacrificed on my behalf. As I think upon the things I have to be grateful for during this Thanksgiving season, may I never forget what You did on my behalf. Amen.

November 16th <u>Words of the Spirit</u> *(John 14:21 NIV)*

"Whoever has my commands and obeys them,
he is the one who loves me."

Have you ever felt the conviction or the words of the Holy Spirit? I have, and that conviction can be very painful. One of the first times the Spirit convicted me was while I was working at a local store with a friend. I was checking in new merchandise and she was waiting on customers. That day she sold several large pieces of furniture; and I got more and more jealous. Suddenly, words came out of my mouth, which were clearly not mine, "All of the sales are for the good of the store, no matter who rings the cash register." Believe me, they were the words of the Holy Spirit, not of a self-centered, jealous Vicki. Recently, the Spirit spoke again through me, but in a much more powerful way. Two women came into His House looking for a study Bible. I was showing them how to use a topical index. I always use forgiveness as an example because many people have issues with forgiving others or themselves. Instead, out of my mouth came, "Let's say you are dealing with grief..." They both began to cry... that is exactly what they were dealing with! The Spirit knew they needed to talk... and fed words into me to open that door.

The Holy Spirit not only convicts us. He is our teacher and has the authority to teach us the ways and characteristics of Jesus and Father God. The Holy Spirit must be welcomed in to our daily lives. He takes up residence; but we must seek to know and receive Him. Recently, on a drive home from His House—two weeks in a row—the Spirit spoke to me. The first time the words came out of my mouth. The next time they were spoken aloud in the car. During that exchange,

I thanked God for some blessings in my life... and the Spirit spoke, "I've got your back." You can believe this or not, but God speaks... we have to be ready to listen. If you want to understand the Spirit more, read Scriptures about Him and pray for His revelations.

Holy Spirit, I need to know You more. I have focused on God the Father and Jesus the Son and have not spent near enough time learning from You. Amen.

November 17th   Christians in the Marketplace *(Proverbs 14:35)*

*The King's favor is toward a servant who acts wisely,
but his anger is toward him who acts shamefully.*

*M*ordecai was a Jewish man living in exile in Persia during the reign of King Ahasuerus. He overheard two men conspiring to kill the King, and revealed the plot. Mordecai was instrumental in saving Ahasuerus' life and he received no reward for it. That didn't matter to him because doing right was his motive not recognition. Years later, during a sleepless night, King Ahasuerus reads the court records and finds that Mordecai saved his life and was never recognized for it. Mordecai is rewarded for his faithfulness and obedience. This man would have gone to his death and never required recompense or restitution, and his reward would have been in heaven. In an age where we all worry about climbing the job ladder, getting our recognition, and receiving the benefits... Mordecai's humility shines bright. He would have been a great addition to today's workplace.

In a day when customer service practices are at an all time low, ·Christians in the workplace must make a difference. We need to be ever mindful of how we answer phones, greet visitors, address negatives, and treat our fellow workers. We, like Mordecai, are called to be *"light"* in a dark world. I recognize the importance of a smile, a kind word, or a bit of humor in making an awkward moment seem less significant. These same practices apply to not only customer service, but also to our interactions with family, friends, and the stranger we meet on the street. In a hurried and harried world, we need to be peace in someone's day. How is your witness? Are you *"light"* in the area God has given for you to shine?

Father God, we do need to worry less about recognition and more about how the world sees us as agents for Christ. Make my little light shine in the darkness of this vile world, so that one other may see You in me. Amen.

November 18th Send Me! *(Isaiah 6:8)*

Then I heard the voice of the Lord, saying, "Whom shall I send, and who will go for Us?" Then I said, "Here am I. Send me!"

How willing are you to say to God, *"Here I am, Lord. Send me!"* I doubt many of you will ever be asked to do something totally outside of your comfort zone, but then I never thought I would be commanded to do the things I have been sent to do. Whether it is teaching, public speaking, opening the store, or writing this book; He does take me out of my safety zone. Isaiah, in the passage this verse is from, stands up and offers himself in God's service. Have you ever thought about what it must cost a missionary to leave all the comforts and amenities of America to go and serve in a third world country without sanitation, healthy food processing, and protection? Have you considered the price of a pastor leaving a loving congregation to walk into one divided by strife? Does the thought of standing before a crowd of thousands to speak or sing scare you to death? Each of these people is an "Isaiah" who stood up and said to God, "Take me and all I have to offer. Use it to grow Your kingdom."

Lots of us say we want to hear *the still small voice* of God, but what if that voice speaks words which will carry you into unknown territory? Think about this truth: Not all "mission fields" are in foreign lands. Some are at the house of your sick or elderly neighbor. Some require you to share Jesus with a neighborhood child. Some are serving meals at a soup kitchen. Some are driving a cancer patient to treatments. God will not call every one of us to distant lands. He always calls every one of us to serve! Isaiah, Moses, Samuel, Joshua, Abraham, and Mary were all called into the service of their Lord. Each faced hardships, persecution, and frustrations. Each had a distinct impact on the world around them. Are you ready to say, "Here I am; send me, Lord?"

Help me to trust that You will never send me to places where You will not walk beside me, Lord. I am guilty of saying, "Someone else will do it." Shame on me for being unwilling to serve You. Amen.

November 19th <u>A Servant's Heart</u> *(Hebrews 10:24)*

*...and let us consider how to stimulate one another
to love and good deeds...*

Some of the Bible's most interesting characters are those who have a servant's heart. Most of us know of Ruth's sacrifice for her mother-in-law; or of Samuel's work in the temple where he served God for his entire life. Joseph served the King of Egypt so well, he became second in charge in a powerful foreign nation... and sowed seeds of faith along the way. Mary Magdalene traveled with and served Jesus and His disciples to show her gratitude for the healing Jesus brought into her emotional life. Jesus, Himself, took off His outer garment, tied a towel around His waist, and washed the feet of His friends... and His betrayer, Judas Iscariot. Why would the King of Kings stoop down and do the most menial task, which was reserved for the lowest household servant? He did that for the same reason He hung on the cross. He did it to show us a picture of what love, in its purest form, really is. Some of us are great servers; I am not.

Are you a "doer" or a "thinker?" I have a friend, who if you say you have a headache bakes homemade cookies and brings them over. Geri is the consummate "servant." This friend is at the bedside of the dying, at the graveside with the family and is the first to send cards and make calls. She is a nurse and buys boxes and boxes of Christmas cards and small ornaments and novelty gifts. I swear, just about everyone in the hospital gets a little gift from Geri for Christmas. Her mother and sister are both like her, as are her lovely daughters. You see, in their family, they make serving and loving a way of life. Is your heart a servant's heart? Some of us need to work on this area of our Christian walk. Serving shows our concern for others and our commitment to Christ.

Lord, make me more like Geri. Give me the grateful heart of Mary Magdalene, the compassionate heart of Ruth, the righteous heart of Joseph, and the gracious heart of Jesus. Amen.

November 20th   20/20 Hindsight   *(Mark 8:23-24)*

Taking the blind man by the hand, He brought him out of the village; and after spitting on his eyes and laying His hands on him, He asked him, "Do you see anything?" And he looked up and said, "I see men, for I see them like trees, walking around."

I know a lot of people who have "blurred vision" when it comes to the moral absolutes of our holy God. Blurred vision comes from not knowing what the Word of God says or from knowing and not doing what the Word says to do. A small child can never obey a rule he hasn't been taught. Unfortunately, we like to plead the same ignorance and pretend the wrong things we do must somehow be right! Blurred vision is seeing sin we know is wrong and dressing it up to make it look less wrong. Who do we think we are fooling? God is a god of absolutes. He will never look upon adultery and call it "harmless flirtation." He will never look upon stealing and call it "petty theft." When God truly gets hold of a heart, these things are not tempting to us. He removes the lust of the flesh and replaces it with a pure and holy inner spirit.

I lived for years blurring my vision to somehow make the things I did more palatable… to myself and to God. Hindsight is 20/20; and we can always look back and see what we did right, and what we did wrong. I have spent the last twelve years questioning why it took me so long to really hear the things of God. Why did I ignore the sown seeds of the past? Why did I hear sermons and not understand their personal implication in my life? Why did I justify the immoral things I did, which make me cringe today? The clear answer is that the enemy of my soul used to own me and control my vision. Today, I look back in hindsight—remembering what I have done—and praise God that He now holds the title to my heart.

Jesus, looking back to where I was before I knew You as my Lord and Savior is a hard thing for me. I am growing stronger and more determined each day to serve only one Master; and that Master is YOU. Amen.

November 21ˢᵗ <u>Hezekiah's Hard Work</u> *(2 Chronicles 31:21)*

Every work which he began in the service of the house of God in law and in commandment, seeking his God, he did with all his heart and prospered.

The Bible refers to Hezekiah, King of Judah, as a king who had a close walk with God. He was a reformer who set out to eradicate all traces of foreign gods and idols from the temple, the King's palace and from the entire southern kingdom of Israel. Hezekiah's own father had nailed shut the doors of the temple and encouraged his subjects to serve these idols. Now, a mighty and most godly leader steps up and leads by example. What Hezekiah did required hard work, and he never shirked from that. It also required diplomacy in order for his people to follow what must have seemed unreasonable and maybe even foolish ideas. Reinstatement of the Passover feast, reinstatement of the system of tithes and offerings which provided for the needs of the priests and Levites, and reinstatement of prayer in God's Holy Temple... all these things required much work and personal commitment. Hezekiah's legacy is clearly written in 2 Chronicles 31: 20 *"...he did what was good, right and true before the Lord his God."*

Our nation is facing an epidemic of laziness and lack of commitment to see jobs through. Few of our young people have a work ethic, which would make them stand out against older workers. Hezekiah was born to a king who didn't have much of a work or spiritual ethic. He could have followed those footsteps and gotten away with being "a chip off the old block." Instead, God birthed a passion and a fire into his heart. Hezekiah changed the world he lived in for the best... he impacted lives... he wore God wherever he went... he was a prayer warrior. How is your work ethic? Does it reflect Christ in your heart? Would others in the workplace know there is something different about you? Our job is to *salt and light* our world. Shake and shine!

Father God, I seek to begin today to build a legacy like Hezekiah's. I want to reflect You, honor You, bring glory to You and reinstate all the godly things I have allowed to drift away. Amen.

November 22nd Inspired Word *(2 Chronicles 17:9)*

They taught in Judah, having the book of the law of the LORD with them; and they went throughout all the cities of Judah and taught among the people.

$\mathcal{L}$et me start today's teaching by asking you a question. Do you believe 100% that the Bible is the inspired word of God? How you answer that one question, will affect tremendously your faith walk. Would it surprise you to know that some seminary students are being taught that there are untruths, exaggerations, and improbable teachings within the Bibles pages? Many do not believe in the Biblical time line, the six days of creation, or the truths of stories like Jonah, David and Goliath, and Daniel in the Lion's Den. Would it bother you to know that some do not believe in Jesus' divinity, miracles and resurrection? Let me say again... this is coming out of seminaries—Christian schools for higher education! These are the kinds of entries which make me mad enough to spit! Why are our seminaries teaching these things? What effect is it having on our churches? I will state emphatically what I believe to be true. God's Holy Word is alive, it is applicable and appropriate to today's situations, and it is the lifeblood we need in order to walk fully with Jesus Christ. God knew exactly what would be needed within its pages in order for our answers to lie there today. He gave the words to those He trusted to write as He directed. Jesus relied on those Old Testament teachings as His firm foundation. We must do the same and then add the New Testament teachings to them.

I could spend hours a day, each day for the rest of my life, studying the Bible and never make a dent in the wisdom, revelation, comfort, and truths hidden within its pages. You might wonder why I so vehemently believe in your need for the Word in your life. The answer is simple... **the Bible has transformed my life.** I read it—I apply it—I teach it—I do my best to live it—and I may one day die for it. How many doubters would do the same? During this season of Thanksgiving, I encourage you to read the Bible and thank God for its truths and how He has preserved it.

Jesus, Your Word is a lamp unto my feet and a light unto my path. I have hidden it in my heart that I might not sin against You. Your

Word alone is truth. May I burn for it every day. Thank You for Your Holy Bible. Amen.

November 23rd <u>Still Applies</u> *(Matthew 5:18)*

For truly I say to you, until heaven and earth pass away,
not the smallest letter or stroke shall pass from
the Law until all is accomplished.

The world may turn from the teachings of the Bible; but the Bible's truths will never turn from being true in the world. One of the main accusations used against the Bible is that it is outdated and does not apply in our lives today. Each story in the Old Testament carries a moral lesson and truths which still apply today. For instance, Jonah ran away when God gave a specific instruction to him. He ran headlong into trouble, suffered, repented, cried out, and was restored. Have you ever had a child who refuses to obey you, suffers, repents, and is restored? Bingo! Murder, adultery, stealing, and lying are just as wrong today as they were thousands of years ago when the Ten Commandments were written. Joshua had to fight powerful and mighty enemies, and he found victory. Christians are fighting the war against a secular society; and we are finding victories. We learn that with God on our side we have much; without Him on our side we have no one to lean on. God's promises for His children never change.

Several months ago, Ginger, one of my "Seekers" asked if God could bring life back to a dead church. I told her He could, but He would need sparks of life (her and others committed to the task). The next morning, as I studied my Bible, I came upon a passage in Ezekiel 37 where God takes Ezekiel to the valley of dead dry bones. He asks if they can ever live again. God tells him to walk among them and prophesy the words of God. Notice he didn't say tell them jokes or wow them with wonderfully choreographed sermons... simply speak His words. As Ezekiel did this, the bones began to come together with sinew, muscle, tissue, and finally skin came upon them. God then breathed His Holy Spirit upon them and they stood up as a mighty army prepared for God's service. I was so excited when I found this following the question from the night before. Yes, He surely can restore life to a dead dry church! God's word is fully alive!

Jesus, I need more time in Your Word and more understanding of what I read. Open my ears to hear, my eyes to see, and my heart to receive. Amen.

November 24th   <u>Will and Testament</u>   *(Hebrews 9:16-17)*

For where a covenant is, there must of necessity be the death of the one who made it. For a covenant is valid only when men are dead, for it is never in force while the one who made it lives.

The verse for today's lesson is used to explain that Jesus had to die, in order for his covenant (promise) to be fulfilled. He could not stay here, walk as man and take ours sins away. He could not fulfill the promises of the Old Testament prophets—for a Redeemer and Messiah—if He lived here on this earth forever. Before Jesus left the earth, He needed to do all of His speaking, teaching, preparing, and ministering so His children would be able to follow in His footsteps. That teaching and preparing are the words of the New Testament. Jesus had people who walked with Him every day write down the truths they learned from Him. He directed some who were not even alive during His earthly walk, to write down teachings, events, and challenges the early church faced. All of these things today are the Bible truths we apply to our lives. This New Testament is Jesus' last Will and Testament. It is the heritage and legacy of His children. It is His operator's manual for our effective lives.

Most of us think we will live forever; and we live like that is true. Jesus knew His earthly days were numbered. He had a mission and needed to make sure each detail was perfect. Jesus wrote down

412

the wishes He had for us, the promises He wanted to make to us, and the roadmap to direct our paths. If your parent or spouse died and left you a legacy like that, wouldn't you read it? Would you act indifferent to it? Jesus died to leave us that legacy... surely we can find a few minutes each day to give back.

Jesus, thank You for the heritage, promises, teachings, and love in the pages of Your Word. You wrote it for me... I never thought about that until right now. Even if I were the only one... You would have written it! Amen.

November 25ᵗʰ <u>Randie's Psalm</u> *(Psalms 30:11-12)*

You have turned for me my mourning into dancing;
You have loosed my sackcloth and girded me with gladness,
that my soul may sing praise to You and not be silent
O LORD my God, I will give thanks to You forever.

Nine months after I gave my heart to Christ, my family was dealt a devastating blow. My twelve year old niece, Randie Renee died. She was Shelly's oldest daughter and was just coming into young womanhood. Randie carried my middle name and was her Uncle Dan's sweetheart. We were at the hospital the day she was born. She was truly the most beautiful baby we ever laid eyes on. The hardest thing I have ever done in my life is to tell my sister—twice—that her child was gone. I am nauseated as I write this entry just remembering the panic I felt. I swear to you that the old Vicki, who was not a spirit filled Christian, could not have done what needed done over the next week. My family fell apart. I was called upon to select the music, minister and to make other funeral plans. Each step of the way, Jesus was my strength.

During this difficult time, I found out the very real truth that Scripture is alive and ready to speak to our hearts. Psalm 30 was in my morning Bible study, and it spoke to me from the moment I read it. Here are some excerpts: *"LORD my God, I cried to You for help, and You healed me. For His anger is but for a moment, His favor is for a lifetime; weeping may last for the night, but a shout of joy comes in the morning."* The weeping did indeed last for a while, the pain never entirely goes away; but God's faithfulness during that difficult time will never be forgotten. Have you lost someone close to you? Do you question the death of young people? I will never profess to have all the answers. This I do know... He will carry you through. No matter the loss you feel, He felt the same and will comfort you as Christ Himself was comforted by His Father.

Lord, it is comforting for me to know that I never walk alone through the hard times. You alone carry me when my knees are too weak and my feet are too tired. You are my strength and my song in my mourning. Amen.

November 26th   Nothing New Under the Sun   *(Ecclesiastes 1:9)*

That which has been is that which will be, and that
which has been done is that which will be done.
So there is nothing new under the sun.

When we look at the world around us and see the way God's people are being rejected and He is being removed from the public places, we tend to think this is new and horrible. It surely is horrible, but the verse above tells us that there is nothing new... nothing that has not happened before to some degree. Were there murders thousands of years ago? Do Cain and Abel ring a bell? Were there adulterers? Do David and Bathsheba come to mind? Was there a removal of God from the public forum? Nehemiah had the law read and the people were reminded they were to celebrate the Feast of Booths, which hadn't been done for at least forty years! Were there brat children in times past? Did you ever hear of Jacob or the Prodigal Son? Were there godly leaders and selfless sacrificers in Bible times? Think about Joseph and Ruth... or Jehoshaphat and Esther. Nothing is new... and this affirms more than anything I've written that the Bible is the LIVING WORD OF GOD and is just as applicable today as the day it was written.

If you feel persecuted, read and find that Peter and Paul were before you. If you feel like you have failed as a parent, read the story of Isaac. If you think the devil has a hold of you and will never let you go, look up Mary Magdalene's encounters with Jesus. I write this to you because we all feel like what we are living, feeling, or dealing with has never been dealt with before. Nothing is new. Give it over to God and trust that He still brings resolution.

Jesus, I do tend to think my problems are worse than those of anyone who came before me. Help me to draw strength from the past history of Your provision and faithfulness. You are an awesome Savior. Amen.

November 27th <u>Windows of Heaven</u> *(2 Kings 7:1)*

Then Elisha said, "Listen to the word of the LORD; thus says the LORD, 'Tomorrow about this time a measure of fine flour will be sold for a shekel, and two measures of barley for a shekel, in the gate of Samaria.'"

Scripture tells us God is not a man, He is holy and He will never lie. Why is it then, we hear what He says and then doubt the words? In this entry, we find famine raging in Samaria—the northern kingdom of a divided Israel. Elisha, the prophet, tells the king of Samaria the next day there will be flour and barley for sale within the gates of his nation. An officer of the king says, *"Behold, if the LORD should make windows in heaven, could this thing be?"* Elisha responds, *"Behold, you will see it with your own eyes, but you will not eat of it."* In an amazing way, God causes the Aramean army—who has stopped all food from coming into Samaria—to flee from their camp leaving food and other provisions everywhere. The next day, indeed there is food in the city! God's word for His supernatural provision was fulfilled. Unfortunately for the doubting officer, the part of the prophecy regarding him was also fulfilled. He was trampled by the people surging forward after the food... which he *seen it with his own eyes, but was not able to eat.*

I have shared several instances of God opening the *windows in heaven* to provide for Dan and I, His House, and now this book. The windows are sometimes people we know well, sometimes people we have just met, and are usually opened in unexpected ways. Usually this happens when we are barely getting by, or when we have a special need (like publishing fees). God knew the needs of the people of Samaria... and He knows your needs, too. Sometimes, the words we speak stop Him from pouring out the blessings He has for us. When we first opened the store, I said we needed a certain dollar amount of sales each week. From that time on, we received within five dollars above or below that exact amount each week. Someone told me I was tying His hands. Once I lifted the restraints, we were blessed with great sales for several weeks in a row. I think small. He thinks really big! When He speaks, we need to listen.

Father, thank You for the times You have opened Heaven's Windows and poured out blessings in my life. I know You know my needs. Who better than You to provide for them? Amen.

November 28th   Spiritual Warfare: Elisha   *(2 Kings 6:16)*

So he answered, "Do not fear, for those who are with us are more than those who are with them."

Elisha, the same prophet we met in yesterday's teaching, is about to go into battle against a mighty enemy, the King of Aram. Elisha is despised for his prophetic gifts and teachings; which always seem to be fulfilled by God. Elisha is in Dothan and the Arameans are sent to arrest him. Things are not looking good, especially when Elisha's servant looks out and sees that their camp is completely surrounded by the Aramean army who encircled them during the dark of the night. The servant is terrified and says, *"Alas, my master! What shall we do?"* Elisha acknowledges that they are facing a mighty army, but tells his servant not to fear because those who are on our side—God's mighty army—are bigger than theirs! *Then Elisha prayed and said, "O LORD, I pray, open his eyes that he may see." And the LORD opened the servant's eyes and he saw; and behold, the mountain was full of horses and chariots of fire all around Elisha. When they came down to him, Elisha prayed to the LORD and said, "Strike this people with blindness, I pray." So He struck them with blindness according to the word of Elisha.* Elisha takes this powerful army and delivers them into the hands of the King of Israel. No matter how big the enemy seems, our God and His ministering army is bigger!

———————————

Spiritual warfare is a very real force in our lives. Satan makes everything bad look good and everything good look bad. Elisha's servant looked at only what his eyes could see. We often do that don't we? We see a pile of unpaid bills, a rebellious teenager, or a struggling marriage... and we see no hope. Elisha looked through God focused eyes to see what the bare eye cannot see. God has a mighty army, but the enemy wants us to not see it. If he can sow seeds of doubt, fear, anxiety, hopelessness, frustration, and a sense of failure, he wins every single time. Are you ready to fight the warfare of the enemy? Don't make a rash decision because the enemy will step up his attacks once you choose to fight. But, you will have God's army on your side.

———————————

Father, the enemy of my soul is waiting to sow doubt and despondence in me. How grateful I am that You are in control and will always bring me through the tests. Warfare is tough, but You make me tougher. Amen.

November 29th <u>Spiritual Warfare: At Home</u> *(Malachi 2:10)*

Do we not all have one father? Has not one God created us?
Why do we deal treacherously each against his brother
so as to profane the covenant of our fathers?

*Y*esterday, we talked about spiritual warfare and the battle for what our eyes see. Today, I want us to look at how this warfare is effecting our homes and our families. I can count on one hand the number of families I know who are living in homes where love, respect, and unity reign. Mostly, I see families in utter chaos with children disrespecting one another and their parents. Where did the honoring the mother and father part get lost? Listen carefully to this truth. Satan wins every time he sows seeds of contention in a home because a house divided cannot stand and is vulnerable to attack. How does this work? Let's go back to the basics of the law of God. When the doors to our homes are left open to attack, we invite these guests in: theft, lies, disrespect for parental influence, disregard for God—His Name, His Authority, His Sabbath, hatred (murder), jealousy (coveting), and adultery. Any one or any combination of these things will destroy the peace and unity in your home. Remember the words of John 10:10: *The thief comes only to steal and kill and destroy; I came that they may have life, and have it abundantly.*

How do we protect our families, marriages, and homes from these very real attacks? Is there hope for marriages to last and families to not be divided? The answer to both questions is that we need more Jesus, less self, and a willingness to fight for that which is right. There is only one weapon we can use against the attacks by the enemy, and that is faith. Our faith must be exhibited through prayer, time in the Word, and using the Name of Jesus Christ to render the works of the enemy powerless. We must rebuke him, pray for a hedge of protection around our home, and teach these things to our families. He cannot divide a tightly yoked marriage. He cannot steal the child who is sold out for Christ; but he will surely try.

Spirit, I am frightened at the thought of going into battle with the enemy. I do believe You "have my back" and will give me the words to keep my home, marriage, and family strong in faith. Amen.

November 30th   Spiritual Warfare: Workplace   *(John 15:8)*

My Father is glorified by this, that you bear much fruit, and so prove to be My disciples.

*I*n the politically correct society we work in, God has been almost completely removed from the workplace. In many companies, no one is allowed to talk about church activities, faith, or even offer prayer to a co-worker. How unfortunate that is! We are left with cold, indifferent, and competition driven workplaces where real friendships and relationships are hard to find. Stress levels are high and the enemy has done his job of *killing, stealing and destroying* real comaraderie and respect. Why does Satan care about our workplaces? Why would he attack there? The truth of the matter is, he will assault any part of our lives which could pose a threat to the things he wants to accomplish. Faith based fellowship and spiritual unity are contrary to his plans. This is nothing new, except that in America we have always been open and transparent about our faith. Today, it seems that everyone but Christians can talk about their beliefs. Those who practice Wicca, go to psychics, or seek out New Age teachings are given a free pass. Jesus was right when He said we would be persecuted for our faith... even (or should I say especially) in our workplaces. Stifle our words and our fruit production dies.

How is your workplace witness? Are you able to sow "seeds of righteousness" even when you cannot talk openly about the things of God in your everyday interactions? Scripture tells us we will know the Christians by their fruits. Do you want to know how to fight the spiritual warfare of the enemy as you work every day? Live out *the Fruits of the Spirit: Love, joy, peace, patience, kindness, goodness, faithfulness, gentleness, and self-control.* Wear Jesus without saying a word! Don't allow yourself to be drawn in to gossip, divisiveness, filth, and back stabbing. You are a child of the King of Kings. He fought His spiritual battles with love, self control, and patience. Go out and fight the good fight!

Jesus, my hands aren't as tied by the enemy as I give him credit. I have Your Spirit within me and Your hand upon me. I am a "Blood-bought child of the Living God." I can fight back, can't I? Amen.

December 1st   Queen Esther   *(Psalms 32:1-2)*

How blessed is he whose transgression is forgiven, whose sin is covered! How blessed is the man to whom the Lord does not impute iniquity, and in whose spirit there is no deceit!

*F*irst impressions can be so very wrong! I first met Esther when Dan and I picked her up for a small group meeting. She wasn't someone I ever thought I would forge a friendship with. Today, she is one of my dearest friends, my greatest encouragers, and one of the tools God used to bring this book into your hands. I call Esther "Queenie," and fully believe she was put into my life *"for such a time as this!"* Esther has been attending my classes for nearly three years, but in all truth she should be the teacher. She is a "preacher's kid" who probably knows more Scripture than I ever will. She is a staunch supporter of His House and sows into our ministry whenever possible. She is one of those *"much forgiven"* people who had wandered away from her Christian heritage more than once... but the Good Shepherd kept drawing this little lamb back to the flock. Today, she is a committed believer with a lot of regrets and a very grateful heart.

On the morning of my vision for this book, I went to the store very early and emailed two friends, Esther and Gail, who both excel in typing, grammar, formatting, and punctuation. I had one question to ask them, which would seal the deal of writing this book. I wrote and asked if they would do some typing from old journal entries, edit my copy, and proof everything. Within minutes I had their replies; both would do it. Esther said, "Who am I to argue with one of your visions?" Esther received the first draft—with my lousy formatting, typing and punctuation—and she has invested a huge amount of time in this project. My first impression was wrong. Esther and I are now friends and confidantes. You and I need to be wary of making snap judgments of other people. Do you have friends like Esther who support and encourage you? Hold on to them! Friends are a gift from God.

Jesus, there are some things I cannot do on my own. Sometimes I need an Esther to sacrifice for me, encourage me, and comfort me in my losses. Lord, thank You for the people I can truly call my friends. Amen.

December 2nd   Sin: Depravity   *(Romans 1:28)*

And just as they did not see fit to acknowledge God any longer, God gave them over to a depraved mind, to do those things which are not proper.

When you think of someone with a depraved mind, what do you picture? Most of us think of a serial killer, a child molester, or a rapist. Read the verse again. When man decided to no longer acknowledge God, He removed the hedge of protection He had created for him and allowed the lusts of the flesh and the inborn depravity to reign. Did God make man evil? No. Sin made man evil. Think again of the original sin of Adam and Eve when pride began to rear its ugly head; they wanted to be as wise as God. Depravity was Cain murdering his brother Abel. Depravity was Jacob betraying his brother to steal his birthright. Depravity was Joseph's brothers selling him into bondage. Depravity was Judas betraying Jesus for the price of a common slave. Depravity is husbands leaving their wives for other women. Depravity is children walking in disrespect to their teachers, parents, and neighbors.

You may not like this entry, because of preconceived ideas of what "real sin" is. I have written before and will say again, <u>all sin separates us from God</u>. He doesn't see good sin or bad sin; there is no such thing. Depravity, as described above, is doing those things which are not proper... period! Unfortunately for us, we take a soft approach to sin; and the condition of our nation reveals that. Look at our television programs, our movies, our video games, and music. They all reflect depravity. Look at what our children are subjected to in school with teaching on homosexual relationships as normal, abortion as a viable option, and condoms being distributed because our children are animals who cannot control their lust. That is depravity. Look at the internet...that too is depravity. I hope you are getting mad enough to fight back. When we fail to acknowledge God, we deliver ourselves into this filth. Our only hope is in Christ.

Father God, it must break Your heart to see the things Your children do. I am coming to the understanding that sin is sin and it all separates me from You. Lord, show me how to help fight the good fight against evil. Amen.

December 3rd <u>Sin: Strife & Deceit</u> *(Romans 1:29)*

...being filled with all unrighteousness, wickedness, greed, evil; full of envy, murder, strife, deceit, malice; they are gossips...

*L*et's look today at other sins which are prevelent in our everyday lives; but which separate us from God. Strife is defined as: "heated, often violent dissension, bitter conflict, contention, or competition between rivals." Does that sound familiar to you? We live in a very angry and contentious world. Who would have thought fifty years ago that we words like "road rage" would be part of our everyday talk? Who would think that our workplaces, homes, public squares, and churches would be filled with malice, deceit, gossip, and envy? This all falls back to yesterday's entry, which told us that when we remove our acknowledgement of God, we are given over to depravity. Our days are eaten by this disease, and our nights are sleepless as we dwell on thoughts of vengeance, animosity, jealousy, and hatred for others. No wonder people die of stress related diseases, we are being eaten alive. We have no peace. Is there hope for us? Yes, but only if we return to the original basics of a relationship with God.

———

Is your home full of strife? Do your children fight and contend with one another? Are there more angry words than kind ones? Do you speak love and teach of Jesus to your family? Return to the basics of loving God and loving each other and praying for your family. Remember, the enemy loves the dissention... don't give him the victory! Diffuse gossip, deceit, and greed in your work place. When you are surrounded by these things, remove yourself. If you cannot remove yourself physically, do it mentally by reciting Scripture or praying silently to yourself. Ask God to bring you peace and serenity. Seek the help of the Holy Spirit.

———

Lord, the world's ugliness is eating me alive. I need to escape into Your arms and away from the confusion, hatred and animosity. I need You and Your Spirit like never before. Amen.

December 4th Sin: Arrogance *(Romans 1:30)*

...slanderers, haters of God, insolent, arrogant, boastful, inventors of evil, disobedient to parents...

*Y*es, today we look at more sins which separate us from God. Insolence, arrogance, and boastful pride are today's focus.

Insolence is rudeness with contempt. The insults hurled at Jesus during His trial and crucifixion are perfect examples. They were rude, but they were also spoken with contempt. We see and hear this today on talk shows and in political debates where gentility has flown out the window in the face of partisanship. Arrogance is showing an offensive air of superiority. The Jewish leadership used lots of arrogance as they belittled and insulted Jesus during His teaching times. We see this today in the way "celebrities" think they are better and smarter than everyone else; and we feed their arrogance by treating them as such. Boasting and pride in one's self or possessions is our last sin today. Scripture shows this in King Hezekiah, who was one of the few good kings in Judah, but who showed—in a moment of boasting—all the riches of his palace and the temple treasury to the king of another nation. Not a wise move by an otherwise smart man.

Let me confess here that if I stood before God today, I would be called to task for these sins. I can be very insolent, arrogant, and prideful; and God has worked on me for twelve years about these things. Sometimes, I find myself arguing or debating just for the sake of the debate. When I do these things, I am called to the carpet by the conviction of the Holy Spirit. What about you? Do you tend to speak in rudeness and contempt? Do you feel proud and arrogant? Are you boastful? God has truly worked on changing these things in my life. Owning a struggling bookstore and writing a book I don't know if anyone but my friends will buy are humbling experiences. God, even in the good things of my life, is teaching me humility.

Jesus, may the words of my mouth and the meditations of my heart be to Your liking and to Your standards. My tongue is sharp and piercing, but You can soften it. Go ahead, work in me. Amen.

December 5ᵗʰ <u>Sin: Without Mercy</u> *(Romans 1:31)*

*...without understanding, untrustworthy,
unloving and unmerciful...*

*A*re you a compassionate person? How is your love walk? Do you give forgiveness and mercy as commanded by God? Let us look at the portion of Scripture for this entry. Those who walk in depravity and are apart from God walk without under-standing, love, being worthy of trust, and mercy. This should hit home to some of us (yes, I did write <u>us</u>), who find it hard to forgive. We love to hang on to our bitterness and our self-righteousness at the things people have done to hurt us. We like how it festers and keeps us stirred up, don't we? This is sin, and it separates us from God. He can not—and will not—use bitter vessels. They will taint the living water He wants poured out of them. Those who lack understanding and compassion, who are unloving, and who are unable to forgive are unusable in His plans. Catch the word untrustworthy; that means He cannot trust those with bitter and hard hearts to carry Him to a lost world.

My "Seekers" class knows this kind of teaching as "being fed the hard word" of God. I am not going to sugarcoat the Gospel or tell you things you like to hear, but I will tell you the Word of truth. The fact is this... God needs His children to be ready, willing, and able to work in His kingdom. I have heard bitter believers who made my hair curl—and that's quite a feat! What does that attitude say to a lost world? If we are no different from the lost souls around us, how can we ever have an impact in their lives?

Lord, I have harbored unforgiveness in my spirit; and it has kept me from ever finding real peace in my life. You will need to crack the hard veneer to get to the teachable spirit within me. Show me Your face, Jesus. Amen.

December 6th <u>Sin: Made Acceptable</u> *(Romans 1:32)*

... and although they know the ordinance of God, that those who practice such things are worthy of death, they not only do the same, but also give hearty approval to those who practice them.

I bet you are glad this is my last lesson in this series! I asked a Seeker a few weeks ago if she felt that I "beat up" on her when I teach these truths. She said she is convicted...but loves knowing what she is doing wrong so she can make changes and do things right! Praise God! Did you read the verse carefully? Those of us who have read these verses, now know the things which are contrary to the teachings of God. I have written several times that <u>all sin separates us from God</u>. Sin also has another consequence. It brings death. God created the world to be without end; sin changed all of that. The verse above tells us that those who practice sin also give approval to the sin they see committed by other people. I have addressed condoning *"sin in the camp"* in the past. This is not only sin in our churches, but in our families, our homes, our businesses, and our government.

How do we condone sin? We tell a friend it is okay to have an affair... because she isn't happy in her marriage. We say it is okay to cheat on our taxes...because the government has enough money. We tell our kids it is okay to talk back to a teacher; because she is a fool. We say it is okay to go camping every weekend in the summer and skip church; because it is quality family time. We fall into gossip about a coworker; because they cause a lot of problems in the office. We wear a blouse cut way too low; because everyone else does. We allow our children to go to Spring break where we know drinking, drugs, and alcohol are rampant; because we don't know how to tell them no! We shut our mouths to false teachings in our churches; because we don't want to make waves. We are condoning sin as acceptable, which is sickening to the God of all Creation.

Father, I am guilty as charged! I have given approval to things I know are fully contrary to Your teaching. I am as guilty as the one commiting the sin. The conviction is heavy, but now I know what is expected of me as a Child of the King. Amen.

December 7th <u>Absolute Waste</u> *(Malachi 3:8-9 NIV)*

"Will a man rob God? Yet you rob me. But you ask, 'How do we rob you?' In the tithes and offerings. You are under a curse—the whole nation of you—because you are robbing me."

The leaders of Israel were not counseling their people to follow the law of God; and because of that, the tithes were withheld. God's workers had to work other jobs to support themselves. These truths still apply today. When I think of the money we spend on entertainment, video games, toys never played with, jewelry we don't wear, and furniture for houses we don't really live in, I am blown away! Billions and billions of dollars spent on things which leave us just as empty after we have them as before we bought them. Our credit card debt is through the roof, our homes are being foreclosed on in unbelievable numbers, and we continue to spend. Money is wasted on gambling, drinking, drugs, sports, and a myriad of other things, which cause division in our marriages and a lack of parenting in our homes. All this is true, but guess who suffers the most? The local church, which is unattended, unstaffed with volunteers, and unsupported by tithes and offerings. We are out of control and God will not wait forever for us to wake up and settle down. We are despised by the rest of the world for our psuedo-Christian values. We claim to be a nation blessed by God; at the same time we fall into the cesspool of sin.

Nothing I have written in this entry is news to you. We hear a constant rant about how bad things are, how disrespectful our children are, how bad our finances are, and how low our morals have fallen. What do you do about any of that? Where do your dollars go?

Are you giving them to the gambling establishments around your state? Are you spending too many of them on things which do not satisfy the longing of your soul? Are you contributing to God's plan through tithes, offerings, service, and support of missions? America is under the curse mentioned above. We will never be a godly nation again, unless we start in each home honoring the things of Christ. We are robbing God of our money, time, love, respect, honor...

Lord, I need help and direction to get my giving into perspective and in line with Your teachings. Direct me to someone who can help me make better use of the dollars You have given to me... whether many or few. Amen.

December 8th   A Weaker Vessel   *(Luke 22:3-4)*

And Satan entered into Judas who was called Iscariot, belonging to the number of the twelve; and he went away and discussed with the chief priests and officers how he might betray Him to them.

*S*atan is always looking for a weak vessel, which he can fill and use to accomplish his plans of destruction. In today's verse, we find Judas Iscariot, one of Jesus's twelve Apostles, being filled with the evil of Satan and going to the Jewish leaders to betray Jesus. Why would someone who watched Jesus heal, restore sight, open ears, and cast out demons, fall so quickly away? Why would he betray the kindest, most gentle teacher he had ever known? Maybe those descriptive words give us a clue. Judas wanted a great military leader as his Messiah. He wanted a mighty warrior who would overthrow the Roman occupation. He wanted someone quite different than this patient teacher with compassionate eyes. Jesus withstood the temptations of Satan by using God's Word as His weapon. He was filled with the Holy Spirit, and there was no room for the enemy of his soul. Judas was filled with frustration, anger, and confusion...which clearly made him the weaker vessel the enemy sought.

During a recent class session, we talked about the power of Scripture used in rebuking the assaults of the enemy. I used examples of how to claim God's promises when Satan attacks emotionally, physically, and spiritually. Then I said these words to them: "Once you have God's words in your heart and your spirit is in touch with His Spirit, the enemy will have no choice but to go and find a weaker vessel to inhabit. That weaker vessel will not be Joe Doe on the street that doesn't have any faith, because that person is no threat to Satan's schemes. He will go and take up residence in someone with shallow and unsupported faith — someone who is not grounded in the Word and fully connected with the Spirit." Are you a weak vessel? It is time to get to work!

Lord, I am afraid the enemy might consider me to be a weak vessel. I know there is power in Your Word and strength in Your teachings. Equip and teach me today. I long to be strong beyond temptation. Amen.

December 9th Saturday Girls *(Psalms 84:10)*

*For a day in Your courts is better than a thousand outside.
I would rather stand at the threshold of the house of
my God than dwell in the tents of wickedness.*

His House was meant to be a gathering place, a place of fellowship for believers to minister to one another, and a place of teaching. The faces in my original vision, and those I thought would gather there; are not the ones God has brought. How awesome it is to see those He has brought to share our days. Our "Saturday Girls" are Debbie and Judy. They could not be more different in appearance and personality, but could not be more alike in Spirit and commitment to the Lord. Debbie has a near photographic memory and has done extensive study on the meanings of names and the

Biblical significance of numbers. Debbie is a pure blooded encourager who, unlike most of us, takes the initiative to call someone or write a letter and share her insights, prayers, and love. Judy is a tiny woman with a huge heart. She is one of the bravest people I know, and is a Jewish Christian. Judy longs to be in Israel, her true homeland. She has gone several times, without a group or tour,and really learned about her people, her heritage, and her eventual home. She is gifted with insights, as well as an occasional prophetic word. Dan and I would be lost without our "Saturday Girls" and the love and laughter they bring to His House.

Stop and think about the circle of friends, coworkers, and associates God has placed in your life. Each looks differently, acts uniquely, and blesses you in their own way. Do you have an encourager like Debbie? God put that person into your path because He knew you would need them *"for such a time as this."* Do you have someone who you learn from and who inspires you to reach for the unknown? That person is your Judy, the one who steps out and wants to take you with them. Think again of your circle. What are their gifts, their abilities, and their passions? Thank God for your friends today.

Jesus, You have given me a unique and varied circle of people. They impact me; and I in turn will impact them. Thank You for their gifts and graces. Help me to be an example of Your grace in their lives. Amen.

December 10th My Elaine *(Ruth 3:11)*

"Now my daughter, do not fear. I will do for you whatever you ask, for all my people in the city know that you are a woman of excellence."

God works in the most mysterious and exciting ways. Elaine and my mother have been friends forever. They don't see one another often, but when they do the years melt away. I had very little contact with Elaine's family for many years, but she knew I was Christian because of some letters I had written to our local paper. One day Elaine called and asked if I would pray for her husband. I told her I would and mentioned that I taught a Bible Study on Wednesdays at the church across from her home. I can say I under-estimated God and His planning and never dreamed she would come. Elaine came... as did her daughter Karen, one of my dear, dear friends; her daughter Karla, a special friend, a volunteer at His House, and the subject of the December 15th entry; and several assorted children and grandchildren. When God put things in motion for His House, Elaine was the first to offer help and has continued to do so eventually becoming one of our volunteers. She blesses me by being my sounding board, my friend, and my constant encourager. I thank God for my Elaine and her family.

Why do I take a page to share about someone you do not know? God puts people into our lives for a give and take. Elaine has helped Dan and I in awesome ways, but we have prayed her through her husband's cancer, her breast cancer, her treatments, her other health concerns, and family needs. This fulfills the Scriptures about a friend needing *someone to pick them up when they fall*; and it explains the portion which says *woe to the man who falls and has no friends to pick him up.* Friendship is a give and take. How are you as a friend? Are you a constant giver or a constant taker? Jesus taught us how to weep with our friends, encourage them, and speak truth into their lives. We need to excel in being Christ-like friends.

Jesus, as we enter into this season of love and new birth, please place into my heart the teachings I need to make me the kind of friend You were. Help me to reach out in pure friendship during this CHRISTmas. Amen.

December 11ᵗʰ   Bouquet of Seekers   *(John 7:18)*

He who speaks from himself seeks his own glory;
but He who is seeking the glory of the One who sent Him,
He is true, and there is no unrighteousness in Him.

*J*ust in case you have missed it while reading this devotional, I want you to know that we must seek after God, do His perfect will, and follow His Word as our roadmap through this life. There are some who are indifferent to their Creator. There are lukewarm Christians who believe their hour on Sunday is all they need. Then, there are real seekers who hunger for the Word and hunger to just get more of Jesus in them, on them, and around them. I am looking for this last group of people. God is sending them to His House one at a time from every denomination, age group, and status. Please allow me these lines to tell you about a few of my "Seekers" and the lessons I have learned from them. You have already met Queen Esther, Elaine, Debbie, and Judy. Deann teaches me that God never stops working in us to create the perfect kingdom tool. Laura hungers for the Word and will go against anyone who tries to stop her in order to learn. Jim is one of the gentlest men I have ever met and has been in church for years but is growing in huge steps. Sue brings us years of wisdom in her faith walk. Marta and Bette are some of our shining Catholic lights in the group. They exude love and encouragement. Ginger, Bonnie, Vickie, and Dawn are new to the Word and are as hungry as I was twelve years ago. Bonnie and Marsha are lifelong Christians, dedicated to kingdom witness. I learn as much from them as they do from me. Stacey and Shawnna bring youth and vitality... and as always, Dan is there beside me.

God is raising up an army of believers who will drop denominational tags and simply serve Him and walk in His words. I believe some of this army will not come from the mainstream churches. God will raise a people from the highways and byways, the street corners, and the taverns. He is not partial. He is not selective. He wants all to come into a saving knowledge of Jesus Christ and His promise of eternal life. God will break down all necessary walls in order for this to happen. Maybe, just maybe, this was the entire purpose for His House. Everyone is welcome because it truly is His house... not mine. God is looking for Seekers... are you ready?

Jesus, Your word tells us to ask, seek, and knock in order to find You and find Your truth. I am ready for a deeper walk. May my Christmas present this year be a deeper, more committed walk with You. Amen.

December 12th   No Cloak for Their Sin   *(John 15:22)*

"If I had not come and spoken unto them, they had not had sin, but now they have no cloak for their sin." KJV

The words of the Scriptures define sin, and that is why so few ever delve into them to learn the truths hidden there. Jesus was despised as He walked the earth. He was rebuked and rebuffed because His righteousness convinced the sinner of their shortcomings. The above verse comes from a passage of Scripture where Jesus is explaining to His disciples exactly why they would be hated. Look closely at His words. "If I didn't come and tell them the difference in right and wrong, they had the excuse of not knowing they were sinning. Now that I did define the differences, they have no excuse to hide behind. Sin is exposed and the cloak of ignorance is removed." This is such a great word picture of why the world would rather condemn all Christians than try to find out what we believe. I can honestly tell you that I didn't want my sins to have names. Little white fibs would become lies. Lust after someone I was not married to would become adultery. Harmless cussing and swearing would become using the Lord's name in vain. No wonder we don't want our sins defined.

Depending on where you are in your faith walk, and where you started in this book, you need to look closely at what the Bible defines as sin. A review of Romans 1:28-32 is a great start. Let's be honest. You can call it whatever you want it, dress it up frilly and pretty, laugh about it with your friends; but sin is sin and <u>all sin separates us from God</u>. Gee, where have you heard that one before? Think about how much easier it would be to not need a cloak to hide your sins. Life would be so much less complicated. If you are in need of a cloak now, you can change that. Give yourself a great Christmas gift this year... peace and godliness.

Lord, I want to not need a cloak; and the only way for that to happen is for me to walk right before You. Your words define the sins I have tried to cover up in my own life... may I truly strive to follow Your words. Amen.

December 13th <u>Wishing Time Away</u> *(Psalms 118:24)*

This is the day which the Lord has made;
Let us rejoice and be glad in it.

*D*o you remember when you were a child and it seemed like Christmas and birthdays took forever to come? On the other hand, summer vacation flew by and was way too short. Our concept of time surely changes as we get older. Time is precious, and we wish too much of it away. This is an excerpt from a recent journal entry. "I like to picture God hiding little blessings and gifts for us to find as we work and live our lives each day. Many times Dan and I say at the end of the day on Sunday, "Where did the weekend go? Why can't it be Friday afternoon again?" We walk into the new week with regret that it isn't the weekend. How God must hate to see us wish our days (and our work weeks) away. He has hidden blessings; but we are too lazy to uncover them. Maybe He had planned a Monday bonus, a Tuesday new friend, a Wednesday ministry opportunity, a Thursday kindness by a coworker, and a

Friday without back pain! We miss all the blessings during the week; because we are looking for the weekend.

Scripture tells us that God has numbered the days and gives each of them significance. Think of times when you had an okay day turn into a great one. We need to value our seconds, minutes, hours, days, weeks, months, and years. How tragic it would be to come to the end of life and feel that each day was wasted or worse, wished away. My motto is, *"This is the day the Lord has made, and* **I choose to** *rejoice and be glad in it!"* We truly need to learn to live like each day were our last.

Father, You ordained time and where we were to live in its span. I am grateful that I live "for such a time as this" right where You placed me. I confess my wished away days… Father forgive me. Amen.

December 14ᵗʰ <u>That Which Costs Nothing</u>
(1 Chronicles 21:4)

But King David said to Ornan, "No, but I will surely buy it for the full Price; for I will not take what is yours for the Lord, or offer a burnt offering which costs me nothing."

*K*ing David is referred to as a *"man after God's heart,"* and this story shows us exactly why. David is told to build an altar for God on the floor of Ornan's threshing house. When David goes to Ornan, the humbled man falls before the King with his face to the ground. David tells Ornan what he has been commanded to do and that he would like to buy the threshing floor. Ornan says, *"Take it for yourself; and let my lord the king do what is good in his sight."* David could have done as this generous man offers, but he realizes one important truth. The altar requires sacrifice, and you cannot sacrifice something which costs you nothing. Giving requires the donation of money, time, effort and goods. Something given by another can never be our sacrifice. David pays full price for the property. He builds the altar and does the offering as commanded.

If God told me to write this book as an offering and a labor of love on His behalf, and I had you write it for me... how much offering or sacrifice would I have put into it? Would God honor my non-sacrifice? No, if He were to honor one of us, it would likely be you, the one who actually did the work! So many people feel like $20 in the offering plate is all it takes to keep God happy and on our side. He wants us to offer ourselves, our obedience, and our commitment to serve. Those sacrifices come in different shapes and forms, but require obedience on our part. I would have loved to have you write some of these entries, but the truth is that God prepared me for years to write it and to dig on past experiences for the applications. I have "paid full price" with every word, thought, prayer, and tear, but He will honor the sacrifice.

Father God, David could have taken the cheap or easy way out of the sacrifice. He chose full obedience instead, and was richly rewarded for his faithfulness. Help me to be willing to sacrifice. Amen.

December 15ᵗʰ   Andy and Karla   *(Proverbs 3:6)*

In all your ways acknowledge Him,
and He will make your paths straight.

Sometimes, God works in ways which seem almost unbelievable. Today's story is one of those events. Karla is a volunteer at His House and has been divorced for years. She is the mother of four and a grandmother many times over. One day, she told her mother she needed a "nice Christian man" to share her life with. Andy works in the factory with Dan; has never been married and has waivered in and out of his faith walk over the years. He was visiting the store one day and out of my mouth came these words, "I should fix you up with my volunteer, Karla." I swear to you that I had never given this a thought and would never have even dreamed the two would be compatible. Days later, Andy asked Dan about Karla and was interested in meeting her. They met at my "Seekers" class on Thursday, had a double date dinner Friday, and have been inseparable ever since. Andy is wonderful with Karla's kids and grandkids. Her family loves him... and they are getting married on December 15, 2007. Dan and I are their attendants (because I couldn't convince them to choose skinny ones!). God works in unbelievable ways!

There have been many instances of words coming out of my mouth, which were not connected to thoughts in my mind; and each time a life-change was in the works. You see, God had a plan for Karla and Andy, my mouth was merely the tool He used to implement the plan and fulfill her desire for a Christian husband and his for a godly wife. This couple had no idea one year ago where God was leading them. Our prayer is for a long, happy, and healthy marriage for two dear friends; and that they would tell everyone how God *"joined them together in a three-strand unbreakable cord."* Are you ready for God to do amazing things in your life? Are you listening and watching for the doors He is opening? Step out in faith! Who knows but that *"for such a time as this,"* He may have an awesome plan for you?!

Karla and Andy's story is a blessing, Lord. I want to be ready and willing for You to work Your mysterious ways through me. Please show me Your hand; and give me discernment to know the difference between Your hand and fleshly temptations. Amen.

December 16th   Nativity Story: Zacharias   *(Luke 1:13)*

*But the angel said to him, "Do not be afraid, Zacharias,
for your petition has been heard, and your wife Elizabeth
will bear you a son, and you will give him the name John."*

*T*oday begins a series of character stories leading up to the birth of Jesus. My earnest prayer is that you will go into the book of Luke and read the full story. Step back in time to recapture the true meaning of this season. Zacharias, a Jewish priest, lived in the days before the Messiah was born. The descendants of Aaron were divided into twenty-four groups, each serving for two weeks in the temple each year. Zacharias is chosen as the priest to enter the Holy of Holies, the portion of the temple where the Ark of the Covenant, a box containing the tablets of the Ten Commandments rests. An angel of God appears to him. Zacharias is terrified, but the angel tells him that the prayers of he and his wife Elizabeth have been answered. The elderly couple is barren, and God is going to give them a son whom Zacharias is to name John. The delayed stay within the Holy of Holies worries the other priests, but when Zacharias comes out they can tell he has had an encounter with God. Doubt in the angel's words led him to challenge the promise. Zacharias is told he will be unable to speak until his son is born. He returns home after his duty in the temple is finished, and Elizabeth conceives a child. Zacharias remains mute as he revisits in his thoughts the encounter he has had in a face-to-face meeting with an angel of God!

Righteousness is rewarded when the unanswered prayers of years are finally answered. I find it interesting that they never stopped praying for a child even in their advanced years. God is putting in place the series of events leading up to His greatest plan ever. He is about to send the long awaited Messiah, the Savior of the world. He needs to fulfill Old Testament prophesies about one who would walk before Jesus and tell others of His salvation. That one is John... and you may know him as John the Baptist. God hears all prayers. Some He answers with a quick "yes," some with a definitive "no," and some with a sincere "wait a while." Some of us would rather have the "no" than the "wait." God's timing is always perfect.

Lord, I am impatient and shortsighted. I want it; I want it now, and I want it all! Sometimes, Your plans are very different from mine. Help me to learn to wait upon You and watch You work the wonders of Christmas. Amen.

December 17ᵗʰ <u>Nativity Story: Elizabeth</u> *(Luke 1:25)*

"This is the way the Lord has dealt with me in the days when He looked with favor upon me, to take away my disgrace among men."

Zacharias has the vision, but Elizabeth is going to have the baby! Think about this, this couple is likely in their eighties when all this takes place! I was mortified when my parents told me they were expecting in their mid-thirties! Elizabeth could have recoiled in shame and wondered what others would think about her. Instead, she considers it a great gift. Her response when questioned about how this conception could have happened is surely an emphatic, "Nothing is impossible with God!" Imagine what it was like at their house with her excited plans and talk about the upcoming birth of their child... as Zacharias sits in silence waiting for his voice to come back! Finally, the day arrives and Elizabeth gives birth to her son. Eight days later, he was to be circumcised and named. Biblical names were significant and determined a family line. Everyone was confused when she said her son's name was John. Her relatives challenged the decision, until Zacharias wrote on a tablet, *"His name is John."* As soon as he obeyed, the shackles were loosened off his tongue and he began to speak. Zacharias was filled with the Holy Spirit and began to glorify God. Elizabeth was righteous and obedient, and she was willing for her child to be used for the purpose set before him by Almighty God. John was strong in spirit and was the one who walked before Christ and proclaimed repentence for the remission of sins. God's plan moved onward.

Obedience carries great weight with God. Scripture tells us *"to obey is better than to sacrifice."* Elizabeth is more worried about what God plans than what others will think or say about her. We could all take a lesson from her book. Are you worried about how others will react to your faith in Jesus Christ? Are you afraid to witness? We must come to the end of self in order for God to work miracles in our lives. Patience pays off. Elizabeth had her great Christmas gift in the form of a baby boy; promised by an angel and delivered by God.

Jesus, John is a precurser for me. I am called to go into all the world and proclaim the good news of the Gospel. Give me Elizabeth's boldness and passion as I walk for Your Name. Amen.

December 18th   Nativity Story: The Magi *(Matthew 2:2)*

"Where is He who has been born King of the Jews?
For we saw His star in the east and have come to worship Him."

The Magi, or as our Tyler calls them, "the three wise guys" came from thousands of miles away to worship the King of the Jews. There has been much speculation about where they came from. Some believe they were Jews still in exile in the land of Babylon who waited for the Messiah to be born. Others believe they were eastern astrologers following a new star. Yet others believe they were divinely appointed by God. Whatever the situation, they travelled far to follow Christ's star and were instrumental in protecting this tiny baby boy. Herod, the Roman leader of the area of Bethlehem has heard of this newborn "King." When the Magi come to him seeking information about where the King of the Jews was located, Herod figures he can trick them into leading him to baby Jesus. He intends to have Him slain before the Jews hear that their Messiah has come. These wise men follow the new star to the place where Jesus is. They carry him gifts of gold (royalty), frankinsence (worship) and myrrh (used for embalming). They worship the newborn King; and then sensing the evil intentions of Herod, return home without reporting to him. These Wise men were directed to the Christ child by God, presented Him with gifts representing His divinity, and were directed by God to leave on a different path. God's perfect plan was being unveiled.

How far would you travel to worship the King of Kings? Most of us think a drive of more than twenty minutes is an inconvenience. We don't want to break up our weekends to go to church when we are out of town. We don't want a mid-week service because we are tired or too busy. I am not lecturing you here... I am guilty myself. Think about these men travelling thousands of miles to worship Jesus. Surely, we can be more willing and open to 'inconvenience' for His sake.

Jesus, obviously the Magi were men who knew all about worship and giving glory to You, Lord. As of this day, I choose to be more self-sacrificing and less self-absorbed. I want to see my Messiah, too! Amen.

December 19th Nativity Story: Joseph *(Matthew 1:20)*

But when he had considered this, behold, an angel of the Lord appeared to him in a dream, saying, "Joseph, son of David, do not be afraid to take Mary as your wife; for the Child who has been conceived in her is of the Holy Spirit."

*P*icture this... Joseph is in a position where everything he has ever wanted is about to happen. He works at a trade he excels in and is noted for his fine carpentry work. He lives in Nazareth near Galilee, and is betrothed to a lovely young woman named Mary who shares his faith in the God of Israel. All is well until Mary disappears and is gone for several months. He hears her voice at the open door upon her return, and turns around full of expectaion at seeing his love, only to see that she is with child...a child which cannot possibly be his! Joseph is crushed. He is weighed down by the betrayal of the one he believed he knew so well. "How could you, Mary? How could you betray our love and our plans?" Joseph knows the Law of Moses, which gives him the right to cast Mary away from him—or even have her stoned for the act of adultery. Being a righteous man, he chooses to send her away secretly. In a fitful sleep, an angel appears to Joseph telling him Mary has not been with a man, but instead the child she is carrying is born of the Holy Spirit. This is God's son; and His name is to be called Jesus... for He will save His people from their sins. How it must have bothered Joseph to watch his son born in an animal barn, to be layed in a feed trough, and to be surrounded by the lowing sounds and smells of the animals. How he must have looked at their son and wondered what the future held in store for him and his beloved Mary.

Imagine this story playing out in today's society where everyone is worried about their rights being violated. Think of this good man and what likely happened to his reputation when he married a woman who was great with child. Think of the doubts about being the father to the Son of God! God chose the right couple for this plan to play out exactly as He had orchestrated. Joseph had huge faith in a remarkable God... how do you measure up? Christmas can only happen if the players all do their parts!

Father God, how amazing are Your plans and Your ways! Give me huge faith like Joseph to trust fully in You and in Your methods. Help me to think often of Joseph's story during this Christmas season. Amen.

December 20th   Nativity Story: Mary   *(Luke 1:30-31)*

The angel said to her, "Do not be afraid, Mary; for you have found favor with God. And behold, you will conceive in your womb and bear a son, and you shall name Him Jesus."

*H*ave you ever been exactly where you wanted to be only to have Him move you? Mary was in that same situation. She was betrothed: engaged but commited to the union which could only be broken by death or divorce. She loves Joseph and will soon have everything she has dreamed of since she was a young girl. An angel appears to her calling her *"God's favored one."* She is told that she's God's chosen one and will be used for the birth of the long awaited Messiah. She questions how that can happen because she is a virgin. She is told of the Holy Spirit whose child she will bear. Mary, no matter the potential cost, agrees. She is told her elderly cousin Elizabeth is also expecting. Mary goes to stay with her until the promise of the angel is fulfilled. The miraculous conception takes place and Mary must return to tell her beloved Joseph the news. Mary was surely shunned in Nazareth. Even if the child were conceived of their union, they have transgressed the law of God. Joseph, because of God's intervention, marries her and keeps her pure. As they make the journey to Bethlehem for the census, these things must have played over and over in Mary's mind. Soon her time to deliver was at hand. "What do you mean there is no room," her panicked husband cries to the innkeeper, "My wife is ready to bear our child." Mary, far from home and in less than ideal surroundings, gives birth to the Son of God. God's amazing drama is unfolding; and all Mary can do is trust in Him.

Without a second thought, Mary lays her life on the line to be obedient to the God she trusts more than life itself. She knows she is causing herself, her family and her betrothed shame. She knows the whispers and the gossip being spread behind her back. She sees doubts in the eyes of even those who are close to her. Nothing stops her or causes her to renege on the promise. She looks into the face of her baby and remembers the words of the angel, *"Do not be afraid, Mary, for you have found favor with God."*

Lord, Mary was raised up "for such a time as this." You used her; use me! This story never ceases to amaze me. How wonderful is

Your direction and planning in order for the prophesied word to be fulfilled. Amen.

December 21st <u>Nativity Story: God</u> *(John 10:30)*

"I and the Father are one."

During this series, we have looked at the earthly players who brought the CHRISTmas story to life. Today, we stop and look at how the birth of Jesus affected God. Most people have a difficult time being able to understand that Jesus is God. From the beginning of time, when Adam and Eve sinned in the garden, God has been preparing to reconcile us back into right standing with Him. A perfect, sinless lamb is the only sacrifice for a man's sins. A perfect, sinless Man is the only sacrifice for the sins of the entire world. God loved us enough to become a baby, born in humble circumstances, and obedient all the way to the cross. Easter and Christmas are simply two halves to the same story! At Christmas, God became flesh. At Easter, He was resurrected to full divinity. Jesus' birth cost God everything when the human side of Him left Heaven, came to dwell among vile men, and was rejected, and despised. God could easily have given up on mankind, caused all life to cease, and started a new race of people without free will. Instead, He was conceived in perfect holiness, came in humble surroundings, and first appeared to the lowly shepherds. God, who owns everything the world, was born in a barn to a virgin girl and an obedient man. When you look at pictures of the Nativity story... look closely at Jesus... for you are looking at the face of a pure, innocent and holy God.

We focus on the birth of baby Jesus when we think about the Christmas season. Yes, the birth of our Messiah is the centerpiece of our lives; but He is God in the flesh. Jesus later tells us if we know Him we know God for, *"I and the Father are one."* To me, that means that the Father is loyal, emotional, passionate, loving, gracious, and wise. I, for one, am thrilled to learn about my Creator during this season of the Savior's birth. Are you ready for Christmas? Is your heart ready for a special encounter with your Creator? He brought the gift... and the gift is our Messiah.

Father God, thank You for this glimpse of Your character. I have focused before on Jesus only. You are the one who orchestrated this whole series of events, and I want to glorify Your name this Christmas. Amen.

December 22nd Eyes of the Shepherd *(Matthew 2:6)*

"And You, Bethlehem, land of Judah, are by no means least among the leaders of Judah; for out of you shall come forth a ruler who will shepherd My people Israel."

This story was originally written for Christmas 1998. It will require more than one day's space. Read it each day, and then you may want to reread it in full along with the Christmas Day entry on Jesus.

Eyes of the Shepherd

As I looked across the hills at my flock grazing under the star strewn sky, I felt a sense of peace that filled my entire soul. Nighttime is like that in the life of a shepherd. Unless threatened, the sheep graze quietly and rest in the calm of the cool evening. I leaned on my bent staff, carved from acacia wood, and smoothed from years of use. I thought about the life I had lived. As a child, I had dreamed of all of the exciting things that I would do with my life. I could be a builder, a teacher, a carpenter... as long as life was exciting, I didn't really care. You can, then, imagine my dismay when my father sent me out to tend his flock! I would never disobey his command; but I was disappointed, devastated, reluctant, and even angry. A shepherd's life is solitary, often without physical comfort and very lonely.

I could not dishonor my father. So, I picked up that stick and vowed to be a good shepherd. It took some time to learn how to tend my flock... partly because I was reluctant to do this job. When a shepherd loves his sheep, he is able to sense their needs, hear their cries, and protect them from danger. He must also be willing to lay down his life to defend them. I was willing to do all of these things, not for my own glory, but for the sake of my father, who needed someone to tend the flock he so loved.

As I leaned on my staff, a soft light lit the sky off to my right. At first, I thought it was a reflection off the water beyond where my flock grazed. Imagine my fear when the light moved toward me—stopping only a few yards away! Suddenly, the light began to take form and there stood a figure in a flowing robe, bathed in soft light with eyes so peaceful that my hammering heart began to calm within my chest.

Jesus, this Shepherd was obedient, just as You were. Had You not been willing to be my Shepherd, I would not be the person I am today. Thank You for loving me enough to sacrifice Yourself. Amen.

December 23rd Eyes of the Shepherd-2 *(Psalms 23:2-3)*

He makes me lie down in green pastures; He leads me beside quiet waters. He restores my soul; He guides me in the paths of righteousness...

*H*e stretched his hand out to me and spoke in a clear, soft voice. "Don't be afraid. I bring you good news. Today, in the City of David, a Savior has been born. You shall travel there and find Him wrapped in swaddling cloths and lying in a manger."

Why would this angel appear to me? I am a poor shepherd with no prestige, with nothing to offer. I am a simple man, a caregiver, a tender of the flock, a man of peace. I am low and humble before the powerful men of the world. Why would he speak to me? It must be a mistake; but do angels make mistakes?

My curiosity overwhelmed my usual cautious thinking and I

called to my sheep, which follow me because they know and trust my voice. I began walking in the direction of a bright star, which seemed to be sending brilliant rays pointing directly toward the city of Bethlehem. Once, I thought about turning back, surely this was only a dream... but that light in the distance drew me on.

As I climbed the crest of the last hill before Bethlehem, I caught sight of a stable, bathed in soft light and gently lit within by a tiny glowing fire. I heard the cry, that unmistakable cry that only a newborn baby makes. I watched as a beautiful young woman knelt beside the tiny wrapped bundle nestled in the hay. I watched the wonder in her eyes and could hear her soft murmurs to calm the cries of her son.

I watched the man standing behind her. He, too, watched the infant with eyes of love, but I could sense frustration in him. I realized that he was ashamed that his tiny son had been born in a stable, was resting in an animal's feed trough, and was wrapped in cloths torn from his own tunic.

Jesus, I want to follow You because I know and trust Your voice. How grateful I am that You are a humble Shepherd who felt all the things I feel today. You're the best CHRISTmas gift I have ever received. Amen.

December 24th <u>Eyes of the Shepherd-3</u> *(Luke 2:20)*

*The shepherds went back; glorifying and praising God
for all that they had heard and seen, just as had been told them.*

I wanted a closer look at their son, but assumed that they would not want me to come nearer. After all, my clothes smelled of sheep...and it had been a long while since I had a real bath. Suddenly, the young woman lifted her head, looked directly into my eyes, and gestured for me to come near. I walked to the stable on shaking legs. I was afraid and unsure of why I was here, but I was somehow compelled to move forward. I had a sense that something was about to happen that would change my life forever.

When my feet finally stood on the stable floor, I looked at the beautiful baby wrapped in remnants but looking to me like a king wearing royal robes. His golden curls—they looked like a crown upon his head. His tiny arms stretched out to the side...like they wanted to draw me into them. I stood there awed, as I always am, by the miracle of birth.

Then, I looked into his eyes, not the eyes of a baby, but the eyes of the wise... eyes that looked at me as if they saw who I really was. Eyes that said that they understood about shepherding, about obeying a father's command, about hearing the cries of the flock... about love deep enough to lay down a life for.

As I looked into those eyes, I knew that never again would I feel that shepherding was a lowly job. I know that my life was forever changed. I knew that I had witnessed something truly special. I knew that I had looked into the soul of the ONE who would one day save the world!

———

My prayer is the Shepherd's story has touched your heart. Have you ever given thought to why the shepherds were the first hear of Jesus' birth? He is the Shepherd, who would (and did) lay down His life for us, His flock. Dwell upon this truth during these last hours before we celebrate His humble birth.

———

Jesus, my Messiah, my Savior, and my King. You are the willing ONE who has and will continue to save this evil world. My Shepherd, I love Your voice and will follow wherever You send me. Amen.

December 25ᵗʰ Nativity Story: Jesus *(Luke 1:32-33)*

"He will be great and will be called the Son of the Most High; and the Lord God will give Him the throne of His father, David; and He will reign over the house of Jacob forever, and His kingdom will have no end."

*W*ould you leave the beauty, splendor, and peace of the most beautiful place ever created to come to earth, be born in a barn, and be despised by those who have waited thousands of years for you to come? Would you willingly walk away from a place of full authority and holiness to come to a place where your authority would be challenged and you would be falsely accused of blasphemy and deceit? Jesus did all of this... Why? He modeled obedience for us. Imagine the conversations between Jesus and His Father before He left and came to earth. "You know the people will deny You? They will challenge Your authority, hate You, and call You a deceiver. Are You sure You love them enough to suffer this?" Jesus thinks about it and replies, "They don't deserve our grace; but this has been the plan since the Garden of Eden. I must remember that some will listen and receive the restoration. For them, it is worth whatever I will suffer. If only one is saved, it is worth the price." Thus, our Lord was led to forsake all He knew and loved to come to earth in the form of an innocent baby born in a humble stable, visited by shepherds, and despised by the world. He is the greatest gift the world has ever known!

How hard it is to go back after years of telling our children about Santa Claus being the star of Christmas and tell them who the real Star is. How hard it is for us adults to change our focus from gifts and garland to one of worship and adoration. How hard it will be to stand before our Lord and hear the words, *"I never knew you."* Jesus truly carried to us the greatest gift the world has ever received—not in money, fame, or material possessions; but in eternal grace to be lived forever with Him in Heaven. Merry CHRISTmas to each of you.

Jesus, Thank You for leaving Your home, Your glory, and Your Father to come to men who would reject and deny You, find reasons to accuse You, and lead You to the Easter Cross. You are the perfect picture of love. Happy Birthday, my Jesus. Amen.

December 26th   <u>Christ Prays for Us</u>   *(John 17:9)*

"I ask on their behalf; I do not ask on behalf of the world, but of those who You have given Me; for they are Yours."

*O*n this day after Christmas, we need to be grateful for a living Messiah who prayed us through the testing we would face. As Jesus prepared to face the agony of the cross, He knew the flock would scatter once the Shepherd was gone. His disciples depended on His faith, His teaching, His provision, and His strength. Just as a parent would do, He planned and prayed for those He knew would be lost without Him. The 17th Chapter of John details the prayers of a Shepherd for those in His flock and those who would later be a part of that same flock. He, as always, acknowledges the Father's part in all He has accomplished... even saying His followers actually belonged first to God. Jesus prayerfully says to His Father, *"I do not ask You to take them out of the world, but to keep them from the evil one."* He knew that His followers would have to live in this dark world with its temptations, deceit, and false teachings. He didn't ask God to totally remove us but to give us strength to withstand the tests, tempts, and taunts of the enemy. He also asks God to, *"Sanctify them in the truth; (because) Your word is truth."* Jesus, as He prayed into the future for you, knew that the Holy Word of God contained all truth and that the words within its pages would sanctify (set apart; cleanse) us.

Do you realize that the gods of all the world's religions never claim to pray for their followers. These unseen and unknown gods are often manmade idols with no ability to respond to or answer prayers. Only Christianity, with Christ as Saviour, has a God who prays and interceeds for His children. Jesus sits today at the right hand of God intervening on our behalf. Thank God we have His word to assure us of these truths.

Father God, I am blessed to know that even though I am in this vile world, I am not of it. I can keep my eyes on You, keep my mind filled with Your word, and keep my faith fit through exercising it daily. No other Name but the God of Israel carries such glory. Amen.

December 27th   Saying 'Thank You'   *(Psalms 92:1-2)*

It is good to give thanks to the Lord, and to sing praises to Your name, O'Most High; to declare Your loving kindness in the morning and Your faithfulness by night.

As we near the end of this year, we need to look back at all the times Jesus has strengthened and encouraged us. We need to think of the times His Holy Spirit has directed our footsteps. We need to thank God for His foresight to preserve His Word for us to use *"for such a time as this."* Has He helped you through a time of testing or temptation? Have you enjoyed the beauty of His creation... saw the miracle of birth... or received a gift there was no other explanation for except God sent it? Have you had the "lights in your eyes come on to the understanding of Biblical truths?" Have you had more healthy days than sick? Have your children been protected? Have you had "enough" to make ends meet, "enough" to eat, and "enough" sunshine to keep your spirits up? Do you have happy memories of the year gone by? Did you learn new things, find new adventures, and make one new friend? Most of us take these things for granted or believe all blessings came from our own hard work. Scripture tells us in James 1:17: *"Every good thing given and every perfect gift is from above, coming down from the Father of lights, with whom there is not variation or shifting shadow."*

If *every good and perfect gift is from Heaven,* why do we spend so many of our precious hours worrying and fretting? Why are we never satisfied with the bounty we have? Why do we fail to give honor, glory, praise and thanks to the Father? My recommendation to you is to take these last days of this year to thank God for every blessing and to begin to pray for His continued hedge of protection going into the next year. *Draw near to Him and He will draw near to you.*

Lord, Your strong arms have carried me, held me, and picked me up when I fell this year. I long to be grateful like never before, giving You all the glory and honor You deserve. Thank You for "every good and perfect gift" I have received. Amen.

December 28ᵗʰ <u>I Shall Not Be Moved</u> *(Psalms 16:8)*

*I have set the Lord continually before me;
because He is at my right hand, I will not be shaken.*

As we near the end of this year, those of you who have been reading this devotional each day have had the Word of God before you. For some of you this may be your single source of Scripture; and for others it might be used as a supplement to your personal Bible study. Whatever the situation, our Lord has been *"set continually before"* you as the verse for today states. Do you feel that you know more about the character of God and the holiness of Jesus than before you began to read? My great prayer is that *For Such a Time as this...* is a stepping stone toward your deeper faith commitment and your thirst for the living water of God's Word. Let's continue with the next portion of this verse, *"because He is at my right hand."* Have you grown in confidence knowing God cares for your needs, is waiting for your call, and is prepared to carry you through the fires of your life? Do you realize He is omnipresent (in all places), omnipotent (all powerful), and omniscient (all knowing), and that your concerns are His concerns? Finally, the last portion of this verse says, *"I will not be shaken."* Make this the new cry of your heart? "He is before me, at my right hand, and knowing my every need, I will not be shaken by the winds of this life."

Scripture tells us that *faith comes by hearing the Word of God.* Faith gained any other way is not real faith; and only real faith will carry us through times of hardship and keep us from being moved. Let me paraphrase several other verses, which confirm this truth. *"No weapon formed against me will prosper; because I am more than a conqueror in the name of Christ Jesus who strengthens me. He surrounds the righteous with a hedge of protection, as with a shield. He leads us beside the still waters and is our rock and our salvation."* There are thousands more promises for the children of God in the Bible; begin today to dig for these golden nuggets of hope.

Lord, I am stronger just knowing You are always beside me, carrying my burdens, sheltering me from the assaults of the enemy, and loving me when I am unlovable. Please continue the good work You have begun in me this year and on into the next. Amen.

December 29th   Dead, Dry Bones   *(Ezekiel 37:5)*

Thus says the Lord God to these bones,
'Behold, I will cause breath to enter you that you may come to life.'

*E*zekiel is a prophet of God, who finds himself an exile in Babylon along with the rest of the nation of Israel. God wants to give Ezekiel a message of hope to carry to his people. He provides that in the form of a vision. The prophet finds himself overlooking a valley filled with dead, dry bones. These bones represent the Jews in Babylonian captivity, who allowed themselves to become dry — without deep commitment to God. As Ezekiel looks over the valley, God asks him if the bones can ever live again. He then tells His prophet to speak the word of God over the bones. Notice what he is to speak, God's Word, not a carefully crafted sermon or a powerful oratory, but only the pure, sweet, life giving Word of God. As Ezekiel begins to speak, muscle and tissue begins to form upon the bones. They begin to join together into perfect skeletons; and then flesh begins to cover the bones until they were complete bodies again. Still there was no breath, no life within them. God tells Ezekiel to prophesy the breath of God, the Spirit of God over them. The spirits quicken within them and real life comes to the valley of dead, dry bones. They are the remnant who will return to the land of Israel, infused with God's Holy Spirit and ready to live wholly for Him.

Are you like these bones? Do you feel dead, dried out, and empty in your faith walk? Do you want restored life and passion for God? Is the body of believers you worship with similar to this arid lifeless valley? God is still in control. What joined the disjoined bones back into a complete body? The Word of God! It is so simple! We need the Word of God, not fancy sermons crafted to tickle our ears. Then, we need the infilling of the Holy Spirit to bring us life, passion, hope, wisdom, and direction. There is hope for your church, your home, your marriage, and your spiritual growth. That hope is in the Word of God. End this year and begin the next with the Bible and the hope which lies within its pages.

Father God, I have walked in that valley; and I hated every minute of it! I long to walk where there is life, where there is hope, and where there is a burning passion for You. Please Lord, breathe Your Spirit into mine that I might become part of the mighty army of God. Amen.

December 30th Looking Back *(Psalms 65:11)*

You have crowned the year with Your bounty,
and Your paths drip with fatness.

*S*top and think about the year which is about to come to a close. Ask yourself these questions. Have I grown in my faith walk this year? Am I more aware of what God's plan and purpose for my life? Have I put what I have learned into action? Am I producing the Fruits of love, mercy, patience, kindness, and humility? Have I spent time learning from the Word of God? Is my prayer life deeper than it was at the beginning of the year? Be

454

honest in these answers, because they will advise you on where you need to work extra hard in the coming year. We have spent a year together. I have been praying for your spiritual growth as you read these entries. Some of you I will never meet this side of Heaven. God has a plan for each of you. Seek Him to find the path He wants you to walk. Maybe this writing has inspired you to write your own book, become a teacher, to simply be the best student of the Word possible or to open a new business. Hopefully, it has revealed that you are a product of the life events you have lived through. I have enjoyed every minute we have spent together. God truly has *"crowned the year with His bounty."* I am a different person today than I was when I began to write these entries. From the initial vision to the completion of writing these entries, seventy days have passed. Yes, that is how quickly the words have flown from my mind to these pages. God has a plan. God has perfect timing. God chose me to write these words for you to read *For Such a Time as this...*

Praise God for the year you have just lived. Even in the darkest moments, you have had hope. He has provided food, shelter, teaching, love, encouragement, and insight. Take time now to thank Him for His unending faithfulness. You are a child of the King!

Lord Jesus, You have walked each step of this year with me. Even when I was unaware of Your presence, You were there. I thank You for each promise You have kept, each bit of wisdom You have shared, and each word of caution You have given. Hear my praises for who You are to me. Amen.

December 31st   Looking Forward   *(Matthew 6:34)*

*So do not worry about tomorrow; for tomorrow
will care for itself. Each day has enough trouble of its own.*

*L*et us look at some of what we have learned this year. Remember the days we learned about David and Solomon, the mighty Kings of Israel who had great success, power, and wealth, but were drawn away from God's plan when they fell to sins of the flesh? Remember Jabez, who asked God for blessings, extra ministry opportunities, and a hedge of protection? Think about the outline of the plan of salvation, the explanations of church rites, and the Bible characters who came to life within these pages. If even one entry made a difference in your life, then the cost and effort for this book were worth it! This devotional was not designed to be read once and then put on a shelf to collect dust. Begin again in the next year to learn from its teachings and apply its methods. You could read the full chapter where each verse is lifted from to see what other golden nuggets of wisdom and promise are hidden there. God has a plan for you; seek to find that plan and put it into action. Listen for His still, small voice as He directs you. Most importantly, seek the life giving, cleansing words of Scripture. It is written for you to grow and to encourage you as you walk through this life and on into your eternal life. You are walking into a new year; make it your resolution to know Him more. Begin by committing to time in His Word each and every day. I close with my prayer for you...

Father God, Sweet Jesus and Indwelling Holy Spirit... this child has spent part of the last year learning more about You and how You work in the lives of Your disciples. This year's entries held Biblical teachings, life-lessons, and wonderful excerpts from Your holy Word. I ask You this: Please bless them for the extra effort they have put forth; and then give them a burning hunger for Your Word, a hunger nothing else can ever satisfy. Jesus, give them a holy boldness to be witnesses for Your Name in a lost world. Father God, I ask Your hedge of protection around their homes, families, jobs, churches, and lives. Holy Spirit, I ask that You would give them wisdom, discretion, discernment, and a spirit of conviction. I ask that You would open their eyes to false teachings, false prophets, and the temptations of the flesh. Lord, I have prayed for every person who will read these words— words You have laid upon my heart. I ask Your call upon their lives. Call them, receive them, cleanse them, save them, and make them Yours. It is my joy to serve You; and I pray they may know this same joy. Amen.

Notes and Thoughts

Notes and Thoughts

Printed in the United States
202661BV00003B/1-51/A